# MANILA:
## History, People and Culture
### The Proceedings
### of the
### Manila Studies Conference

Co-sponsored by
**De La Salle University**
and the
**Philippine Studies Association**
April 11-12, 1986
Barrio San Luis Complex
Intramuros, Manila

Edited by
**Wilfrido V. Villacorta**
**Isagani R. Cruz**
**Ma. Lourdes Brillantes**

Published by the De La Salle University Press,
2401 Taft Avenue, Manila, Philippines

ISBN # 971-118076-6

First Printing 1989
Second Printing 1990
Third Printing 1992

**De La Salle University**

*and*

**The Philippine Studies Association**

*gratefully acknowledge the valuable support of*

**THE FORD FOUNDATION**

*and*
**Intramuros Administration**
**National Historical Institute**
**National Museum**
**Student Council, DLSU**
**Behavioral Sciences Team, DLSU**
**San Miguel Corporation**
**The Conference Secretariat**
**Ma. Angeles Guanzon-Lapeña**
**Alejandro D. Padilla**

# THE PHILIPPINE STUDIES ASSOCIATION, INC.

The Philippine Studies Association, Inc., was formed in 1984 with the following as charter members: Ofelia Angangco, Wilfredo Arce, Fe Arcinas, Isagani Cruz, Doreen Fernandez, Andrew Gonzalez, FSC, Milagros Guerrero, Carolina Hernandez, Florentino Hornedo, Elsa Jurado, Vivencio Jose, Antonio Ledesma, SJ, Patricia Licuanan, Aurora Roxas-Lim, Bienvenido Lumbera, Resil Mojares, Nicanor Tiongson, and Wilfrido Villacorta. Ofelia Angangco was elected president, Doreen Fernandez vice-president, and Elsa Jurado secretary-treasurer, to be replaced by Milagros Guerrero while the former was away in Japan.

The purpose of the association is "to promote study, criticism and research in Philippine languages, literature, culture and society, and to further the common interests of teachers and scholars in these fields" (By-Laws, Art. I, Section 2).

To implement this goal, the association's first activity was the First National Philippine Studies Conference held at the Philippine Social Science Center in Quezon City from February 11 to 13, 1985. The conference brought together in fruitful interaction scholars engaged in the different fields of Philippine Studies. In an exchange of research methods, findings, and perspectives, there was interdisciplinary dialogue on Philippine matters and materials. Scholars outside Metro Manila, scholars new in the field or as yet unpublished, participated. As the first Philippine Studies conference on Philippine soil, it was an exploration of the extent, development, and needs of Philippine studies, an update on the breadth and depth of the field. It also affirmed Philippine Studies as a field, interdisciplinarity as a mode of dialogue, and the examination of Philippine reality both micro- and macro- as an ongoing concern.

The Philippine Studies Association, Inc. is linked with the Philippine Studies Committee of the Southeast Asia Council of the Association for Asian Studies (U.S.A.). It is currently planning a seminar on Northern Philippines Studies in connection with UP College Baguio, and is a co-sponsor with De la Salle University of the Manila Studies Conference.

(For information on membership in The Philippine Studies Association, Inc., please write to The Membership Committee, Box 10, MCCPO, Makati, Metro Manila. Types of membership are: Regular (₱100 per year; ₱250 per three years), Associate (₱100); Students ₱30); and Foreign ($35).

# Table of Contents

# Foreword

During the First National Philippine Studies Conference at the Philippine Social Science Center in 1985, De La Salle University offered to host the second conference of the Association. Because De La Salle has been closely linked with the history and culture of Manila, the theme chosen was Manila Studies.

The conference was originally set in February but that period was a tumultuous one arising from the controversy over the results of the snap presidential election. Contesting the accuracy of election returns, Corazon Aquino launched a civil disobedience campaign which paved the way for the historic EDSA Revolution.

With the support of the Ford Foundation, the conference on "Manila: History, People and Culture" finally took place on April 11 and 12, 1986 at the Barrio San Luis Complex in historic Intramuros. It was a moment of hope, with the euphoria over the fall of the dictatorship still lingering in the consciousness of the participants. Jose Maria Sison (who went underground after the proclamation of martial law but was apprehended by the military in 1977) was recently released, and presented a paper entitled "The Nationalist Leadership in Manila in the Seventies"

Although the conference was an academic gathering, one could sense from the conference proceedings the high expectations of all delegates that human rights and democratic institutions would be fully restored. If the conference were to be held today, the mood would certainly be different.

The papers contained in this volume were those submitted to the committee for publication. They covered a wide range of subjects, including the historical, economic, political, social and cultural aspects of Manila's development. The paper-writers and participants, who came

1

from different universities and agencies, all contributed to a broader understanding of the great city that is central to the Filipino soul.

De La Salle University thanks the Philippine Studies Association for the opportunity of having hosted this important conference and hopes that there will be similar conferences in the future that will cement the network of Manila specialists and promote popular consciousness of the legacy of Manila.

**Wilfrido V. Villacorta**
Conference Chairperson

# Programme

## MANILA: HISTORY, PEOPLE, AND CULTURE

11 April 1986, Friday

| | |
|---|---|
| 8:00- 8:30 | *REGISTRATION* |
| 8:30- 9:30 | *OPENING CEREMONIES* |

*National Anthem*

| | |
|---|---|
| *Welcome Remarks* | Dr. Wilfrido Villacorta<br>Conference Chairperson<br>Dean, College of Liberal Arts<br>De La Salle University |
| *Opening Remarks* | Prof. Ofelia Angangco<br>President<br>Philippine Studies Association<br>Professor, University of the<br>Philippines |
| *Orientation to the Seminar/Introduction of the Keynote Speaker* | Dr. Wilfrido Villacorta<br>Conference Chairperson<br>Dean, College of Liberal Arts<br>De La Salle University |
| *Keynote Address:*<br>*"The Beginnings of Manila"* | Prof. Carlos Quirino<br>Historian and Biographer<br>Former Director, National<br>Library, and Founding<br>Curator, Ayala Museum |

*Master of Ceremonies*
Dr. Isagani Cruz
Conference Committee Member

A. POLITICS AND LEADERSHIP IN MANILA

*Convenor:* Dr. Remigio Agpalo, DLSU

Dr. Raul de Guzman, UP, "Contemporary Politics and Leadership in Manila"

Dr. Patricia Licuanan, Ateneo, "Perceptions of National Leaders: The Consequences of Contrast"

Prof. Socorro Reyes, DLSU, "Women and Protest Politics in Manila: A Case Study of Two Women's Organizations in the Philippines"

Prof. Jose Ma. Sison, UP, "The Nationalist Leadership in Manila in the Seventies"

B. LITERATURE OF MANILA

*Convenor:* Dr. Isagani Cruz, DLSU

Dr. Ophelia Dimalanta, UST & DLSU, "City Fiction: Manila, A Way of Life and Art"

Dr. Estrellita Gruenberg, DLSU, "The Canon of Philippine Literature According to Teachers in Metro Manila"

Prof. Rosario Lucero, DLSU, "Manila as a Setting for Taglish Romance Novels"

Dr. Soledad Reyes, Ateneo, "Ang Lunsod sa Nobela: Madilim na Pangitain"

C. URBAN PROBLEMS OF MANILA

*Convenor:* Dr. Manuel Diaz, DLSU

Prof. Stella Go, DLSU, "Reintegration of Returning Overseas Contract Workers: The Case of Barangay Vergara, Metro Manila"

Dr. Pilar Jimenez, DLSU, "Health, Nutritional Problems and the Utilization of Health Services: The Situation among Preschoolers in Depressed Metro Manila Communities"

Ms. Emma Laforteza, PBSP, "Metro Manila Livelihood Program: the PBSP Experience"

Dr. Trinidad Osteria, ISEAS, "Demographic Trends and Patterns in the City of Manila"

2:00-5:00    A. HISTORY OF MANILA

*Convenor:* Dr. Marcelino Foronda, Jr., DLSU

Fr. Jose Arcilla, S.J., Ateneo, "The Jesuits and the American Occupation of Manila, 1898"
Dr. Marcelino Foronda, Jr. DLSU, "The Neo-Manileños: An Oral History Approach"
Dr. Milagros Guerrero, UP, "Society and Morals in 17th Century Manila"
Dr. Aurora Roxas-Lim, UP, "The Archaeology of the Metro Manila Area"
Fr. Luis Merino, O.S.A., Intramuros Administration, "The Townhall of the City of Manila: Buildings, Purposes, and Functions"

B. CULTURAL LIFE IN MANILA I

*Convenor:* Dr. Ma. Belen Alampay, DLSU

Dr. Isagani Cruz, DLSU, "People Power Kuno"
Prof. Candido Filio, UP, "Cultural Resources in Development: The Case of Intramuros"

C. ETHNICITY IN MANILA

*Convenor:* Dr. Pilar Jimenez, DLSU

Prof. Carmencita Aguilar, UP, "The Muslims in Manila Prior to Colonial Control"
Prof. Theresa Chong-Cariño, DLSU, "The Chinese Women in Manila: Changing Roles and Perceptions"
Dr. Alfredo Tiamson, UP, "Economic Activities of Muslims in Manila"
Prof. Motoe Terami-Wada, DLSU, "Japanese Associations and Institutions in Prewar Manila"

5

12 April 1986, Saturday

9:30-12:30    A. ECONOMIC LIFE IN MANILA

Convenor: Dr. Tereso Tullao, Jr., DLSU

Prof. Ma. Luisa Camagay, UP, "Mujer Publica"
Prof. Edna Formilleza, DLSU, "Poverty Studies in Manila"
Prof. Ma. Elena Chiong-Javier, DLSU, "Women Vendors in Metro Manila Markets"
Dr. Isagani Medina, UP, "The Socio-Economic Life of Manila in the Nineteenth Century"

B. LANGUAGES OF MANILA

Convenor: Dr. Ma. Lourdes Bautista, DLSU

Dr. Virgilio Enriquez, DLSU, "Ang Wika ng Maynila: Sa City Hall, Palengke, LRT, Telebisyon, atbp."
Bro. Andrew Gonzalez, DLSU, "The Creolization of Philippine English:   Evidence for English-as a-First-Language Among Manila Children"
Prof. Judy Carol Sevilla, DLSU, "Bilingualism and the Bilingual Education Program:   Views of Metro Manila Leaders"

C. RELIGION IN MANILA

Convenor: Fr. Jaime Belita, C.M., DLSU

Prof. Basilio Balajadia, DLSU, "Folk Catholicism in Manila: Sects in the Making"
Dr. Fernando Elesterio, DLSU, "The Iglesia ni Kristo in Manila"
Dr. Doreen Fernandez, Ateneo, "Pompas y Solemnidades: Notes on Church Celebrations in Spanish Manila"
Dr. Marcelino Foronda, Jr., DLSU, "The K.A.L.K.: A Rizalist Cult in Manila"

6

2:00-5:00  A. NATIONALISM IN MANILA

*Convenor*: Dr. Wilfrido Villacorta, DLSU

Dr. Romeo Cruz, UP, "Nationalism in 19th Century Manila"
Prof. Prospero de Vera, DLSU, "Politics and Teachers' Organizations in Metro Manila"
Prof. Edmundo Garcia, UP, "Reflections on Significant Popular Movements in the 1980s"

B. CULTURAL LIFE IN MANILA II

*Convenor:* Dr. Emerita Quito, DLSU

Prof. Leonor Orosa-Goquingco, "Ballet Education in Metro Manila"
Prof. Rosalinda Orosa, "The State of Performing Arts Criticism Today"
Dr. Nicanor Tiongson, UP & DLSU, "Theater of Protest in Manila, 1969-1985"

C. PSYCHOLOGY AND VALUES OF MANILEÑOS

*Convenor*: Dr. Virgilio Enriquez, DLSU

Fr. Jaime Bulatao, S.J., Ateneo, "Another Look at Philippine Values"
Dr. Alfredo Lagmay, UP, "On Values Formation"
Dr. Amaryllis Torres, UP, "The Values of Manila Workers"

5:00-6:00  *CLOSING CEREMONIES*


*Awarding of Certificates of Attendance*

*Induction of New Officers of the Philippine Studies Association*

*Closing Remarks*         Dr. Doreen Fernandez
                          Vice-President
                          Philippine Studies Association
                          Professor, Ateneo de Manila
                          University
                              and
                          Dr. Wilfrido Villacorta
                          Conference Chairperson
                          Dean, College of Liberal Arts
                          De La Salle University


*Master of Ceremonies*
Dr. Ma. Belen Alampay
Program Co-Chairperson
Chairperson, Department of History
De La Salle University

# Committees

Dr. Wilfrido Villacorta
*Conference Chairperson*

Prof. Ofelia Angangco
and
Bro. Andrew Gonzalez, F.S.C.
*Conference Organizers*

*Program:* Dr. Ma. Lourdes Bautista, Dr. Ma. Belen Alampay, and Dr. Doreen Fernandez

*Publications and Public Relations:* Dr. Isagani Cruz and Dr. Aurora Roxas-Lim

*Secretariat:* Prof. Ma. Angeles Guanzon-Lapeña and Prof. Jesusa Marco

*Food and Reception:* Dr. Rachel San Miguel

*Exhibits:* Dr. Priscilla Arguelles and Prof. Judy Sibayan

*Invitations:* Prof. Carmelita Quebengco and Prof. Fe Arcinas

*Finance:* Prof. Nilda Rotor and Dr. Milagros Guerrero

*Book Sales:* Prof. Marjorie Pernia

*Liaison:* Prof. Cornelio Bascara

*Physical Facilities:* Prof. Leopoldo Martinez and Prof. Reynaldo Palma

# Closing Remarks

The founding of the Philippine Studies Association, and in fact, the efforts of the first scholars to venture into Philippine Studies, were impelled by a vision. The vision was: to have the most rigorous, the most talented works of Philippine scholarship focused on Philippine concerns, exploring Philippine lifeways, artistic expressions, religious beliefs, and thought—in other words, discovering, examining and evaluating all the rich veins that pour lifeblood into Filipino culture and identity.

The vision arose from the colonial cast of Philippine education—and therefore of Philippine scholarship. The first waves of Philippine scholars mostly devoted their high education, their talent, and their energy, to studies of Western—usually American—materials. Philippine matter was given scant attention, not only because many primary materials still had to be retrieved from the field, but also because the colonial conditioning had made Western materials more desirable, and had made entry into the world of Western scholarship the goal to be aspired for.

Attention to the "hidden wealth" of Philippine Studies improved in the wave of nationalism of the 60's and the 70's—the time when theater and literature and even some scholarship homed in on the vernacular. A second stage of the improvement occurred in the 80's, with two international conferences on Philippine Studies—in the United States. Although only a few Philippine scholars were involved, the conferences focused attention on work done, mostly by foreign scholars, on Philippine concerns. To the colonial mind, this gave Philippine Studies an international cachet, a new importance and desirability. It also clearly showed the Filipino scholar how Philippine Studies was an area in which he could naturally excel over foreign scholars, since, as the insider to the culture, his vision was one no outsider could probably ever achieve.

10

The National Philippine Studies Conference in February, 1985 was a crystallization of the vision, since it had Philippine scholars from various disciplines in rich dialogue about the culture that shapes the identity that makes the Filipino. This very successful Manila Studies Conference that we have just shared and experienced is a further stage in the fruition of the vision of Philippine Studies. Here scholars have engaged in interdisciplinary interaction, focused on a specific area in time and place: Manila. This indicates Philippine Studies come of age, its importance established, its method confirmed, its triumph visible. Even more valuable is the fact that it sets a trend. From here on in, there will surely be spin-offs: Northern Philippines Studies in October, Mindanao Studies and Visayan Studies — and so on into the future, until the whole rich mosaic of Philippine culture is assembled in full and living color, so that we all can know in documented detail and with complete understanding, what really it is about the Filipino that is worth dying for.

Doreen G. Fernandez
Vice President
Philippine Studies Association

# The Papers

# THE MUSLIMS IN MANILA PRIOR TO COLONIAL CONTROL

CARMENCITA T. AGUILAR

## Maynila as a Muslim Kingdom

Today we find in Manila, within the San Miguel district, an economically active Muslim community engaged in barter trade and various Muslim handiworks, particularly cloth weaving. The barter trade area is on R. Hidalgo Street alongside a nearby mosque. Some residential houses including the Philippine Islamic Center are found along Carlos Palanca Sr. Street. There are about 7,000 persons living in this two-hectare piece of land.[1] The Philippine Muslim Association started the acquisition of the area as early as 1964. Now it is a haven for Muslims in Manila, particularly those who are traders, students and professionals, who find it convenient to reside in the city. In Barrio Bicutan, Taguig, there is a 34-hectare area alongside the Fort Bonifacio Military Reservation, housing the Maharlika Village, another progressive Muslim community.[2] There are around thirty families and approximately a hundred students residing in the area. But this is not the first time that Muslim communities have existed in Manila. The fact is that Manila was an affluent and prestigious Muslim kingdom long before the arrival of the Spaniards.

The name *Maynila* is derived from the Tagalog word *Maynilad*, meaning "a place overgrown with *nilad* plants," a type of water plant bearing white lily flowers that grew thickly in the river.[3] It is not known, however, how far back in pre-Spanish history the name *Maynila* was used. In the Spanish account of 1570 — May, 1570 was the date of the Spanish conquest of Manila — Manila was already referred to as a Muslim town, although in 1521 the Pigafetta reference to the place was "the Muslim kingdom of Luzon."[4]

The Muslim kingdom of Manila was situated along the southern bank of a river (known as Pasig today) which opened into a larger bay that formed a gulf.[5] The bay resembled a narrow sea with its entrance at the

13

gulf. It was considered unsafe to cast anchor before the town of Manila itself because the coast was dangerous. Only during high tide was the river navigable by big ships. The bay appeared large and spacious and almost harborless. The land all around Manila Bay was very fertile and well-cultivated. Rice and cotton were planted in the fields. The slopes were smooth and had little herbage. There were forty other towns in the surrounding area and these were inhabited by both Muslim and non-Muslim natives.

The kingdom of Manila was defended by a palisade or fort all along its front facing the sea. The fort was always guarded by soldiers. The houses of the natives were behind the palisades and along the river. Pieces of artillery stood at the gates guarded by bombardiers. The Manila fort was made of palm tree logs built on top of a very narrow mound. Pieces of artillery were placed protruding from the openings on the walls large enough to let an individual soldier pass through. There were twelve pieces of artillery on the fort of Manila.

The Muslim kingdom of Manila was known for its brave warriors who used bows and lances effectively. The kingdom also had oared boats large enough to carry 300 rowers apart from the warriors. These boats were well-equipped with artillery, some large and some small. The Muslims had learned to use gunpower and manufacture cannons.[6] It was said that one vessel could attack two *praus* (native boats) and could sink them when within range.

Manila was noted as an economically progressive Muslim community whose people thrived on agriculture and trade. It conducted regular trade with the Chinese who came twice a year bringing in silk and cotton robes, large earthen jars, gilded porcelain, gold thread, benzoin, musk, and many other interesting items.[7] In exchange, the Chinese obtained cinnamon, pepper, wax, iron, copper, bronze, steel, gold, and pearls. Manila traders, including the royal houses, conducted regular trips to the Bornean ports where the objects of trade included cinnamon, wax, and brass products. The Muslims of Manila had very close affinity with the Borneans. Their royal houses were related.[8] At the same time, the Muslims in Manila served as middlemen for the Chinese goods received regularly from China. These in turn were bartered with the goods, including gold, from the neighboring islands and other interior areas. The Muslim community of Manila, for instance, would come regularly to trade. They would bring cloth and Chinese goods and return home with gold from the natives' mines. If the Cebu natives were not working on their gold mines at the arrival of the Muslim traders, arrangements were made between them in such a way that the latter could work the mines for a particular period and obtain the gold in exchange for the goods they brought.[9]

The Manila kingdom, in 1570, was estimated to have a population of 2,000.[10] Living with the Muslims were forty married Chinese and their wives and twenty Japanese. These Chinese were believed to have left China with their families during a period of political upheaval in that country.

## Culture and Social Relations

Islam as a religion and socio-political institution was not confined to Mindanao but in fact, found its way into other parts of the islands as proven by the existence of other Muslim settlements outside of Mindanao. Its spread to Manila was due to the Muslim traders from Borneo who came almost at the same time that Islam found its way to Mindanao. According to accounts, there were also Bornean missionaries who came to Luzon to preach the doctrine — thus the inhabitants of Manila, the coastal towns of Batangas and Mindoro were followers of Islam.[11] The rulers of Manila were also related to the rulers of Brunei. It was also said that the king of Borneo had the practice of holding as hostages the wealthy men of Manila who traded in Borneo by not letting them sail home for five to six years or more.[12] Some of these men married in Borneo.

But the Spanish account claimed that the Muslims on the island of Luzon did not really understand the law of Muhammed.[13] Only some of them observed the non-eating of pork and the practice of circumcision as influenced by their dealings with the Muslims from Borneo who came as traders. Few could read the Alcoran (Koran) and they swore by the sun and the moon.

And yet, the Muslims of Manila manifested certain lifestyles and practices that distinguished their Islamic culture distinctively from the "Pintados" or painted natives from the Visayas.[14] The Muslims, both men and women, were well-attired. They wore showy headdresses of many colors that were turned and knotted at the back of their heads. They learned to melt gold and form it into trinkets which they wore as body ornaments. The chiefs were more elegantly attired in comparison with the freemen. Both men and women wore anklets of gold and bracelets around their arms.[15] The men wore their hair short while the women pierced their earlobes and wore earrings.

A system of dowry or bride price was practiced in contracting marriages depending on the rank of the women.[16] The dowry was divided among the parents and relatives of the women. The men were permitted to

15

have two to three wives if they had enough wealth to support them. Divorce was practised. A man was permitted to leave his wife by paying the same sum of money he gave for her dowry. The woman could leave her husband by returning double of what he gave for her dowry.[17] But no matter how many wives a man had he always regarded one among them as the legitimate wife. If he died and had no children with his legitimate wife, all his other children by the other wives could not inherit his property. Another direct descendant was allowed to be his heir.

Slavery was an institution accepted by both Muslims and non-Muslims. The wealthiest and strongest owned most slaves, but usually only non-Muslims became slaves to Muslims. Slaves were not absolutely subjected to the master but served only under certain circumstances. An inefficient slave could be sold by his master.

The Muslims in Manila had well-settled and cultivated lands unlike the other natives who were nomadic or tilled their fields only when they ran out of food. Their lives were orderly and disciplined. Their engagement in trade and the development of their household crafts to support their trading activities showed that they were industrious as a community.

### Leadership and Authority

The kingdom of Manila was ruled by Rajah Sulayman or Soliman who was described by his subjects as the greatest chief of all in Luzon. Some chiefs in the neighboring towns, both Muslim and non-Muslim, were paying tribute to Soliman.[18] There were instances when villages that failed to remit tribute were raided by Soliman's warriors both as threat and punishment to the erring chiefs.

Rajah Soliman was the chief of Manila when the Spaniards came to conquer it in May, 1570. The elder chief of Manila who was as equally respected as Soliman was Rajah Matanda or Rajah Laya who was Soliman's uncle and adviser. But Lakandula (Alcandora or Condola in the Spanish account) was the chief of Tondo, the kingdom on the northern bank of the river. While Soliman received the Spaniards as friends when they first came and even celebrated the customary blood compact with Martin de Goiti as a commitment to friendship, Lakandula never trusted the Spaniards. He was hostile and wanted to drive them away the very day they landed in Manila.

Soliman was wealthy as a chief. His house was large and contained many things of value such as copper, iron, porcelain, blankets, wax, cotton, and wooden vats filled with wine. Cannons were also found in Soliman's storeroom.

## The Spanish Invasion and the Fall of Manila

Miguel Lopez de Legazpi arrived in the Philippines in 1565 and established a colony in Cebu. From Cebu, he sent his troops to the Visayan islands, particularly Panay, and established control over the areas. But it was not until May, 1570, five years after his arrival, that he authorized the conquest of Luzon.

From the account of the priest Antonio Pigafetta, who was with the Magellan expedition in 1521, it was learned that when their ships were in Brunei, they captured a young prince who was the son of the Muslim king of Luzon. He was also the grandson of the Sultan of Brunei. He was at that time in Brunei to marry a cousin. That prince was believed to be Rajah Laya, the uncle and adviser of Rajah Soliman. The knowledge of the existence of a Muslim kingdom in Luzon may have influenced Miguel Lopez de Legazpi to delay the conquest of Luzon until five years later when he could have been more prepared tactically to meet the Muslim foes. As narrated, there were only 110 Spaniards who participated in the conquest of Manila. The rest were the "Pintados" from Panay and Cebu.[19]

The account of the conquest said that Martin de Goiti left Panay on May 8, 1570, with ninety arquebusiers and twenty sailors on board the frigate La Toruga and the junk San Miguel, together with fifteen praus or native boats manned by the allies from Cebu and Panay. They had three large pieces of artillery. In a week's time, they were in Balayan (Batangas) after fighting some Muslim groups in Mindoro. Within the second week of May, they were in Manila.

The meeting between Goiti and Soliman was friendly. Rajah Matanda and his entourage met Goiti on the shore and embraced him. Then Rajah Soliman arrived with his followers. According to the Spanish account, "Soliman assumed an air of importance and haughtiness but said that he was pleased to be the friend of the Spaniards. He would not, however, tolerate any abuse by them as they had inflicted on other natives. Anyone who would violate his people would repay with his life."[20] Then he and Goiti embraced and parted. The next morning, Soliman sent his messenger to Goiti to inform him that, since he learned that the Spaniards would ask for tribute from him and his people, he would not allow them to enter the river. Goiti dissuaded him from believing that, and in a house inside the fort, a blood compact took place between the two. The Spanish account of the terms of the compact was that the Muslims of Manila were

17

to support the Spaniards who would come to live in Manila. If that would be done, then they would pay no other tribute.

After the compact, the Muslims promised to supply the Spaniards provisions for their ships. But the Muslims did not lay down their weapons and there was no sign of friendship among the warriors. Goiti learned that Rajah Lakandula was preparing to attack the Spaniards. Even while Soliman was giving assurance that he would assist the Spaniards, Goiti prepared for the worst. And soon there was cannon fire heard from the side of the Muslims. The report later said that Soliman fired the first three shots directed at the ships. In the next instance, a full battle was raging. The Spaniards burned the town and captured all the twelve pieces of artillery on the fort. It was a losing battle for the Muslims who had about a hundred dead on the shore due to either the arquebus bullets or burns. There were around eighty captives while many others died on the *praus.* Manila had fallen on May 24, 1570. After three days, the Spaniards sailed back to Panay.

The following year, in May, 1571, Miguel Lopez de Legazpi, arrived in Manila with his fleet, and intended to settle there. According to the account, Rajah Lakandula met him on his ship and apologized for the hostility instigated by Rajah Soliman the previous year.[21] But during this second coming of the Spaniards, the Muslims themselves burned the city which they had rebuilt then evacuated to the interior villages. The Spaniards took over the site of the Muslim city upon which they built the Spanish Walled City known to us as Intramuros ("within the walls"). Rajahs Laya, Soliman and Lakandula, having come to terms with the Spaniards, offered to help pacify the surrounding areas by convincing the other chiefs to accept the Spanish offer of friendship. But this did not materialize because each chief had his own view of the issue. Some chiefs decided to attack the Spaniards as in the case of the Chief of Butes (Navotas).[22] Besides, the power and prestige of Soliman must have waned at this time because of his defeat by the Spaniards, while Lakandula's reputation suffered because of his compromise with the enemies.

On May 16, 1571, Legazpi announced that lands and *repartimientos* would be given to the Spaniards who would settle in Manila—and these were his officers and soldiers and some Spanish gentlemen with him. On June 3, 1571, Legazpi announced that Manila would be his capital. On June 24 of that same year, he organized his administrative set-up, appointing the officials of the city. The Muslims and their leaders were among the native inhabitants of the city who co-existed with the Spaniards. If the claims of missionary priests were true, then the Muslims of Manila became the Christianized natives under the

Spanish colonial administration.

## Conclusion

The Muslim community prior to the arrival of the Spaniards was an economically progressive community, well-organized socially and politically. While the natives may not have been so learned in the doctrinal aspect of Islam, their well-ordered lives and the manifestation of certain Islamic practices in their social relations were enough proofs of their understanding of their religion. The fact that they had well-settled and cultivated lands with products that provided for the sustenance of the community as well as for the barter trade showed that they were an industrious people.

They also understood the significance of strong leadership and political authority for power per se, as well as for economic gains. This was shown by their assertion of vassal-suzerain relation with some coastal tribes as well as by their resistance against foreign invaders. They also developed their military might through fortification and training of warriors to protect themselves from their enemies. They manufactured their own cannons and other pieces of artillery, and used gunpower, too. All these meant that they understood the value of technology. They knew how to smelt gold, steel, or copper for weaponry and ornaments.

They had a well-developed seafaring capacity as evidenced by the kind of boats they built and which could sail as far as Borneo and the neighboring islands. As a people, they had strong pride and loved their independence as shown by their resistance against the Spaniards. The leadership had a high sense of propriety and protocol in dealing with foreign leaders — a revelation of their exposure to a higher culture, perhaps influenced by Islam itself. If the Spaniards had defeated them, it was because they were not equal enough to Spanish military technology at that time. They were also quite unprepared for the Spanish ways of professing friendship which in effect meant subjugation and vassalage.

## NOTES

1. "Muslims in the Big City," *Philippine Panorama*, March 4, 1979; by the author's research in the area.
2. *Expressweek* (Sunday magazine of *The Daily Express*), February 16, 1979.

3. According to Rev. T.C. Middleton, O.S.A., some writers claim that the name is a corruption of Maydila from the Tagalog words *may* and *dila* meaning "the place that has a tongue" — alluding to a tongue-shaped island formerly at the mouth of the Pasig river. See also, "Relation of the Conquest of the Island of Luzon," in *The Philippines*, Blair and Robertson, vol. 3.

4. Cesar A. Majul, *Muslims in the Philippines*, 1973. Quezon City: University of the Philippines Press, pp. 72-74.

5. "Relation of the Conquest....", pp. 155-157

6. "Relation of the Voyage to Luzon," in Blair and Robertson, p. 100

7. Majul, *Muslims in the Philippines,* p. 73

8. "Relation of the Voyage to Luzon," p. 103

9. Miguel Lopez de Legazpi, "Relation of the Filipinas Islands," in Blair and Robertson, p. 57.

10. "Relation of the Voyage....," pp. 101-102

11. Ibid. pp. 77-91

12. Francisco de Sande et al. "Account of Expeditions to Borneo, Jolo and Mindanao," in *The Philippines,* Blair and Robertson, vol. 4, p. 149.

13. Ibid., p. 151; Legazpi, op. cit., p. 60

14. "Relation to the Conquest..." pp. 143, 147

15. Ibid., p. 163

16. Legazpi, op. cit., p. 61

17. Loc. cit.

18. "Relation of the Voyage..." p. 94

19. Ibid., pp. 100-101

20. Ibid., p. 97 (On the blood compact between Goiti and Soliman)

21. Ibid., p. 105

22. "Relation of the Conquest...", p. 156

# THE JESUITS AND THE AMERICAN OCCUPATION OF MANILA, 1898

JOSE S. ARCILLA, S.J.

My topic is much more limited than it may first appear. We would need an entire book for the whole story of the Jesuit presence in Manila. We would have to study the Ateneo de Manila, the Escuela Normal, the Manila Observatory, or the San Ignacio Church—four institutions through which Jesuit influence spread all over the city. If we look into the more recent past, we may have to include the May devotions, the Conference of Saint Vincent de Paul, the NCAA, the Christmas packages drive: all of these were introduced by the Jesuits.

I shall discuss only the time when the Americans took Manila on 13 August 1898. My sources are the documents preserved in the Jesuit archives in Rome, Spain, and here in the Philippines.

The Americans took Manila on 13 August 1898. Gunfire started at about 9:00 in the morning, and by 6:00 that evening, they struck the Spanish colors and hoisted the Stars and Stripes over Fort Santiago, to the tune of the American national anthem. Except for the soldiers who cheered, there were no witnesses to that historic events. Governor Basilio Augusti had just sailed for Hongkong with his family.

Outside of Manila (that is, Intramuros), both the American vanguard and the Filipino troops needed a place to stay. They first approached the Jesuits at the Manila Observatory on Padre Faura Street, but Fr. Jose Algue, the Director, refused them use of the building, since the first floor was already occupied by refugee families from the suburbs. Why not, suggested the Jesuit, try the velodrome?

After the Americans came the Filipinos, asking to have their flag raised over the Observatory. Refused, someone succeeded nonetheless in hoisting it. And when two officers assigned a man to pull it down, he was met with *bejucazos* from the unit guarding it. The flag was lowered later, however.

These two incidents may seen unimportant, but they show the

21

delicate position in which the Jesuits found themselves. They were openly loyal to the Spanish government, but they were also committed to help the Filipino people attain the good life. What did they do in that time of crisis?

Manila was not unaware of the mounting crisis between Spain and the United States. On 5 April, less than a month before the victory of Dewey, Governor Fernando Primo de Rivera was asking the Jesuit Superior for information in order to introduce some reforms into the country (both in keeping with the Pact of Biak-na-bato and out of his personal conviction that they were needed). Three weeks later, upon receiving news of the outbreak of the war, people walked through the streets of Intramuros demonstrating their adherence to Spain. Two days later, when Dewey moved from Hongkong to Mirs Bay the sick soldiers in the military hospital at Malate were transferred to the Jesuit weekend villa at Santa Ana (today, the La Ignaciana Apostolic Center on Pedro Gil Street).

The defeat of the Spanish fleet off Cavite is too well known to need detailed discussion here. In less than an hour on 1 May 1898, eight Spanish war vessels were destroyed. About 1:00 in the afternoon, an unarmed mail boat, the "Isla de Mindanao," was burned off Parañaque. Its crew subsequently found lodging in the first floor of the Jesuit Ateneo Municipal.

The following day, 2 May, the Jesuits retired their valuables to Sta. Ana. In Cavite, the Spaniards retired and set up a new government center in San Francisco de Malabon (Trias), where, with the help of Filipino volunteers, they transferred their weapons. By noon time, the Americans had already installed themselves on the beach and occupied the arsenal.

Back in Manila, the Junta de Autoridades (the extra-legal advisory body to the Governor General) held an emergency meeting. They all agreed it was vital to keep Filipino loyalty. They, therefore, approved: recruitment of native (indio) volunteers, with the promise of promotion up the rank of colonel and admission to positions in the civil administration; the formation of a new "consultative assembly" with Filipino members; and titles of nobility to deserving Filipinos. But they stopped short of adopting liberal reforms. Finally, at the suggestion of Fr. Pio Pi, Superior of the Jesuits in the Philippines, they approved the plan to send religious priests and friars to the towns and rural areas to make sure of the sentiments of the people.

Nothing unusual happened the next few days. Dewey, unsure what faculties he had, merely demanded the surrender of all war vessels in the Philippines, declared all Spanish marines as war prisoners, and announced the blockade of Manila.

For the Jesuits life went on as usual. On 5 May, they had a family celebration to honor their Superior's saint's day. But on 9 May, Frs. Jose Algue and Antonio Rossell volunteered to go to Cavite. They left the next morning, arriving in Imus at 6:00 o'clock in the evening. They were welcomed by Tomas Tirona, an Ateneo student, son of Guillermo, himself a former Ateneo student. When word went around that there were two Jesuit priests at the Tirona residence, 20 of the most influential town leaders came out of hiding. They had not been seen for some time because they were afraid of being made *capitan municipal*, lest they suffer the same fate of the last two *capitanes* who had been mysteriously killed.

We might perhaps inject an observation now. Why were these two municipal captains, presumarly appointed by the Spanish authorities, killed? By whom? We perhaps will have no answers to these questions since apparently no documents attest to the facts. But it shows there must have been a strong anti-government feeling in Imus that led to the murder of the two town officials.

The Jesuits themselves were expecting the worst. There were rumors that Dewey had offered free passage to all the consuls in the city to save them when a force 30,000 strong would rise up in arms to massacre all the foreigners in the Philippines. Nothing of the kind took place. As reported to the Jesuit Superior in Manila the town leaders were unanimous in their gratitude and loyalty to the Spanish Crown. They declared it was "better to die than fall into the hands of heretics." They assured the Jesuits that

our elders have passed on to us not the slightest complaint against the Jesuits who had administered various parishes in the province. Rather, we have heard from the lips of our parents nothing but praise, and we know that they, like ourselves, are convinced of how those Jesuits of old, like Your Reverences, sought only justice and truth and you have always professed true love for us. We, therefore, would fail in our filial duty to our ancestors; nay, we would be going against our consciences were we to turn a deaf ear to your advice, disagree with your reasons, or refuse to carry out what is being urged on us.

This must have been an embarrassingly happy surprise to those two emissaries. Their worst fears had proven baseless, the two Jesuits were warmly received in all the towns they visited: Imus, Bacoor, Kawit, Noveleta, Trias, Salinas, etc. In Bacoor, Baldomero Aguinaldo, cousin of Emilio, pledged allegiance to the Spanish Crown. His sincerity can be seen from this: that on 22 May, he wrote to the Governor General that he was retiring from public life since he did not wish to break his promise; neither did he want to fight his cousin.

The Jesuits were back in Manila on 14 May, happy over the success of their mission. Through the help of Daniel Tirona, they had been able to see many of the Cavite leaders in the towns they visited: Artemio Ricarte, Mariano Trias, Emiliano Riego de Dios, Mariano Punzalan, Ladislao Diwa, Jose Tagle, etc. As they reported to their superiors, the Caviteños were unanimous in thanking them for

the service done them in explaining the real situation to them, and suggesting what would be most convenient. They said they were ready to die if it was the price of preserving intact the religion of their ancestors taught by the priests at so much trouble and sweat; that at the call of the leaders to be assigned to them, they would all rally to defend their most cherished interests.

Complaints were also discussed, which implies that there must have been a free and open discussion of all pertinent issues. There were two main grievances presented to the Jesuits: the abuses of the native Guardia Civil, and the injustice of court sentences based on secret police reports. The people of Bacoor petitioned that the town be elevated to a Comandancia, and then they would raise 1,000 fighting men for the government.

Let us again pause here for a few observations and questions. Were the Jesuits perhaps a little too optimistic? Fr. Algue, one of the emissaries, was the Director of the Observatory, a respected man, and certainly known for his honesty and integrity. Fr. Rossell, his companion, was a well-known figure in Manila. He had been, earlier, instrumental in the retraction from freemasonry of one of the Luna brothers. These two priests could not have been too easily taken in by words!

It is also important to remember the dates. These contacts with the Cavite leaders took place before the nineteenth of May. Emilio Aguinaldo was still out of the country, and it is not at all impossible that the people in the provinces were sincere in their pledges of loyalty to the colonial government. It is thus important to realize that during this period, anti-Spanish hostility among the Filipinos was not universal, or that the war against the Spanish government was not an insular movement. There is evidence to support the claims of the Spanish friars in the Philippines that the people in the towns and rural areas stood loyally by them. It is true some of the friars were tortured and abused during the first phase of the war (1896-1897), but the perpetrators were the minority, the ilustrados who had had access to liberal literatures and had been influenced by their reading. Fr. Schumacher has published a brief essay showing that the revolutionary leaders in Cavite remained faithful to Roman Catholic practices. And certain quarters in that province blamed the counteroffensive on the execution of the Spanish Recollect friars they had apprehended in Naic. It was American Protestantism, with the blessings of the Taft Administration, that helped decatholicize the country. Of course, we cannot overlook the lack of priests immediately after the change of governments. And how does one explain the strong anti-American stand of Artemio Ricarte, who chose exile in Japan rather than to live under an American government? Questions like this come to mind when one reads the documents about this period which are kept in the Jesuit archives. In other words, it is time to change our attitude that the revolution was a homogenous picture. No, it was rather a much more nuanced story.

Emilio Aguinaldo returned from Hongkong on 19 May, courtesy of the Americans. A Jesuit diary has this entry for the day: "The dispatch, *McCollough*, which had sailed for Hongkong, arrives in Manila, bringing on board Emilio Aguinaldo, with two leaders who had departed for Hongkong last December." And the diarist adds information which could enlighten the still unresolved controversy about the agreement between Dewey and Aguinaldo.

Aguinaldo was in Singapore on 21 April, hoping to contact, the Englishman, Howard W. Bray. He wanted to win the latter's support, or at least, advice, because he wanted to lead the fight for Philippine Independence, provided the United States recognized the Philippines. He had decided on this course of action because the terms of the Pact of Biak-na-bato had not been, according to Aguinaldo, carried out: the expulsion and the secularization of the religious orders in the Philippines; their prohibition from participating in secular affairs; general amnesty for all the rebels guaranteed against any acts of personal vengeance by the Spaniards; radical reforms in the administration; a free press to denounce abuses in the administration; representation in the Cortes; and abolition of secret police reports and sentences of exile.

These terms were demanded by Aguinaldo as the conditions for the validity of the pact. But someone who claimed he had seen the text of the pact itself denied they had been written in the text; instead, there was a note: "The government will attend to just complaints of the native population provided they do not hinder the country's progress." Unfortunately, the anti-Spanish paper in Hongkong, the *Daily Press*, did not publish this note, giving rise to conclusions unfavorable to the Manila government. But there was a secret protocol, or at least verbal acceptance of these conditions by the Governor General of the Philippines. We must remember, however, that the Governor General in Manila had no powers to make decisions. He was empowered only to implement decrees emanating from the royal government in the peninsula. And, when interrogated, Paterno, the negotiator of the pact, was tight-lipped. Lastly, the indemnities were not paid on time, nor were reforms introduced within the six months' deadline.

What may one conclude from this? Again, that more analysis of the documents is needed before any definitive picture of the Philippine revolution can be made. We now begin to see that the textbook tradition of our history needs to be modified.

The successful first mission to Cavite prompted the Governor General to send a second pair of emissaries to the province: Frs. Jose Algue and Jose Clos. This time, the priests failed to contact Daniel Tirona, for he had been kidnapped by two men armed with bolos and a rifle, and brought for interrogation before Aguinaldo. The Jesuits were not a little put down, naturally, but apparently to allay some of the fears of the local leaders, the two suggested drawing up a list of their grievances against Aguinaldo to present it to the government in Manila. They were gladdened, on the other hand, by the continued loyalty of such important leaders as Ricarte, Riego de Dios, and Mariano Trias. Although Bacoor was now showing signs of wavering, and some of the town leaders had thrown in their lot with Aguinaldo, others promised the Jesuits they would return some 200 or 300 rifles taken from the Cavite arsenal.

By 29 May, the American *McCollough* was ferrying men from Bulacan to Cavite, where they were enlisting under the colors of Aguinaldo. These men were then sent to the arsenal of Cavite for a rifle and the sum of four pesos. Rumors were strong that two native companies of Regiment 74 had joined Aguinaldo after exterminating a marine infantry unit. And, as the Jesuit chronicler adds, American weaponry distributed among the Bulakeños posed a serious danger, at the same time that Aguinaldo was sending his men to the various provinces to prepare them for an uprising. Finally, the first open exchange of gunfire took place on 30 May.

Interestingly, no Jesuit document mentions the 12 June declaration of independence by Aguinaldo in Kawit. Manila is not too far away, but people there seem not to have known anything about that incident. Later, however, on 18 June the story reached the city that Aguinaldo had "set up a republic." But no one gave it much thought!

This brings up the legitimacy or the validity of the so-called independence day of the Philippines on 12 June. Which countries or governments recognized the existence of that republic? Who, or how many, in the entire province of Cavite accepted the new Philippine nation at that time?

The following day, 13 June, a meeting was held at the Paterno residence in Manila, with about forty *criollos* (creoles), Chinese mestizos, and indios, none of whom had any political ties. All of them wanted to work for peace. The initiative of the meeting had come, not from Paterno himself, but from some Filipino revolutionary leaders who wanted to surrender to the government in secret. They had originally sounded out the General of the Marine, but he refused to receive them since he was "vowed to military action." It was then that they went to the Governor General to present to him a list of demands and reforms, asking him to grant autonomy as a sign of peace. The governor accepted all the demands on condition, however, that the Filipinos first lay down their arms. The Filipinos, it was pointed out, were already members of the "consultative assembly" first convoked on 28 May. What was the role, then, of this second group?

It is not too well known, but on 9 July, Macabulos in Tarlac had challenged Aguinaldo's authority. Nor is it known that on 11 July, an autonomy plan drawn up supposedly by Paterno was modified by some of the Cavite leaders who refused to approve the clause on the freedom of worship, insisting that in the Philippines there should be no change in religion. And the possibility of civil marriage sat ill with these leaders.

On 15 July, a plebiscite was held in Bulacan; should autonomy be accepted, or should they continue to fight for independence? There was no agreement, but in the meantime, three groups emerged: the separatists, under Aguinaldo's leadership; the autonomists, led by Isabelo Artacho; and the annexionists, with Teodoro Cortes (still in Hongkong) as their head. Because of Aguinaldo's energy and absolutism, the autonomists were kept in the background, inhibited from expressing their true sentiments. Of course, with Cortes still in Hongkong, his group exercised the least influence.

Fighting continued, but strangely, on 29 July, Filipino and Spanish troops met and joined for a meal in one of the trenches! The following day, 21 Filipino leaders met in Bulacan to ask for autonomy. It was initiated by Pedro Serrano, but was strongly opposed by Aguinaldo, who threatened the former for thinking of such a course of action.

By 7 August, the Belgian consul and the English Vice-Consul called on the Governor General to convey a message from Dewey: the probable bombardment of the city within 48 hours, and the need to evacuate it of non-combatants. Impossible, answered the Spaniards, for at the gates of the city (i.e., Intramuros), the Filipino fighters were waiting. He asked, however, for six days to consult his government, surprising Dewey who had been thinking all the time that the Governor General enjoyed full powers. The people, of course, panicked upon learning of this, and they braved the heavy sea in order to sail away to safety.

Let us again pause for a few observations. The most obvious thing we

27

note is the lack of unanimity in the Filipino leadership at this moment. Aguinaldo did not enjoy universal authority, nor were all the Filipinos totally against the Spanish government. They wanted to be independent, but they were not necessarily anti-Spain. And clearly, they were not pro-American!

# POMPAS Y SOLEMNIDADES: NOTES ON CHURCH CELEBRATIONS IN SPANISH MANILA

DOREEN G. FERNANDEZ

The pages of the Philippine history are studded with accounts of feasts and celebrations starting in, occurring in, or initiated by the churches of Spanish Manila. As early as January 1597, for example, there was "rejoicing and festive show as had never been known before in the islands"[1] when the relics of 155 martyrs, including those of 20 Popes, and of Sta. Potenciana, patroness of Manila, were installed in a richly decorated tabernacle in a new church. The fiesta was celebrated with:

.... solemne procesion general, Novenario, y certamen Poetico: de el insigne Convento de San Agustin salio la solemne Procesion, paso por la Iglesia Cathedral, y por las mejores calles, vino aparar [sic] al Colegio de San Ignacio ... colgadas de las Ventanas ricas y costosas tapicerias; aproporcionadas [sic] distancias estaban construidos arcos triumphales, fuentes de varios licores ... venian en la Procesion en proporcion en seis Andas y catorce relicarios de costoso adorno, las Santas reliquias en hombros, manos de Sacerdotes, Prelados, Prebendados, y Religiosos graves, revestidos de Capas de Coro, ricamente guernacidas de Perlas, Joyas, Cadenas de Oro, en cantidad, y calidad abundantes ... acompañaban todas las Confradias, communidades, y estados, festejando a trechos la funcion alegres danzas de varias naciones y trages: estaba la iglesia de el Collegio adornada de colgaduras exquisitas, pinturas, y poesias ... ofrecieron los Padres de San Agustin con musica escogida, y predicaron eminentemente con espiritu ... el ultimo dia huvo justa Poetica ...[2]

The above—solemn masses and eminent preachers, processions, jewelled robes and ornaments, rich banners and hangings, triumphal arches in the streets, literary/dramatic performances, the music of voices and instruments, dignitaries and the faithful in procession—soon came to be the standard elements of a church celebration in Spanish Manila. It was invariably with pride that friar-chroniclers recorded the pomp and solemnity with which "M.N. y S.L. Ciudad de Manila" celebrated its festivities.

These included both religious and civil occasions, since church and state were so inextricably linked. Church feasts inevitably included civil authorities—at the very least attending, but more usually involved. Civil or state feasts always started in the church, at the very least with a Mass and a *Te Deum*, but more usually with the Archbishop and the clergy as well as the faithful involved in novenas, sermons, processions, etc.

One of the earliest notes on such celebrations, for example, was in 1571, after the conquest of Manila, when "those Moros or Tagalas received the peace offered them, and rendered homage to King Don Felipe ... and to his successors, the sovereigns of España." This was done on the feast of St. Andrew, patron saint of Manila, and the *adelantado*, Legazpi, unfurled the standard, which was then carried about with great pomp, and attended (as in Cebu) by processions, masses, and preachings, with ecclesiastic and secular dignitaries participating.[3]

In 1595, a letter from Felipe II to Don Francisco Tello details quite explicitly the procedure of receiving the royal seal:

....you shall go ... accompanied by the auditors, the fiscal, all the soldiers in military array, the citizen encomenderos, my officials, and all others in public positions. The said seal will be contained in a box borne under a canopy, the supports of which shall be carried by the regidors of the city. The box will be borne by a horse, richly caparisoned ... All of you shall go straight to the cathedral with bared heads, where the archbishop will be waiting, clad with his pontifical vestments, together with all his clergy ... There you shall place the box, and the archbishop will repeat his prayers, beseeching our Lord to direct the founding of the .... Audiencia for his good service, the pure administration of justice.[4]

Both the above examples show how special state occasions (not yearly events) assumed the participation of the church and its people.

**Religious Feasts**

The more usual festive occasions included, first of all, religious feasts, of which there were a number each month, including feasts for the whole church (such as Christmas and Easter), feasts special to Spanish subjects (e.g. "San Tiago Apostol,"),[5] and those special to the diocese, region, or congregation (e.g. San Andres, chosen patron saint of Manila because on his feastday the city was delivered from Limahong's blockade; and St. Ignatius Loyola, founder of the Society of Jesus).

The feast of the Immaculate Conception, for example, was celebrated in 1619 with nineteen days of bullfights, masquerades, nightly illuminations and fireworks, and the concerted—and competing—efforts of all the religious congregations:

On the first day ... Sunday, December 8 ... there was given a drama on the beauty of Rachel. On Monday the religious of St. Francis held their fiesta in the [cathedral] ... In the

30

morning, one of the grandest processions ever seen in this vicinity set out from their house ... First came the whole force of Manila in perfect order, the arguebusiers and musketeers firing their pieces at intervals. Next came a rich standard bearing the image of the conception of the Virgin, and at her feet Escoto [ Duns Scotus ] ... After the standard ... borne by the father guardian ... a lay friar called Fray Junipero ... regarded as a holy and simple man ... was dancing, and calling out a thousand silly phrases about divine things. Now followed banners, crosses, and candlesticks. After these came on floats eight saints of this order, so richly adorned that there should be so large a quantity of gold, jewels and precious stones in Manila, or that the fathers should have collected so many of them. These saints were accompanied by eight groups of Indian dancers ... One represented canons, one cardinals, another pastors, etc. The last sang while dancing .... Last of all came the most holy Virgin of the conception. The procession reached the cathedral and the fiesta was held. In the afternoon they presented a very devout drama, on the martyrs of Japon.

On Tuesday the fiesta of [the Augustinians] ... began... On Wednesday, we of the Society began our festivities; and although we had no procession, as is our custom, the celebration at night was by no means inferior ... there was burned a great quantity of illuminations ... Our people played a thousand musical instruments. During the day we held mass, in our impressive manner, and then had a sermon; and in the afternoon we presented a remarkable drama on the conception. All the people said they had never seen anything like it.

On Thursday the fiesta was again held in the cathedral. In the afternoon there was another drama ... On Friday the Augustinian Recoletos began their fiesta. In the morning there was a great procession ... In the afternoon was presented the drama of the Prince of Transilvania ....

On Sunday there were two fiestas. One was held in the cathedral ... while the other was at our house—where it seemed expedient to hold it in order that the cathedral and the religious of St. Francis should not monopolize the entire celebration, and acquire such a right for the future .. At nightfall our collegians of St. Joseph formed a procession remarkable enough to have appeared in Madrid ...all the collegians ... on horseback two by two, wearing their usual robes of brown silk with facings made of fine scarlet cloth, and with shoulder-stripes of lace. Their caps were a blaze of gold and precious stone. About their necks they all wore many chains and jewels. Each of the prominent nobility of the city had ahead of him, as a bodyguard, six or eight servants, with large tapers of white wax in their hands. They carried staffs having upon them large placards with various pictures, letters, and hieroglyphics, all appropriate to the occasion ... Finally came a very beautiful triumphal chariot drawn by two savages, and decorated with many arches of flowers and gilded figures of angels. In the midst of these and among a great number of lights went, enthroned, a beautiful carved figure of our Lady of the Conception. Before the chariot was a band of clarion- players. They followed eight children dressed in silk garments and carrying silver candles. They represented angels .... singing and reciting in praise of the Virgin. After the chariot came Original Sin, tied with a chain, and so well made up for his part that he became a mark for the blows and pinches of the people. Next day there was another very magnificent fiesta, in which a dance was given by more than sixty Japanese, who sang and danced to the accompaniment of various instruments, according to their custom.

After this, on Sunday, the order of St. Francis began their eight-day fiesta. Another was held at the port of Cavite in which, as in Manila, all the orders took part—except one, which during all this time did not leave its house, enter the cathedral, nor display illuminations. About this there was no lack of gossiping in the city.[6]

The above is reproduced in some detail, because not only does it contain the standard elements—religious and otherwise—for festivities mentioned earlier, but it also emphasizes one other that came to play an important part in all Philippine feasting—fireworks, rockets, and illuminations. The attitude displayed by the anonymous friar, moreover, is also telling: his admiration for the "great magnificence" reveals the standard for celebration—pomp and solemnity or, in more contemporary expression, *bongga*, compound of visual splendor, symbol and allegory, *pasikat*, important personages (Don Luis Faxardo, brother of the governor, Don Fernando Centeno, general of the galleys, alcaldes, regidors, etc.), richness, music and theater, exotic dances, and an undeniable spirit of competition or *pasiklaban* between the religious orders. We cannot help but smile at his almost wicked aside—one of the religious orders, easily identifiable, did not take part, and became the object of gossip in the city. If it all sounds familiar, it is because it is this kind of feasting and celebrating that set the standard for the years that followed, the spirit filtering into our criteria for celebrations, our theater aesthetics.

## Royal Feasts

Aside from religious feasts, cause for celebration was also provided by events in Spain that reverberated into her colonies, especially those relating to royalty. The accession of Philip IV in 1623, for example, called for festivities attended by the entire town, civil and political,[7] and that of Carlos II in 1677 occasioned four "sermones panegiricos," an "octavario," and a booklet describing the royal feasts.[8] The festivities for Carlos II of Spain (1677) had sermons from the different orders, bullfights and *comedias*, and "a beautiful and splendid masquerade, with magnificent costumes, and parades of servants in costly liveries. The most distinguished citizens of Manila went therein, two by two, representing the realms of the monarchy ... with shields and mottoes proper for each kingdom."[9]

At the feasting for the birth of Prince Luis Felipe Fernando in 1710, there were *toros* (50 on each of two days), a novena, special *villancicos* by the Jesuits, *fuegos* ("... cinco mil bombas, setenta docenas de voladores y busca pies, veinte quatro nudos grandes, trescientas peloteras de Sangley y trescientas pelotares de acero fueron los principales elementos de un solo castillo .... Hubo ademas buques de fuego no menos estupendos...."), *indios* and *mestizos de sangley* in "escaramuzas, parejas, caracoles y otras habilidades," comparsas, comedias, loas, races, a literary competition, and a sermon that detailed the expenses on the Philippines of His Majesty, the

King of Spain.[10]

The celebrations were obviously not limited to Spanish subjects or customs, since at the accession of Carlos IV in 1790, aside from the pontifical mass and the *Te Deum* at the cathedral, levees (*besamanos,* or court days, for the nobility to "kiss the hands of the king"), banquets, comedias and bullfights, Fray Manuel Barrios describes Chinese lions spitting fire, and a serpent [dragon] fifty cubits long swallowing fire and dancing through the streets; the distribution of ₱3,000 in alms to widows, orphans, and undowered girls, and one Pedro Gallaraga who "carried to the stars the name of his august sovereign, by means of a large aerostatic globe, which crossed the bay and was lost to sight among the clouds," and also "flung to the people a quantity of coins bearing the stamp of the new monarch."[11] On the same occasion, the Filipino poet, alferez real Luis Rodriguez Varela, decorated his house fittingly:

.... en cuyo frontispicio .... un hermoso Palacio,.... dividido en tres cuerpos diferentes .... En el primer cuerpo se registraban unos Salones magnificos conbalcones [sic], galerias claraboyas, y ventanas en Simetria admirable, y en sus lienzos se veian pinturas finas y extraordinarias....

En el segundo cuerpo se veian unas columnas de orden compuesto, y en medio de ellas entre colgaduras de Damasco debajo de pabellon de ceda guarnecido de galon de plata, se manifestaban los Reales Retratos en quadro obalado, y a sus pies el Cetro y la Corona, todo dorado de Oro .... En la parte inferior del quadro se leia la siguiente inscripcion.

> De CARLOS REY... sin igual,
> el merito, y la grandeza proclama el Alferez Real;
> y de Luisa liberal
> la incomparable belleza.

En el tercer cuerpo sobre barandillas doradas se elevaba una Cornisa ... en cuio centro se veian de pintura fina las armas de la Corona Espanola ....[12]

Still other such royal occasions included: the arrival and installation of the portrait of Fernando VII in 1825; the proclamation of Isabel II in 1834 (5500 *luces, cucanas* or greased poles, *carros triumfales* from Tondo, Binondo, Sta. Cruz, Ermita, Malate, and Dilao drawn by *zagalas*, in front of which danced other zagalas "entrage morisco" or "vestidas a la indiana," boat races, dances, banquets, regattas, declamations, and of course theater); a royal wedding in 1847; the birth of Don Alfonso de Borbon in 1858, which was the occasion for the construction of what became the Teatro del Principe Alfonso in Arroceros, three days of games, races and feasting, and prizes given to babies born on the same day.[13]

A royal funeral, that of Prince Balthassar Carlos, in 1649, was given special and lengthy attention in a publication printed by Simon Pinpin. The announcement had arrived in July 1648, and in it the king "ordered the demonstrations of sorrow to be made on the same scale as if intended for his own person." The fiscal auditor, Don Sebastian Cavallero de Medina, was chosen manager of that solemn function, assisted by the treasurer and two regidors. The people changed into mourning garments and the whole community "became a theater of grief."

Expressions of condolence were given on Monday, November 9, 1648 at the halls of the Royal Audiencia and Assembly, which were draped in funeral adornments. At two in the afternoon the bells of all the churches tolled, and all the religious communities assembled "with their crosses, priests, deacons, and subdeacons, clad in their vestments," in the garrison royal chapel, where a "royal tomb" and mausoleum had been erected. While each community in succession chanted its responsary, "the ecclesiastical and secular cabildos were assembling, as well as the tribunal of the royal official judges, the superiors of the orders, the rectors of the colleges," the Jesuit San Jose and the Dominican Sto. Tomas, and the members of the Sta. Misericordia. From there the august procession left to express condolences to the Governor General, in order of strict protocol.

A processional next accompanied the royal crown to the chapel of the royal camp for solemn vespers and the funeral oration. This solemn parade started with some 150 orphan boys from San Juan de Letran, holding candles of pure white wax which were later distributed throughout the city; then the confraternities with their pennants and banners; the suburban parishes with their crosses and black-cloaked *curas*; the college students with their *becas* turned back as a token of grief; the bureau of Sta. Misericodia in black surtouts and hats, their heads covered, and bearing their small bells; the holy orders; the ecclesiastical cabildo in black choir-cloaks, with the skirts extended and their heads covered; the cabildo and the judges' tribunal, bearing maces and insignia, and the nobility in flowing black mourning cloaks; the royal standard carried by captain Gabriel Gomez del Castillo assisted by alcaldes; the royal Audiencia with the governor followed by the government and court secretaries, and the gentlemen and pages of the palace. Between the city cabildo and the royal Audiencia was carried the Caesarean crown on a cushion of rich cloth.

At the Plaza de Armas, as the "brilliant procession went around it" was the royal regiment of the Spanish troops — 486 infantrymen on four fronts, each commanded by two captains and one alferez, who later fell in behind the procession in "great order and discipline," their arquebuses held with butt-ends reversed. The royal crown was placed on the catafalque, "or rather a funeral pyre of fire, crowned with candles as is the firmament with stars, where the brilliant and the majestic glowed in competition."

The vespers for the dead were followed by a funeral panegyric that "roamed the spacious and extensive field of the virtues of our most serene prince " a responsary, and the grand procession in reverse, returning his Lordship to the palace.

The following day, November 10, the different religious orders sang masses at their assigned altars, and responsaries in front of the royal catafalque, then went to the palace, for a reassembly of the previous day's parade — to return to the chapel of the royal camp to sing the office for the dead and the mass. Fr. Francisco Colin, college rector and outgoing Jesuit provincial, preached the sermon, and "arrested the attention and even the admiration of those present." Some responsaries followed, and thus ended the funeral ceremonies, showing "the devotion and loyalty of vassals ever attentive to the service of their Catholic monarch, in recognition of the rewards that they receive from his august hand."

The account ends with a detailed description of the royal catafalque, with its columns, entablatures, friezes, architraves, cupola, canopy, cushions, inscribed verses ("Esta fatal urna encierra fallida una Magestad ..."), symbolic figures, candles, obelisks, and escutcheons — and with the funeral poems and eulogies in Latin and Spanish.[14]

The "pomp and circumstance" were for a prince the people had not known nor seen, but surely the detail and grandeur of the ceremonies were impressed upon the observers, suggesting "the royal way" of doings things, of mourning, of remembering, of sealing a person's importance — and thus created a mental set, a lasting impression, or at the very least a vivid memory.

## City Festivals

*Festejos* were also called for by events important to the life and welfare of the City of Manila. Thus, the loss of the galleon San Felipe, and the martyrdom of San Pedro Bautista and his [Franciscan] companions were the occasion for rituals in 1597. The Franciscan church was decorated by the *ciudadanos* [probably Spanish] with rich hangings of damask and brocade, and by the *Indios* with their "invenciones piadosas de tejidos de palmas y flores," making the convents and streets look like spring. For three days the religious orders, the town, the civil and military officials were in attendance at the cathedral for the *Te Deum* and procession in which were carried a painting of the Holy Martyrs (raised high so that it could be seen by all) and the casket of relics; the solemn

High Mass and sermon on the glorious martyrdom (which had such an effect on the listeners that "todos confesaron el sentimiento que habia causado en sus almas, y nuevos deseos de morir por la confesion de la Fe"); and the installation of the relics in a place of honor.

The re-establishment of the Audiencia (suppressed some years earlier) in 1598 was marked by a procession in which the royal seal was taken from the monastery of San Agustin to the cathedral upon a horse caparisoned in crimson and gold, under a canopy borne by the regidors of the city, clad in crimson velvet and white silver cloth, followed by the president and auditors, afoot and bareheaded, with a throng of citizens in gala dress and the soldiery with drums and banners. They walked along streets adorned with tapestry, finery and triumphal arches, to the music of flutes, trumpets and other instruments—and were received at the cathedral door by the archbishop in pontifical robes, and by the chapter and clergy. The seal was taken to the main altar and placed on a brocade-covered stool, as the singers intoned the Te Deum Laudamus.[15]

The Spanish victory over the Dutch in 1610 was marked by the ringing of church bells, a solemn procession from the cathedral to the Jesuit church, where a sermon was preached; a mass and sermon in the Franciscan church; the erection of a catafalque (to commemorate those who had died in the battle) of three storeys with pyramids, tapers, Latin and Spanish epitaphs, inscriptions, and a tomb, in a church hung with different colored silks and "signs of gladness rather than weeping." On the dead were conferred the following honors: the pontifical chant, mass by the bishop of Macao, and the presence of all the civil and church dignitaries. The spoils were distributed right after, in an interesting mixture of the religious and the worldly: "a quantity of silk and silver (not to mention the hulls of the vessels, the ammunition, and more than fifty pieces of artillery, and other things such as wine, oil, etc.—all worth three or four hundred thousand pesos."[16]

Especially interesting from the point of view of "practical" civil matters being the impulse for church festivities was the defeat of Cachil Corralat (Sultan Kudarat) by Governor General Sebastian Hurtado de Corcuera in 1637. The fact that Corralat was Muslim and that much has been made through our Spanish history of the "infidels" in the south, suggests that there was a religious dimension to the victory. However, the fact that this was one of the few victories over the courageous Mindanao Filipinos, hard-won after a long siege on Kudarat's hilltop fortification, proves that the triumph was definitely and primarily a military one.

Corcuera had arrived in the Philippines in 1635, with express orders from Philip IV to punish the Muslim pirates severely and stop their raids in the Visayas and Luzon. His victory over Kudarat in May 1637 had climaxed a long campaign begun in February, and in which Jesuit missionaries and his chaplain, Fr. Marcello Mastrilli, S.J., had played more than priestly parts, bearing news, recruiting Visayan soldiers, and finally accepting the submission of the datus. With troops consisting of Spaniards, Pampangos, and Visayans, Corcuera's assaults had caused Kudarat to withdraw to a stronghold on a hill (*cerro*), which was finally taken.

When Corcuera entered the bay on May 24, "Manila [had] prepared a Roman triumph for the conquistador," and his ship was met by decorated sampans, which escorted it to a special landing place. A triumphal procession passed through the royal gate, Puerta Real (reserved for governors and archbishops), up Calle Real, past the Jesuit college (where a triumphal arch had been erected, and the povincial, Fr. Juan de Salazar, came forward to offer congratulations) to the cathedral. The procession included Nicolas Gonzalez's company that had won the battle of Punta Flechas, carrying the captured standards; the seamen of the expedition, with the Chinese and Filipino captives liberated in the campaign; the Maguindanao prisoners with the women and children walking free, and the men in chains; the service troops carrying stacks of captured weapons; the Pampanga troops; Corcuera's artillery dragging captured guns; then finally Corcuera himself "preceded by six boys dragging in the dust in front of him the captured standards of Kudarat."

Corcuera was received at the cathedral by the members of the Audiencia, the cathedral chapter, and the city corporation—without the archbishop. He entered the church and, humbly prostrate on the floor, "offered a prayer of considerable length, attributing his entire success to God." Afterwards he addressed the army, which gave him a general salute, while the standard-bearers lowered the flags. The master-of-camp hosted "a bountiful and choice of repast," walls were illuminated, skyrockets were fired, and at night "the soldiers in masquerade went through the streets on horseback with many torches, to display their joy; both men and horses were elegantly and splendidly adorned."

There were also: a city masquerade, huge bonfires, illuminations, solemn funerals for those who had died in the war, eight altars erected with masses beginning before dawn and filling the morning, a thanksgiving fiesta, Mass and sermon at the cathedral, a procession with dances, floats, instruments and two portable organs, and Father Mastrilli carrying a banner depicting, standing back to back "that figure of Christ which had been stabbed and insulted by the enemy," and St. Francis Xavier—through streets adorned with arches and branches and hangings.

It is this same celebration that produced a significant sidelight: children playing "Moros y Cristianos" on the walls of Intramuros, inspiring Fr. Hieronimo Perez, S.J., to write the comedia *gran comedia de la toma del Pueblo de Corralat, y conquista del Cerro*, a Spanish comedia about real Filipino *Moros* and *Cristianos* in battle (all subsequent vernacular *komedyas* were about imagined *Moros* and Christians of Europe).[17]

One might also mention the following events, commemorated in the city by both church and state: victory over the Chinese (more than 1300 Sangleyes killed in a hill above Calamba by a company of Spaniards and some Indios), celebrated with a *Te Deum* in 1639; yearly commemorations of the victory over Limahong on the feast of St. Andrew (parade of the banner of the city, and "the divine services celebrated with the customary pomp, and attendance and presence of the governor, Audiencia, and regidors"); a disastrous earthquake in 1645 (processions, public prayers, many acts of penitence "as in Holy Week," and general confessions); the fortification of Manila against the pirate Koxinga (public prayers, reception of relics of martyrs, processions, octave festival in the cathedral); the arrival of a new Governor General and of new religious (two triumphal arches with "ingenious emblematic allusions in Latin and Castilian verse, and very expressive aludations," and processions in 1684) — and many other similar occasions when the *ciudad de Manila* was pleased, blessed, or saved, mentioned but not always described in the *relaciones, memoriales,* reports, letters, and other friar accounts, that chronicle the events of the Spanish years.[18]

## Church Events

Still and all, of course, church events — not only feasts — provide the principal motive force for festivities composed of varihued and multi-layered events that provide, as this paper suggests, the models and eventually the aesthetics for most Philippine celebrative observations that followed through the years — church feasting, civic celebrations, town fiestas, and even theater. Wenceslao Retana, writing of publications that describe royal fiestas in the Philippines, says that these have a double interest: literary, which is considerable; and "el concerniente a las costumbres sociales, que no es menor."[19] He obviously meant the social customs of those times, but this paper proposes that these feasts and celebrations help us understand the social customs of our own day, since they set patterns and models that we still follow in part or in spirit in our own time.

## Other Assorted Feasts

Before analyzing that, however, there are a few more occasions that one can mention, as contributing to this canon of feasting. These are not related to liturgy, nor to the Spanish crown, nor to events directly affecting the life of the city of Manila, but are relevant or at the very least peripheral to one or two, or all of the three.

There are, for example, feasts observed by individual religious orders (Augustinians, Recollects, Dominicans, Franciscans and Jesuits) of the country. The canonization of Saints Ignatius and Francis Xavier and the beatification of Aloysius Gonzaga in 1623, for example, did not only affect the Jesuit order but the whole city, which, as the Spanish saying goes, "threw the house out the window," covering Xavier's statue with "more than 15,000 precious stones, of which 1,000 were diamonds; that of Ignatius with more than 20,000 stones, of which 800 were diamonds." San Jose and Sto. Tomas students presented plays; the city corporation a bullfight. The archbishop was petitioned to declare the feasts of both saints holy days of obligations for the Spaniards of the archdiocese "in view of the many and great favors which these islands have received from God our Lord by means of the sacred order of the Society of Jesus, and in recognition of the great debt of gratitude ... [owed] to the same holy order" because of educational and other services rendered. The petition was granted for Manila and Nueva Caceres, and later for Nueva Segovia and for Cebu dioceses as well.[20]

Because of the canonization of the 21 Japanese martyrs (three were *dogicos* of the Augustinians; the others were Franciscans) in 1630 by Pope Urban VII, there were eight days of feasting, the preparations for which took six months, and cost two million reales. "The religious marched in glittering vestments, all at the cost of the pious and religious inhabitants of Manila." The orders invited one another; there were grand processions, the first bullfight in the islands, comparsas, *fuegos y castillos*, also dances and *comedias* which made the festival so magnificent that it "could have been envied by the best cities of España."[21]

Fr. Francisco Marcelo Mastrilli of the Society of Jesus, already mentioned with reference to Corcuera, was seized, tortured and beheaded in Japan (1637), and *Te Deums* were sung, bells rung and illuminations prepared, while the dean, the archbishop, the Royal Audiencia, the orders and a great crowd of people "celebrated the glory and virtues of the holy father Marcelo, with tender tears; for he was generally loved and regarded as a saint."[22]

The sudden death in Pila of Doctor Don Fernando Montero,

eminent preacher, in 1645, as he was preparing to assume the office of Archbishop of Manila, turned the triumphal parade that had been prepared into a funeral procession; while the death of Archbishop Don Miguel de Poblete in 1668 is remembered by a booklet of "llorosa descripcion" which includes funeral declamations and poems.[23]

One of the most detailed sources of data on drama of the period is a rare booklet called *Sagrada fiesta:/ Tres Vezes Gran- /de: que en el discurso de tres dias zelebro el convento de/Sancto Domingo de Manila, primera Cafa de la Provincia /del Sancto Rosario de Filippinas* ... and published in 1677 upon the beatification of Sts. Pius V, Diego de Berbana, and Margarita de Castello. It describes the altar, the decoration of the church, the Latin and Spanish verses, labyrinths and anagrams, the feasts and sermons, the entremeses, the loas (personages: Cuidado, Verdad, Divertimiento in one; Imposible, Obediencia, Petrus currit in the other) and the new comedias, all in verse, and all written by a Dominican, who had been ordered to clean up some improprieties "bien intolerables y mal sonadas" in "la Comedia antigua."[24]

Even excommunication rites in 1718 called for "the greatest solemnity that has been seen in these islands," and featured banners, white and black crosses on the capes and mantels worn by the familiars, who marched in procession through all the city accompanied by eminent citizens in gala attire on caparisoned horses with "many lackeys wearing rich livery." The father commissary rode a mule with trappings, accompanied by ecclesiastical and lay servants of the holy tribunal, alcaldes with maces, drums, and other officials on horseback. The ceremony of excommunication itself consisted of a reading of the edicts on one day, and on the next a reading of the letter of excommunication in a ceremony "that strikes fear and terror into the hardest heart."[25]

The killing of Don Fernando Manuel de Bustillo Bustamante, governor general, and his son, called for a public funeral "so ostentatious that in it ...[were] consumed seven-and-a-half quintals (or hundred weights) of wax" and costing a thousand pesos "taken from the goods of the deceased," and with "the great pomp usual in such cases "[26]

The Sixth Centenary of St. Thomas Aquinas (1874), and the Fifteenth of the conversion of St. Augustine (1887, three days of feasting) were celebrated by all Manila, as was the Fourth Centenary of the discovery of America (1892, three days of feasting).[27] The inauguration of the church of St. Ignatius (1899) called for five days of masses, sermons, decorations, music, choirs, lights, Academia Literaria and Velada Musical, dialogues and theater, magic acts and acrobats, new masses composed for the occasion, bands, programs, etc.[28] The inauguration of the *aguas potables* (1882), however, eclipsed all the above, since its five days of celebration included: an order by the Governor to illuminate the facades of houses and keep them lit from dusk to 10 p.m.; a reception at the Palace; the inauguration of the Caja de Ahorros y Monte de Piedad; a *Misa de Gracia* by the Archbishop and a *Te Deum* at a specially-built altar at the Sampaloc rotunda; music and games (*diana* and ·"cucanas y otras distracciones") all over the city; arches and fireworks; the *salon de Luneta* decorated with "arcos, telas, foliaje," alms for the poor and special treats for prisoners; races (*carerras de cinta*) and prizes; a formal ball ("gran baile de etiqueta"); weddings and baptisms, with prizes for children born that day, many of them named after Queen Ma. Cristina (whose birthday it was), etc.[29]

The above kind of feasting filtered down to individual and even personal levels — scaled down to the occasion or the budget — for example the beatification of a saint, Beato Alonso de Orozco (1882), or the feast of St. Thomas in the same year; or a feast given by the St. Casa de Misericordia for Governor General Mariano Ricafort (1825), which featured a speech by D. Jose Fernandez on the order's works of charity, dances, the recitation of poems, and a ceremonial gift to the Governor of "una hermosisima pluma de escribir adornada de escarchado y platilla fina ... sin olvidarse de poner las iniciales ... de S.E. colgadas del pico de un pajarito." On this occasion, Retana makes an aside: "It deserves notice that all Spanish poetry written in the Philippines is detestable, and especially so are those meant to praise [loar] authorities."[30]

Special notice might be given to the feast of the Third Centenary of St. Theresa of Jesus (1882), because a new element is added to the three-day celebration (October 13-15) — the first Art and Industry Exposition organized in the Philippines. The program details the difficulties encountered, the scaled-down expectations that resulted in (only) 253 exhibits — and the accompanying masses and tridium, litanies and salves, apostolic blessing and procession, preachers and prize-winning poets, including the "indigena filipino" Pedro Paig, and the rains and hurricane that interrupted the festivities.[31]

One notices that of the feasts mentioned above, only two are truly secular — the centenary of the discovery of America, and the inauguration of the *aguas potables* — the rest being church-related. This suggests what a motive force for celebration the colonial church came to be. Yet the friar accounts give little attention to the feasts celebrated yearly, like Christmas, and the patron saints of individual barrios and suburbs of Manila. These provide year-round pomp and splendor, for example the glittering Maundy Thursday and Good Friday processions, in which jewels glint among velvet and satin mourning garments, and statues of the Virgin are surrounded by globes and light and silver flowers. De Huerta mentions that the Santo Entierro had also come out of the Franciscan church, the first missionaries having founded "la hermandad de Nuestra Senora de la Soledad," but the honor (of the procession) had later been ceded to the Dominicans.[32]

Pastoral visits were also events celebrated with routine solemnity, even though occasionally the circumstances could be quite unusual. When Governor Pedro Manuel de Arandia died in 1739, Bishop Miguel Lino de Ezpeleta of Cebu filled the position, and was reluctant to give it up when Manuel Antonio Rojo was named Archbishop of Manila (an *ex officio* was expected to fill the post). After some trouble, Archbishop Rojo eventually was able to assume the post and go through the process: "Auto de Visita, Edicto General, Residencia, Publicacion de la Mision y Jubileo, Visita de la Santa Iglesia Catedral, Visita de Sagrario, Recononcimiento de Reliquias, Ornamentos y demas Muebles," etc.[33]

Surely the pomp and solemnity with which church ceremonies were conducted at every level, from the saying of mass to the visit of an archbishop or the canonization of a saint, must have added up to continuing statements through the centuries of just what grandeur meant — to the church, and therefore to her faithful.

It might be interesting to take a look at this time not just at one individual celebration, but at some related observances through the years within the Franciscan order, since it seems safe to assume that analogous events happened within the other orders.

On the occasion of the Chinese revolt of 3 October 1603, St. Francis is said to have appeared on the *muralla*, defending the city with a sword of fire. This was attested to in the juridical inquiry by very respectable witnesses, including 400 (enemy) prisoners who had been sentenced to death, and accepted baptism, at which they were all named Francisco. St. Francis was then named "Serafin Custodio de Manila," with the ecclesiastical and secular *Cabildos* promising to celebrate his feast yearly as it was celebrated in 1604, with all dignitaries assisting. The miraculous statue was venerated in the Sta. Clara monastery, and was brought out on October 4 of each year in majestic procession, with masses, sermons, and packed churches.

The first statue of the same saint that had been brought to the Philippines in 1577 was venerated in a chapel of the same church. During the earthquakes of 1645, D. Alonso Cuyapit, *indio principal* of Dilao, had taken it to his house to use in the processions of the Third Order, and there this statue was seen away from its niche, kneeling at a window overlooking Manila, and shedding tears — through all four days of the earthquakes. Many people saw this, and wet their handkerchiefs in its tears. A procession was formed to take the statue back to Manila, at which point the quakes ceased. A wind came up, but the candles did not go out; the chiming of bells and the salvos of artillery competed with the *vivas* and praises of the devotees.

The statue was declared miraculous, and St. Francis was named patron and protector against earthquakes. In 1742, when a galleon failed to arrive, this statue, now called San Francisco de las Lagrimas, was taken out in procession, accompanied by the crosses of all the parishes, the orders, the Real Audiencia, and the Governor.[34]

In 1689, however, the Archbishop Fray Phelipe Pardo, a Dominican, forbade the celebration of its feasts, and posted letters of excommunication on the doors of the church, so that the faithful could not enter. Fray Joseph Torrubia, Chronista General and Procurador General of the Franciscans, wrote a *Memorial al Rey*, petitioning His Majesty to allow the feast to continue to be celebrated on December 4, saying that the prohibition was meant "to mortify the [Franciscan] community," and that although they were aware of the intention to trim down the Calendar of Feasts of Manila, the number being excessive, this feast should stay, because of its significance to the city.[35]

In the next century, a footnote to the above is suggested in the dedication of a new church of St. Francis in Sampaloc, commemorated with a rare and fragile book of 143 pages, its dedication written by the Franciscan Provincial, and a message by the chantre of the Cathedral. In it is described in luxurious detail one of the five "vistosos Arcos Triumphales," with its structure and decor:

...ocho bizarros Angeles..un espacioso Tablero...en que traveseaban por las barandas atractivas ramblas de vivas frutas, y flores, aureos fondos, y valiente sombra...una Piramide con oro, y purpura refaltada, repisa de un celeste Globo, en que parado un Angelon con talar ropaje de esplendente estofa, garifo con la argenteria de sus deslumbrantes guarniciones, de la una mano despedia Laureles, y de la otra Palmas: entretegido el uno, y otra de derrame con lluvia hermosa de Rosas, y Estrellas...

the procession with "innumerable Gentio de el Vulgo," sermons, and a "Solemne Accion de gracias dadas a Dios por la venerable Orden Tercera de Penitencia de NSP San Francisco" in a very festive and luminous dedication of the church of Our Lady of the Angels of the Convent of the Discalced Religious of the "Seraphico Patriarcha de esta Ciudad de Manila,"[36] so named, as we have seen, in 1603, and still extravagantly honored a century later, although one wonders how San Francisco de las Lagrimas fared with the King.

A very interesting ceremony—purely secular and political, but with links to the above—occurred when Carlos Maria de la Torre y Navacerrada came to Manila as Governor General in 1869. Pedro Gutierrez y Salazar called it "la primera manifestacion politica en Manila;" Montero y Vidal dubbed it "una serenata;" and Fr. Casimiro Herrero said it was "una manifestacion, la primera conocida en Filipinas, pero con senales marcadas de oposicion a nuestra bandera y a nuestra dominacion"—a "demo," in other words, yet one partaking of the nature of the feasting under discussion so far. Gutierrez says it was:

...Verdadera farsa de Carnaval por su forma, fue por su organizacion y significacion esa manifestacion el atentado mas grave que se ha cometido en estas Islas, desde su descubrimiento, contral la integridad de la Nacion Española.

Componiase de una llmada comision de hijos del pais, con algunos estudiantes, parte seglares y parte clerigos, unos cuantos dependientes de los Juzgados de esta capital, algunos municipes de los arrabales de Santa Cruz, Quiapo y Sampaoloc, y unos pocos indios y mestizos...toda gente de poco valor, con tres charangas y una musica de cuerda para acompañar un himno patriotico, que se canto, con banderolas y faroles de papel del peor gusto.

...se elimino por completo al elemento peninsular; no tomaron parte en ella los propietarios, comerciantes, Abogados y empleados de cuenta, españoles, filipinos, ni aun los mestizos e indigenas de valer.

Hubo sus vivas a la libertad y a la Constitucion, a la Soberania Nacional, a Filipinas con España y por España...Un himno patriotico filipino y su recepcion en Palacio, en la cual S.E. y doña Maria Gil y Montes de Sanchiz obsequiaron a porfia y tendieron y estrecharon fraternalmente su mano, y aun les sirvieron refrescos y dulces, a los que tomaron parte en la manifestacion, y muy particularmente a los individuos de la llamada Comision de los Filipinos.

Montero y Vidal adds that the General and his wife received courteously the "demonstrators," who sang a patriotic hymn, after which there was a toast, and the Señora de Sanchiz read a poem. Casimiro Herrero says that "se vertieron ideas contrarias a las instituciones que conservaban aquel Archipielago para España." *Eco Filipino* adds that the group went to a lot of trouble to get the proper permits, and had bands of music and "infinidad de emblemas," including two transparent ones on which were written VIVA ESPAÑA CON FILIPINAS, Y VIVA FILIPINAS CON ESPAÑA. They marched through the principal streets of the city, and in front of the balconies of the Palace, in the middle of a silent crowd, sang a hymn written by a "director de un taller de carruajes" (therefore "not a correct literary product," but a frank expression of the sentiments and aspirations of the Filipino nation), while the leaders (the *comision*) were received by Governor La Torre. After this, the group dispersed "in equal order and composure," leaving the governor to comment that he had never seen anything like it in other analogous gatherings.[37]

Why is this demonstration included in an account of feasts? Because although the purpose was not religious, or royal, or related particularly to the "muy noble y siempre leal" Manila, the political statement was choreographed with the same solemnity and ceremony as a religious procession—the *comision* of leaders replacing the civil and church dignitaries; the emblems and banners replacing the *estandartes, lienzos*, and statues of saints; the nationalistic hymn and the little bands taking the place of religious songs and their accompanying instruments; *faroles* in hand instead of candles; the silence while the hymn was sung, and the respectful courtesy with which the leaders met the Governor and his lady, drank a *brindis*, and heard her recite a poem, partaking of the form and *punctilio* of a standard colonial church ritual.

As a result of this "demo," notes Gutierrez y Salazar, 1) the members of the Comision, who had never before set foot in it, began to frequent the Palacio de Sta. Potenciana; 2) the Spaniards and other government staff started to withdraw their regard (distance themselves, would be the modern expression) from the Governor; and 3) the Governor began to foster a resentment against the peninsular and official sector, a feeling in turn exploited by the "new and heretofore unknown friends of His Excellency and his lady." The members of this Comision, whom Gutierrez calls "gente de poco valor" included, among others, Joaquin Pardo de Tavera, doctor of laws; Jose Icaza of the Royal Audiencia; Jacobo Zobel, Regidor of the Ayuntamiento; Lorenzo Rocha, artist; Fr. Jose Burgos, doctor of laws and Cura Parroco of the Manila Cathedral; Angel Garchitorena, Andres Nieto, Vicente Infante, etc. In the shocked and indignant tones of the chroniclers, who read in the "serenata" and hymn—

> Filipinas asi a tu llegada,
> con ardor como nunca sentido,
> el caudillo te aclama querido
> del progreso a que aspira y de union....
> Ese dulce y armonico acento
> que respeto y cariño pregona,
> es de un pueblo que ufano blasona
> de ser fiel al Gobierno español.

"subversive" ideas to threaten the establishment, the contemporary Filipino can see, prefigured, current establishment phobia for all mass actions and their banners or statements.

The above "manifestacion" did not mark the end of the feasts of the old type. Our attention is called by a thick publication called *La Paz y el Ayuntamiento de Manila,* or *Relacion de los festejos realizados con motivo de la terminacion de la guerra en Filipinas.* In it are detailed the program of the feasts with which the Spanish community celebrated in December 1897 the peace with General Emilio Aguinaldo, and also the newspaper and other accounts after the event. It is lavishly illustrated with photographs of the young King, the Queen Regent, the Governor, the Alcalde, and the Comision de Festejos, and the Casas Consistoriales (exterior and interiors). Even more interesting to note is the program (January 30 to February 2) which, right after the Filipino revolution against Spain, had bands again playing in the streets from morning until midnight; *cucanas* with prizes in the districts; *festejos populares* held in Bagumbayan, where just a year earlier Rizal had been shot, and where now stood "puestos de feria, fondas, tios-vivos, bazares-rifas, teatro y circo al aire libre, y toda clase de diversiones y recreos." Afternoons featured boat races, horse races, sack races, bicycle races, obstacle races ("reservada exclusivamente para *batas* insulares...en su traje o en camisa chinica"); evenings were for concerts (studded with numbers from Spanish zarzuelas and *sainetes*); zarzuelas and comedias; fuegos artificiales ("Dos rosas juguetonas," "Aspa de doble movimiento," "Valvula vertical," etc. and the burning of 2000 *bombas* called *calacuerdas*); a *funcion de gala* in the Gran Circo Filipino, honoring the army; and for the very elite, a *baile de etiqueta* in the Casas Consistoriales.

Almost half of the publication is taken up by the latter — photographs and descriptions of the building and its decorations, from the vestibule "con sus numerosos focos de luz, sostenidos por artisticos candelabros abrillantando los caprichosos dibujos de elevados jarrones japoneses;" to the salon "un gran roseton...de papuas, palmas, follaje y flores entrelazados," with the Spanish flag, the seal of Manila, the portrait of the Reina Regente, etc.; to the dining rooms where the buffet was laid (catering) by the *Restaurant de Paris*: Foiegras de Strasbourg, sandwiches of *Poted-ham, Mortadella y Jambon*; *langue a l'escarlatte, Tete de Sanglier a la gele, Jambon de York*, etc.); and even the *salon de descanso* for the ladies, with its decorations by Genato and Iriarte, its *"puff* elegantisimo," its mirros and laces; and the dance itself, breathlessly described, each single guest named.

A contrast is strongly suggested, and none wonders what the Filipinos were doing and feeling, they who had led a revolution against all this, the aftermath of which was being celebrated in grand Spanish style?

## Pompas, Solemnidades, Pistahan, Bonggahan

What does all this feasting through the centuries signify? Surely it did not go unnoticed by the "Indios," the native Filipinos who did not plan the feasts, sing the High Masses on feastdays, or preach—but walked in the processions; filled the churches during masses and *Te Deums*; listened to the poems declaimed, and the sermons by illustrious preachers from the five religious orders; watched the fireworks and the burning *castillos*; plaited the palm leaves and garlanded the flowers and hung the fabrics to decorate the streets; climbed the greased poles and ran, rode, or cycled in the races; absorbed the music (from morning *diana* to evening concert) and the drama (from *entremes* and *sainete* to *comedia* and *zarzuela);* carried the candles and pulled (perhaps decorated as well) the *carrozas* in processions, etc. Considering what moral ascendance anything Spanish had because of colonial dominance and example, certainly all these had their effects on the Filipino mentality.

The elements of Spanish feasting—both secular and religious—set the standard for celebration and, in derivative form, were reflected in native fiestas. These, noticeably, always feature "arcos triumfales," but no longer with columns and cornices, pyramids and poems—instead, inexpensive and readily available bamboo, bent and tied and shaped, with the curls and curlicues it is possible to do with this material and the humble instruments available. These always feature, too, a Mass honoring the patron saint, and a sermon outlining his virtues; perhaps a *diana* in the morning, and even a band around town. If the town can afford it, there might be a comedia or zarzuela to reflect all those "funciones de teatro," and this might begin with a loa—in the vernacular, however—speaking of the *patron*, or the mayor, or the *hermano mayor*, or town personalities. And if there is a budget for it, there might even be *kuwitis* (*cohetes*) and *lusis* (*luces*) and *paputok* (*bombas*; *fuegos artificiales*)—even a *castillo*, or the Blessed Virgin, or the face of a politician, if the donor is generous, or the town has the techonology of, say, Bocaue.

Perhaps if one analyzes the ethos and the spirit of the town fiesta in great detail, one would be able to trace quite a lot of it to a nativization of the Spanish-period celebrations. Certainly the arrangement, or design of the fiesta, was on the Spanish model (church observances, fused to celebrations, games, music and theater, with town dignitaries in attendance)—and so was its spirit. Those grandiose sermons in elegant Spanish, which few Filipinos could probably understand, even as late as the end of the 19th century (the law and arrangements for compulsory education coming only in 1863, with the Educational Reform Act), washed

47

over the listening Filipinos in great splashes of rhetoric and bombast, sounding important and grand and musical—but without communicating ideas. In the same way do they listen to political speeches (waiting for "bomba" after all the splashy platforms), and even to the long verses of *komedya*, in which love and war occur in a purely rhetorical register—dodecasyllabic quatrains tumbling out in relentless rhyme and rhythm, the audience relishing the deliciousness of the rhetoric, and not necessarily the weight of ideas or the heft of dialectic.

The fiesta may therefore be said to have inherited from church festivities the actual physical elements—mass, sermon, band, theater, arches, parades (processions), fireworks, the benign presence of dignitaries or leaders, etc.—but even more significantly, the ethos or spirit of centuries of church-related festivities.

Also in the same line of descent, sharing the same forebears, would be the aesthetics of our native theater. Not only do the verses of *sinakulo* and *komedya* tumble over themselves in enthusiastic profusion, endlessly and luxuriantly, like a preacher's Castilian rhetoric; they also outline worlds heard about in Spanish feasts—the kingdoms of Europe, the households of nobility, the courtships and intrigues of the *zarzuela*, the Romans and Jewry and the holy cast of the Passion and the Bible. The favorite scenes of rural theater audiences focus on romance and battle—and on out-of-this world effects like *magia* in the *komedya* and *artipisyales* in the *sinakulo*. That is "showtime" all over again, in the rituals and celebrations of Spanish Manila, when architectural wonders, drapes and decorations, magicians and acrobats (*volatines*), games and declamations, fireworks and other dazzling entertainments made people forget the humdrum and the workaday. One also remembers that in the *sinakulo* all the special, "miraculous" scenes like Christ ascending to Heaven, angels descending, the Virgin rising to meet the Holy Trinity in the clouds, God creating Adam and Eve, the Transfiguration, etc., are always punctuated and illuminated by *lusis*, artificial lights ("fuegos artificiales") always marking moments of grace and wonder in the native aesthetic.

Covering statues with jewels and streets with damask and brocade marked important occasions; embroidering with sequins and beads and hanging galloons and epaulets mark the garb of royalty in the *komedya*, and the *horror vacui* of native art characterizes house decoration, the setting of fiesta buffet tables, and the general native idea of ornamentation. If the quelling of revolutions, the ceasing of earthquakes, victories over pirates and foreign invaders (the Dutch; the British) and the beatification and canonization of saints provided occasion for celebration in Spanish Manila, then on barrio level the harvest, the fiesta, Holy Week, Christmas, a wedding to come, the birth of an heir, a death in the family, a graduation from college (to which elders and brethren contributed), provide occasion for *komedya* or for going into debt in order to prepare a *handa* for the community.

And if no feast was complete without prelates and priests, governor and regidores, military officers and civil officiales, no wonder no fiesta or evening of folk theater can begin without the mayor's remarks, the *hermano mayor's* speech or the *hermana's* bow, and the parish priest, as well as a *politico* or *konsehal* or two in the audience — since one of the responsibilities of the dignitary is to shed light and dignity on community occasions with his/her importance.

Finally, because all feasting traditionally begins in, is motivated by, or includes, the church, most native feasts and much native theater begins in, is motivated by, or includes the church as well — from the church-originated *sinakulo* and *salubong* with their folk apocryphal interpretations, to the love-and-war *komedya* in which Christianity triumphs and all mix-matched couples get married in the end (by Catholic priests, of course), to the quite secular but church-linked *sunduan* and *santacruzan* (now only in name connected to the finding of the Holy Cross).

This is a very preliminary inquiry into the feasting in Spanish, Catholic, colonial Philippines, through an exploration of church celebrations in the ever loyal and most noble city of Manila. Perhaps within this feasting, between the pealing of bells at dawn and the final burst of fireworks at midnight, lie the rhyme and reason of the Philippine *pistahan* and *paputok*, the rhetoric of *bonggahan*, the ethos of *pagdiriwang* and *pagbubunyi*, the aesthetics of Philippine fiesta and theater.


NOTES


1.  Fr. Pedro Chirino, S.J., "Relation of the Filipinas Islands and of what has there been accomplished by the Fathers of the Society of Jesus," in Blair and Robertson, Vol. 12, 246.

2.  P. Juan de la Concepcion, *Historia General de Philipinas 1788-1792* (Manila: Impr. del Seminar. Conciliar, y Real de S. Carlos, 1788), Tomo III, pp. 318-320.

3.  Fray Juan de Medina, OSA, "Historia de la orden de S. Agustin de estas Islas Filipinas" [1630], in Blair and Robertson, Vol. 23, 199-200.

4. Letter from Felipe II, Blair and Robertson, Vol. 9, 190-191.

5. Tabla general de todas las fiestas y vigilias de este obispo de Nueva Caceres, manuscript, 1735.

6. "Relation of Events in the Philipinas Islands, 1619-20," Blair and Robertson, Vol. 19, 63-66. For other celebrations of the feast of the Immaculate Conception, see Casimiro Diaz, O.S.A., "The Augustinians in the Philippines," Blair and Robertson, Vol. 37, 212-213; "Events in the Filipinas Islands," Blair and Robertson, Vol. 18, 80; *Descripcion del Novenario* ..., 1855, MS; Compania de Jesus, *La Inmaculada a Traves de los Siglos,* 1904.

7. Blair and Robertson, Vol. 12, p. 182 (footnote).

8. Francisco Moya y Torres, *Lealtad Empenada / Finezas de Amor*..., in Mauro Garcia, *Philippine Rariora* (Manila: Eugenio Lopez Foundation, Inc., 1982), pp. 71-72.

9. Diaz, "Augustinians," Blair and Robertson, Vol. 37, 166.

10. Fr. Nicolas de San Pedro, "Sermon,/que en las fies-/tas Reales..." in Weceslao Retana, *Aparato Bibliografico*, (Madrid: Imprenta de la Sucesora de M. Minuesa de los Rios), Vol. I, pp. 225-231.

11. "Events in the Filipinas, 1764-1800," [compiled from Montero y Vidal, *Historia de Filipinas*], Blair and Robertson, Vol. 50, 66-67.

12. Manuel Barrios, "Descripcion de la proclamacion y jura..." in Retana, *Aparato*, Vol. I, p. 423.

13. Retana, *Aparato,* Vol. II, pp. 530-532; p. 430; pp. 555- 558; *Programa/de los festejos y manifestaciones piadosas/con que ... celebran el natalicio/del Principe de Asturias/Don Alfonso de Borbon* (Manila: Imprenta y Litografia de Ramirez y Giraudier, 1858).

14. "Royal Funeral Rites at Manila," Blair and Robertson, Vol. 36, pp. 23-43; "Aparato Funebre, y real Pyra de honor ..." in W.E. Retana, *Archivo del Bibliofilo Filipino* (Madrid: Casa de la Viuda de M. Minuesa de los Rios, 1896), Tomo II, 105-158.

15. Dr. Antonio de Morga, "Sucesos de las islas Filipinas," Blair and Robertson, Vol. 15, 133-35.

16. Fr. Gregorio Lopez, S.J., "Relation of Events in the Filipinas during the Years 1609 and 1610," Blair and Robertson Vol. 17, 124, 127.

17. Fr. Juan Lopez, S.J., "Corcuera's Triumphant Entry into Manila," Blair and Robertson, Vol. 27, 330-340; Horacio de la Costa, S.J., *The Jesuits in the Philippines, 1581-1768* (Cambridge: Harvard University Press, 1967), p. 386; "Events in the Filipinas, 1637-38," Blair and Robertson, Vol. 29, 38-39; Doreen G. Fernandez, "Historical Notes on the Jesuits and Early Philippine Theater," *Philippine Studies*, Vol. 29, 3rd-4th quarters, 1981, 386-389.

18. "Relation of the Insurrection of the Chinese," Blair and Robertson, Vol. 29, 215; Fr. Joseph Fayol, "Affairs in Filipinas, 1644-47," Blair and Robertson Vol. 35, 218; "Events in Manila 1662-63," Blair and Robertson, Vol. 36, 218-260; Diaz, "Augustinians," Blair and Robertson, Vol. 42, 229-230.

19. Retana, *Aparato*, Vol. I, p. 231.

20. de la Costa, *Jesuits*, p. 365.

21. Medina, *Historia*, Blair and Robertson, Vol. 24, 174-175; Fr. Felix de Huerta, *Estado Geografico, Topografico, Estadistico, Historico-Religioso...* (Binondo: Imprenta de M. Sanchez y Ca., 1865), pp. 15-19. The latter details who was in the procession, in what order, bearing what statues or effigies, and conducting the orchestra.

22. "Events in the Filipinas, 1637-38," Blair and Robertson, Vol. 29, 33.

23. Diaz, "Augustinians," Blair and Robertson, Vol. 27, p. 162; Garcia, *Rariora*, p. 47.

24. Retana, *Aparato*, Vol. I, 154-155.

25. Diaz, "Augustinians," Blair and Robertson, Vol. 37, 281- 283.

26. De la Concepcion, *Historia*, Blair and Robertson, Vol. 44, 159-160; "Noticias de lo sucedido en la ciudad de Manila en octubre de 1719" in Retana, *Archivo*, Tomo V, p. 145.

27. P. Vindel, *Catalogo Sistematico y Iluystrado de la Biblioteca Filipina* (Madrid: Calle del Prado num. 9, 1904), entry 1253; entry 1244; Retana, *Aparato*, Vol. III, p. 1085.

28 *Resena Historica de la Inauguracion de la Iglesia de San Ignacio de Loyola de Manila en 1889* (Manila: Imprenta y Litografia de M. Perez, Hijo, 1890).

29. D. Francisco, de Mas y Otzet, *Carriedo y sus Obras* (Manila Establecimiento Tipografico de Ramirez y Giraudier, [1882]).

30. Vindel, entries 1259, 1255; Retana, *Aparato*, Vol. II, 527- 529.

31. Retana, *Aparato*, Vol. II, 932-934; *Descripcion de las solemnes fiestas ... Tercer Centenario de la gloriosa virgen y doctora mistica Sta. Teresa de Jesus ... Octubre de 1882* (Manila: Establecimiento Tipografico de Ramirez y Giraudier, [1882]).

32. de Huerta, *Estado Geografico*, p. 19.

33. Pilar Elordi Cortes, "Una visita pastoral de arzobispo Manuel Antonio Rojo a la diocesis de Manila," *Missionalia Hispanica*, XXXVIII: 14, 1981, 319-391.

34. de Huerta, *Estado Geografico*, pp. 12-13; "Relacion de la Forma y modo que Salio en Prossecion [sic] General, Ntra. SSmo. Padre, San Francisco de las Lagrimas, el dia 22 de Octubre, de 1742,"

Manuscript.

35. Fray Joseph Torrubia, *Memorial al Rey*, 1689.
36. *Sagrados Triumphos, Celebres Expressiones, y Festivos Aplavsos...de Mayo de el Ano de 1743...* (Impressos en el Convento de Nuestra Senora de Loreto, del Orden Seraphico, en el Pueblo de Sampaloc Extramuros de la Ciudad de Manila, Año de 1743).
37. Jeremias Rebanal y Ras, "El Gobernador de Filipinas Carlos Maria de la Torre y Navacerrada," *Missionalia Hispanica*, XXXVIII:112, 113, 114, 46-55.

## BIBLIOGRAPHY

Bobadilla, Diego de, S.J. et al. "Glorious Victories against the Moros of Mindanao," 1638. *The Philippine Islands, 1493-1898.* Emma Helen Blair and James Alexander Robertson, eds. Vol. 29, 86-89.

*Catalogo de documentos referentes a diversiones publicas conservados en el Archivo Historico Nacional,* 1858-1958. Madrid, 1958.

Chirino, Pedro S.J. "Relation of the Filipinas Islands and of what has there been accomplished by the Fathers of the Society of Jesus," 1604. Blair and Robertson, Vol. 12, 175- 321.

[Compania de Jesus] Junta-Organizadora de Festejos del Año Jubilar de la Concepcion Inmaculada, Congregaciones Marianas de los Colegios de la Cia. de Jesus. *La Inmaculada a Traves de los Siglos,* [Cartel y Programa], 15 Agosto 1904.

Concepcion, P. Juan de la. O.S.A. *Historia General de Philipinas, 1788-1792,* Tomos I-XIV. Manila: Impr. del Seminar. Conciliar, y Real de S. Carlos: Por Agustin de la Rosa, y Balagtas, 1788.

Cortes, Pilar Elordi. "Una Visita Pastoral del Arzobispo Manuel Antonio Rojo a la Diocesis de Manila [1760]." *Missionalia Hispanica,* Vol XXXVIII, No. 114, 1981, 319-391.

Costa, Horacio de la, S.J. *The Jesuits in the Philippines,* 1581-1768. Cambridge, Mass.: Harvard University Press, 1967.

"Decreto del Gobernador General que trata del programa de festejos por la Inauguracion de las Aguas Potables," Manila, 18 Julio 1882. MS [A1 MRP Provincial de S. Francisco.]

*Descripcion de las solemnes fiestas que con motivo del Tercer Centenario de la gloriosa virgen y doctora mistica Sta. Teresa de Jesus se celebraron en la ciudad de Manila en los dias 13, 14 y 15 de Octubre de 1882.*

Manila: Establecimiento Tipografico de Ramirez y Giraudier, 1882.

"Descripcion del Novenario celebrado en Sta. Maria de los Angeles de Manila, 1855." MS.

Diaz, Casimiro, O.S.A. "The Augustinians in the Philippines," 1718. Blair and Robertson, Volumes 37 and 42, 149-284; 117- 312.

"Events in the Filipinas 1764-1800" [compiled from Montero y Vidal, *Historia de Filipinas*]. Blair and Robertson, Vol. 50, 23-74.

"Events in Philipinas 1638-39" [probably by Juan Lopez]. Blair and Robertson, Vol. 29, 141-171.

"Events in the Filipinas Islands, 1617-1618." Blair and Robertson, Vol. 18, 65-92.

"Events in the Filipinas, 1637-38" [probably by Juan Lopez]. Blair and Robertson, Vol. 29, 23-49.

'Events in the Filipinas Islands, 1639-40" [probably by Juan Lopez]. Blair and Robertson, Vol. 29, 194-207.

"Events in Manila 1662-63." Blair and Robertson, Vol. 36, 218- 260.

Fayol, Fray Joseph (of the Order of Mercy). "Affairs in Filipinas, 1644-47." Blair and Robertson, Vol. 35, 212-275.

Felipe II. "The Audiencia of Manila Re-established," El Pardo, November 26, 1595. Blair and Robertson, Vol. 9, 189-192.

Fernandez, Doreen G. "Historical Notes on the Jesuits and Early Philippine Theater." *Philippine Studies*, Vol. 29, 3rd and 4th Quarters, 1981, 375-393.

Ferrer, Fr. Alejandro, O.F.M. "Parecer sobre las Conmemoraciones de S. Francisco y Sto. Domingo." Pregunta. Santa Ana, 6 Septiembre 1754. MS.

"Fortunate Successes in Filipinas and Terrenate, 1636-37." Blair and Robertson, Vol. 29, 116-134.

Garcia, Mauro. *Philippine Rariora*, A Descriptive Catalog of 17th Century Imprints in the Lopez Memorial Museum. Manila: Eugenio Lopez Foundation, Inc., 1983.

"The Government and Death of Bustamante" [by Diego de Otazo, S.J. and others; introduction summarized from Concepcion, *Historia de Philipinas*]. Blair and Robertson, Vol. 44, 148-195.

Huerta, R.P. Fr. Felix de. *Estado Geografico,, Topografico,, Estadistico, Historico-Religioso de la Santa y Apostolica Provincia de S. Gregorio Magno de Religiosos Menores Descalzos de la Regular y mas Estrecha Observancia de NSPS Francisco en las Islas Filipinas*. Binondo: Imprenta de M. Sanchez y Ca., 1865 [2nd ed.].

La Paz y el Ayuntamiento de Manila (Relacion de los Festejos Realizados con Motivo de la Terminacion de la Guerra en Filipinas), Diciembre de 1897. Manila: Tipo-Litografia de Chofre y Comp., 1898.

Lopez, Fr. Gregorio S.J. "Relation of Events in the Filipinas during the Years 1609 and 1610." Blair and Robertson, Vol. 17, 100-143.

Lopez, Fr. Juan, S.J. "Corcuera's Triumphant Entry into Manila," May 24, 1637. Blair and Robertson, Vol. 27,, 330-340.

de Mas y Otzet,, D. Francisco. *Carriedo y Sus Obras*, Memoria de las Obras Pias de los Pobres y del Agua Instituidas por el Insigne Patricio D. Francisco Carriedo y Peredo y Cronica de los Festejos que el Excmo. Ayuntamiento de la M.N. y S.L. Ciudad de Manila en Union su Vecindario ha Celebrado para Conmemorar la Inauguracion de Aguas Potables. Manila: Establecimiento Tipografico de Ramirez y Giraudier, 1882.

Medina, Fray Juan de, O.S.A. "Historia de la Orden de S. Agustin de estas Islas Filipinas" [written 1630, published 1893]. Blair and Robertson, Vol. 23, 121-297.

Morga, Dr. Antonio de. "Sucesos de las Islas Filipinas." Blair and Robertson, Vol. 15, 25-287.

"Noticias de lo sucedido en la ciudad de Manila en Octubre de 1719 (Asesinato de Bustamante), relacion impresa hace 1721." W.E. Retana, *Archivo del Bibliofilo Filipino*, Tomo Quinto. Madrid: Libreria General de Victoriano Suarez, 1905, 129- 145.

Perez, Fr. Angel y Guemes, Fr. Cecilio. *Adiciones y Continuacion de "La Imprenta en Manila" de D.J.T. Medina, o Rarezas y Curiosidades Bibliograficas Filipinas de las Bibliotecas de esta Capital.* Manila: Imprenta de Santos y Bernal, 1904.

*Programa de los Festejos y Manifestaciones Piadosas con que el Excmo. Ayuntamiento, Junta de Comercio, Provincia de Manila y Comision de Festejos Nombrada por el Ejercito y Cuerpos Administrativos, celebran el Natalicio del Principe de Asturias Don Alfonso de Borbon.* Manila: Imprenta y Litografia de Ramirez y Giraudier, 1858.

*Programa de las funciones con que la M.N. y M.L. Ciudad de Manila, los Pueblos Estramuros, el Ejercito, la Marina y Real Hacienda, han dispuesto celebrar los Regios Enlaces de S.M. y A.* Manila, 7 Abril 1847.

Rebanal, Jeremias y Ras. "El Gobernador de Filipinas Carlos Maria de la Torre y Navacerrada." Missionalia Hispanica,, Vol. XXXVIII, 95-128, 171-226,, 305-316.

"Recurso de nuestro procurador Fr. Antonio de Santo Domingo, con el expediente instruido para que la audiencia de Manila asista a la fiesta de N.P. San Francisco segun costumbre antigua y por acuerdo de la misma audiencia hecho en 1696." MS, 1773.

"Relacion de la Forma y Modo que Salio en Prossecion General, Ntro. SSmo. Padre, San Franciso de las Lagrimas, el dia 22 de Octubre, de 1742." MS.

"Relacion de las Lagrimas de S. Francisco, 1700." MS.

"Relation of Events in the Philipinas Islands, 1619-20." Blair and Robertson, Vol. 19, 42-70.

"Relation of the Insurrection of the Chinese" [probably March 1640]. Blair and Robertson, Vol. 29, 208-258.

*Resena Historica de la Inauguracion de la Iglesia de San Ignacio de Loyola de Manila en 1889*. Manila: Imprenta y Litografia de M. Perez, Hijo, 1890.

Retana, Wencelao E. *Aparato Bibliografico de la Historia General de Filipinas*, I-III. Madrid: Imprenta de la Sucesora de M. Minuesa de los Rios 1904. Offset reprint by Pedro B. Ayuda y Compania, 1964.

Retana, W.E. *Archivo del Bibliofilo Filipino*, II. Madrid: Casa de la Viuda de M. Minuesa de los Rios, 1896. ["Aparato Funebre, y Real Pyra de honor... a las memorias del ferenifsimo Principe de España Don Balthassar Carlos, que efte en Gloria," Manila, 1649.]

Retana, W.E. *Noticias Historico-Bibliograficas de el Teatro en Filipinas desde sus origenes hasta 1898*. Madrid: Liberaria General de Victoriano Suarez, 1911.

Retana, W.E. *Origenes de la Imprenta Filipina*. Madrid: Libreria General de Victoriano Suarez, 1909.

"Royal Funeral Rites at Manila," 1649. Blair and Robertson, Vol. 36, 23-43.

San Miguel, Fr. Joaquin de, O.F.M. "Informe sobre la celebracion de las fiestas en comun de Sto. Domingo y S. Francisco. Acompaña la carta del Prov. pidiendo el informe. Binangonan, 20 Junio 1778. MS.

Sta. Ines, Fray Francisco de. *Cronica de la Provincia de San Gregorio Magno de Religiosos Descalzos de N.S.P. San Francisco en las Islas Filipinas, China, Japon, etc.* [1676]. Manila: Tipo Litografia de Chofre y Comp., 1892.

*Sagrados Triumphos, Celebres Expressiones, y Festivos Aplausos con que la Santa Provincia del Santissimo Rosario del Sagrado Orden de Predicadores; la de San Gregorio el Magno de Menores Descalzos, y su Venerable Orden Tercera de Penitencia Celebraron, en los dias 11, 12, 13, y 14 de Mayo de el Año de 1743. La Dedicacion solemne de le nuevo templo de Nro. S.P.S. Francisco, con la Advocacion de la Reyna de los Angeles, en la ciudad de Manila, Capital de estas Islas Philipinas: con asistencia de la Real Audiencia, nobilissima Ciudad,*

*Sagradas Religiones, y general Concurso ae todos Estados.* Impressos en el Convento de Nuestra Señora de Loreto, del Orden Seraphico, en el pueblo de Sampaloc Extramuros de la Ciudad de Manila, año de 1743.

# NATIONALISM IN 19TH CENTURY MANILA

ROMEO V. CRUZ

Nationalism, in the context of the Philippine experience, develops as consciousness of belonging to one people – the Hispanic and Catholic Community all over the empire. This sentiment was quite limited, based on the political, religious, social and intellectual perceptions of the archipelago as an integral unit co-equal with other components of the Spanish empire but all united under the monarchy. The people of the Philippines, on the basis of this perception, were one with, and had equal footing with, other peoples of the Empire in Spain, America and elsewhere.

The assumed cultural unity, though universalistic in aspirations, was modestly nationalistic in program and goals. It conceived of the unity between the colonies and the mother country and stressed the Hispanism of all peoples composing the imperial society. In short, the basic concept of nationalism was national identity despite the Spanish society's universal and imperialistic structure. In reality though, when first conceived and disseminated, certain objective facts were gleaned over or ignored. The cultural integration of the Philippines was quite incomplete. Politically and territorially *pax Hispanica* was only established in Luzon, the Visayas and the coastal areas of Mindanao. Even here, two problems at least were never resolved by Spanish power – the interior and remote areas peopled by ethnic Filipinos and the *remontados* who represented a counter-culture; and the administrative dilemma presented by the struggle between localism and centralism.

The fissiparous trends and tendencies were further aggravated by religious diffusion as the effectiveness of Catholicism was challenged by local conditions – the competing loci of power within the Church, failure of missionary or conversion work in the hinterland, and failure of indoctrinating the lowland Filipinos as evidenced by the appearance of nativism and folk Catholicism. Socially, the pre-Hispanic racial unity of the Filipinos, already shattered by ethnicity and linguistic differences, was further worsened by the infusion of the Spanish mix in the racial cauldron especially during the second half of the 19th century as manifested in the struggle between the Spanish regular clergy and the Filipino secular priests. These objective realities could also be seen in the lack of integration in the other aspects of Philippine life and culture during the Spanish period. And finally the physical isolation of the archipelago, and the inaccessibility of many interior areas offered a complete picture in relation to this defective integration. Yet, despite this diffusion and diversity, nationalism in its appearance assumed a basic unity though it was more apparent than real.

Moreover, the Filipinos, whose consciousness of oneness was being aroused, were apparently aware of certain objective commonalities like a well-defined territory, common racial stock, common parent language, etc. And with the coming of Islam and Christianity, the Filipinos' possession of commonalities amidst their diversities was enhanced with the foundation of churches with universalistic pretentions. The historical phenomenon led to the formation of an Islamic Community and a Catholic Community. This separate community consciousness was naturally far from uniting the people of the whole archipelago into a nation since both communities' political and cultural institutions, social and belief systems led to further bifurcations. Though based on certain unities, both communities merely reenacted the earlier Muslim-Christian war drama in the Middle East, Africa, and Europe. In their separate ways, the Muslim and Christian Communities developed different identities based on universalism but not nationalism which would be anachronistic during the early centuries of Spanish rule — nationhood and nationalism being of later occurrence than universalism of the ancient and medieval type.

Thus, the first stage in the occurrence of Philippine nationalism was more or less based on the Christian experience and not on the Muslim experience. It was Hispanic with the object of achieving Spanish nationhood — thus Hispanism. The next stage was the achievement of "Filipinism" — taken from the term "Filipino" in the sense of a Spaniard born in the Philippines, or the so-called creole. Community here was based on the oneness of the idea of being "Filipinos" or creoles who had been the subject of social, political, and religious discriminations in a Philippine colonial situation where the peninsular Spaniards as actual rulers of the country did the discriminating. The next stage was the community of Creole-Indio identity turning the previous concept of "Filipino" as creole into Filipino as Indio belonging to the the enlightened and upper class of Indios. In the previous two stages of the evolving nationalism, the dominant ideas that cohered with the national concept were assimilation, liberalism, democracy and imperialism. No attempt was made to create a separate nation. On the contrary, the goal was achievement of Hispanic nationhood characterized by a cosmopolitan structure and composition of peoples within the Spanish nation. In all three stages the type of nationalism that developed differed only in degree and not in substance. Hence, it was aptly termed as imperial liberal nationalism. Roughly, each stage could be periodized as follows: for the first stage, 1809 to 1820; the second, 1821 to 1880; and the third, 1880 to 1896.

The fourth and last stage in the evolution of nationalism could be roughly dated from 1896 to the end of the nineteenth century or circa 1912. Here, the imperial liberal nationalism of the three earlier stages was supplanted but not annihilated by a new type of nationalism — radical nationalism. The main national idea preached was a new and independent nation dominated by Indios now transformed into Filipinos. The idea centered on the concept of *Katagalugan* — the sense of living near or surrounded by bodies of water — a nation of Tagalogs.

Nationalism thus started out as a concept — Hispanism — which later became "Filipinism" or "Creolism" then assimilationist or coalesced "Filipino-Indio" concept, and finally the idea of *Katagalugan*. This presentation of nationalism in the Philippines is unorthodox; its periodization is not the usual chronology associated with the beginnings of this sentiment in our history; and finally its definition is historically contextual based on our experience. Briefly, the traditional interpretation usually started with a superimposed definition that is separate from our experience, allowing readers much liberty to make their own connection between the intellectual construct and the experience. The consequence was fragmentary exposition that started with an independent and separate definition and a layered causation using the factor-analysis similar to digging tunnels with no exit. The objective realities of a well-defined territory, racial commonality, political and religious integration, commonality in languages, etc. had been existing since pre-Islamic and pre-Catholic eras, yet nationalism had not taken root even if its presence was discernible.

It was not until the first decade of the 19th century that these objective realities were animated by an awareness of national community in the form of Hispanism. This was precipitated by events in Europe when, in the course of Napoleon Bonaparte's invasion of Portugal, he decided to cross from France to Spain — and stay in the latter. He appointed his own brother, Joseph, as king of Spain and exiled Ferdinand

59

VII, the absolutist king of the Spanish empire. The Spanish revolution that followed Napoleon's usurpation in 1807 summoned the colonies, including the Filipinos, to unite and defend Mother Spain. The Spanish rebels, after establishing a Central Revolutionary Junta at Aranjuez asked, in the form of decrees issued in the name of a parliamentary government, the integral units of the Spanish empire to assist in overthrowing the usurper. The decree of 1809 stressed that the old colonies were equal and integral parts of the Spanish monarchy for whom the Aranjuez Junta was acting — and thus must send their representatives to the reinvigorated Cortes, the law-making body of the Spanish government. Another decree embodied further the concept of nationalism. It maintained that a federal empire was to be established in Spain where former colonies, now provinces would be at par with Spain and entitled to representation to the Cortes. The peoples in Spain and the provinces were Spanish citizens entitled to the privileges of the citizenship within the federal empire. The new motherland, according to the decree, was to be the object of loyalty and must be strengthened so that unity among the component units would remain solid. The former imperial possessions were not to be considered as factories or colonies. They were, on the contrary, integral and necessary members of the monarchy. As rewards for their assistance and loyalty, the provinces had to be represented before the royal person of King Ferdinand VII and to participate in the Junta's interim government.

The more complete form of the new national idea or Hispanism was more or less detailed in the Constitution of Cadiz of 1812. The new nation according to the Constitution, was composed of the united Spanish peoples all over the world. It was the repository of sovereignty and powers of government. The people were free, independent and not vassal or owned by any single person or family. Moreover, the form of government was a constitutional monarchy like that of England and autonomy was to be observed in the provincial units. The liberal contents were expressed in the provisions stressing the sanctity of the individual and the sacredness of property, freedom of petition, of the press, and of assembly.

The Constitution was promulgated in Manila and other provinces in 1813. Earlier, nationalism was institutionalized when the elections for representatives to the Cortes were held in Manila and the other provinces in 1810. Their oath of office swore them to defend the Catholic Church and the new Spanish nation, to free the nation from the usurper, to defend the King's possessions and his royal family, and finally to respect the laws of Spain. In the same year the Spanish Cortes issued a proclamation that showed the nature and character of Hispanism which it wished to spread in the empire. It said that all provinces in "America and Asia" were integral parts of the monarchy and their peoples were "equal in rights and privileges to those of the Peninsula...". The new nationalism was for the first time also disseminated by the first government newspaper *Del Superior Gobierno* that came out in Manila on August 8, 1811. Its publication, according to Jesus Z. Valenzuela, was motivated by nationalism or Hispanism. Through Hispanism it was held that the Filipinos' loyalty could be maintained at the time Spain was engaged in the war of independence. Thus primarily nationalism in the form of Hispanism was transplanted in Manila and the Philippine soil from 1808 or 1809 to 1813 which nearly coincided with the Mexican revolution in Spanish America.

The Spanish community in Manila and the provinces swelled from a little over 1,000 to 4,000 between 1808 and 1813, according to Tomas de Comyn who was in the Philippines at that time. These were the people, in addition to some Indio *ilustrados*, who imbibed the new nationalism. Their number was increased by new arrivals from Spain who served as officials in the State or the Church, or those who escaped the chaotic conditions consequent to the Spanish war of independence. These people were responsible for disseminating Hispanism as government officials who implemented the decrees and the Constitution of 1812 which embodied the nationalistic ideas. The impact of Hispanism was both positive and negative but nonetheless it showed that the concept was rapidly spreading among the people who appeared to understand its significance. The Junta which established the Cortes also ordered its assembly in 1810. It also decreed the election of delegates in Manila, among them, Ventura de los Reyes, a 70-year old wealthy merchant of the city whose credentials were approved in 1811. He was one of the signers of the Constitution of 1812. Moreover, he proposed and succeeded in obtaining approval for the abolition of the monopolistic galleon trade with the *boleta* system and the introduction of plans for the development of agriculture, commerce, industry and navigation in the country. The next extent through which Hispanism became effective was seen in the implementation of the principle of representation. Capitals of the Spanish provinces overseas (the former colonies) were ordered to form a preparatory junta each to issue instructions on the method of election of the *deputados*. The Philippines was then divided into four provinces—Manila, Nueva Segovia, Nueva Caceres, and Cebu—each in turn was subdivided into electoral districts with a definite number of electors. Manila was entitled to 27 district electors who would elect nine deputies and three alternates. The election held in 1814 was a big affair and two of those elected were educated Indios, Mariano Pilapil and Andres Gatmaytan. The others were most likely peninsulares and creoles: Manuel Cacho, Cayetano Zeferino, Miguel Fernandez de Luna, Roberto Pimentel, Juan de Zuñiga, and others. What happened to them was unfortunate. Due to lack of funds, only two deputies were sent and they were not able to hold office because Ferdinand VII returned from exile, restoring absolutism in May 1814.

That year also marked the withdrawal of the effectivity of the Constitution of 1812 in the Philippines, which Ferdinand VII nullified when he abolished the Cortes. The spread of nationalism was however demonstrated by the revolt in Sarrat, Ilocos province in 1815. The Ilocanos, 1,500 of them from the lower classes, took up arms believing that the *principales* and Spanish officials conspired to withdraw the Constitution. Now that they were Spanish citizens and no larger vassals, the Ilocanos thought they were exempted from *polo y servicio* and the hated tribute. As late as 1819 the spread of nationalism had been observed by an English traveller, Henry Peddington, who said that the creoles were beginning to take courage in openly discussing the concepts of liberty and democracy of Thomas Jefferson, and the idea of the right of revolution — all components of Hispanism then taking root in Manila and other places in the country — especially in the Manila cafes (probably along Escolta in Binondo).

In addition to the lower classes among the Indios, the upper classes and the *ilustrados* were also affected by Hispanism which began to assume the form of a movement after 1810. The clergy, especially among the Indios, Spanish mestizos and creoles led the movement since they were in a position of power and authority in the parishes. These Filipino secular priests had been educated and trained since the time of Archbishop Basilio Sancho de Sta. Justa in 1774 and 1776. The power, profit, and prestige which the friars possessed went to the Indio secular priests who became the regular clergy's objects of ire and envy. The Indio secular priests were increasing in number by the 19th century, causing Comyn to fear that they might eventually undermine the Spanish government. They numbered, he believed, about 1,000. Hence, he recommended the cessation of their ordination and training. By 1820 tension between the Filipino seculars and Spanish regulars intensified. The seculars charged that the regulars were enriching themselves at the expense of the people while the latter looked down upon the former, denying them important posts in the church administration. The seculars, according to Judge Manuel Bernaldez Pizarro, had already imbibed Hispanism as seen through their assumption of leadership in the conduct of the elections in 1813 when the Constitution of 1812 was proclaimed. For Bernaldez Pizarro, the continued ordination of the Indio secular priests seemed to inspire "revolution" among the masses.

Realities of colonialism in the Philippines soon boggled the minds of the Indios. Hispanism under the artificial and superficial leadership of the peninsulares who were compelled to promulgate the laws of the Constitution coming from the peninsula, was severely limited as seen in the interpretation of Governor-General Gardoqui. He told the people that though the Indios were "Spanish citizens" with privileges and protection under the Constitution of 1812, they should still shoulder the political and economic burdens of the State as Indios.

By the 1820's when the second stage in the evolution of nationalism unfolded, the Indio and creole secular priests found themselves being selectively victimized and eliminated by the limited interpretation given by the Government and the Church on Hispanism. The Indios, creoles and Spanish mestizos were being discriminated in the governm ent, the military establishment and the Church. They had to give way to the newly-arrived peninsulares for high government and church posts. The Indio and Spanish mestizo secular priests were dispossessed of their parishes while the avenues toward advancement were also systematically closed. The decrees of 1826, 1849, and 1861 ordered the return of parishes occupied by the seculars to the friars and gave the latter parishes under the former within the archbishopric of Manila. The decree of 1861 especially precipitated the secularization campaign of Father Pedro Pablo Pelaez, a Spanish mestizo who served as interim archbishop of Manila in 1862-1863. The restoration and later suppression of Philippine representation to the Cortes in 1820-1823 and 1834-1837 unsettled conditions further. The institutionalization of nationalism or Hispanism further strengthened the concept as the Constitution of 1812 was once again promulgated and elections were held in Manila and other provinces. Most of those elected were former officials in the country and presumably peninsulares and creoles like Jose Maria Arnedo and Manuel Felix Cancio (1820), Francisco Bringas, Vicente Posada and Manuel Taenz de Vigmanos (1820-1823), and Juan Francisco Lecaros and Andres Garcia Camba (1835). More importantly, freedom of the press (writing, printing, and publishing without license or prior revision and approval) was decreed in 1821 and proclaimed in Manila only to be abolished in 1834. In the same year (1821) direct and periodic mail service from Spain to the Philippines was also decreed.

The spread and fortification of the ideas of nationalism were further assured with the opening of Manila to world commerce in 1834 and the opening of the Suez Canal in 1869. All the foregoing developments strengthened the nationalistic movement now dominated by the

"Filipinos" or creoles but in coalition with the Spanish and Chinese mestizos and upper-class Indios including the ilustrados among them. The lower classes among the Indios were not unaffected by the spreading nationalism as evidenced by the revolt of Apolinario de la Cruz in Tayabas (now Quezon and Aurora provinces) in the 1840's. But the creoles dominated the scene as exemplified by the Andres Novales mutiny in their struggle for equality in the Government and the Church in the 1820's through the 1850's.

In much the same way that witnessed the strengthening of nationalism, reactionary ideas were also enhanced — for the ingress and egress of ideas included the forces of reaction and conservatism. The forces of reaction and reform which saw Spain in the grip of revolution and civil wars during this period had not been completely reflected in Manila. Madrid at that time became convinced, regardless of the governnment's anti-church policy, that the friars were a necessary evil in the Philippines. Thus for the sake of maintaining Spanish sovereignty, the friars were entrusted with powers of government and with them the suppression of radical ideas — i.e. nationalism and its component concepts. By the 1860's and 1870's or during the second stage of the nationalistic evolution we called creolism or "Filipinism," the climax of the movement was reached with the use of the temporary church powers Pelaez held in his campaign for the secularization. Upon his death in 1863 leadership was inherited by Father Jose Burgos. Simultaneously, the political phase of the movement was already reaching its climax with the organization of the so-called Liberal Party by activist students in San Jose College and the University of Sto. Tomas, also in the 1860's and 1870's. This climax was triggered by the Spanish Revolution of 1868 which led to the proclamation of a new Constitution and the coming of Carlos Ma. de la Torre in 1869.

Encouraged by Governor-General de la Torre, the nationalists that included creoles like Manuel Genato, Joaquin Pardo de Tavera, Angel and Andres Garchitorena, Andres Nieto, Jacobo Zobel, Antonio Regidor, and other progressive leaders joined several activities involving the reformist governor. The secular priests were led by Fathers Burgos, Mariano Gomez, Jacinto Zamora, Mariano Sevilla, Agustin Mendoza, and Simon Ramirez. Students who led the movement were Felipe Buencamino, Sr., Ramon Soriano, and others. They campaigned for the secularization of the parishes and liberal-democratic rights for the people. They participated in the famous Liberty Serenade of July 12, 1869, the September 1869 Liberty Parade and the Red-Ribbon Reception that followed.

It was not surprising then that these elements headed by the Manila

Spaniards or the creoles were the first to suffer martyrdom when they were implicated in the Cavite Mutiny of 1872. It was interesting to note the cross-sections of the colonial society they represented. Among the businessmen were Jose Ma. Basa, Pio Basa, Maximo Paterno, and Balbino Mauricio. The lawyers' group included Pardo de Tavera, Regidor, Jose E. Basa, Mauricio de Leon, Gervasio Sanchez, and Pedro Carillo. The priests included the famous Gomburza, Mendoza, Jose Guevarra, Sevilla, Toribio del Pilar, Justo Guazon, Pedro Dandan, Anacleto Desiderio, Vicente del Rosario, and others. Most of them were exiled to Guam and other penal colonies while others were executed.

By the 1880's the third stage in the evolving nationalism took the form of "Assimilationist Filipinism" with the coalition now dominated by the Indio-ilustrados and the wealthy businessmen all belonging to the burgeoning middle class. They or their parents were the beneficiaries of the economic transition to commercial agriculture in the late 18th century period of the *libre comercio*. The opening of Manila to foreign commerce and the arrival of foreign traders who established informal banking systems and introduced technologies greatly assisted the new middle class in the 19th century. And their demands for liberalization of trade flow, infrastructures, and other communication linkages like steamships, telephone and telegraph services further forced the Spanish government, desiring to make the Philippines a major appendage of the empire, to grant more and more concessions. The new wealth out of commercial agriculture was used for luxuries and education of the children of the middle class.

This emergent social class consisted of the ilustrados who imbibed the spreading "Assimilationist Filipinism." This stage of Philippine nationalism was popularly called the Propaganda Movement. But it might as well be referred to as a revolutionary crisis rather than just a propaganda movement which historical tradition assigned to it. Though it was true that the nature and character of the demands made by the ilustrados were reformatory and assimilationist, what made the movement revolutionary and critical were the hidden and unstated assumptions behind these demands. Rizal, Marcelo H. del Pilar, Graciano Lopez-Jaena, Jose Ma. Panganiban, Mariano Ponce, Antonio Luna, and others were not merely demanding assimilation and democratic reforms. Underlying these demands were ideas for the restructuring of the empire into a federal system instead of the present unitary system. Corollary to this assumption was the implication that if the demands went unheeded, a separate and independent state would be established and administered by the Indios. This State would be established either peacefully or violently—more of the latter depending upon the wishes of Madrid. The federal system, one could logically guess, would be established based on equality among the members or component units—rather a radical departure from the past policy of assimilation of the colonies as colonies, i.e. as vassals of the king.

Following these assumptions was the logic that Madrid must trust and let the Filipinos themselves run their own affairs based on the principle of autonomy for all the components of the federal state. This would call for a radical change in the status quo since Madrid had entrusted the control of the Philippines to the friars. It would also logically follow that not only the friars but also all the Spanish elements would be dispossessed. The Indios, by sheer force of number and participation in the political and religious processes, would dominate the State. All these assumptions made this stage in the evolution of nationalism different from the earlier stages. The leadership in the coalition was now dominated by the Indios who called themselves Filipinos. The attacks against the friar rulers were more intense than during the earlier period as shown by Marcelo del Pilar's derogatory reference to the government in the Philippines as a frailocracy or monastic sovereignty.

To replace this government, the nationalists of the period wanted genuine and meaningful popular sovereignty unlike the earlier demand when the concept was only conferred to the Spanish elements. Moreover, the possibility of a Filipino governor-general or Filipinos occupying not merely minor but major posts in the government and the church was made a certainty by the large-scale participation of the Indios in the political process. The coalition among a few peninsulares, many creoles and mestizos, and many more Indios as caciques, businessmen, and ilustrados showed signs of breaking up. The Spanish elements (peninsulares and creoles) were only reformists in Spain but not in the Philippines where they turned reactionaries. The only link that they had with the coalition was their hatred of the friars and their powers. The liberalism in masonry was another link that held the coalition together. But it was beginning to loosen at the seams.

Finally, the last stage in the evolution of nationalism was reached in the founding of the revolutionary *Katipunan ng mga Anak ng Bayan* or KKK in 1892. While the *Liga Filipina* of Rizal seemed to point to an organization of a united people who would logically control affairs in a presumed State under the Spanish federal system, the Katipunan founded by Andres Bonifacio and company envisioned a new nation independent from the Spanish empire—federally organized or not. The coalition in the nationalist movement—in the form of Indio-Filipinism to be more accurate—now broke up as the lower middle and lower classes, both urban and rural joined together against the Spanish elements, the Spanish mestizos and the Indio upper and middle classes. With the objective of independence and the building of a new nation composed mostly of indigenous Filipinos, nationalism in this last stage was naturally radical unlike the conservative nationalism of the earlier three stages. Furthermore, while the conservative nationalistic movement was tainted with reactionary ideas represented by the old 16th century assimilation, the radical nationalism of Bonifacio and Emilio Jacinto, the acknowledged "brains" of the Katipunan, was more forward-looking, a marked departure from the former. Not only did the Katipunan nationalism aspire for independence and separation, but it also dared to organize a new society which was liberal, democratic, and ethically virtuous based on the brotherhood of all Filipinos—hence the concept of "a nation of Tagalogs" or *Katagalugan*. The new nation would be governed by a code of ethics and moral principles contained in Bonifacio's "Decalogue" and Jacinto's "Kartilla." Its democratic ideas were expounded in Jacinto's essay "Liwanag at Dilim." At least two mythologies discussed the necessity for founding a new nation and for separation from the imperial Spanish nation.

One was in Bonifacio's "Ang Dapat Mabatid ng mga Tagalog" (What the Filipinos Should Know). According to the myth, in pre-colonial times the Filipinos governed themselves, lived in abundance and prosperity, had trade with neighboring countries, had "nobility of heart," and everybody "knew how to read and write" in their own "native alphabet." When the Spaniards came, they promised "friendship," "better conditions," and "knowledge." To make their promises binding, the Spaniards followed the usual custom of *kasunduan* by blood compact performed by Legazpi and Sikatuna. On the Filipinos' part, the promise was to "feed them (the Spaniards) lavishly" and supply their needs, to spend "our wealth, blood and life itself in their defense" and to "fight" for them. These the Filipinos more than fulfilled for more than 300 years. The Spaniards, on the other hand, failed to fulfill their part of the *kasunduan*. The Filipinos' "munificence" was answered with "treachery." Instead of leading the people to "knowledge," the Spaniards "blinded" and "contaminated" them with their "meaness of character...." . When the Filipinos "beg for a little love" the reply was exile and separation from their kin and parents. "What then must we do?" asked Bonifacio. The answer was, by means of reason, the Filipinos could discern the Spanish hypocrisy and cruelty. There was no other recourse but to "open our eyes" and "voluntarily consecrate our strength to what is good" in the hope that "the prosperity of our land ... will now come to pass."

The other mythology was that of a mother country which, instead of giving love to her "children in the East" gave her "sufferings" and "cruelties." Spain had been a "negligent" and "malevolent mother" and therefore the Philippines was "no longer yours whatever happens...". The mother must now prepare "the grave where many dead bodies will find rest."

Related to both mythologies was one component in the Katipunan's formula for admission of members. The applicants were to answer three questions: "What was the condition of the Philippines in early times? What is the condition today? What will be the condition in the future?" Properly coached, the newcomers were to answer: that the Filipinos were "happy and independent"; that the Spaniards "did nothing to civilize" the people; and that Spanish cruelties "will be remedied in time and freedom will be redeemed."

All the foregoing episodes and the four stages in the evolution of nationalism happened in Manila. The city had been, since it was founded by Legazpi, the metropolis in Asia. Before that Manila and the nearby areas were a thriving settlement under a sort of confederation ruled by Rahas Matanda, Lakandula and Soliman. When Legazpi arrived and occupied Manila on May 19, 1571, nearly 395 years ago, he founded a large settlement already actively engaged in trade especially with the Chinese. He then made Manila the capital of Spanish Philippines but the imperial name of "Distinguished and Ever Loyal City" was given only in 1574, and the coat-of-arms in 1596. Since then and up to the last century of Spanish rule, Manila had been and still was a private city. It was, almost immediately after occupation, given the status of a city by Legaspi. As such, Legazpi organized on June 24, 1571 an autonomous government called *Cabildo* consisting of two *alcaldes en ordinario* (or two mayors), twelve councilors called *regidores*, and a secretary. With the *Cabildo*, Legazpi laid down the plans for a modern city: parallel streets at right angles, spaces for plazas, the construction of public buildings like the palace for the governor-general, churches, hospitals and private residences, and for security, the rebuilding of the old fort of Soliman.

At the time of Legazpi's death, however, Manila was not magically transformed into a Spanish city he envisioned. It took time even before the walls which would surround what was later called Intramuros (a headland south of the Pasig River and Manila Bay) were completed. But Manila without walls was secured by natural barriers in time of war by the Pasig River on the north, Manila Bay on the west, and marshes on the east. But in time of peace the city was accessible from other settlements on the opposite banks of the Pasig River: the northern approaches were Tondo, Lakandula's kingdom; Binondo (Minondok), where the Chinese had their business and residence; and Quiapo, a small village then; and, on the south banks were Bagumbayan (now Luneta Park), Ermita, Malate (Maalat), Dilao (Paco), and Lamayan (Santa Ana). These were Manila's suburbs which also included other *arrabales* or nearby places like Santa Cruz, Sampalok, San Miguel, Sta. Mesa and Pandacan. By the 19th century, as a result of commercial agricultural development and the growth of internal commerce, Manila and its environs experienced rapid economic growth. By the middle of the 19th century the city had undergone economic transformation from self-contained agriculture and impotence where Chinese goods were transhipped to Mexico, to export-oriented agriculture and changing demography.

These developments compelled the Spanish authorities through a decree in 1886 to expand the city of Manila into a province with jurisdiction over 28 municipalities including the arrabales.

Manila was perceived differently during the last century of Spanish rule by observers. Rizal likened Manila to a "sickly girl" dressed in her "grandmother's" garments that had seen "better days." Foreman thought the city "a dull capital" where life's monotony was broken only by "the numerous religious processions...". In Intramuros there were the Cathedral and eleven churches and convents serving as headquarters of the monastic orders, the Ayuntamiento, the UST, and different colleges for boys and girls, the garrison, and the stone houses of Spanish residents.

Outside the Walled City were the rapidly urbanizing suburbs. Binondo was the "real commercial capital" where shopping centers were located along Rosario and Escolta streets. Tobacco factories were located here. In Tondo, excess population from the provinces were accommodated as a pool of labor for the city and environs. There was, in Tondo, the slum section of laborers, sailors, and fishermen. Also located here was the Tutuban Station for the Manila-Dagupan Railroad. In Quiapo, artesians abounded: goldsmiths, sculptors, and silversmiths. Santa Cruz was one of the better places where rich merchants lived, together with the mechanics and Chinese mestizos. Sampalok was called the place of the laundrymen and women while San Miguel, where the palace of the governor-general was relocated, was inhabited by government officials and wealthy families of the creoles. Santa Mesa was a cool area abounding in acacia, kakawati, ylang-ylang and fruit trees. It was then the summer residence of both wealthy Filipino and Spanish families. The principal recreation here was horse-racing held in its hippodrome. Santa Ana's good cool climate made the place the residence of many foreigners like the British, Americans, French, and Germans. It had beautiful orchards and gardens. Paco was the residence of the middle and lower classes, and was famous for its circular stone *pantyon* or cemetery and the *plaza de toros*. Two other aristocratic areas in addition to San Miguel were Ermita and Malate where Spanish middle class mestizos and Filipinos lived. These districts also became the center of a cottage industry—embroidery.

Society in the province of Manila was cosmopolitan and composed of pure Filipinos, pure Chinese, Chinese and Spanish mestizos, Spanish and creole elements, and non-Spanish foreigners. Its population had reached 340,000, (nearly half a million) by 1896. The city proper alone at that time had a total population of 16,000. There were at least four daily newspapers in circulation—*El Diario de Manila, El Comercio, La Voz de Espana*, and the *La Correspondencia*. In addition, there was a bi-weekly *La Opinion* and a government paper, *Gaceta de Manila*. Modern facilities of communication were steadily made available: the telephone in 1890, telegraph in 1873 and cable in 1880. The mail sevice for Spain had already been existing since 1767. The transportation system was already relatively adequate: weekly steamers plied the Manila-Hongkong route and there was a monthly service to Barcelona; three lighthouses serviced shipping; *batel* and *paraws* abounded linking the different islands to Manila; and three kinds of horse-drawn carriages (*quiles, carromata,* and *carruaje*) filled the streets. There was also a horse-drawn car-system called the *tranvia*.

Banks served the interests of commercial agriculture and domestic trade: Banco Español Filipino with a provincial branch in Iloilo held the power to issue banknotes, Chartered Bank of India, Australia, and China was established in 1873, and the Hongkong and Shanghai Bank in 1875. There were many other informal banks established by traders who lent money to cultivators, landowners or hacenderos.

The water needs of the Manila residents were furnished by the newly established Carriedo Water-Works, wells, public fountains, and San Juan del Monte reservoir.

This, then, was the Manila which served as the center of religion, progress and modernity, politics, trade, education, nationalist agitation, revolutionary plots, civil and military administration. Truly, she was the Philippines' primate city, the seat of government, and hotbed for reform and revolution.

# JAPANESE ORGANIZATIONS AND INSTITUTIONS IN PREWAR MANILA

MOTOE TERAMI-WADA

As Japan reopened herself to the outside world in the middle of the 19th century after some 200 years of isolation, she had to undergo rapid modernization in order to survive as an independent nation. This process resulted in social turmoil, and subsequently thousands of displaced people were produced. While there were those who did take advantage of the new circumstances in order to secure economic betterment, many, from various social classes, could not adjust themselves to the transition. For instance, the fixed monetary tax and military conscription forced upon the peasants made their existence more difficult than during feudal times. Even the samurai class, a former ruling class, lost their economic privileges as well as prestige. It is not surprising that some decided to leave the country to try their luck elsewhere.

Those who left, therefore, came not only from the lower strata of society, but also included displaced samurais and merchants. In later years, some of these immigrants included well-educated intellectuals disillusioned with the people's rights movement, which had been crushed by the Meiji government. The government then gave more priority to economic and military development than to political freedom and people's rights. Most of the immigrants went to Hawaii, the North and South American continents, and the Southeast Asian countries. In the case of the Philippines, the flow of Japanese into the country was minimal until the United States began its colonial rule over the Filipinos.

One of the earliest known Japanese settlers in the Islands after the 1870's was Tagawa Moritaro (also known as Jose Tagawa or Moritaro Nakagawa), who landed in Iloilo and arrived in Manila some time before August 1890. Tagawa was typical of those who had left Japan at that time — a displaced samurai who wished to avoid military conscription. He later opened a bazaar at Plaza Moraga, Escolta, and engaged in the trading business. He also played an important part in the leadership of the

71

early Japanese community in Manila.[1]

As the peace and order situation in the Philippines improved under the new colonial administration, many jobs which required both skilled and unskilled workers became available. Cheap labor was needed for the construction of railways, roads and military barracks, as well as for mining and other industries. This demand for cheap labor enticed many Japanese to come to the Islands.

Japanese consulate records show that, as of 1903, there were 1,215 Japanese in the Philippines. Of this number, 991 resided in Manila. On the eve of the Japanese military takeover of the Islands in 1941, the Manila Japanese population was 4,700. By this time, approximately 40 Japanese organizations were in existence.[2]

This paper will present these organizations chronologically so as to illustrate the development of the Japanese community. It will also attempt to unearth the nature of the establishments as well as their impact on the host community.

The organizations can be categorized, according to purpose into three:

1.  Official or "semi-official" groups — extension of the national or local governments in Japan, or groups heavily supported by the Japanese government;
2.  Service groups — for mutual aid, enhancing solidarity and intimacy among themselves, preserving their culture, and protecting their economic interests; and
3.  Goodwill groups — for cultivating friendly relations between Japan and the Philippines.

**The Official and "Semi-Official" Groups**

The oldest and sole extension of the Japanese government in prewar Manila was the Consulate. It was established on December 1, 1888, in Sta. Mesa. At that time, there were around 30 Japanese residents in the city. Due to the political instability here (anti-Spanish operations) and back home (Sino-Japanese War), the Consulate was closed between September 1893 and October 1896. When the Philippine Revolution broke out in 1896, the Consulate was reopened mainly to protect the Japanese residents as well as their businesses, although they were still insignificant in number and activities.

The number of Japanese expatriates and the volume of business grew, especially in Davao, and so the Manila Consulate was designated a

Consulate General in 1919, with a Davao branch established in 1920. As of 1938, the Consulate General was housed in the Wilson Building, Juan Luna, Binondo.

To boost the export of Japanese goods abroad, particularly in Asia, the Bureau of Industries of the Tokyo Municipality set up one of its branches on Escolta, Manila, in 1937. Chiefly, it studied local market conditions, hosted trade fairs, and introduced traders and manufacturers.

In the mother country, notably in the areas from where the immigrants came, the Overseas Association was put up principally to assist these immigrants, who were considered the vanguards of Japan's advance to the South. The prefectures which established Manila branches were Fukuoka (c. 1930), Nagasaki (1937), and Yamaguchi (1938). Many Japanese residents in Manila came from these places.

Not fully satisfied with the territorial acquisition of Taiwan and Korea, some Japanese sought economic expansion to the South. They realized that their knowledge of these areas was inadequate, and suspected that the people in those places likewise possessed scanty information on Japan. That is why in 1915, the Nanyo Kyokai (South Seas Society) was organized by both government officials and civilians for research and cultural exchange. The office was located in the Overseas Branch of the Office of the Taiwan Governor-General in Tokyo. In 1924, the Manila branch of the Society was set up, with Eichiro Nuida, then Consul General, as president. Its main task was to accommodate and orient Japanese traders, manufacturers, and students who were in the Philippines for one economic reason or another. Starting in 1934, it accepted those who went to the Islands to work in the local Japanese bazaars and other types of business enterprises, so that they could have a first-hand experience of the business practice here. As of 1938, there were 45 such trainees scattered all over the archipelago, while the Society had some 70 members in Manila.[3]

## The Service Groups

The very first organization to protect the Japanese expatriates' interests was set up as early as the end of the 19th century, when the Katipunan rose against the Spanish colonial government. There is a record of this organization as of April, 1898, and Sakamoto Shiro, a military agent sent from Japan to observe the Revolution, was the president. Sometimes, all the Japanese citizens in Manila were accommodated at his residence at Reina Regente, Tondo, for safety reasons.[4]

The Spaniards were defeated, and then the U.S. colonizers came. After the latter had subdued the Filipinos, the Japanese community in Manila, as elsewhere in Southeast Asia, began to be dominated by people engaged in the brothel business and other illegal activities such as smuggling.[5]

In 1901, the Japanese Association was created with about 40 people as members, 80% of whom were in brothel-related businesses.[6]

Around 1905, the membership of the Japanese community started to change as the flow into Manila of unskilled and semi-skilled Japanese males increased. More workers were encouraged to immigrate due partly to the demand for cheap labor, and partly to the economic difficulties Japan was suffering from as a result of the Russo-Japanese War of 1904.

In 1906, in order to represent the interests of the newly-arrived members, the Representative Society was established. It was open to any Japanese man or woman who was employed or operated their own business, who had been in the Philippines for at least six months, and who were then residing in Manila. Each district in the city had its representative, the number of which was directly proportional to the district's Japanese population.

The Nihonjin Shoko Kai (Japanese Commerce and Carpentry Association) came into being in 1914. It was composed mainly of carpenters, as implied by the name. Its central preoccupation was to look after the carpenters' welfare, since their increasing number had resulted in the lowering of their daily wages. If a carpenter accepted less than the standard wage of ₱3 a day, then certain measures were to be taken against that carpenter. Later on, the bazaar and refreshment (*halo-halo*) parlor owners joined this organization for the same protectionary purpose. As of 1920, it had 660 members.[7]

Toward the end of 1924, to fulfill the needs of an ever growing and more complex Japanese community, the Nihonjin Kai (Japanese Association) was formed by the merging of two previously established organizations, the Representative Society and the Commerce and Carpentry Association. This Japanese Association was more close-knit, and its by-laws and regulations were registered under the Philippine government.

The membership, which was open to all Japanese residents in Manila, numbered a little over 1,000 at the start. This figure doubled in the mid 1930's.[8] Members were rouglhy divided into three groups:

1. Those who were in Manila temporarily representing mother companies, such as the Mitsui, Mitsubishi, Ito Chu Trading

Companies, and Yokohama Specie Bank;

2. Those who operated large-scale bazaars and companies with local capital, such as the Nippon Bazaar and the Manila branch of the Ohta Development Company (main office in Davao);

3. Consisting of the majority of the Association, those who were engaged in small-scale businesses, or were semi- or unskilled workers such as carpenters and fishermen.

For the first four years or so, the presidents of the Association were always drawn from the first group, although their residency in the Philippines was only temporary.[9]

The Association's activities included extending financial assistance to the less fortunate members and the construction of a Japanese cemetery in Polo, Bulacan. In external affairs, they gave donations to charitable causes such as the National Relief Fund after typhoons and floods, the Red Cross, the Anti-Tuberculosis Society, and to the lepers on Culion Island. The members, however, poured most of their efforts into the management of the Japanese Primary School, which shall be discussed later.

In order to supplement the activities of the Japanese Association, the youth and women established their own organizations. The Manila Japanese Young Men's Association (1927) worked on the attainment of physical and mental balance by the members, aged between 15 and 36. Thus, the Association had two departments: the Intellectual Activity Department and the Sports Department. The former held oratorical contests and lectures, while the latter sponsored varied sports matches like baseball, tennis, and judo. As called for in the Association's song, the members hoped to become stalwart youths representing "glorious" Japan, vanguards of maritime Japan, pioneers in their country's southbound ambitions.[10]

There was also a small Japanese Women's Association which appealed to the upper class females of the Japanese community. It used to be part of the Japan Club but became independent in 1936. In 1938 it had only 30 members. They donated to the Philippine Boy Scouts and the Red Cross, or socialized in international functions, as in tea parties for Aurora Quezon, Manuel L. Quezon's wife. They also actively participated in Manila's annual big event, the Philippine Carnival held every February. They even sent representatives to the Ladies' Committee of the said Carnival.

While any Japanese could join the Japanese Association, there was another group which catered mainly to the business sector. Established in 1916, it was originally called the Miitano Club. Miitano stood for Mitsui

Bussan (mi), Ito Chu (i), Tagawa Trading Company (ta), Narasaki Store (na), Ohta Development Company (o) and Ogura Trading Company (o). As the name indicated, it was a venue for the owners and managers of big bazaars and trading companies to socialize.

The clubhouse was built in traditional Japanese style, with a Japanese garden and a tennis court. It had a huge ballroom for entertaining both Filipino and Japanese guests, a bar, a bowling alley, billiard room and library. The clubhouse was located on Taft Avenue, beside where the De La Salle University stands today. It often entertained not only visiting Japanese politicians and high-ranking military personnel, but also Filipino dignitaries like Sergio Osmeña, Sr., Carlos P. Romulo, and Jorge B. Vargas. Manuel L. Quezon was said to be one of the Club's frequent guests.[11]

In order to make the Filipinos more aware of the nature of the Club, the name Miitano Club was changed in 1919 to Japanese Club. Then in 1936, when the war clouds hung thick over China, it was re-named the Nippon Club (Japan Club), in order to expel English words from the Japanese. "Club" was written in Chinese characters instead of *katakana*, the system used to describe words borrowed from foreign languages.

There were other organizations formed for the sake of solidarity and mutual aid among the Japanese residents. Expatriates coming from the same region in Japan grouped together: Fukushima Prefectural Association (established in 1919), Okinawa Prefectural Association (1936), and Kumamoto Prefectural Association (1936). On the other hand, some Japanese residents gathered together according to the district where they lived, like the Sampaloc Mutual Association (1928) and Quiapo District Association (1929).

One of the memorable accomplishments of the Sampaloc Mutual Association was the life-saving aid they extended to a certain Nishiyama. He was a gardener working for a rich Filipino family. When one member of the family was murdered by, as it was later proved, a relative, Nishiyama was accused. Sampaloc Japanese residents who believed in his innocence put pressure upon the Japanese Association and raised enough money to hire him a lawyer.[12]

## Papers

There was active publishing within the Manila Japanese community since practically all the organizations had their own papers. However, there was only one daily newspaper, the *Manila Nichi-Nichi*. Its origin could be traced to the *ShoKoKai Articles*, a newsletter published by the

ShoKoKai three times a month in the form of stencil sheets. Primarily, it reported what had been discussed in the organization's meetings as well as major news from Japan.

In 1917, it was called the *Sho Ko Kai Ho* (Sho Koo Kai News) and a year later it came out in print instead of being stencilled. Its name changed again, this time to *Shoko Shinpo*, when it was placed under the Printing Division of the Japanese Association in 1924 and was published three times a week. It finally assumed its present name, *Manila Nichi-Nichi,* in May 1937.

## Religious Groups

To answer the religious needs of the community, Buddhist temples were built and a Protestant Christian mission was established. The first Buddhist temple was the Nantenji Temple of the Soto Sect, established as early as 1905 in Sampaloc, where the majority of the Japanese expatriates resided at the time. By 1938, it had 300 followers with branches in Davao and Baguio. Besides giving spiritual guidance and performing Buddhist ceremonies, it operated a nursery and dormitory for those who had come from the provinces to attend the Japanese School in Manila.

The Honganji Sect of Japanese Buddhism set up its own mission also in Sampaloc in 1918. The Manila Honganji Temple was very active since its beginning not only within the Japanese community, but also in vigorously promoting friendly relations with the Filipinos. Like the Nantenji Temple, it ran a nursery and dormitory for the children of its adherents.[13]

Later, in 1921, the Manila Buddhist Young Men's Association and its female counterpart were established independent of each other. Charitable deeds like donating to the Culion Leprosy Sanitarium and to victims of natural disasters were typical activities of the women's associations. It also managed a mutual financing association called Tanomoshiko, for the members of the Men's and Women's Association. Membership count in 1938 for the Men's Association was 30, while it was 250 for the Women's Association.

A Protestant mission for the Christian Japanese was established only in the latter part of the 1930's. They went to the United Church, then located at the corner of Lepanto and Azcarraga, for their Sunday worship. However, they held their activities at 19 Aranga Street. They conducted a Sunday school for the children, who were also taught the Japanese language, music, English, and etiquette for young girls. In addition, there were men's and women's groups within the congregation, with different undertakings.

77

## Educational Institutions

As stated earlier, brothel operations were closed down by the US colonial government by the end of the second decade, and the Japanese community was mainly composed of semi-skilled laborers such as carpenters, fishermen, household helpers, small-scale bazaar owners, and refreshment parlor operators.[14] Most of the males were single, and the married ones had left their wives and children in Japan. Even if they had their families here, they usually returned to Japan when the children were of school age.[15]

Thus, the establishment of the Manila Japanese School in 1917 was a sign that the composition of the Japanese community was changing from consisting of transient members to being composed of more permanent residents.

The move to found a school came from the residents themselves through the Representative Society, which was a representative body of the community. The financial burden was shouldered by the children's parents through the Society. A school building was erected at 150 Alejandro Street, Sampaloc, the district where majority of the Japanese residents lived. The school first opened with 24 students and two teachers. As clearly indicated in the first prospectus, the parents wanted, through the school, to inject the "Japanese spirit" into their foreign-born children, who did not even know how to speak their language correctly.[16]

It was not only the Japanese residents who were eager to build the school; the Japanese authorities were more than interested. They wanted the expatriates to grow roots in the Philippines without being worried about their offsprings' education. The expatriates would then have more drive to develop the area which, in turn, would bring more wealth to the mother country. At the same time, those Japanese who were born and raised in a foreign country would be made more aware, through the school, of their Japanese heritage. They would become the vanguards of that area's development by the Japanese, and would be contributing to their nation-building.

This interest by the Japanese authorities was concretized in the form of financial support for the school. In 1921 and 1923 (and onwards), the Taiwan Governor-General Office and the Japanese Ministry of Foreign Affairs respectively, sent subsidies.[17]

A look into the school's activities from 1917 to 1927 further confirmed the statement above.[18] In July 1924, the school authorities decided to make the pupils bow toward Japan every morning. In the same month, one faculty member was sent to Japan for a three-month observation of the educational system there. Many visitors from Japan went to the school to give lectures or simply to observe. Their mere presence made the children more conscious of their roots. Visitors included the following:

| Officials from | Date of visit |
| --- | --- |
| Japanese Foreign Affairs Ministry | July 1924 |
| House of Representatives | January and September 1926 |
| Korean Governor-General's Office | January and February 1926 |
| A Seoul School | March 1927 |
| Taiwan Governor-General's Office | June and August 1926 |
| Interior Affairs Department and Visiting naval warships | July 1924; June, August, September, October and November 1926; January, February and April 1927 |

Manila was considered one of the future Japanese colonial centers in Southeast Asia, as indicated by the frequent visits of high-ranking personnel from the Offices of the Taiwan and Korean Governor-General. In line with the Japanese authorities' aim to develop the expatriates' children as the vanguards in the area, the children were taken to Manila Bay whenever there were Japanese warships anchored there—a practice which fostered a good deal of nationalist pride among the students.

At the end of the 1930's, twenty years after its foundation, the school body had grown to 640 students and 16 faculty members.[19]

Another educational institution was the Seinen Dan Ya Gakko (Night School of the Japanese Youth Association). It was initially set up by the Manila Honganji Mission in March 1920 at Elisond Street in Quiapo. Later, a Youth Association was formed among the night school students and the school's management was turned over the Association.[20]

The Night School was for the young Japanese who worked during the daytime as bazaar or office employees. They all realized, living and working as they were in a U. S. colony, that English should be learned; thus, their classes were conducted in that language. They had two hours of instruction each night, and a course was supposed to be completed in three years. As of 1924, there were 48 students enrolled.

## Economic Groups

There were quite a few organizations formed based on the economic interests of the Japanese residents. Their enumeration in chronological order would reveal the economic development of the community.

One of the first was the Paco Commercial Association (1918), which aimed to financially assist the Paco Japanese residents. A reserve fund was built up through the collection of at least fifty centavos from each member per month.

Next was the institution set up by those in the *halo-halo* business. There were quite a number of them in Manila; in fact, the Japanese were once nicknamed locally as *mongo-con-illero*. But soon the number of members had increased so much that they began to stifle one another's development. In order to control the situation as well as to investigate other problems, the Manila Japanese Refreshment Parlors' Federation Association was set up in 1921, and had 106 members as of 1938.

The carpenters working on ships organized themselves into the Manila Japanese Ship Carpenters Association in 1931, initially with around 50 members.

The masseurs' organization was formed in 1932.

The presence of Japanese fishermen and fishing boats in the local scene increased steadily. Eventually, local fishermen criticized the Japanese monopoly of fishing rights in Manila Bay and other areas. In fact, one of the local magazines featured articles on the Japanese fishing method. The article was entitled "Aboard a Japanese Fishing Boat – Why the Japanese Do Things Better."[21] At one point, a Filipino politician was made to promise protesting local fishermen that he would present a bill which would limit the activities of Japanese fishermen.[22]

Criticism was aimed not only at the small-scale Japanese fishermen but also at other industry-related corporations. As of 1937, the Philippine-Japanese Fishing Corporation, with 39% of its capital coming from the Japanese, was exporting canned tuna to the U.S.A. This was denounced as a "hurdling of American tariff walls by Japanese with the Filipino as tools."[23]

As an outcome of local pressure, the Japanese Fishermen's Association of the Philippines was established in 1939 in Quiapo. The membership was divided into two classes: one for the boat owners and fish industrialists who had to pay monthly dues of five pesos; and the other for fishermen who were obliged to fork over twenty centavos every month. In its year of establishment, the Fishermen's Association had 90 members in the former class and 830 in the latter.[24]

In theory, the Bicycle Importers Association (established in 1935) was not exclusively for the Japanese but for anyone who imported Japanese-made bicycles or bicycle parts. In practice, however, the members were Japanese bazaar owners or import-export businessmen.

The two main goals of the Association were to maintain certain prices in order to avoid unfair competition, and to enlarge its markets. The future target was that all the bicycles used in the Islands ultimately would come from Japan. One of the proposed ways for this target to materialize was to strengthen ties with the non-Japanese retail associations and, if possible, bring them to Japan for tours of bicycle factories.[25]

There were two other organizations that extended economic assistance to the Japanese residents in Manila. One was the Manila Japanese Loan Association (established in 1927), whose members were small- to middle-scale businessmen. By 1939 it had 212 members.

The other was the Manila Ko Sei Kai (established in 1937), whose main activity was to secure jobs for its unemployed members – a kind of employment agency. It had some 70 members as of 1938. It also operated dormitory facilities for those who were temporarily out of jobs.

Japanese business in Manila, especially trading and retail, developed considerably right after the First World War due to the lack of imported goods from Europe. The establishment of the Manila branch of the Yokohama Specie Bank in 1918 encouraged this growth by extending financial aid to the local Japanese enterprises. Thus between 1921 and 1930, the number of retail business firms increased three-fold.[26]

Another historical event boosted the development of the Japanese retail business. At the end of the 1930's, the local Chinese merchants, who used to control the Philippines' retail trade, staged a boycott of Japanese goods as a protest against the Japanese presence in China. This protest seemed to have been widespread. At one time, 80,000 pamphlets advocating the boycott due to Japanese atrocities in China were distributed in downtown Manila.[27]

The Chinese refusal to deal with Japanese goods prompted the local Japanese to open up their own import companies and retail shops. By 1934, there were approximately 200 such firms and shops, of which 139 were locally established firms and 61 were branch offices. Avenida Rizal and Echague Street were filled with these Japanese establishments.[28]

Japanese economic activities were not limited to the retail and fishing industries, but were also involved in the mining and lumber industries. The Philippine Congress became concerned with protecting the country from this foreign economic invasion as political independence became imminent. Issues concerning retail businesses of the foreigners, foreign employees, residents and registration taxes, luxury items tax, foreign shipping tax, lumber exports, foreign-owned fishing vessels and the like were brought to the attention of the lawmakers and discussed in the Philippine Congress.

Japanese businessmen, concerned about protecting their economic interests, moved to establish the Japanese Chamber of Commerce. This was done in 1934 under the initiative of Shogo Dazai, a manager of the Yokohama Specie Bank. It had thirty-four members at that time.[29] Two years later the Chamber's by-laws were formulated, declaring that the Chamber was open to any individual or corporation who/which had offices or were engaged in business in Manila and suburbs. Those who lived outside Manila could also join upon the presentation of two letters of introduction.[30]

As time passed, more owners of the locally established business firms were elected to the board of directors.[31] Japanese Consulate personnel and correspondents sent by the Japanese Ministry of Business and Industry served as the Chamber's advisers.

By 1939, the Chamber had a membership of 123. As of that time, it was successful in stopping the passage of laws banning the export of lumber and the limiting of the number of foreign employees. This was accomplished by pressuring the Filipino business groups connected with the higher echelons of the government, and by constantly keeping in touch with them through personal and social ties. These ties were strengthened through dinners and cocktails given in the Filipinos' honor.[32] To assist in the activities of the Japanese Chamber of Commerce, the Foreign Office in Tokyo sent subsidies from 1937 on.[33]

On the other hand, the Japanese goods boycott movement initiated by the local Chinese businessmen was counteracted by the distribution of pamphlets explaining the Japanese side. This was one of the important tasks of the chamber.

## The Goodwill Groups

One such organization was the Hiripin Dai Ajia Kyokai (Philippine Great Asia Society), established in 1934. Some of the objectives of the Society were to propagate Asianism; to promote friendlier relations among the Asian nations; and to investigate the conditions in other Asian nations.[34] Its establishment did not attract the leaders or those in the high echelons of the Manila Japanese community. For instance, the Consul General thought that it was not wise to disseminate ideas which might cause unnecessary doubts and fears among the Filipino people.[35]

An old-timer in Manila and a successful bazaar owner, K. Kanegae, thought that the "friendship" being offered was not based on equality between the two countries but with Japanese interests in mind.[36] The dubious standing of the Society's president, O. Mochizuki, further alienated the local Japanese elite.[37] Thus, the members came mostly from the lower echelons of the community, such as the fishermen, carpenters, shopkeepers, and the like. The advisers and board members were drawn from the Filipinos. Jose P. Laurel and Pio Duran were advisers, while Jose L. Baluyot, Gertrudo Kalambacal and Isidro Vamenta were board members.[38]

Two years after the Society's founding, the Asia Club was organized on Arlegui Street in commemoration of the birth of the Commonwealth Government. Of a social nature, the Club hoped to attain better understanding and closer ties between the Japanese expatriates and the Filipino citizens. Its founding was advocated by O. Mochizuki (mentioned earlier) and by E. Imamura, who exported lumber and raised chickens in commercial quantities. Both were long-time residents of the Japanese community and were supported by some prominent Filipino citizens like Laurel and Duran.

The Clubhouse was a renovated old university building with a large Japanese-style hall and included facilities for traditional Japanese sports like archery and sumo wrestling, and indoor amusement facilities such as billiard and game tables.[39]

Members of the Great Asia Society automatically became members of the Asia Club. Within two years of the Club's founding, there were 80 members, both Japanese and Filipino.

The Philippine-Japan Society, another organization promoting friendship, was established in July 1936. It was a sister organization of the Philippine Society of Japan set up in Tokyo in 1935.[40] The Philippine-Japan Society aimed to promote and strengthen cultural and economic relations between the two countries. This entailed arranging visits, excursions and student exchange programs. The Society distributed a wide variety of printed materials about the Philippines.

With Philippine independence close at hand, both the Japanese and Filipinos became more conscious of the importance of good relations between the two countries. The Society contributed toward this end by seeing to it that there was frequent contact in the form of student, government and professional exchanges, tours and the like.[41] The Society members made themselves responsible for welcoming and hosting those Japanese visiting Manila to promote goodwill.

Reflecting the semi-official nature of the Society, its membership included no less than Manuel L. Quezon and Sergio Osmeña as honorary president and vice-president respectively. The Society's president was Maximo Kalaw and the vice-presidency was shared by Marion V. de los Santos (president of the University of Manila) and Yasaku Morokuma (a former president of the Japanese Association and a president of the Ohta Development Company).[42]

Three organizations were born as a result of the frequent cultural exchanges: the Philippine Student Travel Association (1935), Manila Japanese Language School (1935), and Japanese Information Bureau (1936). Their offices were all located at 841 Lepanto Street, Sampaloc, where the Manila Honganji Temple was likewise situated. It was but natural to find them in the care of the Buddhist Temple because their educational tours were initiated by the very Reverend Hideo Yamanouchi of the aforementioned Temple.

The Student Travel Association and the Language School were for those Filipinos who had returned from Japan and wanted to maintain and further develop their proficiency in the Japanese language, as well as to keep in touch with others who had undergone the same experience. They also aimed to assist future travelers to Japan. The Language School not only taught the Japanese language but also tried to train future language teachers among the Filipinos. Japanese culture, history, and religion were taught aside from the language.

Under the prompting of Reverend Yamanouchi, the Philippine-Japanese Library, which was originally a part of the Honganji Temple, was converted into the Japan Information Bureau in 1936. This Bureau was given the task of propagating Japanese culture among the Filipino citizens. It accommodated the inquiries of Filipinos who were interested in Japan and its culture. Among the duties of the Bureau were assisting Filipino and Japanese tourists, especially students who wanted to study the other's country; conducting Japanese language courses via correspondence; managing the library; and sponsoring lectures on culture. The Bureau published a bi-weekly English and Tagalog paper named *Eastern Recorder* and a Chinese organ, the *Toa Shin Po* (East Asia News).

## Concluding Remarks

The factors that pushed Japanese immigrants to leave their country had existed since the 1870's, but the reasons that pulled them to the Philippines came about in 1900, only after the U.S. colonial government was established in the Islands.

The very first organization among the Japanese residents in Manila was born out of the necessity of surviving the cross-fire between the Filipino revolutionary forces and, at first the Spanish colonizers, and later the U.S. military forces. The years saw changes in the membership of the Japanese community so that the second Japanese organization, established in 1901, was dominated by brothel owners, prostitutes, and the like. By the time the Representative Society was put up in 1906 and the Japanese Commerce and Carpentry Association in 1914, the community was composed mainly of carpenters, fishermen, cooks, household helpers, and other semi- or unskilled workers. Later on, the number of bazaar and refreshment parlor operators increased.

Up to this time, the tendency of most of these Japanese was to return to Japan eventually with the money that they had accumulated. This period lasted roughly from the end of the 1890's to the middle of the new century's second decade.

As symbolized by the establishment of the Japanese School in 1917, the transient nature of the community gradually became permanent or semi-permanent, slowly taking root in the foreign land. The desire to found a school originally came from parents who were worried that their children were growing up without knowing the language, culture, history, and most of all the "spirit" of the mother country. The Japanese authorities eagerly welcomed the move since it would encourage Japanese expatriates to think of settling permanently in the Philippines, thus obtaining more opportunities to develop and cultivate the area. This, in turn, would bring more wealth to the mother country. Concrete evidence of the Japanese Authorities' approval were the subsidies sent by the Governor-General's Office in Taiwan and the Japanese Ministry of Foreign Affairs.

The opening of the Yokohama Specie Bank in 1918 further promoted the development of the local Japanese business, then more or less firmly established in the country. At this point, the Japanese Consulate, which had to accommodate an ever growing Japanese population in the Islands, became a Consulate General in 1919, and a Davao branch was opened the following year.

As seen earlier, various associations and organizations mushroomed among the expatriates in order to meet a wide array of demands and necessities. The local Japanese economy, which started as simple buy-and-sell endeavors, later developed to such a degree that the Japanese were heavily investing in industries like agriculture, lumber, manufacturing and mining.

The establishment of the Japanese Chamber of Commerce in 1934

85

and the opening of the Taiwan Bank in 1938 attested to the maturity and prosperity of Japanese economic activities in the Philippines.

The end of the 1910's to the outbreak of the Second World War marked the golden age, economically, of the Japanese community in Manila. One local observer aptly pointed out that the secret of Japanese success in business lay in the wise use of capital and in administrative ability. Moreover, he noted that the Japanese expatriates cooperated among themselves and extended mutual protection to one another through their organizations. In addition, they were guided by a strong patriotic spirit.[43]

Indeed, the patriotic spirit characterized the Japanese community since its beginnings. As early as 1904, Japanese residents held a mass meeting at the Libertad Theater under the auspices of the Japanese Association. Those who attended were "all the heads of Japanese firms and 'business ladies' in their national costume." The Japanese Consul spoke on the war that Japan was engaged in with Russia, and urged the expatriates to contribute to the mother country in the form of cash donations or having the males go back home to offer their lives to their "just" cause.[44] As a result of this meeting, $5,046 was collected, most of which came from the brothel owners and the prostitutes.[45]

Kanegae, who had lived in Manila since 1909 and was a successful businessman, recalled that half of his income was spent for promoting Philippine-Japanese relations, developing and looking after the welfare of the Japanese community, and supporting Japan's "national policy."[46]

This intense patriotism was inherited by the second and third generations through constant indoctrination by the Japanese School Administration. At the end of the 1930's, especially after the Marco Polo Bridge incident (July 1937), the various organizations under the leadership of the Manila Japanese Association started to collect donations to be sent to the military offices in Japan.

It would be natural for immigrants, be they Chinese, Filipinos or Japanese, to send their money back to their own families and perhaps to contribute to the local community. But to give money to the national government appeared to be rather unique.

On the other hand, it must have boosted the pride of the Japanese immigrants to see their country winning the wars against China and later against Russia, while most of them were engaged in hard labor in a strange land and a strange culture. At the same time, even if their spirits were elated by the news of Japanese victories, their being in a foreign country alienated them from the mainstream of nation-building. It was perhaps these factors which drove them to be more active in sending contributions to the mother country.

In the middle of the 1930's, Japanese expatriates actively participated in increased cultural exchange activities, taking pride in introducing Japan and its culture to the Filipinos. They perceived that closer ties would help further their own future economic development and they supported Japan's policy of developing Southeast Asia.

When the Japanese Imperial military forcibly entered Manila at the start of 1942, the Manila Japanese residents were filled with joy and pride in seeing their strong army chase "the American devils" away from the city. Their eyes welled with tears and they waved Japanese flags. Most of them, especially male residents of military age, considered it an honor to be conscripted into the Imperial Army, so as to be able to serve the mother country. Others took advantage of the situation and harassed the helpless Filipino residents by acting as interpreters of the Kempeitai and other military authorities.

Yet, there were some Japanese expatriates who became very critical and disillusioned with the military policy and the soldiers' cruelty toward the Filipinos. After all, many of the second generation Japanese grew up with Filipino children. They could not bear to see their friends and neighbors being maltreated and tortured by the Japanese military personnel. They tried to persuade the Japanese military officers that to conquer through sharp bullets was in vain. Instead, mutual trust and friendship should be cultivated to achieve their goal.[47]

At the end of the Occupation, when they had to leave behind their hard-earned economic gains due to Japan's defeat, the Japanese residents might have realized that they were also victims of the Japanese militarism, just like their Filipino friends.[48]

While the members of the Japanese community could be regarded as victims of the Japanese military, the organizations they founded and nurtured assisted and served the Japanese military operations. They supplied the information necessary for the invasion and secured materials as well as manpower necessary for the operations while the Japanese military were in the country.

Even if some, at the start of the Japanese occupation, foresaw the destruction of their lives within the Philippine setting, it was impossible for them to go against the members of the Manila Japanese community who had grown up and lived in an atmosphere of fervent patriotism and nationalism, perhaps stronger than that in the mother country.

## NOTES

1. Information on Tagawa's arrival in Manila came from the Radicacion de Extrangeros, 1891-1897, Philippine National Archives, Manila. Other items on Tagawa's life are seen in Yoko Yoshikawa, "Development of the Japanese Commercial Sector in Manila, 1898-1920; The Case of Jose M. Tagawa," *Tonan Asia Kenyu* 18, (1980): 31-65.

2. For the 1903 Japanese population, see Japanese Ministry of Foreign Affairs (JMFA hereafter), 7.1.5.4., vol. 4, Japanese Ministry of Foreign Affairs Archives, Tokyo.

   The 1941 figure was taken from the Bureau of Insular Affairs 1918/311-A, quoted in Grant K. Goodman, "Japanese Immigration and Philippine Politics" in *Four Aspects of Philippine Japanese Relations, 1930-1940* (New Haven: Southeast Asia Program, Yale University, 1967) p. 40. The number of Japanese organizations by 1941 can be found in Junichi Ohtani, ed., *Hiripin Nenkan 1937-1941* (Philippine Yearbook 1937-1941), vol. 5 (Kobe, 1941), pp. 482-483. All the listings of the Japanese organizations mentioned in this paper are based on the *Hiripin Nenkan,* unless other specified.

3. Aside from Ohtani, *Hiripin Nenkan,* see also JMFA, I.1.10.0.2-4 and *Nanyo Kyokai Niju Nen Shi* (History of Twenty Years of the Nanyo Kyokai) (Tokyo, 1935), pp. 367-368.

4. Ozaki Takuya, *Chomin Sakamoto Shiro* (Tokyo: Chominkai, 1932), p. 331.

5. For more on the nature of the Japanese community in Manila 1890-1920, see Motoe Terami-Wada, "Karayuki-san of Manila," published in the *Philippine Studies* in July 1986.

6. See Chusuke Imamura, *Hiripin Dukuritso o Kataru* (On Philippine Independence) (Tokyo: Heibun-sha, 1935), p. 370; Kiyotaro Kanegae, *Aruite Kita Michi: Hiripin Monogatari* (A Path I Took: Philippine Story) (Tokyo: Kokusei-sha, 1968), p. 43; and Iheji Muraoka, *Muraoka Iheji Den* (Autobiography of Iheji Muraoka) (Tokyo: Nanposha, 1960), p. 134.

7. Senkichi Kobayashi, *Hiripin Kiko* (Travel to the Philippines) (Tokyo: Toho Jeron Sha, 1920), p. 222.

8. As of 1922, Manila was divided into the following districts and corresponding number of Japanese representatives. See *By-Laws of Manila Japanese Representative Society* (1922).

| District | | | No. of Representatives | |
|---|---|---|---|---|
| Binondo | | | 3 | (6) |
| Quiapo | | | 4 | (5) |
| San Juan - Santa Mesa | | | 1 | (2) |
| Paco-Malate-Singalong | | | 2 | (2) |
| Trozo | | | 1 | (1) |
| Santa Cruz   (A) | | | 4 | (5) |
| Santa Cruz   (B) | | | | (2) |
| San Nicolas | | | | (1) |
| Tondo | ) | 5 | | (2) |
| Tondo (fishing area) | ) | | | (3) |
| Ermita | ) | 2 | | (1) |
| Intramuros | ) | | | (2) |
| Sampaloc | | | 3 | (4) |
| Santa Ana | | | 1 | (1) |
| Malabon | | | | (1) |
| Parañaque | | | | (1) |
| Pasay | | | 1 | (1) |
| San Miguel | | | 1 | (6) |

In parenthesis are the numbers in 1936. See Ohtani, *Hiripin Nenkan,* Vol., 2, p. 330.

9. Masaru Kojima, "Manira Nihonjin Shogakko no Shakaiteki Seikako" (Social Characteristics of the Manila Japanese School), *Ryukoku Daigaku Run Shu* (May 1984): 176.
10. Ohtani, *Hiripin Nenkan,* p. 437.
11. For Filipinos visiting the Club, see the *Tribune* issues for 6 January and 2 May 1934, and Kanegae, *Aruite Kita Michi,* p. 448.
12. Kanegae, *Aruite Kita Michi,* p. 247.
13. This aspect will be dealt with in the section on goodwill groups.
14. JMFA, 7.1.5.4., vol. 9.
15. JMFA, 2.6.2.1-6.
16. Manila Japanese School, ed., *Soritsu Nijunshunen Kinenshi* (Twentieth Anniversary of the Founding of the Japanese School) (n.p., 1938), pp. 1-3.
17. JMFA, I.15.0.2.-7-12.
18. Ibid.
19. Ohtani, *Hiripin Nanken,* p. 454. For more details, see Kojima,

89

"Manira Nihonjun Shogakko."
20. JMFA, I.1.5.0.2-7-12.
21. *Graphic*, 6 August 1936.
22. *Graphic*, 25 August 1928.
23. *Graphic*, 7 January 1937.
24. JMFA, K.3.2.2-7.
25. Ibid.
26. K. Watanabe, "History of Japanese Trade in the Philippine Islands," in Modesto Farolan, ed., *Philippine Japanese Yearbook and Business Directory*, vol. 1 (Manila: M. Farolan, 1938), pp. 323-324.
27. *Graphic*, 24 August 1939.
28. The figures came from Watanabe, "Japanese Trade in the Islands," p. 324. The last sentence is attributed to the impressions of Kanegae, *Aruite Kita Michi*, p. 254, and Kiyoshi Osawa, *Hiripin no Ichi Nihonjin Kara* (A Japanese in the Philippines) (Tokyo: Shincho-sha, 1978), p. 90
29. JMFA, 2.6.0.1-23. Besides Dazai, the following were elected to various Chamber committees:

| Name | Company and Position |
| --- | --- |
| S. Ikeda | Mitsubishi Shoji - Manager |
| Y. Morokuma | Ohta Development Company - President |
| N. Nokamura | Daido Boyeki Kaisha - Manager |
| Yamasaki | Mitsui Bussan Kaisha - Manager |

Source: *Tribune*, 4 January 1934.

30. JMFA, 2.6.0.1-23
31. The board members as of 1936 were Osak Boeki Kaisha, Kinka Meruyasin (knit) Inc., Nippon Bazaar, Mori Bicycle Store, Philippine Lumber Exportation Co., O'Racca Confectionary Inc., Takahashi Bazaar & Co., the Sakura Bazaar, Daido Boeki, Mitsubishi Trading, Mayon Bazaar, Yokohama Specie Bank, Mitsui Bussan Ohta Development Company, and Guarantee Cycle Supply.
32. JMFA, K.3.2.2-7.
33. JMFA E.2.6.0.1-23.
34. Ohtani, *Hiripin Nenkan*, p. 468.
35. Grant K. Goodman, "Japanese Pan-Asianism in the Philippines: The Hiripin Dai Ajia Kyokai," *Studies on Asia* (1966): 135
36. Kanegae. *Aruite Kita Michi*, p. 434.
37. Goodman, "Japanese Pan-Asianism in the Philippines," p. 135
38. Ohtani, *Hiripin Nenkan*, p. 468. Later, as an offshot of the Great

Asia Society, the Pan-Asiatic Association was founded for the Filipinos who agreed with the objectives of the mother association. Isidro Vamenta was its president. See Goodman, "Japanese Pan-Asianism in the Philippines," p. 142.

39. Ohtani, *Hiripin Nankin*, p. 468.
40. For details on the establishment of the Philippine Society of Japan, see Goodman, "The Philippine Society of Japan."
41. For more on the exchange of students and professionals, see Goodman, "Philippine-Japanese Student Exchanges, 1935 or 1940," pp. 63-132 in *Four Aspects of Philippine-Japanese Relations*. Also see "Philippine Japanese Professional Exchange in the 1930's" in the *Journal of Southeast Asian History* (September 1968): 229-240; and Ohtani, *Hiripin Nenkan,*, p. 449.
42. Trustees included the following:

| | |
|---|---|
| Ramon Fernandez | former Senator |
| Francisco Benitez | College of Education dean, U.P. |
| Pedro Aunario | *La Vanguardia* |
| Conrado Benitez | President, Philippine Commercial University |
| Francisco Varona | former Assemblyman, representative |
| Leopoldo Aguinaldo | former President of the Philippine Chamber of Commerce |
| Jitaro Kihara | Vice Consul, Japanese Consulate General |
| Tsuneo Yamamoto | Manager, Yokohama Specie Bank Manila branch |
| Masajiro Kawamura | Manager, Mitsui Bussa Kaisha, Manila branch |
| Modesto Farolan | former Manager of the *Philippine Herald* |

Farolan also served as the Secretary and Treasurer of the Society. Source: *Hiripin Nenkan*, vol. 2, pp. 449-480

43. *Sunday Tribune*, 1 January 1930.
44. *Manila Times*, 7 March 2904.
45. Muraoka, *Muraoka Iheji Den*, pp. 147-149. The names of two

Chinese nationals are in the list of donors.

46. Kanegae, *Aruite Kita Michi,* p. 207.
47. Ibid., p. 400.
48. The feelings of the Japanese-expatriates were based on their memoirs, such as K. Kanegae, K. Osawa and interviews with A. Nishio, K. Nishimura, Y. Yamaguchi.

# IGLESIA NI KRISTO IN MANILA

FERNANDO G. ELESTERIO

In a good number of Philippine cities, towns and barrios, one can easily find well-built structures for worship which the *Iglesia ni Kristo* calls chapels regardless of size. While in the past the Catholic churches dominated the skyline in large population centers, now the huge "Cathedral-chapels" of the *Iglesia ni Kristo* have risen to challenge, so to speak, the dominance of the Catholic churches[1]. Architecturally well-designed, solidly built, painted, with manicured lawns and always looking clean, they dramatically contrast with the ancient, still strong but drab-looking Catholic churches. While the latter seem to convey the religious wisdom of the centuries, the former appear to stand for the dynamism of the space age as may be symbolized by the soaring spires like needles piercing the sky.

These magnificent houses of worship are perceived by the *Iglesia* members as a sign that their church is the true church. Some observers, however, see in these buildings the sign of an "emerging triumphalism."[2] The organization itself is perceived as "an attempt at indigenization of Protestantism."[3]

A very important reason for taking the *Iglesia ni Kristo* seriously is that it is "the largest (non-mission related) independent church in Asia" which is projected to have a million members in the year 2000.[4] Although the Protestant churches came to the Philippines more than a decade before the establishment of the *Iglesia ni Kristo*, none of them, individually considered, has been able to match the growth of the *Iglesia*.

The achievements of the *Iglesia* in "church planting" and expansionism become more astounding when one considers the fact that it has to compete with the well-financed Protestant churches and the dominant Catholic Church.

It may be worth noting here that both the Philippine Independent Church (the Aglipayan Church) and the *Iglesia ni Kristo* grew out of the turbulent period in Philippine history when Americans imposed American sovereignty over the whole country. But while the Philippine Independent Church gradually weakened to a point where it eventually requested a *concordat* with the American Episcopalian church to keep itself afloat, the *Iglesia,* relying on native Filipino personnel and resources, continued to grow and is still expanding not only locally but even abroad.

What is the secret of the success of the *Iglesia*? Who was its founder? What does the *Iglesia* teach that can capture the minds of Catholics and Protestants alike? How much influence does it have, particularly in the City of Manila? These are some questions we shall attempt to answer in this paper.

### The Founder of the Iglesia

The year 1986 marked the one hundredth birth anniversary of Felix Manalo Ysagun, the 'founder' of the *Iglesia ni Kristo.* He was born in barrio Calzada, municipality of Tagig, province of Rizal on May 10, 1886.[5] His parents were Mariano Ysagun and Bonifacia Manalo. It was sometime in 1904 after the death of his mother that Felix decided to change his family name from Ysagun to Manalo. Thus the founder of the *Iglesia* ceased to be known as Felix M. Ysagun and came to be Felix Y. Manalo. Some believe that the change in family name was dictated by the significance of the word Manalo, which has to do with "triumph" or "victory." Others say that the Manalo family unlike the Ysagun was well-known and respected in the community. Felix, therefore, preferred to be identified with the more prestigious family; hence, the change in family name. Still, a third reason is that the change was due to Felix's reverence for his mother.[6] While no one can be sure of Felix's real reason, still none of the three reasons just stated excludes the others. Most probably, Felix changed his family name because of all three reasons.

Felix Manalo never went beyond third grade of formal school because of the death of his father in 1896 and the outbreak of the Philippine Revolution in the same year.[7] He was also not able to pursue his studies because the family was not economically well-to-do.[8] The family's livelihood of fishing, shrimp-catching, farming and mat-making was not sufficient to make them financially well-off.

The parents of Felix, particularly his mother, were practicing Catholics. Felix was baptized and raised in the religion of his parents. But in 1904 Felix embraced Protestantism by becoming a member of the Methodist Episcopal church.[9]

As a member of the Methodist Episcopal Church, Felix "attended

Bible training classes and may have become an 'exhorter' or even a lay preacher for the denomination."[10] The *Iglesia* claims, however, that Felix "attended the classes given by that sect in the Methodist Theological Seminary wherein he eventually became an evangelist."[11]

In 1905, he transferred to the Presbyterian Ellinwood Bible Training School.[12] It must be noted that the Methodists and the Presbyterians "were moving toward a jointly operated training program for their workers."[13] This move culminated in the founding in 1907 of the Union Theological Seminary in Manila.[14] The *Iglesia* claims that Felix studied at the Union Theological Seminary and was eventually made a pastor.[15] If Felix ever studied in Union Theological, then, it could not have been for more than a year. That Felix was ordained a Presbyterian pastor as claimed by the *Iglesia* is doubtful since our Protestant source does not support the claims. It is most probable that he was designated a lay preacher of the Presbyterian church.

In 1908, Felix left the Presbyterian Church and joined the Christian Mission.[16] While the transition from Methodist to Presbyterian did not involve "a change of conviction on Manalo's part," it was not so with the move to the Christian Mission. The "missionaries of the Christian Churches of America which also call themselves 'Churches of Christ' preached a strong, uncompromising, immersionist and restorationist message."[17] The members of the Christian Mission were called Disciples of Christ and it was from this group that Felix Manalo borrowed a good deal of his religious ideas particularly about the church.[18] He became a member of the sect in 1910.[19] He attended classes in Bible Science at the Manila College of the Bible.[20] Manalo was later appointed an evangelist. He stayed just long enough with the Christian Mission to court and marry a certain Tomasa Sereneo of Ulilang Kawayan, Paco, Manila.[21]

In 1911, Felix left the Christian Mission and entered the Seventh Day Adventist Church.[22] He was a Seventh Day Adventist "worker" and not a "pastor" as claimed by the *Iglesia*, for he was not ordained a minister of the sect.[23] Within two years, Felix became a widower and by early 1913, he began courting a Seventh Day Adventist girl, Honorata de Guzman, of Rizal Avenue, Manila. Felix eloped with the girl. For this, Felix was punished with suspension. Sometime later he was again disciplined for "moral indiscretion."[24] These are the reasons given by a source in the Seventh Day Adventist Church explaining why Felix Manalo left this church in mid-1913. The *Iglesia* understandably was silent on these and states that "after pondering on the Adventists' persistent observance of the Sabbath, Manalo found it unscriptural" and had to abandon the Adventist church.[25]

Not finding satisfaction in the established religions, he severed relations with them and sought the company of atheists and free-thinkers.[26] He soon came to the conclusion that "wrong interpretation of the Bible caused both the atheists' disbelief and the diversity of the doctrines of different religions."[27] With this conviction, "Manalo resolved to undertake a thorough examination of the doctrines of the different religions."[28] This supposedly took place within the duration of two days and three nights in the early part of November 1913.[29] The *Iglesia* claims that "he [Felix] gained the insight that religion or man's way back to God must be fully in accordance with the will of God contained in the Bible, and that he was being sent to preach the true religion so that God may bring near His righteousness to men in these last days."[30] Although one gets the impression that the idea of establishing a new religion or church first came to Felix Manalo at this time, even when he was still with the Seventh Day Adventists, he was already trying to interest some of his fellow workers in the establishment of a new church.[31]

Although he was residing in Pasay at the time he decided to establish the *Iglesia*, he did not preach the new religion there but waited until early 1914 when he left Pasay for Punta, Sta. Ana, Manila, where he began to propagate it among the workers of the Atlantic Gulf and Pacific Company.[32] He and his wife were actually given accommodations in the worker's quarters.

But why Sta. Ana? The reason lies in the fact that Felix had worked in the area first as a Christian Mission worker and later as "a member of the first Philippine Seventh Day Adventist Church which was also located in the area."[33] Presumably, therefore, Manalo had some reliable friends in the locality and at the same time suspected, on account of his previous experiences in the place, that he would get converts to his new church.

It was not long before about a dozen people were converted to the new religion and baptized by immersion in the Pasig River. This group of converts to the *Iglesia* in the City of Manila constituted the first congregation of the new religion. A few months later Felix, together with his wife and daughters, left Sta. Ana for Tipas, Rizal. The Sta. Ana congregation was placed under the care of Federico Inocencio whom Felix ordained as minister and Atanacio Morte who was made first deacon and secretary of the *Iglesia*.[34]

In Tipas and Tagig, Felix's new religion was rejected and no congregations were established. However, two former co-workers of Felix in the Christian Mission, namely Justino Casanova and Norberto Asuncion, joined the new Church.[35] After months of preaching, the total number of converts could not have reached ten in the two Rizal municipalities.

Without waiting for more a favorable response by way of more converts to the new church, Felix proceeded to the barrios of Pasig, specifically Buting, Pulo, and Rosario. He preached in these barrios starting in the summer months of 1915 and during the greater part of that year. Again, as in Tipas and Tagig, the results were disappointing. With so few converts no congregation could be established in these barrios.[36]

Toward the end of that year (1915), Felix, realizing perhaps that his endeavour would be more acceptable to those whose roots in the traditional religion had already been weakened by the onslaught of Protestantism, decided to end his rather unfruitful provincial mission and returned to Manila.

He started his preaching in Tondo in the house of Quintin Rivera. Makeshift market areas later provided the space and audience for Felix Manalo's religious rallies which were usually held in the early evenings. As converts became more numerous, the Tondo congregation decided to build a house of worship. The chapel was the first house of worship ever constructed by the *Iglesia*. It was of nipa and bamboo and located along Gabriela Street. When sometime later a conflagration hit the area and the chapel burned down, the *Iglesia* members held services in four different private residences.

From Manila Felix Manalo managed and directed the expansion of the *Iglesia* to other areas, particularly in the provinces north of Manila. He trained and ordained ministers.

The rather rapid increase in membership brought with it an improvement in finances, so much so that by 1919 Felix Manalo was able to leave for the United States with a monthly allowance of ₱350, paid for by the *Iglesia*. After all, the Iglesia was registered as a *unipersonal* corporation or as a corporation with Felix Manalo as sole owner. He allegedly studied for a year in "the Pacific School of Religion in California," a congregational school in Berkeley. It is very likely that he was not a regular student since neither is he listed among the alumni nor do surviving faculty members recall any Felix Manalo or Ysagun as a student. No enrollment list of students at the time of Manalo's stay in the Pacific School of Religion has yet been uncovered to settle the matter.

In 1922, three ministers led revolts against Felix Manalo and the *Iglesia*. Teofilo Ora, Basilio Santiago, and Januario Ponce left the *Iglesia* together with members of their congregations. The entire Nueva Ecija membership and the majority of those in Bulacan left the *Iglesia*.[37] It was also during these years that the moral integrity of Felix Manalo was "questioned at first privately and later publicly in the courts."[38] The revolts and doubts about his morals were a challenge to the authority of Manalo. In order to meet the challenge, he proclaimed himself the "angel rising from the East" mentioned in Apocalypse 7:2. The "angel doctrine" became the principal and unquestionable support of Felix Manalo's authority in the *Iglesia*. "It is reasonable to assume that it grew out of Manalo's determination to establish supreme authority over the *Iglesia ni Kristo*."[39]

Towards the end of 1935, Felix Manalo, already a man of means, went to Hongkong on a "pleasure and rest trip."[40] It is not known how long he stayed in Hongkong. The following year, he organized the youth of the *Iglesia* "to add color to the propaganda and evangelical rallies frequently held at that time."[41] This youth organization was called *Tambuli ng Silangan*. It existed without any formal constitution and during the war years it died out. Revived in 1959, it was then envisioned to help in missionary activities and to act as a means to have the *Iglesia* youth get to know each other and thus "lessen the temptation of marrying non-*Iglesia* members." The youth group in Manila called itself *Kapisanang Maligayang Pagtatagumpay*, or KMP for short. The organization's name was derived from the founders' name — Felix Manalo ("tagumpay" also means "triumph"). The youth were told to make house-to-house visits to invite people to come to *Iglesia* rallies. One of its most important achievements was the establishment of the first-ever *Iglesia*-owned school, the New Era Fashion School in Quiapo, Manila. This was the start of the *Iglesia ni Cristo* development center located along C. Palanca St., Quiapo, where one finds the New Era Evangelical College, the New Era Educational Institute, and the New Era Training Center. Today, the New Era College has been transferred to the Central Office compound in Diliman, Quezon City and has an enrollment of 4,000 students from the elementary school to college.

In the latter part of 1938, Manalo left again for the United States to hold a series of meetings to solicit contributions for the *Iglesia*, and for treatment of his stomach ailment.[42] A certain Cirilo Gonzales, secretary of the *Iglesia*, accompanied Manalo to serve as interpreter. It must be borne in mind in connection with the proposed fund raising trip of Manalo that as per documents of incorporation, the organization's existence was dependent on "public charity" (*caridad publica*). Apparently, the *Iglesia* needed more funds than public charity could afford to give.

Unfortunately, soon after his arrival in the U.S., Manalo bacame so ill that all his engagements had to be cancelled.[43] He returned to the Philippines convinced that God wanted the *Iglesia* to depend only on the resources of the members. From then on the doctrine on the duty of contributing to the finances of the *Iglesia* in proportion to one's means assumed greater and greater importance in the indoctrination process of the *Iglesia*. Continuous prosperity and growth in affluence has been the lot of the *Iglesia* ever since.

In February 1939, the Iglesia started a Tagalog magazine, *Pasugo*, for the purpose of further disseminating the doctrines of the organization. Eventually, an English section was added. It ceased publication during the war years and only resumed in January 1951.[44] The importance of the magazine can be gleaned from the fact that while members are not "encouraged to own and read the Bible" they are expected to read the *Pasugo*.[45]

After the war years conversions became more numerous. This meant greater income for the *Iglesia* and consequently led to the construction of a palatial residence in San Juan for Manalo which also served as the organization's central office. Prosperity also made possible the building of concrete houses of worship. The first of these is the one located along Washington Street, Sampaloc, Manila which was constructed in 1948.[46] The construction of "cathedral chapels" along with the small ones went hand in hand with the rapid growth of membership. By April 1963, at the time Manalo died, some 40 concrete chapels had been built. By 1973, the *Iglesia* claimed to have built close to 146 big chapels in a span of ten years (1963-1973).[47] In Metro Manila alone as of September 1985 there were 75 cathedral chapels and a number of small ones.[48]

## The Bible and Its Interpretation

The Bible or Holy Scriptures is considered the sole rule of faith for the *Iglesia*. It contains the words of God, of *Christ,* and of the Apostles.[49] There is no version considered as *official* by the organization. Writers in the *Iglesia* usually quote the version and/or edition which uses the words most appropriate for their purposes. Thus, an article written by an *Iglesia* member may have passages from the Bible which have been taken from different versions and/or editions.

With regards to the "canonical" or genuinely inspired books, the *Iglesia* believes that only those which meet any of the following criteria are considered genuine:

1. Those books which Christ, the Evangelists, and the Apostles quote or refer to; and
2. Those which the Evangelists and the Apostles wrote.

Tradition which Roman Catholics believe in, is considered by the *Iglesia* as composed of or constituted by the word of men, not of God. In other words, Tradition is not part of Divine Revelation.[50]

True preachers of the Gospel are found only in the true church, the *Iglesia ni Kristo* (INK) and when they preach "they merely articulate on what is written, relegating themselves to the background and making the Scriptures prominent."[51] *Iglesia* ministers claim that they do not interpret. Interpretation is by the Bible itself for "the Holy Bible does not accept any private interpretation; it interprets itself."[52]

The INK claims to have been given the function of teaching all men. But the said function is exercised by duly commissioned teachers whose task is to search the Bible for what may be termed as interpretation. In cases of apparently contradictory statements, both of which are supported by Biblical passages, our informant said that the ministers in a conference officially determine which doctrine should be upheld with the aid of a supposedly literal translation of the Greek version of the Bible in the Vatican Museum. A copy (or copies) of this version is not, of course, in their possession but this writer was shown a version published in English by the Jehovah's Witnesses.

## Iglesian Teaching About the Person of Christ

The *Iglesia ni Kristo* teaches that there is one God but denies the existence of three Divine Persons. On this premise alone it is already evident that the *Iglesia* believes neither Christ nor the Holy Spirit are divine persons.

As far as the INK is concerned, Christ is only a man,[53] and the Holy Spirit only one of the Seven Spirits mentioned in Rev. 5.6 which reads:

And between the throne and the four living creatures and among the elders, I saw a lamb standing, as though it had been slain, with seven horns and with seven eyes, which are the seven spirits of God sent into all the earth.

Since Christ is not divine then he is inferior to God. He is a "little lower than God" (Ps. 8.5-6). God raised him up and "put all things under his feet" (Eph. 1.20,22) and Christ himself acknowledged his inferiority to God when he said "My Father is Greater than I" (Jn. 14.28).[54]

Although Christ is only a man he is nevertheless above men because he was conceived by the Holy Spirit (Mt. 1.20) or by the power of the Most High (Lk. 1.35). "No one knows the Father except the Son" (Mt. 11.27). "He committed no sin (1 Pet. 2.22) nor deceit (Is. 53.9) and he has been called the Holy One" (Acts 3.14). Moreover, "God made him Prince and Savior (Acts 3.15) with all power in Heaven and on earth" (Mt. 28.18). "He is even above the angels that these even worship Him" (Heb. 1.6).

With regard to certain passages which seem to point to a unity of the Father and Christ the Son, for example as in Jn. 10.30 "The Father and I are one," the *Iglesia* argues that Christ did not say: "I am the Father" (*Ako ay ang Ama*).[55] The unity expressed in Jn. 10.30, according to the *Iglesia*, is not unity in nature because man is not God (Ezek. 28.2) and God is not man (Hos. 11.9). Therefore, Jn. 10.30 must be understood in the light of Jn. 10.27-29.[56]

When it is stated that Christ is the Son of God this must be understood to mean not a natural sonship but merely adoptive. In this sense Christ is Son of God *not* God the Son.

## The Mission of Christ

Christ was sent into the world, in the manner of the Prophets, to save men from the judgment brought about by sin.[57] When sin entered the world, mankind was condemned to two kinds of death: physical death and spiritual death of eternal damnation.[58] Christ redeemed men from the latter, not from the former. So, all men must die but not all men are condemned.

But Christ did not die for *all* men. He shed his blood only for a particular group. This, the Iglesians claim, is the *Iglesia ni Kristo*.

Was the death of Christ for all, as is the common prevailing belief? In Acts 20.28 it is written: "Take heed unto yourselves, and to all the flock, over which the Holy Spirit has made you overseers, to feed the Church of the Lord, which he hath purchased with his own blood". Christ did not die for the sake of everyone as is commonly believed. He shed His blood and gave His life for the sake of His church exclusively.[59]

The INK believes that in order to enjoy the blessings of the redemptive act of Christ, a person has to become a member of the *Iglesia ni Kristo* because this is the true Church, the Body of Christ. Faith in Christ cannot save anyone. Commenting on Ephesians 5.25, Cipriano P. Sandoval writes:

The teaching of the Apostles is crystal clear. Christ loved the church and gave himself up for her. We cannot now be mistaken as to the true import and significance of Christ's death. His death is intended for the church, hence the futility of the view of those who say that all they need is Christ, without the benefit of affiliation with the Church. This is thinking beyond the scope of scriptural teaching.[60]

Repentance and forgiveness of sin is not possible outside the *Iglesia ni Kristo*, because the saving power of Christ including his mediatorship between men and God is exercised only within the *Iglesia*.[61] Thus, it is absolutely necessary for one to be saved to enter the *Iglesia ni Kristo*, the Body of Christ, because outside Christ no one can be saved.

## Extra Ecclesian Nulla Salus

Outside the church (INK) there is no salvation. Aside from the arguments already alluded to, there is another Iglesian way of proving the statement.

Among all God's creatures, man was chosen to love God (Eph 1.4). Man's knowledge and love of God imply coming into His presence and serving Him (Ps. 100.2). But man cannot serve God just anywhere, for in Ps. 100.4 it is written:

Enter His gates with thanksgiving, and His courts with praise! Give thanks to Him, obey His name!

Men must enter therefore into something in order to praise and serve God. That something is "His gates." And what is that? In Jn. 10.9 we read: "I am the door; if anyone enter by Me, he will be saved ..." and in Jn. 14.6 it is further stated: "I am the Way, the Truth, and the Life; no one comes to the Father, but by me."[62]

Consequently, only those who enter Christ can serve God. Entering Christ simply means becoming members of the *Iglesia ni Kristo* which is Christ's Body.[63]

## Entrance into the Church

A person becomes a member of the *Iglesia* through baptism which has to be by immersion and after undergoing indoctrination from duly authorized ministers. Since indoctrination is a prerequisite for baptism, infant baptism is not practiced by the *Iglesia*.[64]

Moreover, an infant has no sin and has not inherited any and therefore needs no cleansing through baptism. That an infant inherits no sin (original) is proven in Ezek. 18.20 and Deut. 24.16. The former reads:

The Soul that sins shall die. The son shall not suffer for the iniquity of the father, nor the father from the iniquity of the son; the righteousness of the righteous shall be upon himself, and the wickedness of the wicked shall be upon himself.

The passage from Deuteronomy states:

The father shall not be put to death for the children, nor shall the children be put to death for the fathers; every man shall be put to death for his own sin.

That the recipients of baptism should first be instructed is allegedly founded on Mk. 16.15-17 which the *Iglesia* interprets as follows:

Those sent by Jesus to baptize were ordered by Him to preach the Gospel and all that believe in their preaching were the only ones that should be baptized in order to be saved. The infant cannot believe even if the Gospel is preached to him, so that he should not be baptized. The insistence that the infant must be baptized is against the order of Jesus and whoever goes against Jesus is going against God, because the commandments He preaches are not His own but came from the Father that sent Him (Jn. 12.49).[65]

Only those who are in the *Iglesia* have the exclusive right and privilege of serving God and can be considered sons of God and fellow heirs of Christ, as stated in Rom. 8.17: "outside this Church (INK), man is God's enemy."[66]

The *Iglesia's* teaching about non-members of the INK may be summarized as follows:

1. Non-members are under God's judgment and if they die outside the INK, they will be condemned.
2. Unredeemed and in the state of sin, they are enemies of God and separated from Him.
3. They are not children of God nor fellow heirs of Christ.
4. Their repentance and prayers have no value.
5. They cannot serve or worship God. Unless they enter the INK, they will be condemned.

**Why the INK is the True Church**

The *Iglesia* claims to be the Church founded by Christ as recorded in Matthew 16.18 not by historical continuity but because:

1. The INK bears the name of Christ;
2. The INK has the genuine doctrine of Christ; and
3. The INK has ministers duly commissioned by Christ to preach the Gospel.

The Church of Christ must necessarily bear the name of Christ for the following reasons:

1. In Matthew 16.18 Christ speaks of "My church." Therefore, the Church He founded is Christ's Church or Church of Christ as stated in Rom. 16:16.[67]
2. The Church is the flock of Christ (Jn. 10.3). Substituting church for flock we have Church of Christ or *Iglesia ni Kristo.*[68]

The *Iglesia's* alleged possession of the genuine doctrine of Christ distinguishes her from all other churches.[69] In this regard an *Iglesia* writer states:

The true Church is determined and can be singled out from the false by evaluating her doctrines.

. . . . . . . . . . . . . . . .

The true Church brings people back to God by teaching the unalloyed gospel of Christ. The pristine gospel of the Lord is strictly expounded without guile or deceit, no more no less, though it may offend people.[70]

The quotation implies that no other churches except the INK teach the pure gospel of Christ.

The pastors of other churches are false teachers because "they nourish their members with their own opinion, hence, from Protestantism comes the idea of private interpretation of the Bible. This is bad. Why? Because what should be given to the people of God are the 'unalloyed words of God,.....'[71] The *Iglesia* writers are just as severe with their judgment of Roman Catholic priests whom they consider as "wolves in sheep's clothing."

While other churches may claim the name "Church of Christ" they are nevertheless false churches because they do not have genuine doctrines or duly commissioned ministers or true teachers.

### How the Original Church Disappeared

Because of false teachings the original Church gradually disappeared. The name of the Church was changed and false teachings were preached. Thus occurred what the *Iglesia* calls the great Apostasy which was already allegedly foretold by Christ when He said that many would come in His name and lead followers astray. It is further alleged that in the time of St. Paul the Apostasy was already starting when he said: "For the mystery of lawlessness is already at work; only he who now restrains it will do so until he is out of the way." (2 Thess. 2.7)

Felix Manalo states in *Ang Sulo* that the Apostasy was completed after the time of the apostles or after more then three centuries.[72] In *Mga Katotohanan* Manalo is more explicit and puts the total disappearance in the sixth century during the reign of Emperor Justinian I.[73] It must be noted that Justinian I was emperor from 527 to 565.

Erroneous doctrines which are claimed to have contributed to the Apostasy include:[74]

1. That the Catholic church was founded by Christ;
2. That the Catholic Church or any other church should be considered Christian;
3. That the members of the Catholic Church or any other church will be saved;
4. That there should be any other church besides the *Iglesia ni Kristo;*
5. That the Church was meant to last until the end of time;
6. That the saints should be venerated and considered intercessors;
7. That it was on Peter that the Church was founded;
8. That the Pope is Peter's successor as head of the Church;
9. That the Pope is the head of the Church founded by Christ;
10. That the Pope is the highest shepherd of souls;
11. That anyone should be addressed as Father as applied to the Pope, the Bishops, and the Priests;
12. That baptism can be conferred on infants or by sprinkling or pouring of water;
13. That there is such a thing as original sin;
14. That the practice of celibacy is valid;
15. That the abstinence from meat is also valid.

### The Reappearance of the Church

The Church founded by Christ reappeared in the Philippines in 1914 through the instrumentality of Felix Manalo. The reappearance is allegedly prophesied in Revelation 7:1-3 which reads:

After this I saw four angels standing at the four corners of the earth holding back the four winds of the earth, that no wind might blow on earth or sea or against any tree. Then I saw another ascend from the rising of the sun, with the seal of the living God, and he called with a loud voice to the four angels who had been given power to harm earth and sea, saying " Do not harm the earth or the sea or the trees, till we have sealed the servants of our God upon their foreheads."

Explanation:

"after this" — (a) great earthquake (Rev. 6.12) — Lisbon earthquake, November 1, 1755
(b) sun became black — New England States, May 19, 1780
(c) moon became like blood — New England States, May 19, 1780
(d) stars fell like figs to the earth — North America, November 12, 1833

"four angels" — (a) Lloyd George of England
(b) Clemenceau of France
(c) Orlando of Italy
(d) Wilson of the U.S.A.

"four winds" — war affecting the four corners of the earth (Jer. 4.11-12, 19). The war has the following characteristics:
(a) universal or by all nations (Is. 34.1-2)
(b) war tanks were used ("chariots like the whirlwind")
(c) there were planes ("horses swifter than eagles")
(d) sirens sounded ("trumpet call")
(e) people hid in the mountains and air-raid shelters ("hid in caves" Rev. 6.15)

"another angel" — Felix Manalo

"the rising of the sun" — Philippines (Is. 43.5-6; Is. 46.11; 24.15-16)

The following verses are also believed to have prophesied the reappearance of the Church:

Fear not, for I am with you;
I will bring your offspring from the east,
and from the west I will gather you;
I will say to the north, "Give up,
and to the south, Do not withold;
bring my sons from afar
and my daughters from the end of the earth."
(Is. 43.5-6)

Calling a bird of prey from the east,
> The man of my counsel from a far country.
I have spoken, and I will bring it to pass;
> I have purposed, and I will do it.
> (Is. 46.11)


Therefore in the east give glory to the Lord;
> in the coastlands of the sea, to the name
> of the Lord, the God of Israel.
From the ends of the earth we hear songs of praise
> of glory to the righteous One.
But I say, "I pine away,
> I pine away. Woe is me!"
For the treacherous deal treacherously
> the treacherous deal very treacherously,
> (Is. 24.15-16)


Those who believe in the doctrine preached by Felix Manalo constitute Christ's "other sheep" (Jn. 10.16).[75] Thus, the third part of the flock of Christ reappeared in the Philippines in 1914 through the instrumentality of Felix Manalo.

Its reappearance, it is claimed, had to be during the first World War, not the second, because of Rev. 8.1 as interpreted by 2 Pet 3.8.[76]

And when he had opened the seventh seal, there was silence in heaven about the space of half an hour (Rev. 8.1).

But beloved, do not be ignorant of this one thing, that one day is with the Lord as a thousand years, and a thousand years as one day (2 Pet. 3.8)

|  | Year | Month | Day |
|---|---|---|---|
| Start of WWII | 1939 | 9 | 1 |
| The Armistice of WWI | 1918 | 11 | 11 |
| About the space of half an hour | 20 | 9 | 20 |
| Exactly one-half hour | 20 | 10 | |

The silence of "about the space of half an hour" is thus interpreted to mean the period between the two World Wars.

## Assessment of Iglesian Doctrines

There are two doctrinal areas which the *Iglesia* principally and almost exclusively devotes its oral and written doctrinal expositions to. These are on the Church and on Christ. It is very rare that anything doctrinal is ever discussed without reference to the Church which, of course, is the *Iglesia ni Kristo*. One gets the impression that the *Iglesia* has to convince and continuously reassure itself that it is the true Church. At the same time, it is hoped that members of other churches would eventually start doubting that they are in the true Church. When one is in such a state it becomes easier for the *Iglesia* to get him/her into its fold.

The *Iglesia* considers its doctrine on Christ as one which distinguishes it from other Christian churches. This is a way of saying that the *Iglesia* is not just like other Christian churches. In other words, the *Iglesia* is *unique*.

However, even in these two areas the *Iglesia* has not developed a theology worthy of the name. There is a general lack of depth, a total disregard for the historical development of doctrines, and an absence of solid scholarly research. While these defects are unexcusable they are, however, understandable.

The primary purpose of the *Iglesia's* exposition of doctrine, whether oral or written, is primarily to win converts. And among the masses of the people it is not scholarly research that will more effectively bring about conversion but rather a convincingly repeated doctrine, using selected texts from the Bible, sometimes cited out of context, which will produce results. The repetition of a doctrine *ad nauseam* appears to brainwash some people into believing the doctrine as true. This is how the *Iglesia* wins converts.

It must also be borne in mind that no minister of the *Iglesia* has ever merited the recognition for scholarly research in the field of theology. In fact there are very few ministers who have graduated from the *Iglesia's* Evangelical College with the degree of Bachelor of Evangelical Ministry—a government recognized degree. So far the *Iglesia* cannot yet claim that any of its ministers has a legitimate master's degree in Theology, much less a doctorate.

What has been said about the two main doctrinal areas of the *Iglesia* can also be said of the other branches of theology. If the former are deficient and defective the latter are even more so.

### The Iglesia in the Year 2000

The *Iglesia's* visible presence in terms of structures of worship will be more evident in most populated areas of the country. A new policy has been adopted, according to our source at the Central Office of the Iglesia, regarding construction of places of worship. These structures will now be built with division funds instead of money from the Central Office.

It is very likely that the leadership shall have passed on to Eduardo Manalo, son of the present head. Eduardo Manalo is now the Division Minister of one of two divisions in Metro Manila.

Membership in the Philippines shall have risen to about one million and a half. Estimated membership at present is a little less than one million, not including children of INK members who have not yet been baptized. It should be noted that the *Iglesia* considers the figures of the Bureau of Census and Statistics as low. On the other hand, the *Iglesia* refuses to state its total membership, not even a rough estimate.

In the area of doctrines we foresee a more scholarly presentation, at least for selected readers and audiences. As more and more young *Iglesia* members earn college degrees the demand for more enlightened elucidation and research on doctrine is expected. In addition, in the next ten to fifteen years, the *Iglesia* plans to realize its dream of eventually having a university. This will surely add to intellectual sophistication in the *Iglesia*. The nucleus of this future university is the present New Era College with a population of 4,000 from grade school to college.

With its tremendous financial resources the *Iglesia* will have its own television network and several radio stations. At present, it airs its television program twice a week, one hour on Saturday and another hour on Sunday. The *Iglesia's* total broadcast time a week on radio station is 119 hours and 20 minutes.

Public rallies shall have disappeared and emphasis will be more on television and radio broadcasts and house-to-house visits. The latter activity is the most effective for winning converts while the former is for the purpose of arousing interest.

With block voting, the *Iglesia* will play an increasingly greater role in the election of public officials in exchange for certain business deals and other concessions from the government. On a limited scale the *Iglesia* has been able to put into public office some of its members as in the case of a Supreme Court justice during the Marcos regime. Despite its declaration of belief in the separation of Church and State, the *Iglesia* will become a real political power. Presently, its claim to have the power to decide who should get elected to national office(s) is more a myth than a reality. The *Iglesia* vote only makes a difference in a closely contested election.

In the year 2000 the *Iglesia* will still be around and strong but showing some signs of divisions or divisive elements.

## NOTES

1. The term "cathedral-chapels" was coined by Arthur Leonard Tuggy in his book *Iglesia ni Cristo: A Study in the Independent Church Dynamics,* 1976. *Cristo* is used here instead of *Kristo* since the former is more common these days although the latter spelling is found in the organization's *Articles of Incorporation.*

2. cf. Tuggy, *Ibid.* pp. 179-180.

    The *Iglesia ni Cristo* has erected quite a number of concrete houses of worship which have become landmarks throughout the breadth and length of the Philippine Archipelago.

    . . . . . . . . . . . . . . . . . .

    It is the will of God that His people build houses of worship [Haggi 1.8]

    The house of worship is the place designated by God where His people must go and worship Him and render the glory due His holy name (Psalms 5.7, 29.2) ... God's people are not free to choose the place of their liking to worship and pray to Him. God chooses the place ... and that is the house of worship...

    In pursuance to this will of God, the Church of Christ builds big houses of worship....

    *This is the Iglesia ni Cristo,* p. 69.

3. Tuggy, *op. cit.,* p. 190.

4. Tuggy, *op. cit.,* pp. 244, 224. In 1975, Elesterio estimated the membership of the *Iglesia* in the vicinity of 600,000. Previous estimates: In 1948 the Bureau of Census and Stastics had 88,000; in 1954 Sta. Romana placed it a little over 200,000; in 1960 the Philippine Census had it at 270,104; in 1968 Douglas J. Elwood estimated the membership to be 500,000, but the 1970 census of the Philippines placed it at 475,407. cf. Elesterio, p. 27.

5. The biographical data here are based on *This is the IGLESIA NI CRISTO* published by the Iglesia ni Cristo, (C.1977), Elesterio's *The Iglesia Ni Kristo: Its Christology and Ecclesiology* (1977), and Tuggy's *Iglesia ni Cristo: A Study in Independent Church Dynamics* (1977).

6. cf. Elesterio, p.8.

    He grieved over the death of his mother for whom he had a great affection. Thus for sentimental reasons and for expressing his reverence, he adopted her name, Manalo.

    *This is the Iglesia ni Cristo,* p. 5.

7. cf. Tuggy, *op. cit.,* p. 19; Elesterio, *Ibid,* p. 6.

8. cf. Tuggy, *op. cit.*, p. 20.
9. cf. *This is the Iglesia ni Cristo*, p. 5; Elesterio, *op. cit.*, p. 8.
10. Tuggy, *Ibid.* p. 25.
11. *This is the Iglesia ni Cristo*, p. 5.
12. Elesterio, *op. cit.*, p. 9.
13. Tuggy, *op. cit.*, p. 26.
14. *Ibid.*
15. *This is the Iglesia ni Cristo*, p. 5.
16. The Christian Mission is different from the Christian and Missionary Alliance. cf. Tuggy, *op. cit.* p. 27.
17. Tuggy, *op. cit.*, p. 27.
18. cf. Tuggy, *Ibid.* p. 132 f.; Elesterio, *op. cit.*, p. 9.
19. cf. *This is the Iglesia ni Cristo*, p. 5.
20. cf. Elesterio, *op cit.*, p. 9; Tuggy, *op. cit.*, p. 30.
21. cf. Tuggy, *op. cit.*, p. 31; Elesterio, *op. cit.*, p. 9; *This is the Iglesia ni Cristo*, p. 5.
22. *This is the Iglesia ni Cristo*, p. 5.
23. cf. Tuggy, *op. cit.*, p. 33; *This is the Iglesia ni Cristo* p. 5.
24. Tuggy, *op. cit.*, p. 34.
25. *This is the Iglesia ni Cristo*, p. 6.
26. *Ibid.*
27. *Ibid.*
28. *Ibid.* The *Iglesia* claims that this took place "in early 1913." However, the approximate date cannot be correct since Felix married Honorata on May 9, 1913 while still a member of the Seventh Day Adventist Church. The marriage was not however solemnized in the Adventist Church but by a Christian Mission Pastor. This may prove that Felix was at that time not a good standing member of the Seventh Day Adventist. He was probably undergoing disciplinary action for his elopement. cf. Elesterio, p. 9; Tuggy, p. 33.
29. cf. Tuggy, *op. cit.*, p. 40.
30. *This is the Iglesia ni Cristo*, p. 6.
31. cf. Tuggy, *op. cit.*, pp. 41-42. Tuggy cites the testimony of Felix's wife Honorata.
32. Tuggy (pp. 43-ff.) puts the date of the departure of Felix and his wife from Pasay for Sta. Ana, Manila "in early November 1913." The *Iglesia* contends that it was in "an early month of 1914" (*This is the Iglesia ni Cristo*, p. 7.)
33. Tuggy, p. 44.
34. Elesterio, *op. cit.*, p. 10.

35. *This is the Iglesia ni Cristo*, p. 9

36. The bulk of the members up to this period belonged to the Sta. Ana congregation. The total membership could not have gone beyond 50 in all the areas where Felix Manalo preached up to the latter part of 1915 when he decided to preach in Tondo. Tuggy speculates that at the end of 1914 there were less than 100 members. This figure excludes those who may have been converted in the barrios of Pasig in the summer of 1915.

37. cf. Elesterio, p. 14-15; Tuggy, pp. 56-57.

38. Elesterio, p. 11.

39. Tuggy, pp. 57-58.

40. cf. Elesterio, p. 12.

41. *Ibid.*, pp. 171-172.

42. cf. Tuggy, pp. 65-66; Elesterio, p. 12.

43. cf. Elesterio, p. 12; Tuggy, p. 66.

44. cf. Elesterio, p. 13; Tuggy, pp. 66-67.

45. cf. Tuggy, *ibid.*

46. *This is the Iglesia ni Cristo*, p. 10.

47. cf. Elesterio, p. 153.

48. Interview with Bro. Bienvenido Santiago, editor of *Pasugo*, September 2, 1985.

49. ".... Kinatititikan ng mga Salita ng Diyos, ni Cristo, at ang mga Apostol .... " Felix Manalo, *Ang Sulo sa Ikatitiyak sa Iglesia Katolika Apostolica Romana* (Published by the Iglesia ni Kristo, 1947), p. 110. Note: Any future reference to this work will be the use of the words *Ang Sulo.*

    The *Iglesia ni Cristo* (Church of Christ) believes that the words of God are written in the Bible, that when the Bible is silent, the Iglesia ni Cristo is silent too—for it recognizes no other basic authority in serving God except the Bible.

    . . . . . . . . . . . . . . . . . .

    The Bible consists of 66 books written within the period of 1600 years (1500 B.C. - 100 A.D.)
    *This is the Iglesia ni Cristo*, p. 13.

50. Felix Manalo speaking of Tradition in *Ang Sulo* (p. 100) states: "Ang ipinangangaral ng Iglesia Katolika ay hindi Ebanghelio ni Cristo, hindi ang mga salita ng Dios, Kundi ang mga sali't saling sabi (tradicion), at ang mga utos at aral ng tao na nilikha ng kanilang mga "concillo."

51. Jose P. Salazar, "The True Church Brings People Back to God," *Pasugo*, 25, 11 (November, 1973), p. 19.

52. Victor Nalus, *The Roman Catholic Church* (Manila: Afan Publishing House, 1953), p. 69.
53. Biblical citations to prove this are the following: Is. 53.3; Ps. 80.17; Acts 2.22; 17.3; Rom. 5.15; 1 Cor. 15.20-22; 15.47; Mt. 1.20; Lk. 2.5-7, 2.27; etc.

    Despite His uniqueness when compared to all other man [sic], Christ remains man in His state of being. Christ is never the true God. He is a true man.

    . . . . . . . . . . . . . . . . . .

    The true God has no beginning nor is He a son of man (Psalms 90.2; numbers 23.19) ... So Christ could not be God. Neither could He be God that became man nor could He be both true God and true man at the same time. Christ is a man. But God is not man (Hosea 11.9 ). Therefore Christ is not God.
    *This is the Iglesia ni Cristo*, p. 23.
54. Other passages quoted in Iglesian writings: Mk. 15.34 Mt. 24.36; Jn. 5.26, 17.13; Acts 4.10; 1 Cor. 11.3.
55. *Pasugo,* 13, 119 (Nov. 1960), p. 1; 26, 6 (June, 1974), p. 25.
56. cf. *Pasugo,* 26,6 (June, 1974), p. 25.
57. The INK does not believe in *original sin.* But it does teach that sin entered and contaminated the world. This was effected by the first man—Adam. However, this is not "inherited" by his descendants.
58. cf. Victor Nalus, *The Roman Catholic Church*, p. 26; also *Ang Sulo,* p. 112f, and Pasugo, 25, 6 (June, 1973) pp. 5- 7.
59. Jose Salazar, "Salvation is by God's Election," *Pasugo*, 23, 3 (March, 1971), p. 12.
60. *Pasugo*, 24, 6 (June, 1972), p. 4; 25, 5 (May, 1973), pp. 2-3,6.
61. cf. *Ang Sulo,* pp. 6-8.
62. cf. *Pasugo,* 22, 6 (June, 1971), p. 4f.
63. *Ibid.*, also *Pasugo,* 23, 6 (June, 1971), pp. 14-16; 23, 12 (December 1971), p. 19.
64. cf. Nalus, op. cit., p. 63; also Cipriano P. Sandoval, "Christ's Decree," *Pasugo*, 24, 1 (January, 1972), p. 3.
65. Nalus, op. cit., p. 64.
66. C. P. Sandoval, "The Enemies of God," *Pasugo* , 23, 22 (November, 1971), p. 12.
67. *Ang Sulo,* pp. 4, 6, 101; *Pasugo*, 15, 141 (Sept., 1962), p. 37; 25, 1 (Jan., 1973), p. 17.
68. Felix Manalo, *Mga Katotohanan Dapat Malaman Ukol sa mga Aral ng Iglesia Katolika Apostolika Romana* (1936, Copyright by the Iglesia ni Kristo), pp. 83-84.

113

69. Nalus, *op. cit.*, p. 68.
70. Jose P. Salazar, "The True Church Brings People Back to God," *Pasugo*, 25, 11 (Nov., 1973), p. 19.
71. C.P. Sandoval, "The Origin of the Different Churches," *Pasugo*, 24, 7 (July, 1972), p. 19.
72. "Ang Katuparan ng Hula'y magaganap pagkaraan ng panahon ng mga Apostol o sa mahigit na tatlong siglo." op. cit., p. 26.
73. "4.T.—Ang pagtatatag ng Iglesia Katolika Apostolika Romana sa Roma noong ika-anim na siglo sa pamamagitan ng emperador Justiniano I at ng Obispo sa Roma, "Katuparan ng hula nino?"

    S.—Katuparan ng Hula ni Pablong Apostol na ang lobo o puno ng bansa, at ang isang obispo ay magsasama upang italikod kay Kristo ang Iglesiang itinayo niya at ilagay sa hulihan ng magsamang obispo at emperador. (Gawa 20.29-30; II Tes.2.7, 3-6)."
74. *Ang Sulo, Passion; Pasugo* (July, 1964), pp. 13, 73; Nalus, op. cit., pp. 60 ff.
75. cf. *Pasugo*, 23, 12 (Dec., 1971), p. 10 ff.
76. cf. Nalus, *op. cit.*, p. 49; also *Pasugo*, 25. 10 (Oct., 1973), pp. 6-7.

# THE NATIONALIST LEADERSHIP IN MANILA IN THE SEVENTIES

JOSE MA. SISON

Let me first define nationalist leadership as that type of political leadership which has a program of asserting national sovereignty and the civil rights of the people, pushing for national industrialization and land reform, promoting a national, scientific and mass education and culture, and stressing an independent foreign policy.

With this program, nationalist leadership seeks to change the semi-colonial and semi-feudal society into a society that is national and democratic. U.S. imperialism and the local reactionary classes of big compradors and landlords react to and are adverse to this program and want to preserve the present society which they dominate. Thus, the nationalist leadership exposes and opposes them and seeks to undo their dominance.

There are social classes whose conditions, demands and aspirations are reflected in the program of the nationalist leadership and which serve as the source of strength for that leadership. These are the working class, the peasantry, the urban petty bourgeoisie, and the national bourgeoisie. These are the classes which have the dignity of being called people.

Among these classes, the working class is the most progressive political and productive force. It deserves to be the leading class. It has the revolutionary party through which it exercises leadership. It is the leading party with the theory, program, and organization capable of mastering the past, present, and future of not only the most progressive class but also the entire Filipino people.

At any rate, the various patriotic classes can contribute through parties, organizations, and individuals to the formation and development of the nationalist leadership.

Being the political, economic, and cultural center of the Philippines, Manila has been the single most important locale for the articulation and actions of the nationalist leadership. Every major phenomenon in Manila pertaining to this leadership has had national or even international dimensions, even when these are not intended.

Manila was a raging battlefield between the leadership and forces of the nationalist movement and those of foreign and feudal domination during the seventies. The battles were carried out aboveground and underground.

The decade opened with a big bang. While the newly established New People's Army led by the Communist Party of the Philippines intensified the armed struggle in Tarlac, the First Quarter Storm broke out in Manila and lashed out at the ruling system in 1970. The more the reactionary authorities used truncheons and bullets against demonstrators, the more the youth, workers, and other urban poor raised a storm of protest against the system.

The evils of U.S. imperialism, feudalism, and bureaucrat capitalism were condemned. And the youth and workers roused themselves to ever rising fury with the battlecry, "*Makibaka, huwag matakot!*"

The nationalist movement derived inspiration and guidance from such works as *The Struggle for National Democracy* and *Philippine Society and Revolution*. Anti-imperialist and anti-feudal rallies, discussion groups, publications of all types, cultural performances, murals, and wall slogans flourished.

The nationalist leadership operated through the Kabataang Makabayan, Samahang Demokratikong Kabataan, Nationalist Students League, the student governments, organizations of teachers and other professionals, community organizations, MAKIBAKA, the labor unions of U.S. Tobaccco Corporation and Northern Motors, and others. The Movement for a Democratic Philippines became the principal umbrella organization.

Under the influence of the rising anti-imperialist movement, more and more members of the Philippine Congress took the nationalist stand and criticized the U.S.-Marcos regime for its puppetry on a wide range of issues.

In 1971 the nationalist youth movement continued to advance and catch national attention, especially with the Diliman Commune of February 1971 and the long marches of youth, workers, and peasants from Central Luzon and Southern Tagalog regions to Manila. The workers' strike movement advanced.

Nationalist blocs within the Philippine Congress and the Constitutional Convention were ascendant. The Supreme Court came out with nationalist decisions on the Quasha and Luzteveco cases in 1971 and 1972. The press bitterly attacked the U.S.-Marcos regime for its failures and betrayals.

Not satisfied with brutal actions against the workers, peasants, and students, Marcos engineered petty bombing incidents and eventually the Plaza Miranda bombing which almost wiped out the entire opposition party, the Liberal Party.

This dastardly incident laid the grounds for the suspension of the writ of habeas corpus. A number of nationalist professors and students were arrested.

The Movement of Concerned Citizens for Civil Liberties arose to demand the restoration of the writ. Despite the writ suspension, mass actions were held. Activists who had been blacklisted started to go underground and stayed there.

In early 1972 the writ of habeas corpus was restored as a result of public pressure. The nationalist organizations became even more emboldened to launch mass actions, like demonstrations in the city and long marches in the city and towards the city from Central Luzon and Southern Luzon.

The biggest event of the year was the declaration of martial law under Proclamation No. 1081 after a series of petty bombing incidents. Nationalist leaders in political parties, education, student movement, labor movement, press, business, church, and other sectors were arbitrarily arrested and detained. Nationalist organizations which had grown rapidly in Manila were outlawed.

Thousands of activists flowed into the underground in order to escape the dragnet of the enemy and waged a fierce struggle against him. Many joined the city underground and many others went on farther to the countryside to join the armed struggle.

An assessment of the new situation was promptly made by the Communist Party of the Philippines, and new tasks were set for the entire revolutionary movement of the people against the full-blown fascist dictatorial regime of the U.S.-Marcos.

In 1973 the CPP expanded its Manila underground organizations with highly qualified personnel from the outlawed mass organizations. These mass organizations tried to ensure the safety of their officers and members and to send them systematically to the countryside through the CPP.

The CPP initiated the organization of the Preparatory Commission of the National Democratic Front. The objective was to arouse, organize, and mobilize the broadest possible united front against the fascist dictatorship.

The year was one of mastering the new situation, deploying more and

117

more cadres to the various regions of the country, and developing both the city underground and the armed struggle in the countryside. There was also cooperation and coordination between these two areas of struggle.

The enemy seemed to be benefitting much from Martial Law. But, in fact, an avalanche of people were volunteering to wage armed struggle. The difficulty of the revolutionary movement then was scarcity of arms to give to highly qualified people pouring into its ranks.

In 1974 efforts to revive aboveground the labor, student, and urban poor community movements were undertaken against great odds. New cadres not in the enemy blacklist were developed.

It was evident that the U.S. was bent on propping up the Marcos fascist regime with heavy doses of foreign loans. These would increase from year to year to finance infrastructure and other showy projects, to cover deficits in foreign trade and balance of payments, and to build up the military machinery.

The regional organizations of the CPP and NPA were all in place to cover the entire country. That of Manila was the most developed and had the largest membership. Even when Central Committee (CC) members of the CPP were arrested, the CPP and NPA regional organizations acquired more strength.

Thinking that he had conquered the people and wanting to save on prison expenses, and of course, warding off increasing criticism by international organizations, like Amnesty International, about detention without charges, Marcos released a considerable number of political prisoners, including those who would later participate in the open revival of the nationalist movement. Fascist atrocities and abuses were exposed in the country and abroad from Manila by revolutionaries and religious progressives. Work for the legal defense, welfare, and release of political prisoners was systematized, especially after the formation of Task Force Detainees.

In 1975 the La Tondeña strike signalled the widespread strike movement in 300 workplaces, mostly in Manila. Community organizing was done more vigorously. ZOTO (Zone One Tondo) was the pioneer of community mass actions.

Human rights organizations intensified their work, with Manila as their headquarters. More religious progressives arose to assist the city underground of the workers, urban poor, and the students.

The city underground continued to be incensed by the atrocities and abuses of the military and paramilitary forces but was enthusiastic over the expansion and intensification of the revolutionary armed struggle.

*The Specific Characteristics of People's War in the Philippines*, by

Amado Guerrero, was issued to provide the latest comprehensive guidance for the nationwide armed revolution.

In 1976 the armed struggle advanced vigorously. The enemy was not reporting in his press the victories of the NPA. But the Manila underground was well-informed on these through underground publications.

The most important revolutionary document to come out in the year was *Our Urgent Tasks*. This would guide the growth of both the legal democratic movement and the armed struggle in the years to come.

The workers, urban poor, students, religious, and other sectors continued to develop their respective movements legally and openly in defiance of the fascist dictatorship.

In 1977 both the legal democratic movement in Manila and other urban areas and the armed struggle in the countryside advanced tremendously. Every regional organization of the CPP and NPA was growing rapidly. The NDF was gaining adherents in Manila and other urban areas.

Arrests made of CC members of the CPP since the previous year, culminating in my arrest in late 1977, encouraged the fascist dictator to claim that he had crushed the revolutionary movement.

In 1978 Marcos called for the election of the Interim Batasang Pambansa. LABAN (Laban ng Bayan) was formed under the leadership of Sen. Lorenzo Tañada to fight the KBL (Kilusang Bagong Lipunan) in Manila. The election served as an occasion to project the nationalist line on issues, especially because the country was already in an economic crisis due to excessive foreign borrowing for non-productive purposes.

The fascist regime rigged up the electoral rules, process and results. As a result, a mighty noise barrage burst out in Metro Manila. It brought to the fore the people's overwhelming hatred of the regime.

Riding on the anti-fascist wave and outrage over the sham election, the nationalist movement could have rapidly advanced and launched further mass actions in 1978 and 1979. But the nationalist leadership failed to override internal differences over the elections.

In 1979 the second oil shock hit the fascist dictatorship. The deleterious effects of foreign borrowing also became obvious. The agricultural exports of the Philippines — the main dollar earners — fell into a dismal state.

The Marcos regime could still borrow but at far more onerous terms than before. And it would use the new loans to accelerate the salting away of foreign exchange.

The leaders of the nationalist movement could see the trend that

Manila would be the center of turmoil and upheaval in the eighties. Revolutionary efforts of the nationalist leadership in the seventies laid the foundation for the overthrow of the Marcos fascist dictatorship in 1986.

# MUJER PUBLICA

MA. LUISA T. CAMAGAY

Concern over the activities of prostitutes during the Spanish period came in the wake of the growing peril of venereal diseases during the 19th century. Syphilis, together with alcoholism and tuberculosis, was considered one of the social ills of the period. The worldwide concern over the spread of venereal diseases was evident when the International Medical Congress which met in Paris in 1867 declared venereal disease as the "new cholera" of the century.[1] This concern was translated by a closer surveillance of the activities of prostitutes.

In the Philippines, this concern was manifested when colonial authorities in the 19th century imposed punitive measures against prostitutes in an attempt to combat the spread of venereal disease. Understandably, the colonial government adopted such measures because of the increasing incidence of syphilis — a disease which was not fatal but had irreversible effects such as blindness of newly-born babies, sterility of women and infant mortality.[2] In short, the effects of syphilis had serious repercussions on population growth.

There is evidence that the naval station in Cavite was hit by an epidemic of syphilis in December of 1895 prompting the *Jefe de Sanidad* to alert the authorities of the naval station that a number of the sailors infected with syphilis were confined in the Hospital in Canacao.[3]

Public awareness of the deleterious effects of venereal disease seemed apparent in the colony as advertisements of drugs curing gonorrhea and syphilis appeared in the major dailies. The *Boletin Oficial de Filipinas* for the year 1859 contained advertisements of such drugs. *Pildoras Holloway,* for example, was announced as a cure for *enfermedades venereas.* The *Vino de Zaraparilla* of Dr. Albert and the *Rob Antisifilitico de Boyveau Laffecteu* were advertised as effective medicines against venereal disease. The newspaper *El Comercio*[4] likewise carried advertisements of medicines which were sure cures against gonorrhea and

121

syphilis. All these medicines or drugs were manufactured in France and were locally available in the drug store of Don Jacobo Zobel. These drugs reached the knowledge of Manila's reading public. What did the non-reading public, presumably the native population, do? — did they use herbal medicine when infected with syphilis? What home cures did they resort to?

Our sources attesting to the arrests of prostitutes go as far back as 1849. This does not mean however that arrests were made only during this time. Arrests may have been made earlier than this date but we have no written evidence to prove the occurrence of such. Since venereal disease became widespread only in the 19th century, police measures on prostitutes developed only at this time.

Our evidence of 1849[5] reveals the arrests made by the *Seguridad Publica* of prostitutes in a densely-populated area of Manila at that time. The report about the incident was made by the *alcalde mayor* of Tondo. Seventeen women were rounded up and declared vagabonds and prostitutes. The recommendation of the *alcalde mayor* to the governor-general was deportation of these women to a sparsely-populated place like Nueva Quipuzcua (Davao). The merit of deporting the women to places like Davao was to spare them from being infected with venereal disease. Later in the 1860's, the Isla de Balabac in Palawan replaced Davao as the place of deportation for prostitutes.

Interestingly, some of the apprehended prostitutes had served prison sentences in the past because of illegal gambling, estafa, public disorder and even prostitution. It was logical, therefore, that *gobernadorcillos* and other governmental institutions of the period like the earlier *Seguridad Publica* handled prostitution cases.

Towards the second half of the 19th century, the arrests of prostitutes were implemented by the *Comisaria de Vigilancia*. Upon the arrest of the prostitute and her incarceration in the *Carcel de Bilibid*, an inquiry on her background would be conducted. The *gobernadorcillo* together with the *principales* of the town where the alleged prostitute lived was given 48 hours to furnish information such as whether she was included in the list of taxpayers of the town, whether she had had previous brushes with the law, whether she had the reputation of being a prostitute, as well as her civil status, profession and names of her parents. The friar-curate of the town was likewise asked to shed light on the antecedents of the prostitute. This procedure required a thorough acquaintance by the *gobernadorcillo* of his constituents, and by the friar-curate of his parishioners. Additionally, a look into the records of the *Carcel de Bilibid* was undertaken to verify whether the accused had been previously detained and on what charges. Of particular importance was confirmation whether or not the prostitute was infected with syphilis. If the prostitute was, then she was confined in the Hospital de San Juan de Dios instead of incarcerated in the *Carcel de Bilibid.*

A probe into the *expedientes* or dossiers of these apprehended women showed that police or punitive measures took the form of imprisonment of 10, 15 or 30 days and deportation.

The prison terms of the prostitutes were served at the *Carcel de Bilibid.* Upon serving their term, the prostitutes were given a certification attesting that they had indeed served the said term. Surprisingly, upon their release from prison, some prostitutes would actually return to the *Carcel de Bilibid* to ply their trade.[6] These women, according to the prison superintendent, would take advantage of the Thursday and Sunday visiting days to practice their profession, pretending to be relatives of the detainees in order to gain entrance into the prison. Inside the prison, the prostitutes were subjected to hard labor, the nature of which was not known.

In the early part of the 19th century, deportation to the south constituted the early treatment given by the colonial authorities to arrested prostitutes, even for first-time offenders. Evidence points to the fact that exile to far-off Davao or Balabac was considered extremely severe and was a much dreaded punishment among the prostitutes. Frequently, efforts were exerted by their families to spare them from undergoing this punishment. Petitions from mothers and fathers of prostitutes to the governor-general attest to this fact. Invoking reasons like ill health, the fact that the daughter was the sole breadwinner of the family, or even an outright denial of her activities as a prostitute, parents spared no effort to prevent a daughter from being deported to Davao or Balabac.

Deportation or exile, though readily resorted to in the mid-19th century, was used sparingly towards the end of that century. At the advent of the 20th century this kind of punishment was reserved for more severe cases, such as habitual offenders.

At the time of our research, we came across two lists of women deported. The first list dated 1849 contained names of women to be deported to Davao while the second list contained deportees destined for Balabac. The first dated 1849 list included the following names:[7]

| | | | |
|---|---|---|---|
| 1. | Remigia Sebastian | 5. | Januaria Balverde |
| 2. | Eustaquia Zaballa | 6. | Anselma Busta |
| 3. | Remigia Zaballa | 7. | Josefa Carballo |
| 4. | Romana Espinosa | 8. | Juana Legazpi |

9. Justa Gonzalez
10. Eustacia Francisca
11. Romana Pablo
12. Sotera Almario
13. Melchora de los Santos

14. Aristona de los Santos
15. Juliana Pasion
16. Felipa Guevara
17. Maria Josefa

The list of 1872 containing names of women to be deported to Palawan had 26 names. They included the following:[8]

1. Juana del Rosario
2. Rafaela Mesa
3. Alejandra Salmiento
4. Juana Rodriguez
5. Emeteria Borja
6. Lorenza Casimiro
7. Maria Quinto
8. Petrona Trinidad
9. Vicenta Rosario
10. Dominga Crisostomo
11. Dionicia de la Cruz
12. Antonia Cierca
13. Francisca Garcia

14. Elena Gabriel
15. Maria Castañeda
16. Roberta Zamora
17. Graciana Marzano
18. Eulogia Buson
19. Victoriana Javier
20. Eusebia Mamangon
21. Maria Evangelista
22. Eduviges Dumasig
23. Tomasa Diwa
24. Vicenta de la Cruz
25. Dolores Avila
26. Aniceta Chaves

There were other prostitutes arrested who were deported to Palawan as revealed in their individual dossiers but did not appear in a list like that of 1849 and 1872.

Marriage or the offer of marriage apparently served to circumvent or avert the deportation of a prostitute. In 1849 Romana Pablo, who was among those to be deported to Davao, was spared from going into exile because of Gilberto Escueta's request to marry her. Sotera Almario was likewise spared from going through this punishment when Don Jose Maria Medina, a Spanish mestizo, requested her release in order to marry her. In a statement, Sotera Almario confirmed that Don Jose Maria Medina was a suitor and that they were engaged to be married, while Don Medina confirmed that he intended to marry her.

Sometimes marriage plans would come when the deportee was already serving her sentence. The marriage plans of Remigia Sebastian, who was exiled to Davao in 1849, was found in a petition from her mother requesting Remigia's return to Manila in order to marry Jose Espinosa, a musician in the first expeditionary regiment. Vicenta Aleja filed her petition in June of 1849 and the orders of the governor-general to release

Remigia Sebastian came in January 1850. Clearly, the offer of marriage shortened the punishment of deportation for Remigia.[9]

A sojourn to Balabac was unexpectedly made pleasant when one deportee was accompanied by a loved one, as was the case of Eusebia Miguel.[10] A *cigarrera* from Bulacan, 21-year old Eusebia was arrested in August 1871 for getting involved in a fight where she threatened the life of a soldier, Ventura Fabula, who apparently was her lover. Prison records showed that Eusebia Miguel had been imprisoned in 1866 on a charge of theft. The *gobernadorcillo* and the *principalia* of Binondo also testified that Eusebia did not pay her *cedula personal* for the years 1869 and 1870, making her a *vagamunda*. The Chief of Police of the District affirmed that she was a *mujer publica*, having lived with different men in the past. Thus, the recommendation of the Governor of the Province of Tondo was deportation to the south of the Islands, preferably in an agricultural colony, referring to the Isla de Balabac. This recommendation was approved by Governor-General Izquierdo. Eusebia Miguel, however, did not go on exile alone. Antonio Bonifacio, a fellow prisoner of Eusebia at the *Carcel de Bilibid,* who was serving a sentence for estafa, asked permission from authorities to marry Eusebia and to serve his sentence with Eusebia wherever she was to be deported. Not finding any objection to this proposition, authorities allowed Antonio Bonifacio to join Eusebia Miguel to Balabac.

Thus marriage, it seems, was viewed by colonial authorities as a means of reforming prostitutes. The native population apparently agreed with this view, considering the number of petitions by parents seeking the release of their daughters so that they could be married off. One is tempted to ask whether the marriage offers mentioned in the petitions were genuine or whether the Filipinos used this argument merely because they knew that Spanish authorities were sympathetic to it. One gets the impression at the same time that ostracism of prostitutes by the native population did not seem to exist. Otherwise, why would Filipino males consent to marry Filipinas who were known to be prostitutes? And why did parents accept the fact that their daughters were prostitutes? It is perhaps possible that to the laboring class, there was no stigma attached to being a prostitute.

We have no idea as to the number of years a deportee had to serve her sentence. However, after three years, a deportee was allowed to request the governor-general to end her deportation. Josefa Carballo,[11] wrote the governor-general that she was deported to Davao in 1849 and since then had been leading an exemplary life. She requested permission to return to her family to start a new life. The same was true of Elena

125

Gabriel.[12] A *lavandera* from Mariquina, she left her husband and children for Manila. In the city she had no regular source of income and lived with a certain Jose Pingol, who eventually landed in prison accused of assault and theft. We see her name in the list of 26 women who boarded the steamer "Marquesa de la Victoria" for Palawan. This was in 1872. In 1875, Elena Gabriel asked that her confinement to Palawan be shortened. The request was granted. Usually, before the petition was approved, an attestation from the *alcalde mayor* of the province where she had been deported together with a certification from the friar-curate of the town was required. The two entities had to certify that the deportee had truly reformed during her exile. If favorable word was given by both the *alcalde mayor* and the friar-curate, then the petition of the deportee was approved.

Most of the prostitutes were in their late teens and early twenties, although there were older prostitutes in their thirties or forties who were either married or widowed. The provinces where they came from varied. Prostitutes hailed from as far north as Vigan, Ilocos Sur and as far south as Antique. All of them stated having held legitimate occupations. The usual occupations which appeared in their dossiers were *costerera, lavandera, cigarrera,* and *tendera.* It was not uncommon to find sisters plying the same trade. Elena and Placida Gabriel, Eustaquia and Remigia Zaballa, and Melchora and Aristona de los Santos were some of them, to name a few.

What made these women turn to prostitution? Were their earnings from their legitimate occupations insufficient? Or were these occupations merely mentioned to deny their activities as prostitutes? Were they, perhaps, pursuing a legitimate occupation during the day and indulging in prostitution in the evenings?

We suspect that women turned to prostitution for economic reasons. Much evidence shows that women in the provinces ventured into the city ostensibly to improve their economic status. The documents reveal that a number of the prostitutes arrested came from the provinces. Was this indicative of the hard times in the countryside? From the population sampling we have of 160 prostitutes, 105 came from the provinces. The nearby province of Bulacan provided the most number of prostitutes working in Manila. The case of Elena Gabriel is a case in point. Her dossier reveals that she left Mariquina and her life as a *lavandera* in order to try her luck in Manila. Not finding a suitable livelihood which would enable her to earn her keep while in the city, she turned to prostitution. Women in the provinces were tempted to come to Manila because of the economic opportunities that Manila offered. Telesfora Villegas and Basilia Garcia,[13] both from Orani, Bataan, were recruited by a woman who promised them jobs as househelp in Manila with a salary of three pesos a month. The two women, however, later went to the police authorities because they suspected that they were being recruited to become prostitutes instead of *criadas* or domestic helpers.

Documents also reveal that there were four categories of prostitutes, depending upon the way the plied their trade. One category of prostitutes included those who were kept in a prostitution house and were under the supervision of an *ama* (mistress) or *amo* (master).[14] Most of the *amas* were native women. *Amos* were few. We came across a Filipino male and two Chinese male *amos*. A few *amas* stated their occupation as either *cigarillera* or *costurera*. The Filipino *amo* identified himself as a *sastre* (tailor). San Jose de Trozo appeared to be an area where prostitution houses abounded. When a prostitution house was raided by authorities, the *ama* and the prostitutes were all rounded up. It seemed public knowledge that some houses were prostitution houses, but it was only when brawls occurred that the houses were finally raided.

The second category consisted of those who plied their trade by posting themselves in certain streets. These streets were Calle Iris in Quiapo; Paseo de Azcarraga, Meisic, and Santa Elena in Tondo; Arranque, Lacoste, and Gandara in Santa Cruz; Camba, Barcelona, Elcano, Plaza de Calderon and Ylangylang in Binondo; and Singalong, Bangbang, Herran, San Marcelino in Paco Dilao.[15] The women in this category were also under the supervision of *amas* or *amos*.

Prostitutes who plied their trade by going to the house of the client belonged to the third type. These were the prostitutes who rendered service to the Chinese males. We know for a fact that Chinese men who came to the Philippines during the Spanish period, if married, did not bring their wives with them. It is not surprising, then, that these young and robust Chinese sought the services of prostitutes. Three prostitutes, Paula Prim, Andrea Austria and Serapia Roncal were arrested in a soap store owned by a Chinese named Sy Jaco.[16] This evidence reveals that the Chinese themselves were involved in prostitution. Serapia Roncal acted as a pimp or a *corredora*.[17] Margarita San Pedro was also one prostitute who frequented the homes of Chinese men. She was mentioned to have been the concubine of a soldier. She was arrested upon order of the *gobernadorcillo* of Tondo based on reports that she would go to the barrio of Tutuban and spend the night in the homes of the Chinese. Placida Gabriel, a resident of Mariquina and a widow of thirty years, was said to have many clients—among them, according to the *Alferez Comandante* of the Guardia Civil of Mariquina, Chinese men. Other prostitutes, however, were arrested inside the opium dens of the Chinese, raising the suspicion that these places were also functioning as prostitution houses as well. True enough, in 1900 the American acting president of the Board of Health commented that an opium joint was also a house of prostitution "so that those patronizing may 'hit the pipe' in connection with other pleasures."[18]

Finally, the last category of prostitutes included those who serviced clients in their own homes. Belonging to this category were the likes of Trinidad Sanchez, a Spaniard who lived at #6 Calle Uli-uli in San Miguel; Antonelle Dusand, an American who lived at #16 Calle Labasan in Sampaloc; and Lorenza Ida, a Englishwoman who lived at #20 Calle Balmes in Quiapo. Presumably, these women catered to men who belonged to the higher bracket of society.

What were the chances of these women leaving their lives as prostitutes? Once released from prison did these women turn over a new leaf? Notably, a number of prostitutes who were arrested and detained at the *Carcel de Bilibid* were rearrested at a later time. However, one suspects that deportation to either Davao or Balabac or banishment from one's province was so cruel a punishment that it effectively deterred a prostitute from returning to this profession. Marriage may have also reformed the prostitute, making her turn her back on her previous profession. One rare case, however, revealed that one husband forced his wife back into prostitution and lived on her earnings. Ceferino Fernandez,[19] a tailor, ceased practising his profession and spent his days gambling while his wife worked as a prostitute. The *gobernadorcillo* and the *principales* of Tondo recommended his deportation to Mindanao, a punishment which was carried out.

It is difficult to ascertain how these women felt about their profession, their aspirations in life, or even how they appeared in public. Did their manner of dressing or social behavior reveal their true identity? Since it was impossible to interview these women and there is a dearth of information on their views about themselves, a look into the public perception of these women at that time may be useful.

From the various terms prostitutes were labelled by, a value judgment by society was already evident. The prostitutes were called *prostituta, mujer publica, vagamunda* and *indocumentada*. The term *vagamunda* reflected the roving lifestyle of the prostitute, and her inability to be registered in a definite locality earned for her the title *indocumentada*. When arrested, therefore, the prostitute was not only penalized for trafficking her body but also for not paying a *cedula*, the document needed so as not to qualify her as being a *vagamunda* and an *indocumentada*. This wandering lifestyle is alluded to in literary works which have touched on the life of prostitutes:

"You ask me how my life was? It was like that of the others of my kind. Days of bonanza, tempestuous nights, caresses of fortune, and floggings by fate. This, in a nutshell, is my history. I went through towns dispensing smiles never thinking of the mothers, wives, sisters, daughters who perhaps were to cry because of them ..."[20]

Literary works alluding to the life of prostitutes are rare during the 19th century. This is due to the fact that religious literature pervaded the said period. However, at the beginning of the 20th century there were references to prostitutes though few and far between. In Faustino Aguilar's novel *Pinaglahuan*, published in 1907, there was mention of prostitutes. They were pictured in the story as women who called attention to themselves because of their loud laughter, gaudy manner of dressing, and the smell of cheap perfume. The novel described the prostitutes in this manner:

At sa alaala ni Roman ay binasa ang isang mahabang talaan ng mga babaying kung araw ay makikinang, datapwa't kung gabi'y nangagbibili ng pag-ibig sa bawa't makaaabot sa halaga ng isang halik, ng isa nilang yakap. Marami sa mga babaying ito'y nangapalulong sa gayong buhay sapagkat ibig magsikislap ay walang namang kaya, marami ang dahil sa talagang nagmamamasarap sa buhay na pagayong punong puno ng aliw, nguni't may ilan din namang kaya nagsisama ay sa kasalanan ng lahat, sa mga huling ito'y kabilang ang mga ulilang kulang sa mag-ampon, ang nilinlang ng mga walang pusong mangangalakal ng laman, ang mga dukhang sa kakulangan ng mag-akay, ay nangapilit sa pagbibili ng katawan upang may ikabuhay.[21]

From this short literary passage we could gather many reasons why women at that time were in prostitution. These reasons ranged from a desire for sexual pleasure to outright deception by people engaged in the flesh trade. We came across instances when women who were hired as domestic helpers ended up being prostitutes. Such was the case of Florentina Canlas,[22] a 16 year-old native of San Fernando, Pampanga. She was hired as a domestic helper by Gregorio Sarmiento with a monthly salary of two pesos. According to her, after a week of employment under Sarmiento, she was brought by the latter to a prostitution house owned by Gregorio Beteng. She escaped from the sex den since she could no longer stomach the shame and exploitation she was being subjected to. Sarmiento, when questioned, asserted that Canlas became a prostitute out of her own free will—"esta lo hace de su propia voluntad por se de profesion." He further stated that Canlas bought clothes from him amounting to ₱94.20 and that when he wanted to collect this amount from Canlas, the latter left the house. One doubts the allegations made by

Sarmiento, which makes the testimony of Canlas more credible. For how could Canlas, in a week's stay in the house of Sarmiento, incur such a big debt against her monthly salary of only ₱2? If Canlas did enter prostitution out of her own volition to be able to pay back Sarmiento, what could have explained her escape from the prostitution house?

Stories of women who were hired as domestics and later turned over to prostitution dens by the masters of the house seemed to have been a common occurrence during the 19th century. One suspects that some masters of these domestics may have been in connivance with women who run prostitution houses. The charges of debts incurred by prostitutes while under the employ of these masters may have been fabricated to cover up their being turned over to prostitution dens.

The case of Faustina Trias is another case in point. She was 16 years old, a native of Orani, Bataan and married to Candido Ramos, 24 years old, a native of Calumpit, Bulacan and a domestic helper by profession. According to the testimony of Ramos, his wife owed their master Doña Ladislawa ₱23. A certain Martina Rafael volunteered to lend Faustina the amount but the latter was to work for her as domestic helper. After a month, Martina Rafael reportedly told Ramos that Faustina left her household and was now working as a domestic of Doña Gabriela Ventura. When Candido went to the house of Doña Ventura he saw his wife who told him that Martina Rafael brought her to a prostitution house owned by Alejandra Umali. Martina Rafael later denied the accusation.

The alarming incidence of syphilis in the colony by the late 19th century signalled a need for closer supervision of the activities of prostitutes. From the early punitive measures adopted by colonial authorities in the middle of the 19th century, we noticed the formulation by the late 19th century of rules and regulations aimed at preventing the spread of communicable diseases contracted through prostitution and breastfeeding.

The concern over the spread of venereal disease, especially syphilis, led to the creation of the Bureau of Public Health. The rules guiding the operation of the Bureau were greatly inspired by what had earlier been formulated in Spain.

The *Reglamento* of 1897[23] expressed in very euphemistic language that a woman engaged in prostitution was to be referred to as *mujer publica*. A *mujer publica* was defined in the document as one who regularly engages in the trade (prostitution). The *Reglamento* mentioned three categories of *mujeres publicas*. One category included women who stayed in authorized prostitution houses. Another category included women who stayed in their own homes and engaged in prostitution. The third category included women who went to the homes of their clients.

To keep tab of those engaged in the trade, the new Bureau of Public Health undertook a licensing of prostitutes in Manila. The licensing of prostitutes not only allowed a sort of census of prostitutes in Manila but also checked the spread of syphilis in the city. The licensed prostitutes were required to undergo a medical examination twice a week. This examination was done by medical authorities who made the rounds of licensed prostitution houses. *Amas* or owners of prostitution houses who prevented the hospitalization of women infected with syphilis were to be imprisoned and given the maximum punishment. The San Juan de Dios Hospital appeared to be the hospital designated to take care of women afflicted with syphilis.

Soliciting of clients in public was strictly prohibited. Prostitutes were forbidden to solicit clients in streets or street corners and to station themselves in entrances and balconies of homes. Furthermore, they were not allowed to converse with men in the streets nor to use any form of provocation which would offend public morals.

It appears that for the colonial authorities of the period, prostitution would be tolerated but was to be regulated. The regulation of the activities of the prostitutes was intended not only to check the spread of venereal disease but to protect public morals as well. This is evident not only in the ban imposed on public soliciting of clients but also in the insistence that prostitution houses should not be located in places where there was much human traffic. The *Reglamento* also forbade the prostitution houses from revealing through public signs their real purpose.

From the point of view of the colonial authorities, the regulation of the activities of the prostitutes assumed the orientation of a sanitary or health precaution. However, from the point of view of the native population, the regulation of prostitution was a repressive and/or dissuasive strategy against sexuality. It would seem that Filipinos at that time were unaware of the negative implications of prostitution. There was no word for prostitute in Tagalog. The early Filipinos appeared to have more tolerance for sexual freedom than the Filipinos of the Spanish period or even present day-Filipinos. This sexual freedom enjoyed by the early Filipino woman contrasted sharply with the restrictions imposed on the Spanish woman by the early missionaries during the same period.

For the Filipino woman during the 19th century, the flesh trade was definitely a source of livelihood. Whether it was decent or not was immaterial. What counted was that it was an occupation open to women.

## NOTES

1. A. Corbin. "Le peril veneri en au debut du siecle: prophylaxie sanitaire et prophylaxie morale." *L'Holeine des Faubourgs.* (Fontenay-sous-Bois: Recherches, 1978.) p. 245.
2. *Ibid,* p. 247.
3. Philippine National Archives. Prostitucion 1887-1897.
4. These advertisements appeared in the following issues of *El Comercio:*

   13 de Julio 1876
   20 de Julio 1876
   24 de Julio 1876
   9 de Diciembre 1876

5. Asian Center, University of the Philippines. Manila Complex Microfilm Collection. Reel 14, Item 1, Document 4.
6. Philippine National Archives. Prostitucion 1862-1879.
7. Asian Center, University of the Philippines. Manila Complex Microfilm Collection. Reel 14, Item 1, Document 4.
8. Philippine National Archives. Prostitucion 1862-1879.
9. The petitions of Romana Pablo, Sotera Almario, and Remigia Sebastian are found in Reel 14, Item 1 and Document 4 of the Manila Complex Microfilm Collection in the Asian Center, University of the Philippines.
10. Philippine National Archives. Prostitucion 1882-1879.
11. Asian Center, University of the Philippines. Manila Complex Microfilm Collection. Reel 14, Item 1, Document 5.
12. Philippine National Archives. Prostitucion 1862-1879.
13. Philippine National Archives. Prostitucion 1881-1886.
14. These were individuals who had a group of girls under their supervision.
15. Knowledge of these streets is derived from a document making a listing of prostitutes and the areas where they station themselves. This document is found in the Philippine National Archives, Prostitucion 1887-1897.
16. Philippine National Archives. Prostitucion 1881-1886.
17. United States National Archives. Bureau of Insular Affairs Records. Prostitution General Record 2039. Letter of Major Ira Brown, Acting President (Board of Health) to the Acting Adjutant General. Manila, Philippines, May 16, 1900.

18. Philippine National Archives. Prostitucion 1887-1894.
19. Philippine National Archives. Prostitucion 1862-1879.
20. Teofilo del Castillo and Buenaventura S. Medina. *Philippine Literature: From Ancient Times to the Present.* (Quezon City, Philippines: Del Castillo, 1964) p. 248.
21. Faustino Aguilar. *Pinaglahuan.* Unang Pagkalimbag. (Maynila: Manila Filatelico. 1907.) p. 117.
22. Philippine National Archives. Prostitucion 1887-1897.
23. Philippine National Archives. Prostitucion 1887-1897.

# THE NEO-MANILEÑOS:
# AN ORAL HISTORY APPROACH

MARCELINO A. FORONDA, JR.

## Introduction

This paper is an inquiry into the Neo-Manileños or the New Manilans, who are migrants that have settled in Metro Manila for good.

The Neo-Manileños may be categorized into two classes: 1) those who came from the provinces and other parts of the archipelago, and 2) those who came to settle in Manila from other countries.

To the first category belong former students from the provinces who after their studies, found jobs and established their homes in Manila. Others who came from the provinces found jobs in Manila which enabled them to settle here. There are still others who, belonging to the lower strata of society, came to Manila in search of a better life. Ill-prepared for the highly competitive job market in the city, they eventually ended up with no jobs, some living off the largesse of relatives and friends. Many of them, highly frustrated, resorted to a life of crime. Others tried to eke out a living by pushing carts and scavenging in garbage dumps, and became part of the teeming thousands who live in the slums.

To the second category belong migrants from other countries. Some Chinese, for instance, came to Manila in search of the proverbial greener pastures, joining relatives and townmates who had preceded them. Other foreigners initially came to Manila for personal reasons. They liked Manila and later opted to remain here.

Whatever their economic backgrounds and whatever their place of origin, these Neo-Manileños, both local and foreign, certainly had their own expectations of what life in Manila would be. They foresaw certain problems and possible solutions. They also perceived their own roles as Neo-Manileños.

This study focuses on the foreign Manileño: his motivations in coming here, his initial problems and how he solved them, his early impressions of his adopted city and of its people, his perception of his role

134

as a Neo-Manileño, and his view of the future of Manila, and of the Philippines as a whole.

## Informants

For this paper, the Neo-Manileños studied are migrants from the U.S.A., Britain, China, Germany and Spain.

I had originally planned to include migrants from the provinces and other parts of the Philippines. Indeed, I had begun to interview individuals who had originally come from the Ilocos and elsewhere. I realized, however, that including the local migrants would have made this paper unduly long and less manageable.

Informants for this paper, pre-selected mainly because of their availability, included the following:

1. Sandra Schram Cayetano, a former public school teacher in her 30's, born and reared in Michigan, U.S.A., who came to Manila in 1968;
2. Donald Price, a businessman from London in his early fifties, who came to Manila in 1949;
3. Chua Giok Lim, 77, retired employee who came to Manila from China in 1933;
4. Uy Yap Ti, 60, shop-owner who came to Manila from China in 1937;
5. Sy To, 62, shop-owner, who came to Manila from China in 1936;
6. Nels von Ebbe, 51, businessman who as a young boy was brought to Manila by his parents in 1929 from Germany, and whose family returned to Germany before the war and came back to Manila in 1950; and
7. Father Joseph Mena, in his fifties, a Spanish Jesuit priest who came to Manila from Spain after the Second World War.

## Methodology

As the title of this paper indicates, this study uses the techniques of oral history—that is to say, it utilizes well-structured interviews with the above-mentioned informants.[1]

The interviews were conducted in the English, Chinese and German languages (transcripts contain English translations of the Chinese and German texts) in 1985 during the last months of the Marcos era. At that time, local residents—including foreigners—felt constrained to speak

135

cautiously. Indeed, a close study of the transcripts of the interviews with our informants would show guarded comments on the political and economic conditions of the times.

Even so, our informants succeeded in situating themselves in aspects of Manila history and in viewing their roles as Neo-Manileños.

In this paper, our informants are cited by name, but in order to make for an even and easier flow of the narrative, no specific page citations are made from the transcripts.

Rather being a statistical study, this paper focuses on the Neo-Manileños, reflecting the conditions and plight of their times. It deals with immigration history, a relatively new field in Philippine historiography, utilizing oral history techniques, an equally new methodology in Philippine historical writing. It is thus meant to be a modest contribution to the local meager literature of both immigration and oral history.

## The Neo-Manileños: A Study

### Reasons and Motivations

Reasons and motivations of our informants' migration to Manila are as varied as the informants themselves. To be sure, their socio-economic backgrounds influenced to small degree their decision to come here.

Chua Giok Lim was only twenty years old when he first came to Manila in 1933 to find a job.

Uy Yap Ti belonged to a big family in China, which had great difficulty making both ends meet. Orphaned at a very young age, she came to Manila in 1937 with classmates from her hometown. For Uy as well as for her companions, Manila, as compared with the rather primitive China of her youth, "was a much better place to live in. It had a good water system, sanitation and electricity."

Sy To came to Manila in 1936 when he was thirteen "to seek a better life and a brighter future."

Chua, Uy and Ti stayed with former townmates and relatives from the old country who had preceded them to Manila.

Sandra Schram Cayetano had earlier married Renato Cayetano, a former graduate student in the U.S. After their marriage, Cayetano came home to the Philippines for good, and Sandra accompanied him "because my husband lives here." Thus, it was personal circumstance that brought Sandra to Manila.

The same thing may be said of Father Joseph Mena, a Spanish Jesuit who came to Manila in 1952 "under orders" of his religious superiors. He had originally volunteered for the China missions, but missionaries were barred from entering China at that time, so he remained in the Philippines, living most of the time in Metro Manila.

Donald Price belonged to a large family who used to live in a London suburb before he came to Manila in 1949 to work for a business firm. He later met a Filipina from Iloilo whom he married in 1954. They have five children, three of whom, Price is proud to point out, are Filipino citizens.

Nels von Ebbe was brought to Manila as a young boy. His family later returned to Germany before the war. Because of the hard times in Germany after the war, von Ebbe's family, upon the prodding of his Spanish mestiza mother, decided to come back to the Philippines because "they thought things in the Philippines would be much better than in Germany ... and because after all, this is where most of their family and relatives reside."

Whatever their racial background, therefore, our informants, as Mr. Sy succinctly points out, came to Manila to seek a better life and the opportunities that would give them a brighter tomorrow.

## Difficulties and Problems

The opportunities for a better future certainly seemed obvious for the Neo-Manileños. But certain difficulties and problems presented themselves. Foremost among these problems was that of language.

For Chua, lack of knowledge of Tagalog, the language which the clientele of the store where he worked spoke, posed a great problem.

For his part von Ebbe also had to face the language problem, although for a different reason. Von Ebbe had attended grade school and part of his high school in Germany. Upon his arrival in Manila, he took up the remaining years of his high school at De La Salle, where English, a language he did not understand, was the medium of instruction.

"When I returned to Manila," von Ebbe says, "I spoke only German, and hardly knew a word of English. I spoke a little Spanish, however, which is the language of my mother. But English to me was an altogether new language, and Tagalog was much more difficult to learn."

For the Chinese migrants, another difficulty was mainly economic — earning enough to make both ends meet, and saving a little for that business venture that they had planned for the future.

137

For Chua, this problem was somewhat compounded by the fact that aside from earning his own upkeep, he still had to scrimp and save money to send to his parents in China.

Another kind of difficulty presented itself to Father Mena. "The extreme heat made a tremendous difference to me," he says. "It was a terrible experience throughout the first year of my stay in Manila, and I could hardly forget it. You have to live in Europe or in the States to really experience the difference between the climate in Manila and in Western countries. You eventually get used to it, of course, but in the very first year of your stay in Manila it certainly made a difference."

Still other problems had to be solved and other adjustments made. Certainly, adjusting to the lifestyle of the Filipinos was one of them.

Sandra Schram Cayetano, who had always been independent in her native Michigan and had lived alone by herself since she was eighteen, suddenly found herself as a married woman in her thirties living with her husband's parents.

"It was really hard adjusting to the situation," Sandra says. "My mother-in-law seemed to think that she still had control over my husband although he was already 35 and very much married, like telling him what to do and what food to eat, and things like that."

The fact that Cayetano was in politics (he was a member of Marcos' Batasan), somewhat compounded Sandra Cayetano's problems. "Because my husband was in politics," she says, "everybody thought that he had lots of money and everybody who was related to him, even those very far-removed, expected my husband to be responsible for them, like giving them jobs and money for their needs."

But Sandra is a no-nonsense woman, and she decided to take things positively. However, "being in politics changed our lives for the better," she says. "So many people helped us in many ways—morally and financially, even if they didn't have to. This thought made life easier for me, and made me more willing to give of myself to others."

For our Chinese informants, housing was an initial problem. But this was solved because relatives and townmates from the homeland took them in and offered them hospitality while they were looking for jobs and were busy adjusting to their new environment.

Because of a long history of Spanish presence in the Philippines, Father Mena did not find it difficult to adjust to life in Manila. He says, "I began to discover many, many familiar things in Philippine culture that reminded me of my own Spanish culture. So I felt very much at home here right from the very beginning."

*Early Impressions*

Price saw the damage caused by the war when he first arrived in Manila in 1949. The scars of war were still there; some buildings and churches were in ruins, and Intramuros was yet to be rehabilitated. "But even then," Price says, "people were warm-hearted and hospitable."

For her part, Cayetano had an unforgettable experience when she was new in the city. "It hadn't rained for weeks, and the radio announced that a typhoon was expected," she says. "I was really scared because in the States when a typhoon signal is hoisted it is really something. But here in Manila I was really surprised that in spite of the warning, people went about their chores as if nothing was going to happen. Signal number 3 was hoisted, but the weather remained unchanged. In fact, nothing actually happened. It was a traumatic experience for me!"

How did the Filipinos impress the Neo-Manileños?

To Cayetano, the friendliness of the Filipinos was most impressive. "Even if you just meet individuals casually," she says, "they treat you very well. They accept you the way you are. They invite you to their homes. And suddenly you are their friend."

Some negative traits, however, did not escape the attention of Cayetano. For instance, the utter dependence of some people on certain individuals is common among both wealthy and poor families. This has spawned, she says, the lack of initiative on the part of individuals, who prey on relatives who are better-off.

"My relation with Filipinos," Price says, "have always been cordial. I've had no problem adjusting to them; we've always gotten along very well."

Uy, for her part, remarks that for the duration of her long stay in Manila, the Filipinos have treated her very well.

Sy, another old-timer in Manila, says that "most Filipinos in pre-war times treated us Chinese quite well. But only a few, usually the uneducated and illiterate ones, treated us unkindly."

These were the ones who poked fun at the Chinese, throwing invectives at them in a strange mixture of Tagalog swear words and incomprehensible Chinese-sounding words.

Von Ebbe never felt any discrimination against him. On the contrary, he felt fully accepted by the Filipinos.

Father Mena, for his part, felt "very accepted." "I don't remember a single instance at any time that anybody ever discriminated against me because I was a Spaniard," Mena emphasizes. "On the contrary, people were very nice to me all the time."

Mena is also impressed by close family ties among Filipinos which he finds have advantages and disadvantages. The impression he gets is that some individuals take their relatives for granted, and abuse their relatives' hospitality and generosity.

## Recollections

Neo-Manileños feel nostalgic about days gone by in their adopted city. This is especially true with the Chinese informants who have an intimate knowledge of Manila from prewar times, through the Japanese occupation, the postwar era and in more recent times.

Our Chinese informants view the past with fondness and affection. The past represents to them all that was good and noble, when, as Chua says, "everything was cheap ... and everything was fine. Politics and the economy were good, and peace and order reigned all over the land. The Chinese who came here were happy because they were able to find jobs."

The past was, according to them, much better than the present. Indicative of this is the fact that there were fewer squatter colonies in prewar Manila, because, as Chua also remembers, very few people from the rural areas came to work and live in Manila.

But it was the very affordable cost of living in the past that impressed our Chinese informants most. "You could survive," says Sy, "with a peso. With a peso you could buy a lot of things that you needed. A family could survive with a few pesos, unlike today when a family can hardly survive with thousands of pesos."

"Politics was less corrupt," Uy goes on to say, "and economic conditions were much better than those of today. It was more peaceful in prewar times. You felt safe enough to stay out even late at night, unlike today when there are very many killings and kidnappings even in broad daylight."

Uy, who lived in Manila in the early 1930's, says that at that time, one person could survive on one peso a month. For fifteen pesos a month, one could support a family, "unlike today when thousands of pesos would still be inadequate to support a family."

"Peace and order was no problem then," Uy adds, "unlike today when crimes such as murder and robbery are common and are increasing."

Of war-time Manila under the Japanese, Chua has his own recollections. "During the war," he says, "people were hard-pressed. Jobs did not exist, and there was practically nothing to eat. It was only after the return of American troops that life started to pick up and the times became better. Everything began to improve. Everybody had work, and they had something to eat."

Viewing the past made it inevitable for the Neo-Manileños to make comparisons with the harsh realities of the present (1985).

The other informants who knew Manila only after the war can, of course, make no such comparisons, but their perceptions of present-day realities are keen.

### Present Realities

Price points out the unrest that plagues Manila at present. But all countries, he is careful to point out, go through political cycles, having their ups and downs. And he hastens to add that he has "no doubt that in the course of time this unrest will pass away and we will return to a more stable political atmosphere."

Insofar as the economic crisis is concerned, von Ebbe has this to say: "The main problem is that not enough jobs are available; that's the reason why everybody is applying for jobs in the Middle East."

"Money is extremely scarce," von Ebbe continues, "and people have been reluctant to invest under present conditions. Business is very bad."

"But we will survive this crisis," von Ebbe says optimistically. "We have undergone similar crisis in the past, and we survived them. We, too, will survive this present one."

### Their Contributions

What do the Neo-Manileños consider to be their own contributions to their adopted city?

They might have been motivated by simple profit, but our Chinese informants who are shopkeepers feel that they, too, have helped keep life going in their adopted city, something which could also be said, albeit on a higher and wider scale, of our British and German Neo-Manileños, who are businessmen.

Cayetano, for her part, has established a Montessori school and is thus helping prepare young Filipinos for life. As a politician's wife, Cayetano has also helped others; she has learned to give of herself to others.

Father Mena's contribution may be summed up in one word: service — service to educate the youth of the land.

Many are the tasks that the Neo-Manileños have done. But whatever these may be, such efforts would help, as Price himself has said, develop the economy and bring about stability.

*The Future*

How, then do these Neo-Manileños view the future of their adopted city and of the country? How do they situate themselves within such a future?

In the first place, all our informants would prefer to live in Manila and stay here permanently than in some other place.

Certainly, the Philippines of the 1980's is laden with all kinds of problems: economic, social and political but, as Price says, "all countries have similar problems; these problems come and go."

And Price hopes that the Philippines will recover from all these problems, so that by the 1990's the country will have become "a strong financial country."

Father Mena's reason for staying here is on a higher, if not spiritual, level. He would rather stay in Metro Manila than elsewhere "because my vocation is here, among the Chinese," he says. "My original plan was to go to China as a missionary. But God arranged that I stay here working with the Chinese mainly in Xavier School, but also among the Filipinos. I feel very comfortable and fulfilled here."

While von Ebbe disagrees with foreigners residing in the Philippines who consider this country "paradise," he has no plans of leaving the country.

"If you are a foreigner who has lots of money and you don't have to work for a living, the Philippines is paradise," von Ebbe states. "But foreigners who have to work for a living in this country find it hard to make ends meet under the present conditions. Business is very bad and I don't think that under these conditions (in 1985) you can say that the Philippines is paradise."

In spite of these difficulties, however, von Ebbe would rather live in Manila. "I have my work here," he says. "I have my family here. And we're used to this kind of life here."

Von Ebbe could have been speaking for the Neo-Manileños who have lived in Manila these past many years, those who are presently residing here, or even the Neo-Manileños of the future.

**Conclusion**

This present study deals with the Neo-Manileños' perceptions of their adopted city and of their roles in its progress and development. It also underscores the reasons and motivations of the foreign Neo-Manileños' staying permanently in Manila.

Admittedly, the sampling is too limited to make generalizations about the foreign Neo-Manileños.

This study dealt with the personal histories of individual Neo-Manileños and their specific and individual problems, which they solved in their own specific and individual ways. The study also dealt with their perceptions of the reality that is Manila as well as their roles as Neo-Manileños. One cannot, therefore, formulate broad generalizations concerning *all* Neo-Manileños.

Still, one can say that migrants from the lower strata of society, like the Chinese migrants interviewed for this paper for instance, were faced with more problems — economic as well as cultural — than those who came from a higher strata of society. For example, they faced the problem of language. Chinese migrants who lived in Binondo, where they established their own shops, had to learn Tagalog, the language spoken by their clientele. They eventually learned the language, but in the beginning the problem seemed almost insurmountable.

Learning Tagalog posed no problem to our white Neo-Manileños: our American, British, German and Spanish informants. For one thing, they move around a higher level of society where English, a language that they spoke, was commonly used. They did not find it necessary, therefore, to learn Tagalog.

Whatever the color of their skin, the Neo-Manileños in this paper did not feel discriminated against by the Filipinos. Even so, the Chinese migrants found it more difficult adjusting to their new environment than their white counterparts.

There was, for instance, the initial problem among the Chinese of finding a place to stay. But this was solved by temporary living arrangements with their relatives and townmates from the old country.

Because they came here under somewhat different circumstances, the white migrants did not have housing problems. Indeed, they found themselves quartered in the more exclusive areas of Metro Manila.

Still, white migrants also had other specific problems like adjusting to the harsh and intense heat, or getting used to certain aspects of the Filipino lifestyle which for them were somewhat difficult to adapt to. The extended Filipino family system which permitted even married individuals to live with their own parents, or the parents' undue influence and control over married children was puzzling to them.

The motivations and reasons for the migrants' coming to Manila, as our study has shown, were as varied as the migrants themselves. Whatever these reasons and motivations might be, Manila will always elicit some strange fascination from among its visitors.

These people and others like them continue to migrate and settle here—dust, heat, lack of certain amenities, high prices, uncertain times, peace and order problems notwithstanding.

Thus, Manila can very well look forward to a continuous flow of migrants and generations of New Manileños arising in her midst.

## NOTES

1. I closely guided and supervised the planning and conducting, and personally checked certain details, of these interviews. Transcripts are found in the Foronda Oral History which forms part of my private library.

   See "Views," containing transcripts of interviews with Sandra Schram Cayetano and Father Joseph Mena, S.J., ii, 20p. (Contributed by Joy Elsingre and Jonathan Dy and their group); "The British One," containing the transcript of the interview with Donald Price. 14p. (Contributed by Janet Price and her group); "The Chinese Manileños," containing transcripts of interviews with Messrs. Chua Giok Lim and Sy To and Ms. Uy Yap Ti. 37p. (Contributed by Sammy Ang and his group); and "German Residents of Manila," containing the transcript of the interview with Nels von Ebbe, 13p. (Contributed by Otmar von Ebbe and his group).

   I would like to thank these students for helping me gather the data used in this study.

---

A grant from the De La Salle University Research Center made the preparation and writing of this paper possible.

# CHINESE WOMEN IN MANILA: CHANGING ROLES AND PERCEPTIONS

THERESA C. CARIÑO

## Introduction

The history of Chinese women in Southeast Asia has been a relatively brief one. Despite the long history of Chinese migration to the Philippines, many of those who came were either merchants or laborers who left their wives and families in China. It was only when the travel ban on women was lifted by the Manchu dynasty in the late 19th century that women were allowed to join their husbands overseas. In the Philippines, this freedom to travel did not result in the massive influx of Chinese women because of the Exclusion Act imposed by American colonial authorities in 1902. Under this Act, the entry of Chinese women was restricted. It was only when the Pacific war erupted that Chinese women were allowed entry in significant numbers. Between 1937 and 1940, 7,000 Chinese were allowed to enter the Philippines as refugees from war-torn China. Most of these were wives and children of Chinese residents.[1] This influx of women was again curtailed in 1949 when the Philippines held back recognition of the People's Republic of China. Nevertheless, the infusion of women had been sufficient to effect marked changes in the Philippine Chinese community. It had resulted in a Chinese community that became more "Chinese" both physically and culturally. More important, it had given rise to a large, locally born population.

In this sense, Chinese women may be viewed as having been a crucial factor in preserving the "Chineseness" of the Philippine Chinese community. As noted by Wilmott in his study of the Chinese in Semarang (in Indonesia), the influx of Chinese women marked a return to keener observance of Chinese customs, values, festivals and religous practices by the Chinese.[2] The importance of women in their roles as wives and mothers as socializing agents has been generally acknowledged. The fresh influx of women from China, therefore, may have indicated the

145

strengthening of Chinese values and traditions among the Chinese in the Philippines and a greater resistance to assimilation or acculturation.

However, between 1949 and 1975, the severance of ties with China prevented fresh infusions from the mainland, although contact with Taiwan continued. The halt of mass migration in the postwar years has resulted in the evolution of a Philippine Chinese community more responsive to developments in the Philippines than in China or Taiwan.

Furthermore, the mass naturalization of the Chinese in 1975 and 1976 as an outcome of a presidential decree by Ferdinand Marcos further rooted the Philippine Chinese in Philippine soil, triggering in turn a significant expansion in the economic and social roles of Philippine Chinese women. As a result of their naturalization, they became further exposed to the Filipino cultural environment where women experienced greater equality and rights than Chinese women in general. As Filipino citizens, they could now enjoy greater access to a college education and with it, a wider variety of occupational opportunities. The number of Philippine-born and Philippine-educated women has expanded rapidly. They have increasingly assumed economic responsibilities both in family-run businesses as well as in occupations outside the household. Some have won the freedom to run their own businesses and assume managerial functions while others are employed in large business and financial institutions.[3] The rise in their economic and social status and the continuous loosening of familial ties have contributed to the slow but steady erosion of patriarchy among the Philippine Chinese.

This paper will attempt to examine some of the factors that have contributed to the process, their effects on the changing economic and social status of Philippine Chinese women, as well as the implications all this may have for the evolution of Chinese identity and culture in the Philippines.[4] Much of the data for this paper have been drawn from studies based on Chinese women in Metro Manila.

### The Merchant Community and the Status of Women

From the outset, the migration of Chinese women to Southeast Asia thrust them into urban settings where trade and shopkeeping replaced landholding as the economic link with the patrilineal family. This represented a considerable loosening of traditional patterns and Chinese women participated more in the workforce than did their counterparts in traditional China. In the Philippines, and especially in Manila, Chinese women were never cloistered and were usually given a part to play in running the business or the store. In more recent times, they have assumed additional, formerly masculine responsibilities in the family business. Having more education than previous generations and greater exposure to the Filipino milieu, Chinese women are now pressing for and winning the freedom to start their own businesses or sidelines to augment their family income or simply their private allowances.[5]

The greater responsibilities and freedom of women in Chinese business reflect a shift away from patriarchy toward bilaterality of power and inheritance. This has been the result of changing business practices among the Chinese as well as the influence of Philippine social organization that features bilateral kinship and matrilocal residence patterns. In his study of Chinese merchant families in Iloilo, Omohundro noted the growing tendency for business alliances to arise from marriage alliances.[6] Rather than extend their businesses through descent group membership, Philippine Chinese have turned to building alliances through marriage. This has helped to raise the status of women since they become the bridge between two business partners. In marriage, the wife or daughter-in-law is no longer simply a dependent in her husband's household but becomes instead an active agent for her own family. Besides, she is not greatly estranged from her own family because the business alliance has brought the two families closer. This closeness strengthens the woman's position in her husband's family. The fact that the woman's family becomes business associate or benefactor of her husband's family augments her status which is further enhanced if she brings with her business skills and expertise. Furthermore, attention to good relations with one's affines or financial debt to them usually induces a husband to turn over some of the control and money of joint ventures to his wife.[7] To some extent, this has served to reduce patriarchy in Chinese business families. At best though, the wife will be an equal to her husband but is still subordinate to the same extent that her husband is to his father.

It is also noteworthy that affinal alliances have led to a modification in postmarital residence patterns towards matrilocality. While this is still frowned upon by the more traditional Philippine Chinese, it is not entirely rare for a man to move in with his in-laws if they are his benefactors. He may even become an heir, through his wife, to business branches or shares in the company. Under these circumstances, the status of the woman is naturally enhanced not only in relation to her husband but also in relation to his family and relatives.

Because of these changes and the influence of Filipino law and customs, Chinese inheritance practices have also changed towards more participation for women. Daughters who become managers in their father's business may become equal to their brothers as heirs. However, it would be rare for a woman to inherit property and business ahead of and over her brothers.[8] The inheritance pattern may also depend on the kind of business involved. For instance, in a study of 15 hardware firms in Metro-Manila conducted in 1979, not one of the cases showed the line of succession going to a female.[9]

While this confirms the tradition that daughters generally do not inherit, there is also increasing evidence that they are at least being given greater involvement in management functions. Usually, wives or daughters take on duties as treasurers, cashiers and supervisors in a store.[10] They may even become branch managers, although in these cases they are often assisted by their husbands whose decisions prevail.[11]

It has been observed that Chinese women in Southeast Asia do not often succeed individually in big businesses. Their businesses, if they are large, tend to be family businesses...[12] The Philippine Chinese women have been no exception. There are no Chinese women involved independently in large businesses in the Philippines. Co-ownership of a family business is a more common pattern, leading to sole ownership or control among widows. Chinese widows who often outlive their husbands by many years have increasingly assumed active control over their husbands' enterprises and over their grown sons, holding together extended family operations.[13] The emergence of such matriarchs may be a growing phenomenon.

## Moving Out of Binondo

Apart from modifications in business practices, other factors have been crucial in affecting the freedom and status of Chinese women. One of these has been the change in the pattern of urban residence which has contributed to the shrinking of the extended family. The Philippine Chinese family is now more and more nuclear in structure and size as younger generations live separately from their grandparents and other elderly members of the clan. In Metro-Manila, for instance, many Chinese are beginning to move out of Binondo (or Chinatown), prompted in part by its overcrowded conditions and in part by growing prosperity which has led many families to move to plush upper middle-class suburbs. This has meant greater freedom for the young to set up homes less directly under the control and supervision of the older generation and made them more receptive to external influences, especially the mass media, educational institutions, religious organizations and social clubs.

This increasing exposure and contact with Filipinos as well as western-style education has been reflected in greater economic and social freedoms for Philippine Chinese women and a sharper awareness on their part of the need to raise their status at least to the equivalent of Filipino women in general. The relatively high social status of Filipino women who own property and possess many legal rights in inheritance and marriage, has influenced Philippine-educated Chinese women who have begun to view their own status as comparatively too restricted. Equally exposed to a more liberal and less traditional environment, Philippine-educated Chinese husbands have also been inclined to accept a more egalitarian relationship. Many of them no longer restrict their wives from participating in business or acquiring jobs outside of the home.

In the past, Chinese men were adamantly opposed to their wives and daughters working for salaries as employees of others because it was deemed to reflect poorly on the family's wealth and the women's domesticity. Today, in the cities and especially in Metro-Manila, Chinese women are quite visibly working in banks, tourist agencies and airlines as receptionists, secretaries, cashiers and executives or as professionals, teachers and artists. One of the most vivid examples of their growing economic freedom has been the employment of young, unmarried women in Philippine Chinese banking corporations. Many of these young women come from respected business families.

## Women in Banking

The expanding number of Philippine Chinese women involved in the management and other operations of banking corporations is as much a testimony to the growing presence of the Philippine Chinese in the banking sector as it is a mirror of the greater economic freedoms enjoyed by contemporary Chinese women. Increasingly, Chinese women with college degrees have been given access to lower- and middle-management positions in banks. This trend has been evident over the last decade and accompanies the emergence and growth of large, Philippine Chinese-owned banks. A number of these banks embarked on a conscious policy of hiring Chinese women in an attempt to provide better services for clients especially in the Manila downtown area where depositors are mostly ethnic Chinese.[14] Chinese women were hired mainly because they speak a Chinese dialect and were more pleasant to deal with than Chinese men. It was important that those who were hired had impeccable social backgrounds and came from "respected" families—a preference expressed by special clients or large investors.

Although the reasons for hiring women in these banks had little to do with a conscious desire to encourage greater economic freedom and equality for women, the effect of such a policy has been precisely to enable

149

Philippine Chinese women to work outside of the home or family business and to open new vistas for their career advancement.

In a study of Chinese women working in middle management positions in a Manila bank, it was discovered that the majority had simply applied for their jobs on their own—with little family backing or involvement in securing their jobs.[15] Their decision to join the bank had been prompted by the desire to put into practice the knowledge in finance, management or accounting they had acquired in college. Their high career aspirations seemed directly related to their access to higher education.[16]

Most of the women interviewed seemed to enjoy their jobs because of the opportunity provided for them to meet and deal with people. Very few (5.88%) of these women in their mid-20's had immediate plans of marriage. The majority planned to continue at the bank and pursue a career, possibly working their way up to higher management positions and even to launch their own enterprises.

**Tertiary Education and its Impact**

It is evident that education, like employment, has had revolutionary implications for the status of women. The priority placed on education by the traditional Chinese has been transplanted to the Chinese community in Manila. This emphasis on education has equally benefitted women who nowadays receive as much, if not more education, as their brothers. As a matter of fact, in Metro-Manila, there is evidence that Chinese women spend more time in formal education than their husbands.[17]

The majority usually acquire some form of Chinese education at the primary and secondary levels. Several private schools in Manila teach a double curriculum using both English and Chinese (Mandarin) as media of instruction. These schools, mostly run by religious orders, attempt to imbue students with some sense of Chinese traditional values and facility with the Chinese language. Notwithstanding such attempts, many graduates of such schools have tended to be more fluent in English than in Mandarin.

Obviously, the higher the educational attainment, the greater the degree of exposure to western and Filipino values by Chinese women. In the Philippines, it would be difficult for Chinese women to ignore the fact that Filipino women enjoy a relatively higher social status, possess many legal rights and have attained high positions in many professions and in government. As naturalized Filipino citizens, Chinese women can be beneficiaries of these laws on equal rights and inheritance. They have no doubt begun to view their own status, to the extent that it is circumscribed by traditional Chinese practices and values, as being comparatively too restricted.

For women graduates, gaining greater economic independence has been facilitated by the fact that they are under less pressure than their brothers to continue the family business and therefore are in a better position to explore other areas of employment. It is not surprising to find them today in an increasing variety of occupations and positions ranging from airline receptionist to university professor or vice-president of a bank. Such opportunities of alternative employment, unknown to them two decades ago, have understandably made an imprint on women's sex-role attitudes and perceptions.

## Changing Roles and Perceptions

A comparison of two generations of Philippine Chinese women may be useful in determining the rapidity with which changes are occurring in sex-role perceptions and attitudes among them and the direction in which these changes are taking place. In a survey of 20 Chinese coeds at De La Salle University in Manila and their mothers, the considerable differences in levels of education attained between the two generations seemed to have an influence on their sex-role perceptions and attitudes.[18]

Among the mothers (whose median age was 47.5) of these coeds, only 35.3% had attained a college education while 47% had experienced a secondary education. The majority of mothers were housewives. Of those who worked, two were businesswomen, one a teacher and another a writer.

Findings revealed that there was a greater orientation on the part of the older generation of women to make sharper role distinctions between the sexes. Almost all the coeds agreed that men should share in housekeeping chores but only 70% of their mothers shared this opinion. A majority of the coeds (74%) felt that women should participate in politics while only 41% of their mothers agreed and 30% of them disapproved. Sixty-five percent (65%) of the coeds agreed that politics was exclusively a male domain while 75% of their mothers felt so. Both generations shared the belief that women should participate in decision-making but 35% of the mothers believed that family responsibilities belonged solely to the female domain. Surprisingly, more of the coeds (90%) believed that home management was exclusively a female domain than their mothers (80%). As far as business was concerned, 60% of the coeds felt it was an area for both male and female participation. Only 35% of their mothers shared this view.

151

Judging from these findings, there appears to be a trend among younger generations of women who have attained a higher education to believe increasingly in the need for equal responsibilities in housekeeping, although many still believe that home management is predominantly a female domain. Unlike their mothers, they are significantly more open to the idea of engaging in business and participating in politics.

There was close agreement among the coeds and their mothers that men in general were intelligent, had leadership attributes, were aggressive, logical, self-confident, ambitious, competitive and competent. In describing themselves, however, both generations employed many of the same adjectives commonly associated with the subordinate sex. They perceived themselves as intelligent, sensitive, faithful, honest, emotional, religious, submissive and gentle. Interesting to note, however, is that while many of the coeds used the term "competent" to describe themselves, this was not at all the self perception of their mothers. Instead, the older generation women saw themselves as logical and self-confident–adjectives that the coeds did not use in their self-description.

There were also key differences in the way the two generations had experienced sexual discrimination. Generally, the coeds felt less discriminated against than their mothers. To the extent they had experienced discrimination, they had felt it more strongly in school rather than in the home. In contrast, their mothers claimed greater experience of sexual discrimination in the home, followed by school and place of work.

Most of the coeds in the sample felt that their ideas concerning the roles and behavior of women were somewhat different from those of their mothers, though not drastically so. A few expressed the view that women were now more liberated since they could work and select their marriage partners. One respondent observed that in the past, women had been content with being "plain housewives" and even if they possessed jobs outside the home, were never able to pursue their careers to the fullest extent. On her part, she planned to pursue a career and "to develop it to the fullest before getting married." Another coed criticized her mother for being conservative, possessing "lesser ideals," and for seldom articulating her opinions. Yet another lamented that her mother still believed that "women should eat leftovers."

On the whole, the coeds had higher career aspirations than their mothers, were less self-sacrificing in relation to the family, had greater confidence in their own competence and were more open to women's participation in business and in politics.

152

## Marriage, the Family and Patriarchy

Obviously, the younger generations of Chinese women in Manila, partly as a result of higher education and closer contact with Filipino and western values, have rising expectations of sexual equality. Such expectations, accompanied by increasing opportunities for Chinese women to obtain jobs outside the domestic sphere, will in the long run contribute to the weakening of patriarchy in Chinese families.

Numerous constraints still remain, however, to limit the social and economic freedom of Chinese women. Naturalized Philippine Chinese women may enjoy equal inheritance rights under Philippine laws but such legal rights may not necessarily be translated into practice. This is particularly true in business where it is still unusual for a woman to inherit equal shares with her brothers and even more rare for her to inherit an enterprise ahead of and over her brothers.

Marriage is another area where traditional, patriarchal attitudes and values are being eroded but far from eliminated. In Chinese tradition, marriage was an institution designed to preserve and perpetrate the ancestral line and to provide extra hands in performing household chores. It was an occasion for family expansion rather than division and complicated rituals were devised to ensure that family interests rather than individual interests would prevail. This is especially crucial where the family is also a unit of production. Marriage therefore necessarily involves the family and requires the sanction of the patriarch. To ensure the family's control over marriage, complicated, expensive and time-consuming rituals were evolved. Nowadays, these rites have lost their meanings but "proper marriages" still entail ritual observances and a period of engagement before marriage.

Many college-educated Chinese women believe they have more freedom today in determining their choice of marriage partners, but a modified version of the traditional "arranged marriage" is still fairly prevalent among Manila's Chinese women.[19] This is the "introduction" system wherein a third party (or "matchmaker") introduces a man and a woman, prodding them to try out a steady relationship to test their compatibility while emphasizing that the final decision rests with the couple.[20]

Apparently, this is widely practised among the wealthier Chinese who prefer their children to marry those belonging to the same socio-economic class. It is also to ensure exogamy, a long-standing Chinese practice that forbids marriage between those having the same family name.

In many cases, social prestige, wealth and a college degree are still the key components determining the choice of marriage partners. Some marriages may be arranged by parents specifically with business interests in mind, but usually the young couple has veto powers.[21] These cases are rare and in the Philippines, it has been shown that business alliances between affinal kinsmen were usually contracted only *after* a marriage and after long years of marital alliance.[22]

Given the extensive involvement of Philippine Chinese in business, one can surmise the importance of marriage in family businesses. Few of the younger generation would defy their parents' judgment in determining their marriage partners and least so the women. One evidence of this deference to parental control is the fact that most Philippine Chinese women would never consider marrying outside of the Chinese community.

Parental control usually extends beyond marriage but here, the Chinese woman is expected to owe complete allegiance to her husband's family. The woman symbolically severs her ties with her own family after marriage. Once she leaves her parents' house, she has no further claim to the family wealth and her dowry is considered a representation of her inheritance from her family. Naturally, a large dowry provides a daughter more leverage, enabling her to command respect from her in-laws. Also, good health and fertility remain key factors in determining a woman's status in her husband's family. Those bearing sons would certainly enjoy a higher status than those incapable of producing male heirs to the family line.

In a recent survey of married, child-bearing Chinese women in Manila, the majority indicated their high approval of divorce on the basis of a woman's inability to bear children. On the other hand, very few believed that the wife should divorce her husband if he is sterile.[23]

Among the conditions for divorcing the husband, the non-fulfillment of economic duty received the highest percentage of approval.[24] This indicates that Chinese women in Metro Manila, despite their increasing participation in non-domestic occupations, still view their husbands or the men as essentially the breadwinners. Professional women and executives who were interviewed perceived themselves as earning a "supplemental income." In this sense, their careers were considered subordinate to their marriage and family obligations. They believed that their families ought to adjust to the demands of their jobs but were willing to sacrifice their careers should there be a serious conflict between work and familial duties and obligations.

The potential for conflict between career and family demands may be minimized by the fact that Chinese families in Manila are shrinking in size. It has been shown that the Chinese have the lowest birth rate among

Philippine ethnic groups and have an average birth rate of 2.3 per family.[25] Having smaller-sized families will certainly enable more Chinese women to work outside the home. Nevertheless, the domestic realm is still regarded as primarily a female domain and working women are still expected to supervise and manage household affairs.

Thus, despite their growing economic independence, Chinese women in Manila are still extremely family-centric. Professional and businesswomen stress that their primary duty is to the family and considerable numbers continue to seek occupations that will allow them to combine fulfilling family obligations with their work. The majority of working Chinese women in one survey sample either worked at home or in places near their homes.[26] Their family-centeredness may account for their concentration in certain types of jobs. Many of them are employed in professional, clerical, technical or sales work. Only a minority occupy administrative or managerial positions.[27] Middle-level executives express little desire for career advancement when they deem it as conflicting with familial responsibilities.

In Manila, arrangements in which children are left with mothers, relatives or domestic helpers have enabled working women to concentrate on and advance in their careers. Nevertheless, they still assume primary responsibility for home management and for supervising household affairs.

This may be one reason why few working women are involved in community affairs. Few Chinese women are members of community organizations or clubs and none would claim an active role as community leader. Leadership in the Chinese community is still very much a male preserve.

Like most members of the Chinese community in Manila, Chinese women shun politics, although a rising number of those who are highly educated believe that women should participate in politics or at least should be politically aware.

## A Modified Hierarchy

Their conspicuous absence in leadership roles and positions in the Chinese community to a large extent reflects the fact that the social status of the Chinese woman is still one that is primarily "derived." Her social position is defined mainly in relation to the men in her life and she is perceived either as her father's daughter, as her husband's wife or as her son's mother. The Chinese woman's access to education and employment provides her with a wider variety of social relationships and some opportunities for self-fulfillment and recognition outside the home, but her

155

primary status is still "derived."[28] For this reason, there is a tendency to regard her activities outside of the home as supplementary rather than as central. Domestic responsibilities are perceived as having primacy and priority over extra-familial occupations. Thus, those attempting to pursue an independent career are often compelled to fulfill simultaneously two sets of demands — one from their home and one from their employment.

The stress on the centrality of the family limits the ability of working women to advance in their careers. When the welfare of the family reigns supreme, the needs of women are often subordinated to the interests of the family group and the wife is restrained from acting independently. An underlying assumption is that the family comprises a unit under the ultimate leadership of the husband.

Thus, the expanding opportunities for Chinese women to participate in economic activities outside the family may begin to undermine patriarchal traditions, but as long as the family remains the primary focus of loyalty and obligations, women will continue to remain subordinate to the men. At best, the rigid hierarchy that characterized traditional Chinese social structure will give way to a modified hierarchy that will allow women to enjoy more options in social and economic relationships but will restrict and limit their independence.

## Chinese Culture and Identity

Apart from modifying the traditional hierarchical structure of the Chinese family, the increasing release of women from exclusively domestic functions will have some effects on Chinese culture and identity in the Philippines. Over the last decade, it has been observed that Chinese children are increasingly being left to the care of Filipino domestic helpers by their career-conscious mothers. One effect has been the tendency for Chinese children to be more fluent in Pilipino to the point where it sometimes becomes the primary medium for communication among themselves. Furthermore, proficiency in Pilipino and English has allowed for a greater openness to Filipino cultural influences especially through the mass media. No longer as closely supervised by their mothers as among older generations, Chinese children now retain less of the traditional, Confucian values, speak less Chinese and are more westernized in their attitudes and behavior. Not only are the younger generations less adept in the use of Chinese dialects, but they appear to have become more akin to the Filipinos in their religious beliefs and practices. Many Chinese who have received their education in private, sectarian schools regard themselves as Christian and do not actively practise ancestor worship or Buddhism.[29] Filial piety among Chinese women has become "feminized." While they respect their fathers more than they fear them, Chinese women in the Philippines appear to have a greater attachment to their mothers.

Traditionally regarded as the transmitters of social values, customs and beliefs, Chinese women are performing less and less of this role to the extent that they are engaged in economic and other activities outside of the home and family. As more Chinese women participate in extra-familial occupations, the school rather than the family will become the primary socializing unit.

Chinese identity in the Philippines may become less closely associated with the ability to speak and write the Chinese language or with traditional Confucian values and a strict hierarchical social structure. Access to higher education in Philippine schools and universities for Chinese men and women appears to have led to a gradual acceptance of greater economic and social freedom for women. The wider variety of social and economic options available to them will in the long run modify the existing patriarchial pattern towards one that is more egalitarian.

## NOTES

1. Chinben See, "Chinese Education and Ethnic Identity" in Theresa Cariño, ed., *Chinese in the Philippines* (Manila: De La Salle University Press, 1985), p. 34.
2. See Donald Earl Willmott, *The Chinese of Semarang: A Changing Minority Community in Indonesia* (Cornell: Cornell University Project, 1960), p. 290.
3. John Omohundro, *Chinese Merchant Families in Iloilo.* (Manila: Ateneo University Press, 1981), p. 143.
4. For the purpose of this paper, "Chinese Women" will refer to those who have lived most of their lives in the Philippines, have both parents who are Chinese, speak a Chinese dialect and consider themselves as ethnically Chinese. Many of these are naturalized Filipino citizens.

5. Omohundro, *op. cit.*, p. 143.
6. *Ibid.*, p. 145.
7. *Ibid.*, pp. 145, 165-166.
8. See Omohundro, *op. cit.*, p. 166.
9. Grace Yu Cheng, "The Chinese in the Hardware Business," Unpublished A.B. Thesis, De La Salle University, 1979, p. 41.
10. *Ibid.*, p. 43-44.
11. *Ibid.*, p. 46.
12. Joyce Lebra & Joy Paulson, *Chinese Women in Southeast Asia* (Singapore: Times Press, 1980), pp. 94-95.
13. See Omohundro, *op. cit.*, p. 145 and Yu Cheng, op. cit., pp. 41-46.
14. See Dawn Lopez, Unpublished study on "Chinese Women in Banking," 1984, p. 17.
15. Lopez, *ibid.*
16. 64.7% of the respondents cited education as the reason for joining the bank. Only 41.17% cited economic necessity as a motive.
17. Theresa C. Cariño, ed., *Chinese in the Philippines*, p. 5.
18. The survey was conducted between 1984 and 1985 among Chinese coeds whose parents were both ethnically Chinese. All of them were members of the Englicom, a club in La Salle organized by the Chinese.
19. See Theresa Cariño, ed., *Chinese in the Philippines*, p. 24, 25 and 27.
20. *Ibid.*, p. 25.
21. Omohundro, *op. cit.*, p. 165.
22. *Ibid.*
23. Pilar Jimenez, "Ethnicity and Fertility in the Philippines: the case of the Metro Manila Chinese," in Cariño, ed., *op cit.*, p. 7.
24. *Ibid.*, p. 9.
25. Pilar Jimenez, *op. cit.*, p. 7.
26. *Ibid.*
27. See the research findings and the report entitled, "Ethnicity and Fertility in Southeast Asia: The Case of the Philippines" by Pilar Jimenez and Ma. Cecilia G. Conaco, c1983.
28. Smock describes the social structure in which women have greater options but remain subordinate to male supremacy in the family as one of "modified hierarchy." See Janet Z. Giele & Audrey C. Smock, eds., *Women: Roles and Status in Eight Countries* (1977), p. 399.
29. In the survey of 20 DLSU coeds and their mothers, 90% of the coeds professed to be Christians and none of them was Buddhist. Among the mothers, 43% were Christians and 47% Buddhists.

## REFERENCES

Cariño, Theresa C., ed. 1985. *Chinese in the Philippines.* Manila: De La Salle University Press.

Cheng, Grace Yu. 1979. "The Chinese in the Hardware Business." Unpublished A.B. Thesis presented to the Behavioral Sciences Department, De La Salle University.

Giele, Janet Z. & Smock, Audrey C., eds. 1977. *Women: Roles and Status in Eight Countries.* London: John Wiley & Sons Inc.

Jimenez, Pilar and Conaco, Ma. Cecilia. 1983. "Ethnicity and Fertility in Southeast Asia: The Case of the Philippines." Unpublished report submitted to the Institute of Southeast Asian Studies, Singapore.

Lebra, Joyce and Paulson, Joy. 1980. *Chinese Women in Southeast Asia.* Singapore: Times International.

Lopez, Dawn. 1984. "Chinese Women in Banking." Unpublished term paper presented to the Department of History and Political Science, De La Salle University.

Omohundro, John. 1981. *Chinese Merchant Families in Iloilo: Commerce and Kin in a Central Philippine City.* Manila: Ateneo University Press.

Willmott, Donald Earl. 1960. *The Chinese of Semarang: A Changing Minority Community in Indonesia.* Cornell: Cornell University Press.

# HEALTH, NUTRITIONAL PROBLEMS AND THE UTILIZATION OF HEALTH SERVICES: THE SITUATION AMONG PRESCHOOLERS IN METRO MANILA COMMUNITIES

PILAR R. JIMENEZ

## Objectives

Despite advances in the fields of science and medicine, large numbers of children in developing countries throughout the world, particularly those in the 0-6 age category, continue to die of preventable and communicable diseases. Although the Philippines, for example, experienced a declining infant mortality rate in the last decade from 75 per 1,000 live births in 1975 to 60.6 in 1982, this rate is still considered quite high by international standards (UNICEF, 1984).

The problem lies not in the existing technology but in making it available to end users. Many simple technologies designed to improve child survival have, in fact, been developed, yet they have not been widely adopted, particularly by the disadvantaged sectors of the population which experience the highest number of child and infant deaths.

Several programs have been established by both government and non-government agencies to transfer such technologies to the disadvantaged. Critical deficiencies exist in the service delivery implementation mechanism of these agencies (Second Country Report for Filipino Children, 1982). Such deficiencies, especially in the delivery of health services, can have grave consequences on children, considering how large their numbers are.

Projections of the National Census and Statistics Office (NCSO, 1981) indicate that children, defined as the 0-20 age group, numbered 26.40 million in 1980 or 54.6% of the total population. Of this number, preschoolers or those 0-6 years of age, constituted the plurality with 9.86 million (20.41% of the population), followed by the school-age (7-14) group with 9.85 million (20.38%). Besides, the child population was

160

expected to have reached 27.5 million in 1983 and to increase to 28.72 million by 1987. Preschoolers are also expected to remain as the largest population sub-category until 1987 when the anticipated deceleration in the population growth rate will result in the school-age category assuming the lead in numbers (GOP, 1982).

Although statistics are available on the size of the child sector in the Philippines, very little information is known about the situation of poor Filipino children, particularly those belonging to the preschool age category. While a few existing studies indicate that Filipino children born in poverty generally suffer from undernutrition, poor health, high mortality, and slow intellectual, social, and emotional development, there is insufficient information about who they are, their number, their location, and their family background (Second Country Report for Filipino Children, 1982). There is also inadequate information about the health delivery systems in the communities where these poor children live, and hardly any study has been made linking the health and nutritional status of these children with the levels of utilization of health services.

It is imperative, then, that research on the situation of poor Filipino children be undertaken. It cannot be overemphasized that adequate baseline information is vital to program planning and implementation for the various groups and agencies concerned with the welfare of disadvantaged Filipino children.

In addressing this need, a study was undertaken to examine the health and nutritional status of preschool children in four depressed communities in Metro Manila and to determine the factors that account for the observed status. Specifically, the study aimed to: (1) determine the health and nutritional problems of preschoolers (0-6 years old); (2) relate socio-economic and demographic factors to the preschoolers' health and nutritional problems; (3) identify the health services, both static and itinerant, available in the depressed communities, particularly those that affect the preschoolers' welfare; (4) determine the delivery systems for both preventive and curative health services, the difficulties encountered in their utilization, and the extent to which they are linked to the current health and nutritional status of the preschoolers; and (5) propose a model for community mobilization for implementing alternative strategies to improve the health service delivery system.

This study was conducted under the auspices of the United Nations Children's Emergency Fund (UNICEF), the Second Country Program for Filipino Children of the National Economic Development Authority, and the DLSU Research Center.

## Methodology

Quantitative and qualitative methods were utilized in the collection of data. The quantitative methods were a census of 1,778 households with preschoolers (with the mothers as respondents) and an anthropometric survey which measured the height and weight of 536 preschoolers from 316 households. The qualitative methods included case studies of 40 selected households and key informant interviews of 34 health providers and 16 non-health providers. Fieldwork took place from February to September 1984.

The four depressed Metro Manila communities included in this study were: (1) Barangay 184, Maricaban, Pasay City, (2) Barangay 843, Pandacan, Manila, (3) Barangay 133, Bagong Barrio, Caloocan City, and (4) Sitio Luzon Kalaw, Barangay Culiat, Quezon City.

## Findings

The research findings showed that the preschoolers from depressed Metro Manila communities come from large households with young migrant parents whose incomes are barely sufficient to provide their families with the basic necessities in life. They live in congested and squalid surroundings with inadequate sanitation facilities.

Their health profile is typical of those obtained in many disadvantaged communities: high fertility, relatively high infant and child mortality and morbidity patterns that indicate infection, respiratory distress, and poor nutritional status.

This study examined the following health and nutritional practices: childbirth, breastfeeding, food supplementation and consumption, antenatal and postnatal check-ups, child care, and immunization.

Children of inner city communities were born in hospitals or private clinics, while children from outlying city communities were born at home. The prevalence of child mortality for children who were born at home and ministered by indigenous healers appears to be higher than for those born in hospitals or clinics. Mothers recalled that they breastfed their preschool children for an average duration of nine months. The decision to breastfeed is primarily related to an economic consideration, i.e., the current prohibitive price of infant formula. The decision not to breastfeed, on the other hand, is largely related to maternal biological factors such as insufficient supply of breastmilk, inverted nipple, and poor health.

Supplementary foods are introduced to infants during their fourth month, although these are usually insufficient in nutrition due to high carbohydrate load. This dietary pattern is sustained even when children are past their infancy. The preschoolers' households generally eat three meals a day. The households' meager earning is mostly spent on food, yet the typical allotment per person is lower than the average cost of a Metro Manila diet found in the 1982 FNRI second nationwide nutrition survey.

Mothers tend to have monthly prenatal check-ups starting the second trimester of pregnancy. After birth, infants are taken to the health center or to external health providers for a physical examination. Although mothers claim that they bring their children to health providers for preventive health services five times a year, observations made in households and communities indicate that they do not take their children to well-baby clinics; only when children are seriously ill are they taken to health providers for intervention. Mothers are solely responsible for child care; working mothers, however, tend to be assisted by female relatives.

Four out of ten mothers claim that they had all their preschoolers innoculated, while three out of ten never submitted their children for immunization; two out of ten had only some of their children vaccinated. Although most mothers claim that they had all their preschoolers innoculated, it is not known whether the children received the full complement of immunization since the mothers are not knowledgeble about the types of vaccines given to their children. Observations made revealed that most preschoolers were given the first dosage of DPT and OPV. The number of children who received the complete set of basic vaccines tapered off to about one-fourth of those who had received only the initial doses. Most children obtained their immunization from the health center.

The health services available in the four communities come from the government sector, private practitioners, and the indigenous or traditional healers. Day care centers, individual volunteers for health brigades, and private agencies are the other groups that extend health-related services to preschoolers in the communities. A high proportion of the preschoolers' households avails of the services of the traditional healers, particularly the *hilot*, and the government health center. The services rendered by these two health providers do not overlap since they are utilized for specific purposes.

The statistical analyses, i.e., correlation, socio-economic composite index, and multiple regression, have shown that the household characteristics that tend to contribute to the health and nutritional problems of preschoolers are those that distinguish the more disadvantaged in the depressed urban communities. Thus, household with low levels of maternal education, with mothers who originated from rural areas, low monthly income, and with fathers engaged in unskilled types of occupation tend to have a higher number of children ever born, experience higher child mortality, and raise malnourished children. They are also inclined to utilize health providers which render free services, i.e., the health center and the *hilot*.

The findings also indicate potential for participation in health care and delivery projects to community residents, particularly mothers. The mothers are willing to give not only a small amount of money for such projects but also a part of their time. They anticipate these projects, however, to be initiated by others, perhaps by their local officials, the private volunteer organizations, or the health center personnel.

The findings derived from this study indicate that the poor health conditions of preschoolers in selected urban depressed communities are biological manifestations of social problems and their biosocial interactions. Although location in the primate city implies better access to various types of health services, the poor health and nutritional status of preschoolers in slum and squatter communities of the metropolis indicates that proximity to such facilities is not necessarily an advantage, because health and other related aspects of well-being are determined largely by the economic, demographic, cultural, and political opportunities that society affords its members.

To meet some of the health needs of urban poor communities, this study recommends two courses of action. One direction suggests a more remedial stance on some aspects of health and service delivery that requires immediate measures within existing structures and programs. The second strategy suggests the development of a people-based health program in the light of community potential in the provision of health services that this study has extricated.

Among the remedial measures suggested by this study are: (1) direct intervention for some households that need immediate assistance; (2) a more rigorous family planning program; (3) additional assistance to health centers; (4) training and stepped-up usage of the *hilot*; (5) a more active collaboration between barangay officials and health center personnel; (6) environmental sanitation; (7) livelihood programs; and (8) child-to-child and caretaker programs.

The first five suggestions are directly concerned with the improvement of health services for the household and the community. The rest are related to the improvement of the physical environment and of the socio-economic conditions of the depressed households.

For the population-based health program, a conceptual paradigm for community mobilization in health service delivery was developed for future pilot testing.

The conceptual paradigm's long-term goal is the improvement of the health and nutritional status of preschoolers (usually expressed in terms of lower morbidity and child mortality rates) through community participation in the provision of health services. Community participation in this context refers to local involvement in program development, ideally from the planning stage and on through implementation and evaluation. Ideally, all the members, not only the leaders, of the community must participate. It must be a process and not only a structural design and it must exist in practice and not only in theory (Osteria, 1985).

Adequate social participation, however, is required before the community can be mobilized to embark in health care delivery. Such a stage is vital to determine the level of awareness of the community of the children's health problems and to determine the mechanisms by which the community can carry out a health care program. Data derived from this study, particularly on aspects of organization and participation, can serve as baseline information in increasing the level of awareness of communities on the health and nutritional problems of preschoolers and the health-seeking behavioral patterns of households.

One of the major concerns in the development of participatory types of ventures is the political support from the community and other relevant government agencies to ensure the success and the replicability of this experience in similar communities.

In Metro Manila, what mechanisms should be devised to assure communities that will attempt to utilize this conceptual paradigm, of political support from local governments and agencies concerned with the welfare of children?

One possible mechanism that can draw political interest in this pilot activity is the formation of a working group composed of representatives from different agencies and local governments and from the community where the participatory health program is pilot tested. This working group can regularly monitor and evaluate the activities of the pilot community and can perhaps provide the external linkage and support for the community particularly in projects that need outside assistance (e.g., training).

To regularly receive feedback of the community's activities, it can build into its mechanism process documentation, a research method that can assist the group members in: (1) understanding the processes involved in project initiation and implementation; (2) identifying the strengths and weaknesses in project operations; and (3) feeding back research information to project participants for better project implementation procedures.

The population-centered approach as proposed in this study is based on the recognition that intervention must consider the operation of social, economic, biological, and environmental forces on the risk and outcome of disease processes. There is a vast lacunae of knowledge on the determinants of disease. While there has been a call for a child survival resolution, the social roots of illness should be changed: this is the basic tool needed by community health professionals.

# WOMEN VENDORS
# IN METRO MANILA MARKETS

MA. ELENA CHIONG-JAVIER

## Introduction

Women in the economic sectors of developing societies can be broadly classified as belonging to one of two groups: the so-called modern, capital-intensive, formal labor sector, or the traditional, labor-intensive, informal sector. Women workers in the first group are distinguished from those in the second by their active involvement in fields of employment such as government, education, business, and the professions. These women are more in a position to compete with their male counterparts, even in male-dominated activities, and to receive equal compensation for their work. Their number, occupations, and earnings are easily quantified and, as a result, these factors find their way into national statistics.

Working women of the second group engage primarily in occupations which are predominantly related to small-scale trade, craft, and service activities. The income they derive from these occupations is often hardly enough to meet basic needs. Their productivity is quite low; their contributions are rarely considered in statistics or discussions about economic growth.

Development in recent years has accrued more to the benefit of the first, rather than the second, group of working women. This bias is frequently traced to the use of a western-oriented development model, which "exports a middle-class image of what is appropriate for women's work, one that limits or undermines traditional occupations" (Tinker, 1976:1). With the advent of International Women's Year in 1975, there emerged an increasing concern among developing countries for the development of their women engaged in traditional occupations. A major obstacle in carrying out this development task, however, is the serious lack of available data with which to begin. Small-scale trade in the market-place, a traditional women's activity, is one of those largely unreported and unmeasured contributions made by women to society and economy (Hammond and Jablow quoted in Paolucci and others, 1976:54).

In the Philippines, women market vendors do not constitute one of the well-studied occupational groups. When this study was done in 1978, available researches on them had largely emphasized such topics as economic interaction and sociability (Davis, 1976), patterns and processes involved in economic distribution and exchange (Szanton, 1972), description and analysis of urban wholesale fish marketing system (Guerrero, 1975). Hence investigations concerning female market vendors have been quite incidental, that is, women are figured in the studies because they happen to predominate certain spheres of the marketing system like selling vegetables or retailing fish. As might be expected, these investigations lack the intensive treatment that the female vendors would have received had they been the foci of the studies.

In Metro Manila, specifically, petty market vendors have invariably failed to gain the favorable attention and support of urban policy makers. In unfortunate cases where their vending activities conflict with city legislations, as in the case of hawkers or sidewalk vendors, law enforcers have tended generally to ignore their plight and instead deal harshly with them (Guerrero, 1975). Because most of these vendors are women of the urban low-income class, they are regularly placed in a helpless, oftentimes pathetic, situation.

These considerations underscore the importance of gaining more knowledge about women vendors in urban markets in order to be able to address their plight. The present study attempts to contribute to this knowledge through an exploratory but intensive investigation of a small group of 20 low-income, married women who sell vegetables as stallholders and hawkers in two adjacent markets in Metro Manila.

## Objectives of the Study

In general, the study seeks to describe and compare the vendors' personal backgrounds, domestic and occupational characteristics, perceptions, motivations, role behaviors, and problems. In particular, it aims to: 1) ascertain the factors that motivate the vendors to sell in the marketplace; 2) identify the problems that the vendors encounter in their work; 3) ascertain the effects of vending on the vendors' domestic role as wife and mother, and their coping strategies; and 4) determine, in turn, the effects of the vendors' domestic role on their vending activities.

## Methodology

In collecting data, the study employed four qualitative techniques, namely: participant-observation, key informant interview, ethnosemantics, and life history. Participant-observation conducted in the markets and at homes of respondents yielded a reconstruction of the vendors' day-to-day activities and insights particularly on market life and relationships. Key informant interviews with vendors and other market personages supplemented the participant-observation data, as well as elicited the historical background and features of the markets and vendors' characteristics. The use of ethnosemantics made it possible to obtain the distinctive way each respondent group categorized, coded, and defined the people and relationships in their market. And finally, life histories of a few selected vendors were taken to achieve a deeper understanding of their individual drives, aspirations, and urban living conditions.

## Research Sites

### The markets

The study was conducted in two adjacent markets in Quezon City, Metro Manila. Both are similar in the business hours observed as daily markets, the presence of both stallholders and non-stallholders, the availability of certain types of commodities, and the patronage they draw from local consumers.

The ways in which they differ, on the other hand, outweigh their similarities. Grande Market is a bigger, older, better-known, highly stable and organized market. It conducts business under one roof and behind orderly stalls, and observes legal selling practices which discriminate against the squatters, i.e., vendors without stalls. By comparison, Mini Market is newer and smaller. Once part of the residential sector adjacent to Grande Market, Mini Market has evolved as a logical site for the economic activities of many vendors who could not be accommodated in the larger market. This has led to a lack of planning, coordination, and management within the marketsite and a very high proportion of hawkers who call themselves sidewalk vendors. The vendors studied in Grande Market were the stallholders; in Mini Market, they were the hawkers.

### Market personages

As classified by the vendors, the people in the market are divided

169

into two broad groups called *tagarito* (insider) and *tagalabas* (outsider). According to the stallholders, the *tagarito* are comprised of the market's administrative staff and their vendor group. However, they view as *tagalabas* the following categories of people who come to the market: the squatters, piece laborers, middlemen or agents, moneylenders, certain government authorities such as the sanitary inspectors and policemen, customers, and their relatives and friends. On the other hand, the hawkers who sell on fixed streetside locations regard themselves along with stallholders as market insiders. Similarly, they also classify those hawkers without fixed selling places, customers, agents, certain government authorities like barangay officials and policemen, moneylenders, and visiting kins and friends as market outsiders.

The concept of *tagarito* apparently stems from the vendors' perception of their "right to vend" in the market. This right is manifested in their ability to sell from a *puwesto* (literally, place) which is represented by the stall (wooden structure) for stallholders and by the regular selling space on the sidewalk for the hawkers. The *puwesto* symbolizes a status of permanency and stability in the marketplace and in market vending.

**Findings of the Study**

Findings on the vendors' background, domestic and occupational characteristics, and aspirations are as follows. The stallholders are about five years older than the hawkers who are in their mid-thirties. The former have obtained some high school education and are more educated than the hawkers who have only reached the elementary grades. Although the stallholders are rural migrants and the hawkers are city born, both are long-term residents in urban squatter neighborhoods found near their work place.

These vendors who are married in their late teens are their families' sole or major breadwinner. Their spouses are generally unemployed but assist them at home and in the market. The children of the stallholders are fewer (4.5), older, and in the upper educational levels; those of the hawkers are more (6.2), younger, and in the elementary. Hence unlike the former, the latter spend more time at home and use over one-third of this time for child care and household tasks.

Both stallholders and hawkers took after their mother's vending occupation but would rather that their children finish schooling and find other jobs than follow their footsteps. The hawkers started to vend even before marriage and about six years earlier than the stallholders. The former sell primarily because of an inclination toward the trade, while the latter sell because for they see this work as a quick, lucrative means of earning an income.

Both stallholders and hawkers used to sell from non-fixed locations. They acquired their current market positions (stalls for the stallholders and allocated spaces for the hawkers) because of perceived advantages associated with legality (particularly for stallholders) or permanency and stability. The stallholders' choice of market within which to do business was influenced by friends or relatives who sold there. For the hawkers the market's proximity to the home was the major consideration in the selection of work site. Entry into the market was achieved through a formal application by the stallholders and through an informal awarding procedure for the hawkers. Since working in their respective markets, both have been predominantly selling vegetables because these commodities only require a low capital outlay.

The stallholders retail more varieties and a larger volume of vegetables than the hawkers. For both, however, seasonal vegetables comprise the bulk of their stocks. They obtain goods from three main sources: the wholesalers in the larger Divisoria, Balintawak, and Farmer's Markets; the wholesalers-stallholders in Grande Market( the larger of the two study sites); and the vendors and producers in provincial markets. These goods are generally bought on cash terms; purchases are usually undertaken in the evenings.

In terms of capitalization, the stallholders initially invested about three times more than the hawkers. Most of the original investments were obtained from personal or family savings. Over a three-year period, they have managed to enlarge their daily operating capital from ₱221 to ₱576 for the stallholders and from ₱76 to ₱219 for the hawkers. Daily sales return on invested capital is slightly higher for the hawkers who plough back 52 percent of capital input vis-a-vis the stallholders' 49 percent. The hawkers also net a slightly higher margin of profit (17 percent vis-a-vis the stallholders' 15 percent of total sales). The profits come to about ₱19.80/day for the hawkers (or ₱3.30/person/day for a family of six) and about twice this much for the stallholders. Portions of the profits are sometimes saved in the banks; or utilized to buy household appliances, livestock, or insurance policies; and spent on children's education.

Because vending is the vendors' as well as their families' sole or principal source of income, it is regarded as an essential means for continued survival in the city. The vendors neither wish to retire from vending nor desire to shift to another type of occupation. Instead they hope to further establish themselves in it: the stallholders would like to sell durable consumer goods like rice and dry foodstuffs while the hawkers

171

would like to move up to stallholding.

Findings on the specific objectives of the study reveal the following major insights.

First, the women vendors have been drawn to sell in the marketplace because of their poverty and lack of education and skills for other city jobs, the influence of a mother who sold for a living, the immediate cash returns that vending generates, and the relatively easy access to vending as an economic option.

Second, the most pressing problem of women vendors is shortage of capital (particularly for the hawkers) which is remedied by constantly dipping into cash savings, by selling or pawning household possessions, and by obtaining loans from kins, friends, and professional moneylenders who charge atrocious interest rates locally described as "five-six" (20 percent interest on short-term loans). In addition to this problem, the hawkers face the possibility of reprisals from certain market or police authorities for illegally plying their trade. In order to avert such a possibility, they forge ties with these authorities through the *bigayan* (mutual giving) relationship. For example, the hawkers provide the policemen with token goods in return for allowing them to sell uninterruptedly on the sidewalk.

Third, owing to the demands of market vending, the women vendors spend only about nine hours per day at home and most of this period is utilized for sleeping. Thus, they delegate much of their mothering and domestic responsibilities to spouses and older offsprings. They also resort to such strategies as rearing young children in the marketplace, placing these children in the care of surrogates (i.e., grandparents) who live in the provinces, and training children to become independent at an early age.

And lastly, the need to attend personally to their household responsibilities is the women vendors' principal cause for frequent interruptions in vending activities. The propensity for interruptions is higher among the hawkers who have bigger households and younger children. To ensure continued income during their absence from work, the vendors delegate the entire job of vending to family members or part of it to fellow vendors through the cultivation of *tulungan* (mutual helping) ties. These ties are forged with nearby vendors who return the capital but get to keep the profit on goods sold for another.

## Conclusions

The study indicates that there is only a slight difference in the quality of life between the two groups of vegetables vendors, with the stallholders

172

enjoying an edge over the hawkers as a result primarily of the legitimacy ascribed to the former's possession of stalls. The study also shows the vendors' attempt at self-reliance in raising their own capital and trying to keep afloat in the selling business. These attempts are, however, constantly threatened by the problem of capital depletion brought about by the need to meet basic family needs which their meager earnings from market sales cannot support. Nevertheless, despite the odds, the vendors are most likely to persevere principally out of necessity and the fact that selling has already become part of their way of life.

Therefore, efforts to help this group of low-income women should begin with helping them sustain their small-scale vending activities by providing access to credit or soft loans. The existing social network and peer support among the vendors can be tapped and strengthened by organizing them into a cohesive group that is capable of addressing their own problems, seeking and negotiating for external assistance, and safeguarding their members' interests. Moreover, experiences in development work have shown that in order to be effective, these efforts should be integrated with other programs or projects that seek to upgrade the welfare of the urban poor. The study's exploratory nature, however, limits the recommendations that can be made but suggests the need to undertake more representative and comparative researches particularly to support the appropriate programs and projects for the urban poor women who sell for a living.

## REFERENCES

Cuyos, Numeriano A. and Alexander Spoehr. 1976. "The Fish Supply of Cebu City: A Study of Two Wholesale Markets." *Philippine Quarterly of Culture and Society* 4 (3):160-98.

Davis, William G. 1973. *Social Relations in a Philippine Market: Self-Interest and Subjectivity.* Berkeley: University of California Press.

Guerrero, Sylvia H. 1975. *Hawkers and Vendors in Manila and Baguio.* Final Country Report submitted to the International Development Research Centre of Canada. Quezon City: Institute of Social

Welfare and Community Development, University of the Philippines.

Paolucci, Beatrize and others. 1976. *Women, Families and Non-Formal Learning Programs.* Supplementary Papers No. 6. Michigan: Institute for International Studies in Education, Michigan State University.

Szanton, Maria Cristina Blanc. 1972. *A Right to Survive: Subsistence Marketing in a Lowland Philippine Town.* University Park: Pennsylvania State University Press,

Tinker, Irene. 1976. "The Adverse Impact of Development on Women." Paper Prepared for American Association for the Advancement of Science (AAAS) Seminar on Women in Development, 15-18 June, Mexico City. Published in *Women and World Development.* Edited by Irene Tinker and Michelle Bo Bramsen. Washington D.C.: Overseas Development Council, AAAS.

# PERCEPTIONS OF NATIONAL LEADERS: THE CONSEQUENCES OF CONTRAST

PATRICIA B. LICUANAN

When this conference was planned and initially scheduled for February 21-22, the topic assigned to me was "Perceptions of National Leaders." At the time President Marcos was still in power and I prepared to write a paper on Manilans' perceptions of Ferdinand Marcos. The dramatic events of February—the February 7 election and its aftermath and then the revolution of February 22-25—which ended the 20-year reign of Ferdinand Marcos, made him, by his own recent account, "irrelevant." So while the topic of my paper has not changed, the content has had to be completely altered as instead of Ferdinand Marcos, we focus on Cory Aquino and how people see her.

Towards the end of his rule, President Marcos and his government were the subject of various nationwide surveys. This type of data is not yet available for President Aquino. This paper attempts, nonetheless, to describe Manilans' perceptions of Cory Aquino based on limited data. The data for this paper come mainly from content analysis of letters to the editors of four daily newspapers. The newspapers were *The Philippine Daily Inquirer, The Manila Times, Ang Pahayagang Malaya,* and *The Daily Express.* Newspapers with letters to the editorial section were selected. Because these were newspapers in English and because letters to the editor were used, the views expressed were generally middle-class views. It is also accepted that people who write letters to the editor may not be representative of the typical newspaper reader. Most of the letters were from Metro Manila.

The period involved was March 1-21, a period of three weeks. For each week, two issues for each newspaper were randomly selected. For these issues all the letters published that day were analyzed. Only letters about President Aquino and her government were included. Using content analysis, the main themes in the letters were identified. Each letter could have more than one theme. This paper will report only on reactions to

175

President Aquino, leaving out for the time being direct reactions to her Cabinet and reactions to the new government in general. Reactions will be classified into positive reactions, negative, and others. Direct quotes from letters typifying the themes will presented.

## Positive Reactions

The main themes which can clearly be identified as positive are:

*Cory Aquino is the legitimate president.* These letters express the view that the manner in which she assumed the powers of government is legitimate, that she was the real winner in the February 7th election, that she was mandated by people's power, and that now the issue of her legitimacy should be put to rest. For example:

"We are morally convinced, as our people themselves are, that Ms. Corazon Aquino was the duly elected President in the last special presidential election. We join our people in applauding her proclamation and inauguration as the new president of the Republic of the Philippines."

*Praise and approval.* These letters express joy that she is president. They express the view that Cory Aquino has a special calling and special role in history. For example:

"You are destined by God to lead our people to righteousness... to justice, freedom and democracy."

*Congratulations, good wishes, and pledges of support.* This is expressed in the following quotes:

"Reluctantly, you took up the cause of reconciliation and succeeded in crumbling the walls of the dictatorship. By your example our people tore the chains of fear to regain their freedom ... congrats, Madam President, Godspeed."

"We extend our congratulations and pledge our support for a government based on popular participation and public accountability."

"Congrats and expect us to be always behind you when you move to regain our lost paradise."

"Take courage. The power of the people is with you."

"We make a solemn pledge to PRES. AQUINO in her effort to establish a just and independent government that is truly accountable to the people."

*Gratitude.* These letters thank Cory Aquino for her special role in the recent events and especially for the good feeling Filipinos now have for themselves. For example:

"Thank you Cory for reawakening in us the sense of national pride."

"How do I feel now that the Marcoses have gone? Like a person recovering from the painless removal of hemorrhoids. Thank you."

*Trust in the sincerity of her intentions.* These letters express the belief that Cory Aquino ran for the presidency out of a sincere desire to help the country. She is viewed as someone not of the usual political mold and therefore not interested in power.

"President Aquino has no desire to perpetuate herself in power ... is sincere in her desire to bring the country back on the road to progress ... if she declares hers a revolutionary government, it will be to create order out of chaos, discipline out of near-anarchy."

*Satisfaction with initial performance and pronouncements.* These letters approve of her performance in general and express approval for specific pronouncements, such as the release of political prisoners and Cabinet appointments. For example:

"President Aquino's remark for a swift and meaningful action for the immediate recovery of hidden wealth of the Marcoses and cronies deserves people's support."

## Negative Reactions

Negative reactions to President Cory Aquino may be classified into the following:

*Unacceptable/inadequate program of government.* For example:

"We did not vote for Mr. Marcos ... but neither did we vote for you because of our perception that the program of government you espoused appeared to be not only vague but also did not really differ from the IMF-dictated program which Mr. Marcos had been implementing and which brought untold sufferings to millions of our countrymen."

"We hope that the performance of your government will prove our misgivings as totally misplaced."

*Dissatisfaction with initial performance/errors of omission and commission.*

1. The reconciliation and justice issue. This includes negative reactions to: seeming reluctance to remove people from the past regime,

compromising and yielding to pressure, not being hard enough on the criminals of the Marcos era. For example:

"We deplore the apparent reluctance of the new government to remove some propagandists, military hatchmen and intellectually dishonest technocrats of the old regime, ostensibly in the spirit of national reconciliation. We would like to see the warm hand of friendship given instead to our brothers and sisters who have suffered the most under the old regime (the revolutionaries, political prisoners)."

"Is Cory Aquino now compromising for so-called 'practical' purposes or is she giving in to pressures from the powers of the "third force"? I believe she is treading on dangerous ground (by starting to yield to pressures from the likes of Major General Olivas)."

"Madame President, we believe that we must try to heal the nation's wounds and reconcile with those who did us wrong ... but please do not reopen the nation's wound and the bitter memories of the past by allowing your administration to be tainted with the bloody henchmen of the Marcos regime."

"General amnesty has been given, but sad to say, it is to the wrong parties. People who were victims of injustices committed by the past regime remain incarcerated ... while the perpetrators of injustices have been allowed to leave the country in comfortable private jets, and those who chose to remain have been proclaimed heroes."

"I am appealing to our beloved President Aquino that seeking justice is totally different from seeking vengeance. Please, in your capacity as President of the Philippines, let justice rule the land."

2. Violations of the Constitution. These letters point out the unconstitutionality of some of her pronouncements as well as those of her ministers, such as asking the Supreme Court members and the local government officials to resign.

3. Lack of competence. For example:

"Her first *faux pas* at the Club Filipino ... clearly showed her frightening lack of competence in governing."

4. Opposition to Cabinet appointments and the criteria used for appointments. For example:

"After the announcement of your Cabinet ... I could not help feeling somewhat let down. We ordinary people accept them only because of you ... and there is still time to review your selection."

"She should choose Cabinet members and other officials strictly on the basis of integrity and capability ... never out of false sense of gratitude ... should distinguish sycophants, opportunists and turncoats from truly capable public servants."

"It seems to me most unfair for her to retain a man to head the Central Bank of the Philippines under whom the peso came to an unprecedented low and peso bills with the same serial numbers were circulated. Are we so bereft of financial geniuses that Jobo Fernandez had to be retained? I'd like to know from Pres. Aquino just who advised her to keep Jobo on."

5. Opposition to the possible dissolution of certain government entities. For example:

"We are disheartened with the unofficial attempt to dissolve the Ministry of Human Settlements despite your call for reconciliation ... We think this would be unfair for us. We are appealing for your understanding that we are equally dedicated to continuously serve the communities."

6. Opposition to the process used in appointing local government officials. For example:

"Politically, it would be unwise for the President to continue the (local) appointments herself. If she did, she would just unnecessarily sow discontent among her supporters and risk alienating many of them ... she would be imposing upon the entire Filipino nation ... a dictatorial maneuver."

"Aquino should reconsider her decision not to hold local elections until the economy is finally recovered ... Elections are the very foundation of democracy."

**Other Reactions**

Under this category were classified letters or themes that did not express clearly positive or negative reactions. Instead, these letters expressed expectations and qualified support, and made demands, recommendations, and appeals.

*Expectations.* Expectations expressed were to manifest greater independence from outside dictation which brought ruin to her predecessor, to keep her campaign promises, to be different from Marcos, "to use her popular mandate to institute true reforms in society not merely to change the forces of those in government or to put behind bars those responsible for the heinous crime committed against your late husband."

179

*Qualified support.* These letters expressed willingness to extend all-out support for the Aquino government; however, should the changes in government prove to be merely illusory or should things get even worse than before, there is the threat to "oppose your government and struggle to direct the attention of the people to a correct path."

*Demands, recommendations, appeals.* These include a wide range of inputs on such issues as defining the limits of reconciliation, holding of local elections, removal of military bases, declaration of a revolutionary government, abolition of business monopolies, the formation of a consumers' bureau, recalling of military men holding civilian positions, dismantling vestiges of Marcos regime such as Imelda Avenue, Imelda Park, and Marcos Highway.

## General Trends

It would seem that in general the reaction to President Aquino is that of support. This support is seen in statements expressing praise and approval, defending her legitimacy, conveying congratulations and pledges of support, and expressing gratitude, faith in her sincerity, and approval of her performance and pronouncements. Support is also seen in constructive comments on what she should do in order to do a good job as president. These are expressions of expectations, qualified support and demands, recommendations, and appeals.

These statements of support make up 76% of the comments, while only 24% of the themes can be classified as negative or disapproving. It is acknowledged that the choice of newspapers may have biased the responses toward more positive trends. It is felt, however, that the value of the data lies less in possible quantitative trends but more in the qualitative identification of types of reactions. The negative reactions point out the inadequacy of her program of government, that it is no different from that of Mr. Marcos. Dissatisfaction is also expressed with her performance in such areas as the reconciliation and justice issue, violations of the Constitution, her general lack of competence, the dissolution of certain government entities, Cabinet appointments made and criteria used, and the process for local government appointments.

## The Consequences of Contrast

When Cory Aquino was campaigning for president she stressed the fact that she was the exact opposite of President Marcos. And indeed people saw in this inexperienced, sincere, and honest housewife a crusader who would, if she became president, give us a government that was radically different from the corrupt, tyrannical, and self-serving Marcos government. And the people wanted her. Cory Aquino is a people's president the way no other president in Philippine history ever was. She was nominated for candidacy by a genuine people's draft; she was elected despite unparalleled fraud, and was finally installed by people's power after a bloodless four-day revolution.

So people have a lot invested in Cory Aquino. They want her to succeed. She has come to be perceived as an important key to a better future for the Philippines and millions of Filipinos. Because she does represent people's hopes there is a lot of support and goodwill towards her and her government. But ironically enough, precisely because of these hopes, people are more impatient with Cory Aquino than they ever were with the hated Marcos. They are quick to criticize, quick to express disappointment with the flaws in her government.

Cory Aquino was perceived as a radical shift away from Ferdinand Marcos. As such her government must be radically different as well. Any signs of similarity to the old regime—old faces, old practices—are immediately alarming.

One of the most devastating psychological effects of the Marcos regime was the loss of credibility of national leaders. They were generally viewed as incompetent, dishonest, and self-serving, although it is only now that we are beginning to realize the extent of their perfidy. Related to this was their lack of accountability to the people. They did not seem to consider themselves accountable to the people they had vowed to serve, and the people in turn had grown over the years to expect little from them.

Today, with credible leadership, we have recovered our sense of accountability, and so the people's expectations of Cory Aquino are tremendous. In a way these expectations are not really fair, but at the same time, they make perfect sense, and Cory Aquino should not want it any other way.

The expectations are unfair because, perhaps in our jubilation over the end of a 20-year dictatorial regime, the contrast perspective has led us to demand more than what may be realistic in an imperfect world. Thus President Aquino has asked the people to be patient, and this is a fair request.

On the other hand there are legitimate criticisms and demands that serve as valuable feedback to a president who is sensitive and listens to the people. Also, most of these demands, realistic or otherwise, are signs of an

181

awakened citizenry, an optimistic people who now believe that change is truly possible. These are messages to Cory Aquino that the liberation process she vowed to support is well on its way.

# POLITICS AND TEACHERS' ORGANIZATIONS IN METRO MANILA

J. PROSPERO E. DE VERA III

## Introduction

One of the most significant developments in interest articulation and pressure politics in the Philippines during the past five years has been the growth of what might be termed "teachers' power" through the formation of teachers' organizations at both sectoral and regional levels. These organizations have been linked together into a national alliance capable of mobilizing teachers for mass actions on a national scale. From the protest against administrative anomalies in MSU-Tawi-Tawi in 1983 to the more recent advice of Mayor Pablo Cuneta *"na mag-hostess na lang kayo sa Ermita,"* the teachers' movement has indeed assumed a different character from its predecessor in the 1960's and 70's. Indeed, one may be so tempted as to assume that the teachers' movement has finally come of age. But questions do remain. What is the status of teachers organizing in the country today? How does one make sense out of the proliferation of so many acronyms representing teachers' organizations? What problems confront teachers' organizations and teachers organizing? What are the prospects for teachers' power being used to bring about democratization in today's society?

Before these questions can be answered, perhaps it is important to consider the following points:

1) Teachers and education personnel number around 500,000 and as an occupational group make up 60% of all professionals in the country. In the public school sector alone, there are approximately 350,000 teachers working in some 35,113 schools all over the archipelago;[1]

2) The educational system is in constant touch with some 17 million students—or close to a third of the total population of the country;

3) While so much has been demanded from the educational sector, it has been the victim of official government apathy and neglect. The percentage allocated to education in the national budget has drastically dropped from 28.4% in 1965 to 13.7% in 1985;[2]

4) The school system links all islands and municipalities and all sectors in the country. Schools can be found in the upland communities of the Cordillera, the fishing communities in Batanes, and within the walls of exclusive villages in Makati. If developed, it can become the biggest and most well-organized network of communication and mobilization and can emerge as a formidable force in pressure politics;

5) Between 1969 and 1985, there have been ten major national strikes initiated by Metro Manila teachers fighting for their economic rights. In the last five years alone, there has been at least one major national strike every year. The mass protest of September 1985 covered close to six cities and twenty-five provinces, including the cities and municipalities of Metro Manila, and a calculated 30,000 teachers participated in one form or another.[3]

It becomes very clear in the aforementioned statements that more than any other institution or professional group, the schools system and teachers have the strongest link with all sectors and areas in the country today. If properly organized, it can be transformed into a formidable force capable not only of articulating teachers' rights but in bringing about social transformation.

This paper will attempt to tackle the following points:

1) An identification and classification of the various teachers' organizations existing within the country, and in particular, of those in Metro Manila;

2) A probe into the internal dynamics present within each organization and in the teachers' sector with respect to leadership, issues addressed, and tactics used; and

3) Some preliminary observations on the factors that affect the success or failure of teachers' organizations to achieve sectoral demands and affect societal change.

## The Formal School System: An Overview

The formal school system in the Philippines consists of three levels: primary, secondary, and tertiary. Elementary education takes up the first six years of a student's academic life,[4] followed by four years of secondary education in high school, and finally, the tertiary level composed of four to five years of instruction in a disciplinal or degree program. Altogether, the Filipino student spends fourteen years of his/her early life within the classroom. He/she enrolls in Grade 1 at age seven and finishes college at age twenty-one with a degree in the liberal arts, engineering, commerce, or in a similar curricula. Another way of looking at and studying the school system is by classifying schools according to the type of ownership and rationale by which they were created. Using this classification, schools can be divided either into public schools or private schools. The public school sector can be subdivided into two smaller subsectors—public elementary and high schools, on the one hand, and state colleges and universities, on the other. Private schools can be divided into either sectarian or non-sectarian institutions.

Public schools are established at state expense to provide general education to the population as provided for in the Constitution. Public elementary and high schools are spread throughout the archipelago and as a group form the largest single block among educational institutions. In all, there are about 34,794 public schools in the country employing the services of some 350,000 teachers and education personnel.[5] The more notable public schools in Manila include the Ramon Magsaysay-Manila (the biggest in terms of school population—10,000), Ramon Magsaysay-Cubao, Torres High School, Arellano High School, and Mapa High School.

The subsector composed of state colleges and universities is much smaller in number but is likewise distributed nationwide. There are approximately 48 of these institutions. Schools representative of this sector include the different campuses of the University of the Philippines (Diliman, Los Baños, Baguio, Clark, Iloilo, and Visayas), Polytechnic University of the Philippines (PUP), Philippine Normal College (PNC), and the Central Luzon State University (CLSU) in Nueva Ecija. There are also vocational and technical schools built by the government to cover both secondary and tertiary levels. Included under this group are the Eulogio Amang Rodriguez Institute of Technology (EARIST) and the Marikina School of Arts and Trade (MASAT). There are approximately 40,000 personnel employed by state colleges and universities.

Private schools differ from public schools in that they are either run

185

by religious congregations or individuals who are also the owners/founders of such schools. Private sectarian schools are run by religious congregations while non-sectarian schools are established by private individuals, families, or corporations. There are 1,300 private sectarian schools run by various religious denominations employing close to 55,000 educational personnel.[6] The majority of these schools are Catholic institutions with a sprinkling of Protestant, Iglesia ni Kristo, and Muslim participation. Ateneo de Manila University (SJ), De La Salle University (FSC), Adamson University (CM), University of Santo Tomas (OP), Colegio de San Juan de Letran, and the Sisters' schools—St. Joseph's College, St. Scholastica's, St. Theresa's, and Assumption Convent are all Catholic-run or -supported sectarian schools. Protestant denominations are represented by Trinity College (Angelican-Aglipay) and Philippine Christian University (UCCP Methodist) in Manila; and by Silliman University (Presbyterian), Central Philippine University (Baptist) and Brent School outside of Manila.[7] The Iglesia ni Kristo sect runs the New Era College in Quezon City.

Private non-sectarian schools are concentrated mostly in what is called the "university belt" area. Far Eastern University and the University of the East both have student populations numbering between 50,000-75,000; Jose Rizal College, Centro Escolar, Philippine Women's University, National College of Business and Arts, Philippine School of Business Administration, and Manila Central University are just some of the many schools under this category. The majority of the 2,600 non-sectarian institutions are found in Metro Manila and collectively comprise 55% of all schools at the tertiary level. In Manila alone, there are thirteen private non-sectarian institutions located either in the Quiapo district or along Taft Avenue. These schools are owned by big private business and leading bureaucratic families like the Fabellas (Jose Rizal College), Aranetas (Gregorio Araneta University Foundation, FEATI), Benitezes (Philippine Women's University), Reyeses (Far Eastern University), Laurels (Lyceum and National Teachers College), and the Gullas in Cebu (University of the Visayas). The owners of the private schools are organized around the Philippine Association of Colleges and Universities, otherwise known as PACU.[8]

## Teachers' Organization: from the Traditional to the Militant

It is always difficult and sometimes arbitrary to put labels on and classify organizations into distinct groups. Given the number of teachers' organizations, however, makes it imperative that such a grouping be made for purposes of discussion. For want of better terms, I will be using the terms *traditional* or *militant* to classify teachers' organizations. The term *traditional* is used to designate organizations that "address traditional issues using traditional methods" while *militant* refers to groups that have gone "beyond traditional issues, concepts of leadership, and are using other methods in addition to traditional ones." There are three main areas where the difference between traditional and militant organizations can be found. These are in terms of: 1) leadership, 2) approach, and 3) perception and identification of issues.

## Leadership

Traditional organizations are leadership-oriented and personalistic in management style. They are usually dominated by teacher-leaders who have virtually become lifetime presidents. Some of these organizations surface only once a year and many have leaders who have ghost following. The Public School Teachers' Association (PSTA) in particular exhibits traditional patterns of leadership. Local PSTAs involve heads of school departments and some elected leaders are propped up by the administration. As such they are subject to political machination during mass actions. Some of them do not assert teachers' interests when they perceive that such pursuit will conflict with the decision of the Ministry of Education, Culture and Sports (MECS) or the national government. Personalized leadership can also be seen in the manner in which leaders view their role in the struggle to pursue economic demands. Many leaders consider such struggles as personal battles instead of treating them as collective actions in behalf of the whole teachers' sector. If such actions fail or succeed, the results are treated and seen as their personal glory or downfall.[9] This leadership character seems to have been internalized by most teacher-members who rely on the actions of the leaders as a prerequisite for their own actions and treat the results in the same light.

In contrast, the primary aim of most militant organizations and alliances is the advocacy of working through collective leadership and efforts. Although it may be argued by some that those who won in the elections of ACT, SCUFA, POTENT, and similar organizations were themselves the most popular and visible, the electoral process can be considered as more democratized. A point of difference may be seen in the near absence of charges of electioneering and rigged elections among militant groups. The traditional PSTAs, on the other hand, have had long histories of electoral disputes among the candidates who charge each other at both personal and legal levels. The division of work and

187

organizational structure also indicate a consciousness of collectivity between the leaders and the members of such groups.

## Approaches and Methods

Traditional organizations are highly legalistic and over-dependent on the "law" — decrees, LOIs, and directives issued by education and state officials. It seems that these groups are convinced of the validity of their cause but are equally overpowered by the legal system. The teachers probably see their adversary, in this case the government, as too powerful and legally knowledgeable and are correspondingly stifled from taking more militant methods in pursuing their demands. Laws and decrees are to a great extent seen as "sacred covenants" between the teacher as a "public servant" and the administrators and state officials as "paternal" authorities. In the last public school teachers' strike, the bone of contention between the teachers and then Education Minister Laya was not on the moral legality of the "no work, no pay" principle of the latter, but rather, in his assurance or moral pledge not to prosecute the former in court. In choosing the mechanisms to achieve their demands, the teachers have placed a premium on negotiations, petitions, and the follow-up of papers through the bureaucratic machinery of either the school or the state. It might be said that this kind of approach is overly procedural and a stickler to the legal aspect of the demands presented. It can at its worst form be passive, dependent, and self-serving.

The term "militant organizations," and whatever connotations are attached to it, is used to label newly-emerged, cause-oriented groups whose approach and tactics are qualitatively different from their predecessors. Since these teachers' organizations assert the need to situate economic demands within political demands, the avenues open to their members are decidedly bigger than those of the PSTA's. It can take the form of the more traditional ribbon-tying, negotiation, and follow-up, to the more militant mass-actions like barricades, pickets, and other forms of pressure politics. Militant organizations explore not only the options favored by their counterparts, but also extra-legal venues available to acquire their goals.

## Issues

Traditional organizations respond to traditional problems. Traditional issues include demands for salary increase, implementation of wage-orders, following up loans, death benefits, and retirement pay from the GSIS. Many teachers' organizations regard teachers' economic demands as a priority which is correct and valid. But what separates traditional groups from their militant counterparts is that teachers and leaders in the former see the economic issues but fail to relate them to other equally important political issues. For example, traditional teachers' organizations fail or neglect to address non-economic concerns like academic freedom, democratization of the educational institutions' policy-making process, and the right to self-organization. Many teachers in the public schools still view these areas as the concern and prerogative of MECS officials or their own school administrators. In almost all of the massive public school teachers' strikes from the 1970's until today, talks revolved mainly around economic benefits, and once these were promised, the strike was immediately lifted.

Militant organizations see the need to politicize teachers and relate their plight to the bigger economic and political contradictions existing within the country. The issues presented include economic demands — P.D. 451, MECS Orders No. 23 and No. 115, salary increase and standardization, and the Education Act of 1982. In addition, various symposia and fora provide the setting for discussions on teachers' rights and welfare, miseducation, social orientation seminars, and in the furtherance of politicization, mass actions have been held in the U.S. Embassy, Liwasang Bonifacio, and just recently, during the visit of US Defense Secretary Caspar Weinberger.

## Teachers' Organizations: from National to Sectoral

The Association of Concerned Teachers or ACT is a nationwide alliance of teachers and teachers' organizations committed to the idea of fostering "teachers' unity for a nationalist and liberating education."[10] The alliance was formed from the pioneering efforts of teachers from private schools and state colleges and universities who picked up the cudgels in opposing what was seen as legislation contrary to the needs of our academic institutions. This legislation was the Education Act of 1982 which drew howls of protest from both the private and public school teachers in its inability to provide teachers' rights to self-organization and its silence on academic freedom. The organizers included Feliciano Casbadillo of the MPSTA for the public schools, Etta Rosales for the private schools, Ponciano Bennagen from the U.P., and Raul Segovia from the state colleges and universities. Since its launching in mid-1982, the ACT has slowly grown into a national alliance of teachers' groups covering the major regions in the country and setting the framework for a nationally coordinated teachers movement in the years to come. As an alliance which is national in scope, the ACT is organized as follows:

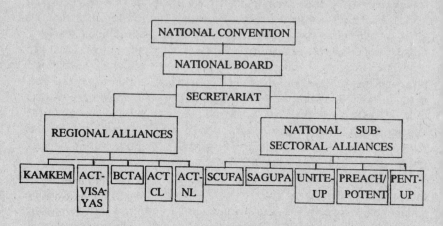

On the national level, the association has a national convention and a national board where regional and subsectoral representation is provided. There is an executive committee handling the different functions of the organization. Five Manila-based teachers' organizations represent national subsectoral alliances – SCUFA, SAGUPA, PENT-UP, PREACH/POTENT, and UNITE-UP. There are regional alliances representing five major areas outside Manila. In Mindanao, the Kahugpunan ng mga Mantutudlo ng Kawani sa Mindanao (KAMKEM) was started by 40 teachers in Cagayan de Oro City from May 21 to 23, 1982 in what was initially known as KAMMI. It now has 9,540 members on a regionwide basis.[11] KAMKEM is affiliated with the rest of the ACT chapters in Mindanao, with ACT-Davao (6,375 members) serving as the leading city-wide organization. There is an ACT-Visayas composed of the Panay Alliance of Concerned Teachers (PACT), Alliance of Negros Teachers (ANT), Negros Oriental Teachers Alliance (NORTA), plus ACT chapters in Bacolod, Aklan, Antique, Northern Samar and Silay City. Altogether, there are some 11,000 teacher-members in this region.[12] In the Bicol region, the Bicol Concerned Teachers Alliance (BCTA) is the region-wide group and there are ACT chapters in Camarines Norte and Sur, Albay, and Sorsogon. ACT affiliates in Central Luzon include ACT-Tarlac, Bulacan Alliance of Concerned Teachers (BACT), Nueva Ecija Concerned Teachers Alliance (NECTA), and ACT-Pampanga which is the biggest with 5,000 members.[13] The fifth regional alliance is the newly formed ACT-Northern Luzon based in Baguio City.

190

**Metro Manila Based Teachers' Organizations**

## CLASSIFICATION

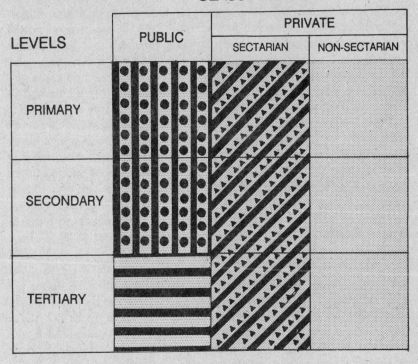

| LEVELS | PUBLIC | PRIVATE | |
| --- | --- | --- | --- |
| | | SECTARIAN | NON-SECTARIAN |
| PRIMARY | | | |
| SECONDARY | | | |
| TERTIARY | | | |

SCUFA
State Colleges and Universities
   Faculty Alliance

SAGUPA
Samahan ng Mga Gurong
   Pampulitika

PREACH
Private Educators for Action and
   Change

PSTA'S
Public School Teachers Associations

UNITE-UP
United Teachers and Employees of
   the U.P.

PENT-UP
Private Educators and Non-Teaching
   University Personnel Alliance

POTENT
Progressive Organization of
   Teachers and Employees for
   Nationalist Transformation

191

The SCUFA or State Colleges and Universities Faculty Alliance was formed under the initiative of teacher-leaders from four state colleges and universities in Manila—the PNC, PUP, TUP (Technological University of the Philippines) and EARIST. A series of meetings was held from August to November 1982 among the four schools which were getting impatient with government inaction on their demands for the standardization and upgrading of teachers' salaries. The series of dialogues and meetings gave the teachers an opportunity to ventilate and compare common issues and problems confronting their sector.[14] The organization was launched in December 1982 and immediately conducted a series of sit-down protests and massive leave within the member schools and in the MECS in March of the following year. The mass action succeeded in increasing the hiring rate of teachers from ₱940 to ₱1,272 a month and corresponding increases in all teaching levels. As an association, the SCUFA is committed to the pursuance of the economic welfare of its members, promotion of academic freedom, and nationalism, and in developing linkages with other professional and multi-sectoral organizations for the advancement of democratic rights.[15] It is currently presided over by Rene Romero of the PNC.

The counterpart of the SCUFA in the public school sector is the Samahan ng Mga Gurong Pampolitika (SAGUPA) under the leadership of Oscar Pascual. This organization emerged from the protest of public school teachers in 1983 against the "deductions" made by the MECS on their salaries because of an alleged computer error committed in the computation of wages. The inability of the local PSTAs to solve the issue prompted a group of teachers to organize the SAGUPA in October 1983 and eventually affiliated it with the ACT. The membership of this organization is drawn heavily from the rank and file of public school teachers who are members of both the ACT and SAGUPA. Among the Manila-based groups, the SAGUPA plays the crucial role in the teachers' movement because it is connected with the public school teachers. Since 1983, it has played a leading role in every teachers' strike in Metro Manila by agitating the local PSTA members and officers to adopt more militant methods during mass actions. The organization also adopted a boycott stance in the 1984 elections. There are about 2,000 members nationwide with about 1,000 of these coming from Manila.[16]

The Private Educators and Non-Teaching University Personnel (PENT-UP) Alliance was launched on December 8, 1984 with the aim of consolidating various employee and faculty unions and associations into an alliance capable of addressing the specific problems faced by private schools. It was created against the backdrop of many questions created by contradicting guidelines in the implementation of PD 451, Wage Order No. 2, and MECS Order No. 23 regarding the allocation of funds produced by tuition fee increases.[17] It filed and won its case in the Supreme Court on the issue of funds allocation. Atty. Greg Fabros of Centro Escolar University (CEU) presides over the organization.

Similarly situated in the private, sectarian school sector is the Private Educators for Action and Change or PREACH. Organized on June 25, 1983 the organization attempted to pursue both the economic rights of teachers and their politicization in order to have "relevant education in line with the promotion of teachers' economic and democratic rights."[18] PREACH members actively participated either as speakers or facilitators in teachers-training programs and regularly sent delegations to rallies and other forms of mass action. However, it soon ran into serious membership problems as it was unable to draw more members into its fold, membership being individual in this organization. This was openly admitted in its report in the ACT Convention in 1984 saying that "it has been able to attract only a few progressive teachers from different private schools." They proposed the creation of a clearer program of action to attract more people to join.[19]

With the intensification of the economic and political crisis brought about by the Aquino assassination, the private school teachers felt the need to enlarge the organizing activities to include all education personnel in both private and public schools into a more militant and politicized body that would pursue national rather than sectoral interests.[20] PREACH was reorganized into POTENT (Progressive Organization of Teachers and Employees for Nationalist Transformation) in July 1985 with the call for a "commitment to fight tyranny, imperialism and all forms of injustice, exploitation and oppression" in unity with other sectors in "the struggle for a truly just, democratic and free society."[21] The membership of POTENT is currently placed at 300 with some 100 active members.[22]

In the public elementary and high schools, teachers are organized around two main traditional institutions – their local PSTA and the national PPSTA. There are local PSTAs in every city, municipality and province in the country. The PPSTA as a national organization accepts members from all areas in the Philippines. Both organizations function as "civic clubs" offering help in securing loans, death benefits, and retirement claims. Among the PSTAs in Metro Manila, the MPSTA of Ana Rose Roxas consistently leads massive teachers' strikes with the support of the other PSTAs.

The leadership of the MPSTA, in particular, has suffered problems in the past years. Federico Ricafort was expelled from the presidency by the executive board in 1983 while Feliciano Casbadillo formed a rebel faction of the association at the same time. The PPSTA, on the other hand, has been meriting media attention because of scandals that rocked the body since 1979. The President at that time already placed the organization under the supervision of the MECS by signing LOI 860. An audit conducted by Sycip, Gorres & Velayo (SGV) in 1985 revealed that about ₱50-₱70 million had been lost due to numerous irregularities.[23] There is a move by the new government to implement government control over this 185,000-strong, mutual benefit organization.[24]

## The Teachers Sector Today: Some Observations

The following can be observed with respect to the status of teachers organizing in the country today:

1) Traditional teachers' organizations (specially the PSTAs in Metro Manila) are more effective than the militant organizations in terms of: a) organization; b) mobilization and pressure politics. This situation, however, may not necessarily follow when one talks of areas outside Metro Manila.

2) The militant teachers' groups, on the other hand, are better prepared in addressing sectoral and national issues, in political education, and linking with other cause-oriented groups;

3) The potential for teachers organizing remains with the public school sector. Unfortunately, this sector continues to be traditional in its organization and direction. Two other sectors need organizational attention—the private non-sectarian schools in general, and tertiary level private schools whose teachers prefer membership in cause-oriented groups rather than teachers' organizations;

4) The teachers' movement in the country is slowly becoming militant. In spite of its growing militancy, however, much still has to be done before we can see a nationally united teachers' movement capable of playing a leading role in social transformation.

The major strength of traditional teachers' organizations lies in its quantitative character. In addition, most PSTAs were organized in the 1940's and through time, they have achieved stability. The numerical superiority of the public and elementary school organizations can be observed in figures or in the percentage of institutions covering each sector. There are 333,912 teachers in the public schools compared to 49,893 in private schools (97,239 if the tertiary level for private schools is added).[25] Distribution of schools on a percentage basis are as follows: primary level — public 90% and private 10%; secondary level — public 60% vs private 40%; and tertiary level — public 10% and private 90%.[26] Undoubtedly, the potential for mass organization remains with the public school sector. The MPSTA has 17,000 members while PREACH/POTENT and PENT-UP number less than a thousand. The private non-sectarian schools remain largely untapped in terms of membership in militant organizations.

There are two other factors that are responsible for the quantitative and organizational strength of PSTAs. First, they act largely as socio-civic clubs fully supported by the school authorities and thus appeal to the rank-and-file teachers. On the other hand, ACT-affiliated organizations can easily be labelled as "red" and "militant" by school authorities, thus discouraging teachers from joining the association. Thus, school administrators play a vital role in organizational growth. Organizations like POTENT and PENT-UP recruit members, mostly progressive teachers in Catholic-run schools like St. Scholastica's, St. Joseph's and St. Theresa's because the thrust on education for justice by the nuns allows a wider space for political dissent within the institution. The same cannot be said of many private non-sectarian schools, and even of reactionary Catholic universities where teachers are mostly at the mercy of the whims of their administrators. Thus, the difficulty in recruiting members.

Finally, one has to understand the nature of the organizations and how it appeals to prospective teacher-members. For the public school teacher, underpaid and overworked as she is, the platform presented by militant organizations asks for more of her time — time for re-education, time for symposia and discussion groups, and time to attend mass actions. In the context of the public school setting, time is simply not available.

It is probably vital to mention at this point why the Metro Manila area is very important to the teachers' movement. As the center of educational, political, and economic life in the Philippines, events and movements in Manila (like the EDSA revolution in February) are closely watched by groups outside the region. The region is also crucial to teachers in organizing because it has the biggest concentration of teachers. It is the center of communications, and developments here are easily projected nationwide. I would not, however, draw the conclusion that teachers' mass actions in Manila precipitate similar moves outside the region. On the contrary, statistics have shown that militant teachers' organizations in the provinces are as equally capable of intensified and prolonged mass action as those in Manila.

The militant organizations are more effective in addressing sectoral and national issues, in research work, and in linking with other sectoral groups. SCUFA and UNITE-UP are two organizations whose aims include research work. Both SCUFA and UNITE-UP conduct research on the salary scale of teachers, look for funding sources, and present proposals to government ministries like the Budget and MECS. UNITE-UP studies the budget and administrative policies of U.P. in order to balance academic and non-academic demands, students' interests, and administration's moves on tuition increases. The similarity in the direction taken by both groups is due largely to their being government-funded institutions sharing common policies and wages. Members of POTENT and PENT-UP come from differently owned and administered schools. Besides, both organizations give emphasis on areas outside research. These groups tend to rely on materials provided by the ACT, TCP, and the Education Forum for their discussion purposes. In all, it can be said that Manila-based teachers' organizations are more advanced in research than those outside the area. Within Metro Manila, militant groups conduct more research than their PSTA counterparts.

Teachers' organizing in Metro Manila in the last five years has developed at a very fast pace. At the national level, regional, provincial and sectoral organizations have proliferated outside the traditional ones. Already, a high level of inter-organizational linkage exists between militant teachers' organizations, education-related institutions like the EF, TCP, and IBON, cause oriented-groups, and to a limited extent (the case of MPSTA) the PSTAs. With improvement in organizational approach and leadership, the emergence of a successful nationalist, pro-people, and democratic teachers' movement is not far off in the future.

## NOTES

1. Ministry of Education, Culture and Sports (MECS), *Philippine Education Indicators 1965-1985* (Manila: MECS, 1985), p. 3.

2 *Ibid.*, p 3.

3 *ACT Forum*, April 1985.

4. For an initial discussion on the educational system in the country consult Diego Quejada's "The State of Philippine Education Today" in Education Forum, *Towards Relevant Education: A General Sourcebook for Teachers* (Q.C.: E.F., 1986), pp. 28-38.

5. MECS, *op. cit.,* p. 3.

6. Quejada, *op. cit.*, p. 32.

7. Arthur L. Carson, *The Story of Philippine Education* (Q.C.: New Day, 1978), pp. 110-112.

8. Teachers Center of the Philippines (TCP), *The State of Private Schools Today* (Q.C.: 1983), pp. 2-4.

9. "Grasping the Correct Methods of Leadership," ACT Discussion Paper, p. 7.

10. "What the Alliance Means to Us," *ACT Forum*, December 1982, also in "1983: The Year of the Teacher—A Year of Struggle," ACT-Philippines, January 21, 1984.

11. Reports on the Affiliates of ACT-Philippines,, mimeographed, p. 2.

12. *Ibid.,* p. 1.

13. *Ibid.,* p. 1.

14. *The State Colleges and Universities Faculty Alliance (SCUFA)* (Manila: PNC Research Center,, 1984), pp. 3-4. Also see "The SCUFA Story," *ACT Forum*, June-July, 1983, p. 5.

15. *Constitution* of the SCUFA, p. 4.

16. *ACT Report,* p. 2.

17. *ACT Forum,* April 1985, pp. 3 and 15.

18. *ACT-Forum*, June-July 1983, p. 2 Also see the *By-Laws and General Program of Action* of PREACH 1984-1985, p. 9.

19. *Summing-up Our Organizing Experience in the Year of the Teacher 1983-1984: Reports on the 2nd ACT National Convention* March 30-April 1, 1984, pp. 20-21.

20. *A Brief History of the POTENT,* mimeo, one page.

21. *Proposed Constitution of POTENT*, Preamble.

22. *Act-Affiliates Report* and consultation with Mr. Chicho Bawagan, national chairman of POTENT, April 7, 1986.

23. *Daily Express*, November 5, 1985 and *The Times Journal*, October 31, 1985.

24. *Malaya*, April 9, 1986.

25. MECS, *op. cit.*, pp. 3-4.

26. Quejada, *op. cit.*, p. 32.

# WOMEN AND PROTEST POLITICS: A CASE STUDY OF TWO WOMEN ORGANIZATIONS IN THE PHILIPPINES

SOCORRO L. REYES

## Some Historical Notes

The participation and involvement of Filipino women in protest politics date back to the brave acts of women like Gabriela Silang, Melchora Aquino and Trinidad Tecson who in their individual and separate capacities contributed to the revolutionary efforts of 1896 to expel the Spanish colonizers from the country. Gabriela Silang continued to revolt in Ilocos after the death of her husband, Diego Silang. Melchora Aquino or Tandang Sora was dubbed as "the mother of the revolution" for the consistent assistance she gave to the revolutionaries. Trinidad Tecson procured arms for the revolution and joined the fighting herself and was appointed quartermaster by General Emilio Aguinaldo, the leader of the revolution after the death of the Katipunan supremo, Andres Bonifacio.

Women first made themselves felt as an organized force in 1893 when a masonic lodge of Filipino women, including Trinidad Tecson, founded the *Logia de Adopcion* composed of "enlightened intellectuals and members of well-to-do and highly respected families" (Maranan, 1984 p. 45). It was considered "an important link in the growing anti-Spanish movement" at that time (Ibid). The women's groups that followed were of diverse character. Though a few still had political concerns, they were mostly mainstream or reformist in nature while the other groups concentrated on women's welfare issues and civic work. To the first category belongs the *Femenina de la Paz* (Philippine Women's League for Peace) organized in 1902 and headed by Carmen Poblete which helped the American colonizers in their pacification drive. Included also in this category were women's groups who accepted American occupation of the country but sought political participation through the extension of suffrage to women. Known as the suffragette movement, it started with the *Asociacion Femenista Ilonga* (Association of Ilonga Feminists) founded by

198

Pura Villanueva Kalaw in 1906. This was followed by the society for the Advancement of Women founded in 1912 by American suffragettes Carrie Chapman Catt and Aleta Jacobs together with some Filipinas led by Concepcion Felix-Rodriguez. In 1921, the National Federation of Women's Clubs was formally organized which, as the vanguard of the suffragette movement from 1921-1937, sponsored the first Women's Convention in 1921 which passed a resolution demanding the right of women to vote. Other groups of a similar nature were the *Liga Nacional de Damas Filipinas* (National League of Filipino Women, 1922), the Women's Citizens League (1928), General Council of Women (1935) and the League of Women Voter's (1939).

Welfare issues pertaining to women were first brought up in the history of women's movements by the *Asociacion Femenista Filipina* (Feminist Association of the Philippines) founded in 1905 by Concepcion Felix-Rodriguez. It sought prison reforms, especially for women minors, labor reforms for women in factories and shops and educational reforms also for women. It also initiated drives against prostitution and started a campaign for the appointment of women to municipal and provincial boards of education, electoral precincts, and municipal committees.

The other women's groups which emerged stressed charity and social service work like *La Proteccion de la Infancia* (Protection of Infants, 1907), the Catholic Women's League, *Club Damas de Manila* (Women's Club of Manila), Federation of Ladies' Associations, Girl Scouts of the Philippines, Young Women's Christian Association, and many others. These groups extended assistance to the young, the sick, the disabled, the prisoners, destitute women, etc. One writer described these activities as "geared to keep the women, most of them coming from rich, elite families, busy outside their homes" (Maranan, p. 46).

After the "grant" of independence on July 4, 1946, two women's groups were organized: the Civic Assembly of Women of the Philippines (1950) and the National Political Party of Women (1951). The former aimed to make the influence of women felt at policy-making levels of the government, though it also stressed that the primary concern of women was the home. The National Political Party of Women did not last long and became inactive. Most women's groups during this period reverted to social welfare work.

It was not until the late sixties that a new women's group was formed—the Malayang Kilusan ng Bagong Kababaihan (Free Movement of New Women) or MAKIBAKA which means struggle. The MAKIBAKA was the first women's group organized in the country with a defined ideological framework—national democracy. It identified the

199

four sources of oppression of women—politics, clan, religion and the males. The MAKIBAKA, however, did not specifically address women issues. One explanation given was that the problems of women did not seem urgent compared to the over-all political and socio-economic issues facing the whole country such as "the widening gap between the rich and the poor, the intensifying economic distress and political instability bred by the country's dependence on foreign capital, and unbridled graft and corruption" (Maranan, p. 48). Another explanation attributed the lack of concern on women's issues to the male-dominated leadership and a third one claimed that MAKIBAKA deliberately avoided being labeled a "feminist" organization because of the word's unpleasant connotations.

At any rate, MAKIBAKA was granted the "singular honor of putting the issue of women's liberation in the proper context." (Ronquillo, 1984 p. 51). It traced the oppression of women to the patriarchal-feudal character of society which defined their function primarily as child-bearers and housekeepers. The semi-colonial character of society, on the other hand, led to the commercialization and commodification of women. MAKIBAKA's effectiveness was in its organization, mobilization and politicization of women students, workers and professionals. It was most remembered for the picket it staged against the Bb. Pilipinas Coronation Pageant at the Araneta Coliseum led by no less than former Miss International Gemma Cruz-Araneta. It was the first time that such a picket was held. When martial law was declared in 1972, MAKIBAKA together with other protest groups was disbanded, and a vacuum was created.

## Women's Groups Today: A Situationer

For almost ten years, from 1972 to 1982, political groups in the Philippines either hibernated or disintegrated in the wake of effective measures of repression adopted by the martial law government. Typical of all authoritarian regimes, the Marcos government used three stages of repression which noted political scientist Herbert Feith (Feith, 1980) describes as "first, destroying the remaining power centres of the defeated enemy, characteristically a coalition of left-wing and nationalist forces; second, establishing tight control over the coalition of supporting elements, reducing the freedom of all groups with a potential for mass organization, expanding the role of military officers within the government apparatus and purging the armed forces of potentially unstable elements; and third, once tight control had been established, the ruling group's problem became one of maintenance, of vigilant management." The first stage in the Philippines involved banning political parties, trade unions, peasant organizations, affiliated ethnic associations and other political groups as well as arresting their leaders and cadre members.

It was only after the assassination of leading political oppositionist former Senator Benigno Aquino, Jr. that political protest was again revived, but this time with such dramatic intensity and extensiveness that the entire political and economic system faced virtual collapse. Overnight, different groups with widely appealing acronyms such as JAJA (Justice for Aquino, Justice for All), ATOM (August Twenty-One Movement), KAAKBAY (Kilusan ng mga Asosasyong Makabayan), NAJFD (Nationalist Alliance for Justice, Freedom and Democracy) developed. Women's groups also emerged such as the Samahan ng Malayang Kababaihang Nagkakaisa (Association of Free and United Women or SAMAKANA which in Pilipino means "Come, Join Us"), Women for the Ouster of Marcos and Boycott (WOMB), Kilusan ng Manggagawang Kababaihan (Movement of Women Workers or KMK), Women's Alliance for Truth and Change (WATCH), National Organization of Women Religious of the Philippines (NOWRP), Association of Major Religious Superiors of Women of the Philippines (AMRSWP), Samahan ng Malayang Kabataan-Kababaihan (SAMAKAKA or Association of Free Female Youth), Kalipunan ng Kababaihang Makabayan ng Pilipinas (KAKAMPI or Association of Nationalistic Women of the Philippines), Kapisanan ng mga Madre sa Kamaynilaan (KAMAY or "hand" in Pilipino, Association of Nuns in Greater Manila), Third World Movement Against the Exploitation of Women (TWMAEW) and Concerned Women of the Philippines (CWP) among others.

The groups which emerged after Aquino's assassination all agreed that Marcos rule had to end but that was about all they had in common. They disagreed about how Marcos should be ousted and who should replace him. They also differed in their fundamental analysis of the causes of the country's social, political and economic ills. Some groups believed that Marcos was the principal and immediate enemy and that after his ouster, everything would fall neatly into place again. There were those who countered that Marcos was the immediate enemy but definitely not the principal one as he was only the instrument of imperialism, feudalism and bureaucrat capitalism—the real enemies of the Filipino people. They agreed that even after Marcos, the problems would remain because his successor would serve the wishes and interests of these forces again. In terms of how the Marcos government should be changed, there were those who advocated peaceful but militant means and those who prescribed violence since those holding political authority were not known to give up their power without the use of violence. The latter contended that it was also the rightful response to the state's use of coercion and superior force. These factors divided political opposition in the Philippines then, and a progressive fragmentation was visibly noted within its ranks. Those who believed in elections as a means for political change could not agree among themselves. Thus, there were two groups which geared for the presidential elections: the Convenors' Group of nationalist Lorenzo Tañada, businessman Jaime Ongpin and Aquino's widow, Cory Aquino, and the National Unification Council of former Senator Salvador Laurel, Assemblyman Homobono Adaza and Assemblywoman and former Supreme Court Justice Cecilia Muñoz-Palma.

Among women's groups however, the trend was more towards consolidation than division. On April 28, 1984, the different women's organizations got together and formed a coalition called GABRIELA which stands for General Assembly Binding Women for Reforms, Integrity, Equality, Leadership and Action. It started with 42 affiliated organizations and now counts among its members 85 other groups for a total of 126 organizations. It is now described as "a full blown coalition representing women from various classes, sectors and groups" (Membership Primer). Perhaps learning its lesson from MAKIBAKA, which failed to address the Women Question but concentrated instead on the broader socio-political issues, GABRIELA proclaims as one of its four major principles its "determination to advance the women's movement, to eliminate all forms that oppress women, particularly the feudal-patriarchal structures which relegate women to inferior and lower-status positions and restrict women from fully and actively participating in all spheres of endeavor." It situates women's issues, however, in the larger context of "national liberation."

As a political force, women are now playing a very important role in the process of social and political transformation. Since its formation in 1984, GABRIELA has undertaken activities intended to raise the political consciousness of women as well as make them active participants in the campaign for change. It has sponsored symposia and fora on current national issues like the Bataan Nuclear Plant, plight of peasant women, militarization, oppression of workers, oil price increase, World Bank-International Monetary Fund conditions, etc. It has also joined rallies, demonstrations, and pickets organized by multi-sectoral groups to denounce injustice and exploitation. On October 22 and 23, 1984, GABRIELA joined the Welgang Bayan (National Strike) spearheaded by the Alliance of Concerned Transport Owners (ACTO) and the Nationalist Alliance for Justice, Freedom and Democracy (NAJFD). On March 8,

1985 GABRIELA organized a women's rally and march to commemorate International Women's Day. It also presented a fashion show on "The State of the Nation" featuring models turned activists like Maita Gomez and Nelia Sancho. To focus attention on issues and problems specific to women, GABRIELA has created task forces on state violence against women, prostitution and pornography, and the welfare of working women. It has also established linkages with other women's groups based in Europe, Australia, New Zealand and Hongkong.

## Studies on Women

A review of studies on women in the Philippines will show the absence of research on women's participation in politics, particularly protest politics. The studies so far on women focus on the sociological, economic, demographic, educational, developmental and legal aspects.

Sociological researches focus on any of the following:

1. Attitudes, decision-making patterns, aspirations of career women (Arceo-Ortega, 1963; Bacabac, Consuelo, 1970; Bley, Nina, 1972; Flores, Pura M., 1965; Castillo, Gelia and Guerrero, Sylvia, 1969).
2. Occupational sex roles (Castillo, Gelia; Hunt, Chester, 1965)
3. Sex roles (Fox, Robert, 1963; Guerrero, Sylvia, 1965)
4. Filipino family (Gonzales, Pilar, 1955; Maglangit, Virginia 1971; Porio, Lynch, and Hollnsteiner, 1975; Umpa, Saira, 1972)
5. Role and Status (Montiel, Cristina and Hollnsteiner, Mary, 1976; Nurge, Ethel, 1965; Popkin, Barry M., 1976; Rojas-Aleta, Silva and Eleazar, 1977; Social Research Laboratory, 1977; Youngblood, Robert, 1977)

Studies on women with an economic thrust usually dwell on:

1. Job efficiency of women workers (Arce, Wilfredo, 1974)
2. Household economic activity (Boulier, Bryan, 1976; Jayme- Ho, Teresa, 1976; King, Elizabeth, 1977)
3. Male-female wage differentials (Boulier and Pineda, 1975; Tidalgo, R.L., 1976.
4. Labor force participation of women (Castillo, Gelia, 1976; Castro, Judy and Salazar, Celia, 1976; De Grazia, Pablo, 1965; Encarnacion, Jose, 1972; Evangelista, Susan, 1974; Guillergan,

Perla, 1969; Mangahas and Jayme-Ho, 1976; Marquez, Asuncion, 1959; Department of Labor, 1974; Ricafrente, Cherry-Lynn, 1973)

5. Quality of life, role and status of rural women (Makil and Fermin, 1976; Popkin and Hart, 1975; Aleta, Isabel, 1978; Salita, Corazon, 1979; Castillo, Gelia, 1979; Illo, Jeanne Frances, 1979)

Demographic studies, on the other hand, concentrate on fertility as it is related to female employment (Concepcion, Mercedes B. 1973); Social class (Jayme, Brigida, 1976) and conjugal interaction (Martinez, Natividad, 1976).

Researches which focus on women's education tackle subjects such as re-structuring and re-orienting their education (Clemente and Amor, 1969); historical development, (de Jesus, Alma, 1970; Flores, Pura, 1965); and education of women in an urban professional society (Raushembuch, Esther, 1964).

Other researches focus on the role of women in development. Specifically, they look into:

1. Filipino women's participation in development (Eventa, 1977; Illo, Jeanne, 1977; Oshima, Harry, 1976)
2. Impact of Poverty (Gonzales, Anna, 1976)
3. Women as partners of men in progress and development (Gonzales and Hollnsteiner, 1976)
4. Social backgrounds of Filipina elite and their relationship to development (Green, Justin, 1970)

The legal aspect of the Women Question is taken up in researches on women's rights (Cortes, Irene, 1974; Shahani, Leticia, 1973) and equality before the law (Javellana, Yolanda, 1975; Romero, Flerida Ruth, 1984).

Notably lacking in the research agenda on women is the nature and significance of women participation in the protest movement, particularly at this point in Philippine history. This paper would like to suggest, therefore, a research project which would look into two women organizations in the current protest movement.

## Description of the Study, Statement of the Problem, Objectives and Methods

This research proposal focuses on two groups within the coalition, namely, Samahan ng Malayang Kababaihang Nagkakaisa (SAMAKANA) and the Women for the Ouster of Marcos and Boycott (WOMB). The former is an aggregate of urban poor women while the latter is composed of middle- and upper-class women. SAMAKANA had its origins in a church-based group of urban poor housewives in Marikina, a municipality in the northern part of Metropolitan Manila. It was later joined by middle-class women who identified with the cause and interests of the urban poor. It was formally organized in October, 1983, two months after the assassination of Senator Benigno Aquino. At present, it has 2,500 members organized in 17 chapters in Metropolitan Manila. WOMB on the other hand was formed immediately before the election of the members of the Batasang Pambansa (National Assembly) in May, 1984. It explicitly states in its primer that it is an organization of middle-class women "upholding women's rights, leading the struggle against women oppression and participating in the broader struggle against the same forces that exploit and oppress women in particular and Philippine society in general." It has two chapters today, one in Angeles City, another in Metropolitan Manila, with a total of 150 members.

This study will look into the group's organizational structure and objectives; composition of the leadership and membership in terms of education, class and political orientation; internal dynamics of group activity; problems of the groups in the course of organizing, mobilizing and action including their strategies and tactics; and the socio-political issues they address.

The specific objectives of the research are:

1. to find out the nature and extent of the membership and participation of women in the current protest movement;
2. to identify the socio-political issues that they address as a distinct pressure group.
3. to determine the extent to which women are motivated by their feminist consciousness to participate in these political activities; and
4. to find out if there are differences in the ideological framework of lower class-based women's groups and middle class-based ones.

The basic approach to be used in this research is the case study and the methods for gathering data include intensive interview of key informants, document research, non-participant observation and informal interviews. Secondary data gathering will also be used to provide adequate background information as well as to contextualize the primary data gathered.

Aside from the research output, this proposal also includes the holding of a seminar-workshop for the dissemination of results. This will be held soon after the study report is finalized and reproduced.

## Theoretical Framework

The group theory in political science espoused by David Truman will serve as the principal theoretical framework for this study. In his book, *The Governmental Process*, Truman argues that unless interests are organized, they will have no impact on the decision-making process. Interests are based on shared attitudes, values and patterns of behavior which lead to common goals and objectives for the attainment of which groups are organized. Truman suggests that there are several ways of looking at the group: in terms of organization, membership, leadership, and tactics and strategies. Organization is significant because it defines the flow of authority, distribution of power and responsibility as well as division of labor and functions. Membership on the other hand is crucial, especially if viewed from the angle of cohesion and solidarity. Leadership which may be formal or informal is equally significant since it is the main force that keeps the group together and determines the direction in which it will go. The tactics and strategies used by the groups are of course the vehicles for the attainment of its goals and purposes. They are meant to exert pressure on the target of activity to make them yield and reflect the group demands in the final policy decisions.

The group theory however, is not enough in looking at the various women's organizations since they will be viewed as part of a movement. Thus, the liberationist framework will also be used—i.e., the groups will be treated as part of a larger process that will eventually lead to socio-economic and political transformation. In this context, it is very important that the underlying structures of society be examined to determine the basic causes of popular unrest. The group will then be situated in this context to find out what particular changes it seeks to bring about and through what means.

The liberationist framework is basically rooted in dependency, a Latin American social science formulation which argues that the conditions of oppression and exploitation in the Third World can be traced to the forces of global capitalism. The economic and political systems of the underdeveloped societies of the world are shaped and determined by outside forces which make use of surrogates as their linkages, purveyors and contact points. These are the political rulers, technocrats, bureaucrats of the Third World or metropolitan powers. This study will seek to find out how women's groups take part in the process of changing structures and power-holders towards the attainment of liberation.

## Future Research Agenda

This proposal is only the first step in the study of women's involvement in protest politics which is now a growing concern among an increasing number of Filipino women. It is the objective of this proponent to go into a larger study of the coalition of women protest groups, GABRIELA. The same framework will be used but this time it will be a macro rather than a micro view. There are several other topics which can be the subject of research in the future:

1. The Government's Attitudes and Perceptions of the Women's Protest Movement (These can involve both the civilian bureaucracy, the political hierarchy, and the military)
2. Profiles of Selected Women Protest Leaders
3. A Study of Women in Power
4. The Women Religious in the Protest Movement
5. Male Attitudes and Perceptions of Women Protest Groups and Leaders
6. A Comparative Analysis of Women Protest Groups in Selected Southeast Asian Countries

## REFERENCES

Eviota, Elizabeth U. 1978. *Philippine Women and Development: An Annotated Bibliography.* Quezon City: Institute of Philippine Culture. Ateneo de Manila University.

Feith, Herbert. "Repressive Developmentalist Regimes in Asia: Old Strengths, New Vulnerabilities" in *Escape From Domination.* International Affairs-Christian Conference of Asia, Tokyo, Japan.

GABRIELA Membership Primer.

Maranan, Aida Santos. 1984. "Do Women Really Hold Up Half The Sky?" *Diliman Review,* Vol. 42, Nos. 3-4, May-June, July-August.

Ronquillo, Salome. 1984. "MAKIBAKA Remembered," *Diliman Review*, Vol. 42, Nos. 3-4, May-June, July-August.

Sub-Regional Workshop on Social Welfare Strategies to Enhance Rural Women's Role in Socio-Economic Activities and Community Leadership in Southeast Asia. 1979. Metro Manila 1-31, October.

WOMB Constitution.

# POVERTY STUDIES IN MANILA

EDNA F. FORMILLEZA

## Introduction

It has been said that the use and allocation of resources have a profound influence on the development of a region and that this development in turn is expected to improve the quality of life of the people in that region.

Metro Manila, which has been the target of a fast pace of development relative to other regions, abounds in facilities, services and resource potentials. It is therefore relevant to ask how this development has affected the quality of life in one of its cities.

This paper centers on the study of a particular facet of Manila's social hierarchy: the urban poor, their needs, problems and aspirations. It will look into the assistance extended by the government to alleviate their condition. This paper will differ from the many exhaustive studies that have been made on different aspects of poverty in that it will present a microcosm of an important though sometimes neglected level of society in the City of Man: the poorest of the poor. Different studies on poverty in the Philippines will be presented to enable us to perceive the poverty situation in Manila alone. Certain limitations on the analysis of these studies however, have to be recognized in that data used in some studies are based on statistics given for the Philippines in general and Metro Manila in particular, whereas other studies are limited to Metro Manila alone.

## Objectives of the Study

The objectives of the study are:

1. To look at how the development of Metro Manila has affected

the quality of life of the people in the depressed areas of the City of Manila.

2.  To provide an insight into the quality of life of the poor, their needs, problem and aspirations.
3.  To determine the nature and type of assistance extended by the government to alleviate the conditions of the poor in the City of Manila.
4.  To present results of empirical studies on consumption expenditures and income distribution of the poor.

## Methodology

In analysis of data the paper will rely heavily on results of empirical studies conducted by various groups of individuals as well as those by private and government agencies during the 70's and 80's. A comparison will be made between Metro Manila and other regions with regard to the incidence of poverty, income inequality, analysis of poverty lines and others.

The paper will center its discussion, however, on the results of an empirical study in 1978 conducted by the Executive Management Group, Inc. (EMG, a private consultancy firm based in Makati) for the National Science Development Board (NSDB) now known as the National Institute of Science and Technology (NIST), for the purpose of establishing a data base for the poor in the City of Manila and to determine the extent of assistance extended by government agencies to the urban poor.

## Estimation of Poverty Incidence

There is no single international definition of poverty by which to judge the standard of living of a particular country. The concept of poverty is circumscribed by the attitudes and traditions of the community as a whole and therefore tends to be relative.

The practice of selecting a precise income level by some researchers to mark off poverty from non-poverty has been criticized by many writers in that such income level may not be critical as long as it is unchanged over time except for necessary adjustments due to price level changes. However, as Mills (1981) succinctly puts it, there can be no natural line that will divide people into those who are poor and those who are not because this task depends on subjective judgments. Hence, a family with an income of $3000 a year would be better off if it had a yearly income of $4000 a year and could still be better off if it had an income of $6000 a year and so on.

In the choice of poverty lines for this analysis, the materialistic definition of poverty is used. "Poverty exists when the resources available to a person are inadequate to provide a socially acceptable standard of living." This standard is generally defined by the amount of expenditures incurred by a family to meet their basic needs such as the following: a) a basket of food which meets dietary requirements; b) a level of education to prepare family members to earn a living and to cope with both the physical and social environment in which he/she lives; and c) the minimum requirement for clothing, medicare and shelter necessary for physical comfort.

Since it is only in food measured in nutritional requirements where an objective standard is available, food has become the primary determinant in most poverty line studies.

## Studies on Poverty

### Choice of Poverty Lines

Several studies on the poor, in Manila in particular and the Philippines in general, conducted during the 60's, 70's and 80's used the basket of food and services as their bases for the choice of poverty lines. Mary Hollnsteiner (1971), Petronilla (1973), the NEDA WAGE COMMISSION (1974), Abrera (1974), Vallientes (1974) and Valenzona (1976), all of whom conducted studies during the 70's, had similar choices of poverty lines. Petronilla's definition was judged to be too decent for the Philippine conditions since it included expenditures for parties and domestic help. Abrera made use of the Economical Menu of the Food and Nutrition Research Center (FNRC) where the poverty line used was the budget for an inexpensive food basket that consisted of items mostly found in the Philippine diet. This was multiplied by 1/.6 to extrapolate the total consumption poverty line, 0.6 being the average food component of the 1971 Philippine household budget. Poverty food baskets for different years and in different areas were obtained by adjusting the Metro Manila poverty line by the ratio of the Consumer Price Index (CPI) of food in areas other than Manila.

Abrera's estimated poverty lines for the different areas and years were:

|      | Metro Manila | Other Urban Areas | Rural Areas |
|------|-------------|-------------------|-------------|
| 1961 | ₱ 3590      | ₱ 2872            | ₱ 2518      |
| 1965 | 4497        | 3597              | 3147        |
| 1971 | 7203        | 5762              | 5000        |
| 1974 | 10550       | 8844              | 7782        |

It was obvious that Metro Manila had the highest poverty line among all other areas. It is evident from the data above that the poverty threshold derived by Abrera is not unrealistically high. This is because the menus which FNRC used were varied (including tomato egg salad and sweet potatoes plus five kinds of vegetables) and therefore a more decent rather than just an adequate or subsistence basket of food for the Philippines was used. A new poverty line was successfully and efficiently constructed by Tan and Holazo in 1975. For this study, they chose a poverty line that provided a subsistence standard of living. This was further defined as the cost of a basket of goods and services providing nutritional, shelter, health and educational requirements for the inter-generational survival of the family. In food, the minimum cost basket that met the recommended nutritional allowances was taken. In addition to these factors, the following were considered as absolute minima:

1. shelter and clothing for protection against the elements;
2. health care needs to prevent and recover from diseases prevalent in the community;
3. the level of education necessary to achieve literacy;
4. abilities that provide one with communication and other skills needed for minimum degree of social, political and economic participation;
5. two changes in garment per person per year;
6. schooling up to Grade VI for children;
7. the average expenditure in medical care of families whose food comsumption was equal to the poverty line; and
8. roughly inputed cost of rent and fuel.

The poverty line was estimated for a typical family of six. Linear programming was used to find the minimum cost basket of food established by the FNRI. The FNRI food table specified the nutrients of a long list of Philippine foods. Two programs were run for each of the ten regions for 1965, 1971, and 1975, using the FNRI food table of the Philippines and the Central Bank raw data on prices. The minimum budget then for each need—food, shelter, fuel, clothing, medicare and education—were added up to compose the poverty line for a region. Two sets of poverty lines were obtained: (A) with an unconstrained food budget, and (B) constrained by varied conditions. The results are given in Table 1.1. (*Please refer to the apppendix*)

In 1965, Manila's poverty line in pesos was higher than the rest of the regions. A closer look at the figures revealed that estimates for rent, fuel, light and water in Manila were higher compared to other regions. Findings in regard to poverty line A showed that in comparison with Central Luzon and Cebu, the Manila poverty line was approximately 26% higher than Central Luzon and 31% higher than Cebu. For poverty line B, the Manila poverty line was 23% higher than Central Luzon and 32% higher than Cebu. In 1975, a larger gap was realized between poverty line estimates for Manila and other regions in the country. In 1975, Manila also surpassed the other regions in its needs for medical care as well as rent, fuel, light and water. The rise in poverty line may be interpreted as the effect of inflation on consumer items for low-income groups. The differences on the impact of inflation were shown by a comparison of the rise in poverty lines to the rise in consumer price index. Table 1.2 gives us the evidence of poverty derived by Tan and Holazo for the 10 regions of the Philippines.

The need to disaggregate the estimation is clearly seen in this data because poverty rates differed widely between regions. Using the food poverty line A, poverty rates ranged from 8.41% for Manila to 58.87% for the Ilocos region, with all regions falling between 28% and 51% in 1965. By 1975, the over-all level was very much higher, but the range narrowed from 27.47% to 63.38% with the incidence for Manila increasing to 35.82%. Such variation as evident in the ten-year span of change in Manila resulted from variations in income and its distributions as well as variation in prices. The latter was reflected in studies of regional price variations as well as the coefficient of variation of the total poverty lines for all needs and for food, medical care, shelter, and schooling.

Table 1.3 shows the incidence of poverty by region in relation to selected indicators in 1971. A high incidence of poverty for Manila defies expectations, Manila being the most modern city of all. While the majority of households in Manila are equipped with electricity and fairly modern conveniences in life, the presence of these conveniences apparently did not alter the highly large incidence of poverty from the prevailing, despite fast, development of this "City of Man."

To shed some light on this matter, a closer look at the system of income distribution is in order.

## Income Inequality

Mangahas (1974) in his paper "Income Inequality in the Philippines: A Decomposition of Analysis" confirms the view that income inequality is greatest in Metropolitan Manila followed by other urban areas and then by rural areas.

The Family Income and Expenditures Surveys (FIES) in 1971 showed a decline in family income of 8% with respect to 1965. Moreover, there was a reversal of the Gini ration (a measure of income inequality) between urban and rural during the same period The metropolitan area of Manila which was the region with the greatest inequality in 1965 became a region of relative equality in 1971. The rural areas which had a moderately equal distribution in 1961 and 1965 exhibited a greater inequality in 1971.

Table 1.4 contains the ranking of the regions according to the family incomes and Gini ratios. As indicated by the tables, the ranking of mean income is quite stable, compared to the ranking according to income inequality. Metropolitan Manila, Southern Luzon and Central Luzon are consistently the top three regions in terms of mean income whereas Cagayan Valley and Eastern Visayas are consistently the lowest. On the other hand, there have been substantial changes in ranks according to the Gini ratio (Table 1.5). Although the rank of Metropolitan Manila appears to have fallen to the sixth place, Mangahas reiterates that the Manila data have to be taken with great caution. The Lorenz curve shows that poverty resulting from income inequality in Metropolitan Manila thus worsened.

In analyzing income inequality between regions, it appears that the Mangahas view that the major part of such inequality is due to the great difference between standards of living in Metropolitan areas compared to the rest of the country is confirmed by data on the weighted Gini ratios. The weighted inequality between Metropolitan Manila and other urban areas is much smaller than that between Metro Manila and rural areas.

## The EMG Study on the Poorest of the Poor in the City of Manila

The poorest of the poor in the City of Manila was the subject of a study conducted by the EMG in 1978 for the NSDB, now the NIST. A list of the poorest of the poor families in the City of Manila as officially recorded by the Metro Manila Commission and confirmed and verified by the Ministry of Social Services and Development (now Department of

214

Social Services and Development), was used as the basis for selecting the respondent population.

All depressed areas located within the four districts of the City of Manila were included in the stratification of the City of Manila into districts and barangays. Barangays found solely along PNR tracks and *esteros* were all included.

A total sample size of 1000 households was selected randomly from the official list of families given by the Barangay Captain and allocated proportionately as follows:

> 576 respondents in the first district
> 144 respondents in the second district
> 187 respondents in the third district
> 93 respondents in the fourth district

The primary objective of this study was to get a socio-economic profile of the poor households in the City of Manila. The study also included the type of assistance extended by both government and private agencies to alleviate the condition of the poor.

## Socio-Economic Profile of the Poor in the City of Manila

### Average Number of Household Members

For all districts surveyed, an average household had 5.5 members. A breakdown by district showed that the third district had the largest average household size with 7.2 members, followed by the first and fourth districts with 5.2 members each, while the second district had the least household members at 4.7.

### Average Number of Dependents

An average of 5.07 dependents for the four districts covered was completed, with the first, second, third and fourth districts registering 5.03, 4.52, 5.68, and 5.02 mean dependents respectively. Only the third district surpassed the average for all districts by 0.61.

### Educational Attainment by Household Head

Distribution of household heads by educational attainment revealed

215

that a handful (46%) out of 1000 respondents had a college education. The distribution is shown below:

| DISTRICT | NONE | ELEMENTARY | HIGH SCHOOL | COLLEGE | TOTAL |
|---|---|---|---|---|---|
| 1 | 247 | 250 | 51 | 28 | 576 |
| 2 | 48 | 88 | 5 | 3 | 144 |
| 3 | 73 | 91 | 12 | 11 | 187 |
| 4 | 43 | 34 | 12 | 4 | 93 |
| TOTAL | 411 | 463 | 80 | 46 | 1000 |

## Average Annual Income of Households

The survey showed that the average household income for all districts was ₱5,910. The average household income by district was listed as follows:

| | | | |
|---|---|---|---|
| 1st District | ₱5,399 | 3rd District | ₱7,511 |
| 2nd District | ₱5,601 | 4th District | ₱6,333 |

As indicated by the above figures, the third and fourth districts registered higher average household incomes than the overall average by ₱1,601 and ₱423 respectively.

## Average Annual Per Capita Income of Households

The average per capita income of the 1000 sample households surveyed was found to be ₱1,068 with the allocation in various districts as follows:

| | | | |
|---|---|---|---|
| 1st District | ₱1,026 | 3rd District | ₱1,037 |
| 2nd District | ₱1,183 | 4th District | ₱1,214 |

## Average Annual Household Expenditures

The study revealed that the average household expenditures for one year stood at ₱5,810. By district level, average annual expenses of the household were as follows:

| | | | |
|---|---|---|---|
| 1st District | ₱5,963 | 3rd District | ₱5,898 |
| 2nd District | ₱4,625 | 4th District | ₱6,522 |

216

On the average, food expenditures constituted the bulk of every household budget with 70% of income spent on it. This finding was equally supported in a more recent survey by DLSU students in 1984 (Alvarez et al.) of a depressed area in Punta Sta. Ana where sampled respondents (N = 815) numbering 140 in two depressed barangays, Vulcan Compound and Barangay Sikat, had also indicated food expenditures as the item that constituted the biggest bulk of their expenditures. The percentage recorded was 62%.

## Major Source of Employment

Forty-two percent of household heads were unemployed. Self employment registered a 34.6% distribution and those employed in private companies numbered almost twice as many as those in government agencies. This is shown in the table below.

### SOURCE OF EMPLOYMENT

| District | Private | Government | Self-Employed | Others | Unemployed | Total |
|---|---|---|---|---|---|---|
| 1 | 84 | 39 | 187 | 12 | 254 | 576 |
| 2 | 27 | 3 | 77 | 3 | 34 | 144 |
| 3 | 10 | 24 | 60 | 5 | 88 | 187 |
| 4 | 14 | 7 | 22 | 4 | 46 | 93 |
| Total | 35 | 73 | 346 | 24 | 422 | 1000 |

## Physical Facilities

The data on type of dwelling used by households revealed that a little less than 60% of the household dwellings of the respondents sampled were "barong-barongs" (shanties). Single-type houses accounted for 14.9% while duplex and apartment types had 3% and 6% respectively.

### TYPE OF SHELTER

| District | Single | Duplex | Apartment | Barong-barong (Shanties) | Others | Total |
|---|---|---|---|---|---|---|
| 1 | 102 | 15 | 40 | 345 | 74 | 576 |
| 2 | 20 | 2 | 1 | 77 | 44 | 144 |
| 3 | 4 | 12 | 14 | 177 | 40 | 187 |
| 4 | 23 | 4 | 6 | 55 | 5 | 93 |
| Total | 149 | 33 | 61 | 594 | 63 | 1000 |

## Kind of Lighting Used

Electric lights and kerosene lamps are the most common kinds of lighting used daily by the poor households in Manila. Only 11 out of 1000 sampled respondents use candles. All the 11 respondents come from the first district. Seven hundred eighty one (781) respondents use electricity and only two hundred eight (208) use kerosene.

## Source of Water Supply

The Metropolitan Waterworks and Sewerage System is the main source of water supply among the poor families in the four districts of Manila. Five hundred forty-three households from the first district use MWSS as their main source of water. One hundred fòrty-four, 183 and 86 households, corresponding to the second, third and fourth districts respectively, also depend on MWSS for their water. The others use artesian wells, rain water and/or open-well water.

## Kinds of Toilet Facility

An almost even distribution of households has been recorded among all the families using three various kinds of toilet facilities, as shown in the table below:

| District | Water-Sealed | Balot (Wrap) System | PublicToilet | Total |
|---|---|---|---|---|
| 1st | 206 | 305 | 65 | 576 |
| 2nd | 35 | | 109 | 144 |
| 3rd | 78 | 34 | 75 | 187 |
| 4th | 16 | | 77 | 93 |
| Total | 335 | 339 | 326 | 1000 |

## Type of Communication Facility Used

The radio is easily the most popular type of communication medium used by respondents with 57.3% of households owning at least one radio. The second most common type of communication medium generally used by households is the newspaper and/or comics. Approximately 19% of the respondents have televisions. Surprisingly, only 24% of them do not possess or avail themselves of any form of communication facility indicated in the survey questionnaire.

*Opinions Regarding Essential Needs in Life*

Food, employment and housing were ranked as the three most urgent needs, as indicated by 32.1, 31.8 and 19.6 percentages these items received respectively from the respondents. Education and health needs were cited as secondary needs only. Clothing seemed to be the least important need among poor households with barely one percent of the total respondents indicating it as essential.

*Opinions/Suggestions for a Better Quality of Life*

It is worth noting that almost 30% of the respondents suggested that government assistance be extended to the poor. Other suggestions given were the following:

| | |
|---|---|
| Provide permanent/good paying jobs | 19% |
| Wife and children should assist the | |
|     head of the family in earning a living | 14% |
| Children should finish their education | 13% |
| Strive harder | 11% |
| Others | 13% |

*Type of Assistance Needed From Government*

Based on opinions given by more than 70% of the respondents (28% did not respond), the needs that necessitate government assistance are employment, housing, food and medical assistance, ranked in that order according to their perceived degree of importance. The first and second districts of Manila shared the same rankings (as mentioned above) of the four most important needs that demanded government assistance, while the third and fourth districts ranked the same four needs as follows: housing, employment, food, and medical assistance.

*Types of Government Assistance Received*

Most respondents, numbering about 400, received medical assistance during the year while 13% received food assistance and family planning demonstrations/samples, etc. The types of government assistance least availed of by the respondents included scholarships, training, and nutritional programs.

219

## Sources of Assistance

The main sources of government assistance for the poor are the Health Centers and the Ministry of Social Services and Development. Other sources of assistance familiar to the poor are the local government/City Hall, Metro Manila Commission (MMC), government hospitals and the Ministry of Education and Culture among others. Health centers were most availed of by the poor in the City of Manila. These were followed by the MSSD and the Metro Manila Commission.

## Analysis of Statistical Results

### Difference in Income Distribution

The results of the Chi-Square Test (Table 2) show a significant difference in income distribution among the poor households in the City of Manila. As revealed in the table, more than half of the poor families are concentrated in the first district of Manila while the rest of the families are more or less evenly distributed in other districts.

Furthermore, the composition of the poor by size of income indicates that roughly 60% of households in the first and second districts are earning an annual income of less than ₱6000. In contrast, less than 50% of those in the third and fourth districts have the same level of annual income. This finding would seem to indicate that there exist certain differences in the degree of poverty among the four districts.

### Analysis of Variance (District and Level of Education)

From the analysis of variance (Table 2.1) there is a strong indication that educational level and geographical location by district do not significantly affect the mean per capita income of the poor families. Their interaction or combined effect is likewise not significant at the 5% level.

What can be inferred from this test is that among the poor, educational attainment may not contribute significantly in explaining income differences. This may be due to the relatively limited access to better employment opportunities among the poor who are more educationally qualified.

### Analysis of Variance (Employment vs. Mean Income)

Table 2.2 shows that the distribution of income by type of

employment bears a strong relation to the relative size distribution of income by income class. It exerts greater influence than the other variables such as educational attainment and geographical location in explaining income difference.

This result implies that policies designed to alter major income sources of the poor would have greater leverage in improving overall income than other policies. This is of particular importance in Manila where most families are dependent on employment earnings (salaries and wages) for their livelihood. Lending further support to effectiveness of such policies are previous studies made by Adelman and Robinson (1978) entitled "Effective Policy Combinations for Reducing Income Inequalities" where it was observed that functional distribution (according to type of employment) was highly sensitive to policy interventions.

## National Development Strategies For Poverty Alleviation

The thrust of development during the last five years has, according to the Marcos government drumbeaters, not really been confined to economic growth per se. Attempts to enhance the quality of life of a greater number of Filipinos have been made through greater government efforts towards a more equitable distribution of the benefits of growth.

Where the main focus of anti-poverty policies has been the upliftment of the quality of life of the rural poor, it is perhaps worthwhile to delve into the needs and problems of the urban poor. This disadvantaged group, found in the relatively more developed regions of the Philippines, deserves attention because of their worsening economic and social conditions, a situation generally concealed when one deals with macro-economic aggregates. It is unfortunate that government policies have not been as effective as we would want them to be in view of poor implementation and the very nature of these policies. It would appear that government efforts have been directed to alleviating the conditions of the poor through stop gap measures which are merely palliatives and are not therefore lasting. The continuous efforts of the MSSD in simply distributing food, medicines and other forms of assistance without complementary programs for long-term effects, have only brought some measure of relief to the urban poor. While advances have been experienced by other sectors of society, for the mass of this unfortunate group of people, long hours of toil and a meager return have been the basic facts of their economic life.

In Manila, in particular, a more rapid pace of development has not only created many problems for this "affluent city" but has also brought

221

about an increasing gap between the living standards of the rich and the poor. This diverse pattern of development has been partly traced to the inequality in the distribution of income and the inefficiency of government in implementing reforms intended to alleviate the conditions of the poor.

Some of the major policy tools employed by the government to alleviate the conditions of the poor are:

- *Taxation policy.* The tax system was restructured to raise more revenues and to effect greater progressivity in the tax rates.
- *Wage and Income policy.* Minimum wage increases were effected from 1972-1980. These were the granting of emergency cost-of-living allowances, the thirteenth month pay and the adjustments in the minimum wage.
- *Housing policy.* Greater provision of low-cost housing and services to settlements within the reach of the lowest income earners have been made available.
- *Educational policy.* Access to educational opportunities has been strengthened through such programs as the Study-Now-Pay-Later plan, the program instituted by the National Manpower Youth Council for out-of-school youth, the greater participation in vocational and technical programs and the like.
- *Health policy.* Government efforts to increase the number of hospitals as well as to expand the health insurances schemes covering all dependents of employees under the Medicare program were directed to alleviate the conditions of the poor.

Other supplementary measures enacted by government during the period were the following:

1. price stabilization program—designed to ensure people's access to some commodities
2. extension of the rent control law—designed to assure people of housing at the least cost possible
3. regulation of transport fares—designed to ensure commuters, particularly students, reasonably priced transport services
4. food production programs—vigorous programs to increase output to ensure the availability of adequate food supplies.

**Summary and Conclusions**

The results of statistical analyses on the EMG study indicate the following broad conclusions on the nature of poverty in the City of Manila.

There exists a significant difference in the income distribution among the poor households in the four districts of Manila. Evidently, more than half of the poor families are concentrated in the first district of Manila while the rest of the families are more or less evenly distributed in other districts.

It was found that the educational level and geographical location (by district) did not significantly affect the mean per capita income of the poor families. This implies that educational attainment is not a major determinant in explaining income differences among the poor households, at least in the short-run. This result conforms with the respondents' own perceptions on how to improve their present level of economic condition wherein education for children was given low importance compared to other suggested ways.

A major finding revealed that the income distribution by type of employment had a strong influence on the relative size distribution of income by income class. It appears that the type of occupation was the most important factor affecting the level of income.

As for existing government policies and programs, it was found that the kind of government assistance reaching the urban poor in Manila was not responsive to the perceived needs of these groups. Furthermore, data tended to show a rather lopsided distribution of government aid among the poor in the four districts of Manila, that is, government assistance failed to reach those poor people who needed assistance. This finding was equally supported in the Alvarez et. al. study in 1984 where the majority of respondents hardly received any government assistance extended to their barangays except during elections.

The rest of the studies on poverty in Manila revealed the following conclusions:

–   The shares in aggregate income of the lowest 20% and the next 20% of the population have increased between 1961 and 1965.

–   Manila's share of poor families has risen from 2.2% of the total in 1961 to 11.2% in 1975. This means, in relative terms, that Manila's condition has worsened between the two time periods. This is

223

evident from the increase in Gini ratio from .45 to .51.

—  Real wages of skilled and unskilled workers in Manila has decreased by an average of 26.95% since 1972. This finding was contained in the CRC study in 1979. The finding is relevant considering that consumer prices have incresed by 135% in that span of time.

—  Several sources, namely the Social Indicators Project of the Development Academy of the Philippines (SIP), the Equity Project within the Research Program on Population, Environment and the Philippine Future (PREPF) and the study done by Tan and Holazo, all reveal that poverty in Manila has been worsening.

It would appear from these studies on poverty that the various solutions to the alleviation of poverty seem to have had negligible effects on the minimization of poverty. While the state of poverty has been opened to debate, the fact remains that as of now, the Philippines cannot claim that it has been truly successful in distributing the fruits of development to this unfortunate sector of its society.

# REFERENCES

Abrera, Alcestis S. "Philippine Poverty Thresholds." Development Academy of the Philippines. Unpublished paper.

Alburo, Florian A. and Eduardo L. Roberto. 1979. *Poverty: Survey of the Philippine Development Research.* Philippines: NEDA-Apo Productions Ltd.

Alvarez, et al. 1984. *An Economic Survey of a Depressed Area in Manila: The Punta Sta. Ana Case.*

Elemar, N. 1982. "A Daily Worker's Income on the Poverty Line." *WHO* Magazine.

EMG Inc. 1978. "Poverty and Resource Allocation with Special Application in the City of Manila." Unpublished paper.

Encarnacion, Jose Jr. "Income distribution in the Philippines: The employed and self-employed." School of Economics, University of the Philippines, Discussion Paper 74-11.

Hollnsteiner, Mary R. 1971. "Socio Economic Themes and Variation in a Low Income Neighborhood." *Philippine Economic Journal.*

Mangahas, Mahar. "Income Inequality in the Philippines: A Decomposition Analysis." School of Economics, University of the Philippines, Discussion Paper 74-15.

Mangahas, Mahar. 1979. "Poverty in the Philippines: Some Measurement Problems." *Philippine Economic Journal.*

Tan, Edita and Virginia Holazo. 1979. "Measuring poverty incidence in a segmented market. The Philippine Case." *Philipine Economic Journal.*

Valenzona, R. L. 1976. "Poverty Philippine Measurement and Nutrition." *Philippine Economic Journal.*

# APPENDIX

**TABLE 1.1**   Poverty Line Estimates  (Pesos per family of six per year)

| Region | Food Basket | | Medical Care | Rent, fuel light & water | Clothing | Schooling | A = (1) + (3) + (4) + (5) + (6) | B = (2) + (3) + (4) + (5) + (6) |
|---|---|---|---|---|---|---|---|---|
| | (1) | (2) | (3) | (4) | (5) | (6) | | |
| | | | | 1965 | | | | |
| I | 511 | 636 | 11 | 732 | 177 | 59 | 1,490 | 1,615 |
| II | 541 | 694 | 14 | 408 | 161 | 59 | 1,183 | 1,336 |
| III | 430 | 643 | 68 | 456 | 169 | 59 | 1,182 | 1,395 |
| IV | 532 | 665 | 21 | 408 | 163 | 59 | 1,183 | 1,316 |
| V | 510 | 656 | 19 | 720 | 177 | 59 | 1,485 | 1,631 |
| VI | 502 | 610 | 11 | 312 | 174 | 59 | 1,058 | 1,166 |
| VII | 496 | 582 | 11 | 348 | 174 | 59 | 1,093 | 1,179 |
| VIII | 80 | 671 | 14 | 312 | 169 | 59 | 1,134 | 1,225 |
| IX | 580 | 720 | 25 | 576 | 203 | 59 | 1,443 | 1,583 |
| X | 518 | 681 | 10 | 576 | 178 | 59 | 1,341 | 1,504 |
| | | | | 1971 | | | | |
| I | 954 | 1,094 | 55 | 1,080 | 298 | 107 | 2,494 | 2,634 |
| II | 1,261 | 1,274 | 35 | 444 | 269 | 107 | 2,116 | 2,129 |
| III | 1,257 | 1,274 | 5 | 492 | ^76 | 107 | 2,157 | 2,168 |
| IV | 1,161 | 1,195 | 31 | 432 | 276 | 107 | 1,991 | 2,025 |
| V | 1,142 | 1,169 | 36 | 756 | 281 | 107 | 2,322 | 2,249 |
| VI | 1,054 | 1,080 | 47 | 348 | 288 | 107 | 1,844 | 1,870 |
| VII | 983 | 1,006 | 64 | 396 | 292 | 107 | 1,842 | 1,865 |
| VIII | 1,245 | 1,308 | 28 | 384 | 281 | 107 | 2,045 | 2,108 |
| IX | 928 | 1,203 | 20 | 624 | 305 | 107 | 1,984 | 2,259 |
| X | 942 | 1,125 | 22 | 636 | 332 | 107 | 2,039 | 2,222 |
| | | | | 1975 | | | | |
| I | 2,109 | 2,460 | 174 | 1,536 | 620 | 194 | 4,633 | 4,984 |
| II | 2,356 | 2,817 | 68 | 528 | 676 | 194 | 3,822 | 4,283 |
| III | 2,456 | 2,819 | 88 | 564 | 681 | 194 | 3,984 | 4,337 |
| IV | 1,752 | 2,321 | 97 | 492 | 584 | 194 | 3,119 | 3,688 |
| V | 1,701 | 2,362 | 78 | 828 | 554 | 194 | 3,355 | 4,016 |
| VI | 2,270 | 2,317 | 68 | 444 | 657 | 194 | 3,633 | 3,680 |
| VII | 2,388 | 2,639 | 72 | 456 | 704 | 194 | 1,814 | 4,065 |
| VIII | 2,221 | 2,625 | 53 | 492 | 719 | 194 | 3,679 | 4,083 |
| IX | 1,895 | 2,059 | 54 | 720 | 758 | 194 | 3,621 | 3,785 |
| X | 2,031 | 2,427 | 110 | 840 | 716 | 194 | 3,891 | 4,287 |

**TABLE 1.2**    INCIDENCE OF POVERTY

| Region | Study's Method | | | |
| | A | | B | |
| | Number of families (thousands) | Percentage of total families | Number of families (thousands) | Percentage of total families |
|---|---|---|---|---|
| | | 1965 | | |
| I | 38.6 | 8.42 | 48.5 | 10.59 |
| II | 154.4 | 51.12 | 173.1 | 57.31 |
| III | 103.0 | 58.87 | 118.2 | 67.58 |
| IV | 208.0 | 28.15 | 238.4 | 32.26 |
| V | 188.4 | 29.44 | 217.9 | 34.05 |
| VI | 137.2 | 33.70 | 156.8 | 37.53 |
| VII | 193.3 | 63.90 | 214.9 | 37.70 |
| VIII | 419.7 | 48.86 | 449.1 | 52.28 |
| IX | 158.5 | 43.91 | 172.5 | 47.78 |
| X | 280.5 | 45.61 | 314.9 | 51.20 |
| Total | 188.6 | 36.71 | 2104.3 | 41.05 |
| | | 1971 | | |
| I | 71.5 | 13.63 | 84.0 | 16.00 |
| II | 194.1 | 56.11 | 194.8 | 56.32 |
| III | 169.8 | 65.32 | 170.4 | 65.53 |
| IV | 257.1 | 30.07 | 262.4 | 30.69 |
| V | 341.9 | 49.12 | 247.2 | 39.81 |
| VI | 243.6 | 48.12 | 247.2 | 49.84 |
| VII | 241.6 | 36.06 | 247.2 | 36.89 |
| VIII | 592.9 | 60.50 | 602.4 | 61.47 |
| X | 237.0 | 45.40 | 269.0 | 51.54 |
| X | 322.2 | 39.06 | 355.2 | 47.05 |
| Total | 2771.7 | 42.09 | 2778.5 | 43.78 |
| | | 1975 | | |
| I | 275.8 | 35.82 | 312.6 | 40.60 |
| II | 242.5 | 43.46 | 288.3 | 51.67 |
| III | 173.2 | 52.66 | 185.8 | 56.48 |
| IV | 181.8 | 27.47 | 250.5 | 37.83 |
| V | 350.0 | 39.42 | 452.0 | 50.90 |
| VI | 285.2 | 55.07 | 289.7 | 55.92 |
| VII | 333.2 | 49.07 | 363.4 | 53.53 |
| VIII | 497.2 | 47.99 | 568.5 | 54.87 |
| IX | 234.5 | 63.38 | 242.9 | 65.64 |
| X | 518.5 | 49.48 | 578.2 | 55.17 |
| Total | 30.91.9 | 45.08 | 3531.9 | 51.49 |

**TABLE 1.3**  Incidence of Poverty by Region Philippines 1971 and Selected Indicators (1973)

| Region | Poverty Incidence (per cost) | Per Capital Gross Domestic Product (1973 Pesos) (%) | Households with Electricity (%) | Households with water pump or artesian well (%) | Households with toilets (flush or antipolo) (%) | Households using wood or charcoal for cooking | Households with houses made of block or wood (%) |
|---|---|---|---|---|---|---|---|
| I | 35.6 | 3988 | 95.8 | 97.8 | 86.7 | 5.4 | 99.1 |
| II | 75.1 | 961 | 11.5 | 60.1 | 44.4 | 82.1 | 57.1 |
| III | 85.8 | 934 | 8.1 | 59.4 | 28.8 | 89.2 | 47.2 |
| IV | 61.2 | 1129 | 37.6 | 82.4 | 39.0 | 63.8 | 66.1 |
| V | 63.3 | 1507 | 40.5 | 81.1 | 44.6 | 59.5 | 68.7 |
| VI | 80.2 | 800 | 16.6 | 56.0 | 32.4 | 83.9 | 56.9 |
| VII | 76.3 | 1712 | 11.0 | 43.7 | 22.2 | 84.1 | 32.0 |
| VIII | 81.9 | 1023 | 15.3 | 60.7 | 61.3 | 86.5 | 58.4 |
| IX | 76.8 | 1045 | 14.1 | 43.8 | 32.1 | 91.0 | 76.6 |
| X | 70.1 | 1312 | 16.4 | 39.5 | 38.1 | 89.8 | 59.9 |
| Philippines | 69.9 | | 28.3 | 63.8 | 41.3 | 72.6 | 62.9 |
| Urban | 48.5 | | 71.7 | 85.8 | 70.1 | 37.0 | 88.8 |
| Rural | 79.1 | | 9.6 | 54.7 | 33.2 | 87.9 | 51.8 |

**TABLE 1.4** Distribution of Families and Income, Mean Family Income, Gini Ratio and Weighted Gini Ratio by Area: 1961, 1965, 1971

| Area | Distribu- tion of Families (%) (1) | Distribu- tion of Income (%) (2) | Mean Family Income (₱/annum) (3) | Gini Ratio (4) | Weighted Gini Ratio (5) = (2)x(4) |
|---|---|---|---|---|---|
| **1971** | | | | | |
| 1. Metro Manila | 8.27 | 17.23 | 7785 | 0.4481 | 0.0772 |
| 2. Other Urban | 21.87 | 30.10 | 5141 | 0.4421 | 0.1330 |
| 3. Rural | 69.86 | 52.69 | 2818 | 0.4614 | 0.2432 |
| Total Philippines | 100.00 | 100.00 | 3736 | 0.4910 | 0.4534 |
| **1965** | | | | | |
| 1. Metro Manila | 8.93 | 23.16 | 6590 | 0.4973 | 0.1152 |
| 2. Other Urban | 20.72 | 28.24 | 3463 | 0.4861 | 0.1373 |
| 3. Rural | 70.35 | 48.59 | 1755 | 0.4226 | 0.2053 |
| Total Philippines | 100.00 | 100.00 | 2541 | 0.5051 | 0.4578 |
| **1961** | | | | | |
| 1. Metro Manila | 8.61 | 21.67 | 4790 | 0.4751 | 0.1029 |
| 2. Other Urban | 25.84 | 34.32 | 2395 | 0.4987 | 0.1712 |
| 3. Rural | 66.00 | 44.01 | 1203 | 0.3971 | 0.1748 |
| Total Philippines | 100.00 | 100.00 | 1804 | 0.5023 | 0.4489 |

**TABLE 1.5**    Ranking of Mean Family Income and Income Inequality By Region: 1961, 1965, and 1971

| | Region | Mean Income | | | Income Inequality | | |
|---|---|---|---|---|---|---|---|
| | | 1961 | 1965 | 1971 | 1961 | 1965 | 1971 |
| 1. | Metropolitan Manila | 1 | 1 | 1 | 3 | 1 | 6 |
| 2. | Ilocos & Mt. Province | 8 | 8 | 5 | 10 | 3 | 1 |
| 3. | Cagayan Valley | 9 | 10 | 10 | 5 | 7 | 9 |
| 4. | Central Luzon | 3 | 3 | 3 | 9 | 9 | 8 |
| 5. | Southern Luzon & Islands | 2 | 2 | 2 | 6 | 4 | 3 |
| 6. | Bicol | 6 | 5 | 8 | 2 | 8 | 5 |
| 7. | Western Visayas | 4 | 7 | 6 | 4 | 10 | 10 |
| 8. | Eastern Visayas | 1 | 9 | 9 | 7 | 2 | 2 |
| 9. | Northern Mindanao | 7 | 4 | 7 | 1 | 5 | 4 |
| 10. | Southern Mindanao | 5 | 6 | 4 | 8 | 6 | 7 |

**TABLE 2**    Frequencies and Expected Frequencies of Respondents Belonging To Different Income Classes, By Districts, Manila, 1977-1978

| Income Class | District | | | | Total |
|---|---|---|---|---|---|
| | 1 | 2 | 3 | 4 | |
| Less than ₱3,000 | 159(133.63) | 43(33.41) | 13(43.38) | 17(21.58) | 232 |
| ₱3,000- ₱5,999 | 246(227.52) | 49(56.88) | 71(73.87) | 29(36.74) | 395 |
| ₱6,000-₱14,999 | 160(199.87) | 50(49.97) | 95(64.89) | 42(32.27) | 347 |
| ₱15,000 and over | 11(14.98) | 2(3.74) | 8(4.86) | 5(2.42) | 26 |
| Total | 576 | 144 | 187 | 93 | 1000 |

**TABLE 2.1** Analysis of Variance for a Two-Factor (District and Level of Education) Factorial Experiment in a Completely Randomized Design (CRD) With Unequal Class Frequencies

I. Subclass Sum (Per Capita Household Income) by District, by Level of Education

| District | Level of Education | | | | Total |
|---|---|---|---|---|---|
| | None | Elementary | High School | College | |
| 1 | 34,574 | 218,750 | 247,497 | 90,224 | 591,045 |
| 2 | 5,022 | 115,212 | 45,583 | 4,560 | 170,377 |
| 3 | 1,880 | 89,426 | 90,595 | 12,008 | 193,909 |
| 4 | 2,489 | 33,372 | 53,435 | 23,629 | 112,925 |
| Total | 43,965 | 456,760 | 437,110 | 130,421 | 1,068,256 |

II. Subclass Means by District, by Level of Education

| District | Level of Education | | | | Total |
|---|---|---|---|---|---|
| | None | Elementary | High School | College | |
| 1 | 1,280.52 | 875.00 | 1,018.51 | 1,611.14 | 4,785.17 |
| 2 | 1,674.00 | 1,280.13 | 949.65 | 1,520.00 | 5,423.78 |
| 3 | 940.00 | 982.70 | 1,091.51 | 1,091.64 | 4,105.85 |
| 4 | 622.25 | 935.49 | 1,335.88 | 1,687.79 | 4,599.41 |
| Total | 4,516.77 | 4,091.32 | 4,395.55 | 5,910.57 | 18,914.21 |

**TABLE 2.2** DISTRIBUTION OF RESPONDENTS BY NATURE OF EMPLOYMENT AND BY TOTAL HOUSEHOLD INCOME

| Nature of Employment | Total Household Income | No. of Respondents |
|---|---|---|
| Technician/Supervisor | 658,500 | 55 |
| Skilled Workers | 675,000 | 93 |
| Operatives | 2,687,500 | 437 |
| Other Workers | 1,700,000 | 280 |
| Unemployed | 580,000 | 135 |
| Total | 6,301,000 | 1,000 |

# PEOPLE POWER KUNO

ISAGANI R. CRUZ

Halimbawa'y may dalawang lalaking naglalaro ng chess sa isang tournament. Kasalukuyang abala ang *tournament director* sa ibang bahagi ng *tournament hall.* Biglang magtataas ng kamay ang unang lalaki at tatawagin ang *tournament director.* Hinawakan na ng aking kalaban ang kanyang tore, sasabihin niya. *Touch-move* dito, kaya kailangang galawin niya ang tore, idadagdag pa niya. Ang sasabihin naman ng kanyang kalaro ay hindi, hindi ko hinahawakan ang aking tore. Halimbawa nang walang miron sa sandaling ito. Walang makakakita sa paghawak o di-paghawak sa tore. Sino ang paniniwalaan ng *tournament director?* Hindi ba iyung akala niya'y laging nagsasabi ng totoo? Iyung may kredibilidad? Iyung matagal nang kilalang hindi nandaraya? Sa madaling salita, ang pagbabatayan ng desisyon ng *tournament director* ay hindi ang kasalukuyang pangyayari o ang katotohanan kundi ang akala niyang nangyari o sa palagay niya'y nangyari. Mas mahalaga ang akala ng *tournament director* kaysa sa tunay na nangyari.

Halimbawa nama'y may isang babaeng naglalakad sa harap ng isang sinehan. Bigla niyang makikita ang kanyang asawang lumalabas ng sinehan na nakikipag-usap sa isang babaeng kilala niyang dating nobya nito. Lalapitan ng babae ang dalawa. Aakusahan ang lalaki na nakipag-deyt sa sine. Sasabihin ng lalaki na hindi naman niya di-neyt ang dating nobya. Mag-isa daw siyang pumasok sa sinehan at mag-isa siyang lumabas dito. Ngunit sa may pintuan ng sinehan ay nakasalubong niya ang dating nobya. Natural, kinausap niya ito. Mag-isa din daw na nanood ng sine ang dating nobya. Nagkataon daw lamang ang kanilang pagkakasalubong at pakikipagkuwentuhan. Ngunit sa akala ng asawang babae'y pinagtataksilan na siya ng lalaki. Pagdating sa bahay ay alsa balutan na ang babae. Iwanan ang lalaki. Sira ang kanilang kasal. Mahalaga ba o hindi kung nagsasabi nga ng totoo ang lalaki at talaga nga palang nagkataon lamang na nagkasalubong sila ng dating nobya sa pintuan ng sinehan habang

233

papalabas silang pareho? Mahalaga ba o hindi kung nag-deyt nga ang lalaki at ang dati niyang nobya? Magtaksil man o hindi ang lalaki'y pareho pa rin ang kahihinatnan. Masisira pa rin ang pagsasama ng mag-asawa dahil ang akala ng asawang babae ang pagbabatayan ng desisyon na hiwalayan ang lalaki.

Sa larangan ng ekonomiya'y halimbawa'y may kumakalat na balita na ang isang bangko'y malapit nang tumaob. Magdadagsaan ang mga may deposito sa bangko at babawiin ang kanilang mga deposito. Magba-*bank run*, sa madaling salita. Tataob ang bangko. Mahalaga ba kung totoo ngang tataob nga pala ang bangko? Matibay man ito o hindi, kapag kumalat na ang tsismis na ito'y malapit nang tumaob ay tataob nga ito. Ang mahalaga'y ang akala ng mga taong may deposito sa bangko. Kapag sa akala nila'y masama ang tayo ng bangko'y sasama nga ang tayo nito.

Ganyan din ang maaaring mangyari sa pagpapalit ng piso sa dolyar. Kapag may tsismis na biglang tataas ang dolyar ay maraming bumibili ng dolyar. Kapag maraming bumibili ay tumataas ang halaga ng dolyar. *Law of supply and demand* lang iyan, ika nga. Mahalaga ba kung tataas nga pala sana ang halaga ng dolyar, kung totoo nga o hindi ang tsismis? Ang mahalaga'y ang akala ng tao. Kung sa akala nila'y tataas ang dolyar ay bibili sila ng dolyar at tataas nga ito. Kung sa akala nila'y hindi tataas ang dolyar ay hindi sila mamimili ng dolyar at hindi nga tataas ito.

Dumako naman tayo sa pulitika. Nagkaroon ng eleksiyon noong a-siyete ng Pebrero ng taong 1986. Nang binilang ng COMELEC ang mga boto'y nanalo si Ferdinand Marcos laban kay Corazon Aquino. Nang binilang ng Batasang Pambansa ang mga boto'y panalo pa rin si Marcos. Pero sa bilang ng NAMFREL ay lamang si Aquino. Ngunit hindi binilang ng NAMFREL ang lahat ng mga boto, kundi porsiyento lamang nito. Maraming boto na galing sa hilaga ang hindi binilang, dahil ayaw payagan ng mga Ilokano na magbantay doon ang NAMFREL. Sino ba talaga ang nanalo sa eleksiyon, kung talagang bibilangin ang mga balota nang walang dayaan? Mahalaga ba kung si Marcos pala o kung si Aquino nga ang nanalo? Kung totoo ngang nanalo si Marcos ay hindi ito paniniwalaan ng tao. Ang mahalaga sa tao'y hindi kung sino talaga ang nanalo sa mga balota, kundi ang akala nila'y nanalo. Nanalo man si Aquino sa katotohanan o hindi'y sa akala ng mga tao'y siya ang nanalo.

Siguro nama'y klaro na kung ano ang pinatutunguhan ng aking mga halimbawa. Maraming pagkakataon sa buhay na ang akala ay mas mahalaga kaysa sa totoong pangyayari. Ayon sa mga makabagong istrukturalista o ang tinatawag natin sa ingles na *post-structuralists* ay hindi lamang sa mga halimbawang tulad ng aking ginamit makikita ang lakas ng akala, kundi sa lahat ng pagkakataon sa buhay. Ang lahat ng bagay sa buhay ng tao ay pinaghaharian ng akala. Kung paniniwalaan natin sina Jacques Lacan at Michel Foucault, at isama na natin dito si Jacques Derrida na siyang ama ng makabagong istrukturalismo, ating aakalain na bale wala ang katotohanan sa buhay ng tao. Ang mahalaga, ang umiiral sa ating buhay, ang talagang nagpapatakbo ng mundo, ay ang akala.

Huwag na tayong mangibang-bansa. Ayon mismo kay Gemino H. Abad na isang dakilang kritiko't makata, mismong ang tao ay binubuo ng mga salita. Sa kanyang tulang pinamagatang "I Teach My Child," inilalarawan ni Abad kung paano nagsisimula ang buhay ng isang tao:

> My child
> Is without syllables
> To utter him,
> Captive yet to his origin
> In silence.
>
> By every word
> To rule his space,
> He is released;
> He is shaped by his speech. (Abad 1985: 43)

Ganyan din ang paniniwala ni Lacan sa kanya namang paglalarawan ng nangyayari kung ang isang pasyente'y nakikipag-usap sa kanyang saykayatris (Lacan 1956). Ang nalalaman lamang ng saykayatris ay ang sinasabi sa kanya ng pasyente. Samakatwid ay binubuo ang pasyente ng kanyang sariling mga salita. Ang tunay na pagkatao ng pasyente, kung masasabi mang mayroon itong tunay na pagkatao, ay ang tinatawag ni Lacan na ang "Iba" (Other). Maaari ba nating makilala kailanman ang "Iba"? Ang sagot diyan ay hindi. Habang tao tayo'y kailangan nating gumamit ng mga salita at ang mga salita, tulad nang matagal nang napatunayan ni Ferdinand de Saussure at ng mga makalumang istrukturalista, ay nakabilanggo sa *signifiant* at *signifie* o sa tumutukoy at tinutukoy. At ang tinutukoy ng mga salita, matagal na nating batid, ay hindi ang realidad, kundi ang mga akala na nasa isip o imahinasyon lamang natin.

Sa pagsisiyasat naman ni Foucault sa pagkatao ng mga awtor ay natuklasan niya na ang isang awtor ay binubuo lamang ng kanyang mga salita at hindi ng kanyang tunay na pagkatao, kung mayroon ngang masasabing tunay na pagkatao ang isang nilalang (Foucault 1969). Kunin nating halimbawa si Jose Rizal. Nagkakabalubaluktot ang pag-iisip ng mga iskolar kapag kanilang sinusuri kung si Rizal nga ba ay naniwala sa

235

madugong rebolusyong o kung repormista lamang siya't tuta lang talaga ng mga Kastila. Kung ang pananaw ni Foucault ang ating gagamitin, matutuklasan natin na ang akala natin kay Rizal ay batay lamang sa kanyang mga isinulat, hindi batay sa kung ano mang tunay na mga pangyayari sa kanyang buhay. Sa katunaya'y kahit na ang mga pangyayaring iyon ay hango pa rin natin sa mga salita, sa mga salita ng mga sumulat ng kanyang talambuhay. Alam naman nating lahat ang mga isyu na laganap sa larangan ng panunuri tungkol sa mga nobela ni Rizal. Ayon sa iba'y si Rizal daw ay si Crisostomo Ibarra, na naniniwala sa mapayapang reporma ngunit nabigo. Ayon naman sa iba'y si Rizal daw ay si Elias o si Simoun na naniniwala sa madugong paghihimagsik ngunit nabigo din. Ayon naman sa iba pa diyan ay si Rizal daw ay hindi makapagpasya kung siya si Crisostomo Ibarra o si Simoun, kung gusto niyang ipasubali na lamang sa edukasyon ang mga kapwa niya indiyo o kung gusto niyang patayin na lamang ang mga mapang-aping mga Kastila't ilustrado. Kung makabagong istrukturalismo ang gagamitin nating paraan ng kritisismo, makikita natin na hindi mahalaga kung ano nga ba si Rizal sa totoong buhay. Ang mahalaga'y kung ano ang akala natin kay Rizal, kung paano natin binabasa ang kanyang mga isinulat. Madali nating makikita ito kung magkukunwari tayo, halimbawa, na may matutuklasang bagong akda ni Rizal. Siguradong magpapalit ang ating pagkakakilala kay Rizal. Magpapalit ang ating akala tungkol kay Rizal. Ngunit hindi magpapalit ang tunay na taong si Rizal. Patay na siya't matagal na siyang hindi maaaring magpalit. Nagpapalit lamang siya sa ating mga isipan at imahinasyon. Samakatwid ay ang ating akala ang dapat nating pag-ukulan ng pansin, dahil iyan ang pabagu-bago, hindi ang tunay na pagkatao ni Rizal na gustuhin man natin o hindi ay maaaring kahit kailan ay hindi natin mawawari.

Matagal nang tinanggap ng mga kritikong pampanitikan ang mga ideya ni Derrida. Alam natin na ayon kay Derrida ay hindi makaliligtas ang tao sa hawak-leeg ng mga salita (Derrida 1971). Patalinghaga ang pagbibigay-katuturan ng mga salita. Walang direktang relasyon ang mga salita sa realidad. Habang nagsasalita ang isang tao ay nabibilanggo siya sa salita. Lahat ng kanyang sinasabi'y patalinghaga. At tulad ng nangyayari sa kahit na anong talinghaga ay nasasatao na ang pagbibigay-kahulugan sa mga salita. Kaya nga ang akala ng tao ang mahalaga, hindi ang sinasabing katuturan ng mga salita. Matagal na nating batid ito sa larangan ng panitikang bayan, lalong-lalo na kung pinag-aaralan natin ang ating mga sawikain. Ngayo'y batid na rin natin na kahit na sa panitikang makabago, at kahit na sa ano mang pangyayari sa mundo, ay umiiral ang batas ng talinghaga. Kahit na anong bagay sa mundo ay teksto na maaaring pag-aralan bilang akdang matalinghaga at malikhain. Iyung mga disipulo ni Alejandro G. Abadilla ay matutuwa. Sa Pransiya pala sa kasalukuyang panahon ay ang nilalaman pa rin ng kanyang tulang "Ako ang Daigdig" ang pinaniniwalaan:

> ako
> ang daigdig
> sa tula
>
> ako
> ang tula
> sa daigdig
>
> ako
> ang daigdig
>
> ako
> ang tula
>
> daigdig
> tula
> ako

Sa madaling salita'y ang daigdig at ang lahat ng mga elemento ng daigdig ay tula, at ang mga paraan ng pag-aaral sa tula ay maaaring gamitin upang pag-aralan ang daigdig.

Kaya nga pag-aaralan ko ngayon ang nangyari noong Pebrero, 1986, bilang tula o teksto. Aking gagamitin ang makabagong istrukturalismo upang palabasin na walang makapagsasabi kung ano talaga ang nangyari noong Pebrero. Hindi naman kailangang sabihin kung ano nga ba ang nangyari. Ang mahalaga'y kung ano ang akala nating nangyari. Tayo'y binubuo ng mga akala o ng mga matalinghagang mga salita. Ang nangyari noong Pebrero ay binubuo din ng mga akala o ng mga salita.

Gawin nating pangunahing teksto ang ilan sa napakaraming naisulat at nailathala tungkol sa nangyari noong Pebrero. Halimbawa'y sa *National Midweek* ay ayaw tawagin ni Petronilo Bn. Daroy ang nangyari noong Pebrero na "rebolusyon." Ito daw ay isang *putsch:*

The February 21-26 events have been alternatively called "People's Power" and "People's Revolution." On one occasion, at the government broadcast station, General Fidel V. Ramos referred to these events as "People's Power Revolution." The semantical awkwardness in all these is a clue to the falsity of the description of what actually happened.

For what actually took place was neither "People's Power" nor a "revolution." More appropriately, it was a putsch. (Daroy 1986)

Kung medyo mapurol na ang inyong Aleman, pabayaan ninyong ibigay ko ang kahulugan ng salitang *putsch* na isang salitang Aleman: "isang insureksiyon o rayot." Sa ingles ng Random House Dictionary (1978) ay mas malinaw siguro: "A revolt or uprising, esp. one that depends upon suddenness and speed."

Maraming napansin si Daroy tungkol sa tinatawag niyang *putsch* (sa Tagalog kaya'y maaari natin itong tawaging *putris*?). Halimbawa'y ang militar ay hindi nagbago: "For instance, the 'New AFP' is not new; it is the same AFP, and although there have been new appointments since the flight of Mr. Marcos, the entire armed forces has not yet been reorganized. Neither has it been reformed." Ang istruktura ng bagong gobyerno nama'y istruktura pa rin ng gobyerno ni Marcos: "The Aquino Cabinet, on the other hand, merely fills up the ministries of the Marcos administration." Ang pinakamahalagang bagay na napansin ni Daroy ay ito, na ang *putsch* ay batay sa isang eleksiyon: "The fact is that an election preceded the events; Ms. Aquino's leadership in turn rests on an electoral mandate." Dahil dito'y wala talagang nagbago kundi ang taong namumuno.

Gamitan natin ngayon ng dikonstruksiyon ang mga salita ni Daroy. Ganito talaga ang paraan ng mga makabagong istrukturalista. Mahilig silang magdikonstrak ng mga tekstong hango sa ibang teksto. Ngayon, kung ididikonstrak natin si Daroy, mapapansin natin na ang kanyang ginamit na salita upang ilarawan ang pangyayari nitong nakaraang Pebrero ay isang salitang hindi lamang banyaga, kundi dalawang beses na banyaga. Hindi lamang salitang ingles, kundi salitang ingles na hango sa wikang Aleman. Maaaring sabihin na ang kanyang pananaw sa pangyayari noong Pebrero ay pananaw na banyagang banyaga. Hindi masama iyon, kung aalalahanin natin ang sinabi ni De Saussure na wala naman talagang relasyong direkta ang salita sa realidad, kaya kahit na anong salita mula sa kahit na anong wika ay maaari nating gamitin kung gusto natin. Ang mahalaga dito'y maunawaan natin na ang *signifie* ng salitang *putsch* ay hindi ang nangyari noong Pebrero kundi ang akala na nasa isip ni Daroy. At ang akalang ito'y banyaga. Sa halip na tangkaing unawain ni Daroy ang pangyayari noong Pebrero sa pamamagitan ng isang salitang Tagalog na kung tutuusi'y siguradong mas tugma sa ating karanasan, dahil ang ating pang-mundong pananaw (*world-view*) ay hango at bumubuhay sa wikang Tagalog, ay ginagamitan niya ng isang akalang banyaga ang ating kasaysayan. Huwag nating paraanin ang pagkakataong mabanggit na kahit na ang mga salitang ginamit ni Heneral Ramos ay mga salitang banyaga. Ang mga salita sa "People's Power Revolution," at kahit na sa "People's Power" at "People's Revolution," ay pawang mga salitang ingles; banyaga din ang mga ito at banyaga din ang mga akalang tinutukoy ng mga ito. Ang ipinahihiwatig ng ating pagdikonstrak sa salitang *putsch* ay ito: na dahil ang nangyari noong Pebrero ay noon pa lamang nangyari sa ating karanasan bilang isang bansa ay wala pa tayong salita para dito. Napipilitan tayong humanap ng salita mula sa ibang bansa, mula sa mga wika ng Amerikano o ng mga Aleman, dahil naubusan ng salita ang ating sariling wika nang ang ating karanasan ay biglang lumikha ng makabagong pangyayari na lampas sa karaniwang sinasaklaw ng ating bokabularyo.

Makikita natin kung paanong napakabanyaga ng mga salitang "People Power" kung babasahin natin ang sinulat ni Roger Rosenblatt sa *Time*. Ayon kay Rosenblatt, ang nangyari noong Pebrero ay isang pagpapatunay na tama ang demokrasya, na magagaling ang mga Amerikano, na ang mga Pilipino'y kumokopya lamang sa mga Amerikano:

The theme is in fact our own: that a people released from oppression will, of their natural inclinations, seek humane values. A revolutionary thought to the likes of Hobbes, who called democracy an aristocracy of orators, but not so wild an idea to Americans, who over the tortuous and often backsliding years have seen the theme take hold. . . .

Try not to forget what you saw last week. It was ourselves in eruption far away. (Rosenblatt 1986)

Ang nangyari daw noong Pebrero ay ang mga Pilipino'y naging gaya-gaya. Ginawa daw natin ang gagawin ng mga Amerikano kung naririto sila noon. Ganyan din ang ipinalalabas ng balita na nakalathala sa isyu ding iyon ng *Time*: ayon sa mga Amerikanong reporter ng *Time*, kung hindi kina Paul Laxalt, Philip Habib, Caspar Weinberger, at Ronald Reagan, ay hindi umalsa ang mga Pilipino at hindi napaalis si Marcos. Ang mga Amerikano daw ang nagsabi kay Marcos na huwag paputukan ang mga taong nasa kalye. Ang mga Amerikano daw ang kumumbinse kay Marcos na lumayas na lamang sa Pilipinas. Ang mga Amerikano daw ang nagpabagsak sa diktadura ni Marcos.

Mas malinaw ang ganitong pananaw sa isang balitang galing sa KNT News Service na nailathala sa *Orlando Sentinel* noong Pebrero 26, 1986:

In the judgment of experts, President Reagan's success in easing President Ferdinand Marcos from power in the Philippines provided a textbook case in how to get rid of friendly dictators.

And from the reactions on Capitol Hill, it was clear Tuesday that Reagan had scored a foreign policy triumph by engineering what appeared to be a relatively peaceful transition from authoritative rule.

"It was carefully orchestrated," [White House Spokesman Larry Speakes] said Tuesday. "It was designed to avoid violence and bloodshed and reach a peaceful resolution, to reach a democratic outcome." (KNT News Service 1986)

### Tuwang-tuwa si Rosenblatt sa nangyari:

The revolution during the past few weeks has been played on television, a serial docudrama of easily read scenes and unambiguous images. Network anchormen went on location for the elections. The principals in the story sought news shows as their war grounds. English was spoken there. (Rosenblatt 1986)

"English was spoken there." Nasa pangungusap na iyan ang susi sa pananaw ni Rosenblatt. Kung ating ididikonstrak ang kanyang sinasabi'y ang nais niyang palabasin ay pag-aari pa rin tayo ng mga Amerikano. Tagumpay ng mga Amerikano ang ating tagumpay. Sa katunaya'y hindi tayo ang nagtagumpay, kundi sila, ang mga puti, ang mga Laxalt at Habib, ang mga Rosenblatt at mga kanong reporter. Ngayon, maaaring hindi tayo sang-ayon sa ganitong pananaw tungkol sa nangyari noong Pebrero, ngunit ang pananaw na iyan, ang akalang iyan ng mga Amerikanong tulad ni Rosenblatt, ang siyang umiiral ngayon sa Amerika.

Siguro nama'y hindi ko na kailangang idiin pa na ang pagsasalita ng wikang ingles dito sa atin ang ginagawang talinghaga ni Rosenblatt sa pagka-Amerikano ng mga Pilipino. Dahil ingles ang salita natin, dahil nagsalita sa mga palatuntunan sa telebisyon sa America sina Marcos at Aquino, dahil nasa telebisyon ang nangyari noong Pebrero, dahil "People Power" ang tawag natin dito at "People Power" din ang tawag dito ni Rosenblatt at ng mga patnugot ng *Time*, ang akala ng mga Amerikano'y sila ang nagtaya ng kanilang mga buhay doon sa EDSA noong Pebrero.

Ito ang dahilan kung bakit nakapangdidiri ang ginawang "Supplement" ng pahayagang *Business Day* tungkol sa pangyayari noong Pebrero. Noong Marso 21, 1986, ay naglabas ng suplemento ang *Business Day* at ipinahayag ng apat na artikulong nakalathala doon na napakagaling daw ng mga Pilipino dahil gumamit daw tayo ng "People Power." ("People Power" pa nga ang pamagat ng "Supplement.") Tayo na daw ang titingalain ng lahat ng mga inaaping tao sa mundo:

The events of the past month taught a lesson in courage founded on faith, in passive resistance that will be a model for all oppressed peoples of the world.

Four crucial days in February saw hundreds of thousands of Filipinos, coming to the rescue of a small rebel force bracing for what could be their first and last battle, pour into the streets armed with nothing but their hope and faith to meet an army that was reluctant to shoot not so much for fear of being overwhelmed as for not wanting to kill their fellow Filipinos. (De Dios 1986)

Kung ididikonstrak natin ang ginawang ito ng *Business Day* ay matutuklasan natin na sa akala ng patnugutan ng pahayagan ay napakahalagang bagay ang nangyari noong Pebrero, hindi lamang para sa ating kasaysayan, kundi para sa kasaysayan ng buong mundo. Ngunit kung titignan natin kung sinu-sino ang nagbabasa ng pahayagang ito ay madali nating mauunawaan kung bakit ganito ang kanilang akala. Pahayagan ng mga negosyante ang *Business Day* at ang mga negosyante ang may malaking pakinabang sa nangyari noong Pebrero. Tumataob na ang ekonomiya ng bansa noon, kung nagugunita ninyo, at nahihirapan na ang mga may pera. Mahirap pa rin ang mga mahihirap at mayaman pa rin ang mga mayayaman, ngunit ang mga nasa gitna, ang tinatawag nating gitnang-uri, ay nagigipit na. Ginigipit sila ng mga kasabwat o mga krony ni Marcos. Kaya nga malaking bagay para sa mga negosyante ang nangyari noong Pebrero. Hindi katakataka na bubuhatin ng *Business Day* ang bangko ng kanilang mga mambabasa.

Mapapansin natin ang paggamit ng mga salitang "courage," "faith," at "hope." Ang mga ito'y pawang mga salitang tumutukoy sa kalooban ng tao, sa relihiyon, sa sobrenatural. Hindi binabanggit ng mga pangungusap na may mga armas sina Juan Ponce Enrile at Gregorio Honasan, mga armas na hindi masasabing sobrenatural, kundi natural na natural at pamatay-tao, pamatay ng natural na buhay ng tao. Hindi binabanggit na inatake ng mga helikopter ni Ramos ang Malacañang. Hindi inaakalang mahalaga ang mga buhay ng mga sundalong nabaril at napatay sa pakikipagpalitan ng putok sa Channel 4 at sa transmitter ng Channel 9. Kung babalikan natin ang pinanggalingan ng mga salitang "courage," "faith," at "hope," ating maaalaala si Hesus, na nagalit pa kay Pedro dahil nagbunot ng espada ang apostol. Ngunit nakahanda ang mga armas nina Enrile at nakasuot pa siya ng *bulletproof vest*. Malaki ang pagkakaiba ng lakas ng loob ni Hesus at ng pananampalataya't pag-asa ng mga apostol sa "lakas ng loob" (na may kasamang lakas ng armas) ng mga sundalo't mga taong naroroon sa Crame.

Dito siguro'y dapat banggitin ko na si Reynaldo C. Ileto ang unang nakapansin na ang mitolohiya ng Kristiyanismo ang umiral sa pagkarebolusyonaryo ng mga Pilipino noong kapanahunan ni Andres Bonifacio. Alam na natin ang madalas niyang tesis, na hindi makakanluran ang unang rebolusyon natin dahil sa katunaya'y iba ang mga layunin ng mga rebolusyonaryo. Ginawang halimbawa si Ileto ni Conrado de Quiros sa kanyang artikulo sa *Manila Times*. Binatikos ni De Quiros ang pagkakaiba ng "people power" sa "people's power." Kahit na hindi sang-ayon si de Quiros sa "people's power" o sa lakas ng masa sa pakikibaka laban sa mapang-aping mga naghaharing-uri ay inaamin naman niya na may pagkakahawig ang "people power" sa "people's power." Ayon kay De Quiros, marami tayong matututunan sa "people power":

In short, "people power" provides us with an index to the actual forms of mass consciousness, its atavistic as much as its progressive aspects, which are an integral part of the objective reality we know as the Philippine social condition. (De Quiros 1986)

Kung talagang susundin natin ang mga makabagong istrukturalista'y mali ang akala ni De Quiros na mayroong "objective reality" na kaya nating marating sa pamamagitan ng salita. Ngunit halimbawa nang mayroon nga. Kung ididikonstrak natin ang mga salita ni De Quiros ay mapapansin natin na nakakahadlang sa kanya ang wikang ingles. Halimbawa'y kahit na sa akala niya'y hindi na bago ang pariralang "people power," ay masyadong malapit ang kanyang tingin: "Actually, 'people power' was already in use before the February 22 uprising, notably in reference to the civil disobedience movement which Mrs. Aquino launched, and the people who used it precisely specified nonviolence as its distinguishing feature." Ikinalulungkot kong ipaalam kay De Quiros at sa lahat ng hindi nananagalog na ang pariralang "people power" ay matagal nang nasa tainga ng mga nakikinig sa radyo, lalong-lalo na sa mga nakikinig araw-araw sa palatuntunang "Metro Manila Banat" sa DZRH. Doon ay kasama sa logo o pagpapakilala ng palatuntunan ang pariralang "People Power." Maaari din namang sabihin natin na ang ingles na "People Power" ay pagsasalin lamang ng Tagalog na "Lakas ng Bayan" o "Laban," ang pangalan ng partido ni Ninoy Aquino.

Marami pa tayong maaaring idikonstrak na mga artikulo, tulad ng sinulat ni Alice G. Guillermo sa *Manila Times* tungkol sa pangyayari noong Pebrero: "The fast-ballooning term 'people's power' is not really new in substance." Sa katunayan, ayon kay Guillermo, ang nangyari noong Pebrero ay isa na namang tagumpay ng pasismo:

Fascism always tries to integrate a strong populist component into its structure.

What happened in the February Rebellion was that a faction of the dominant bloc, the military, broke away from it. . . .

The Enrile-Ramos faction in the February Rebellion took advantage of the strong anti-Marcos sentiment built up by the progressive forces. By taking position against a common enemy—Marcos—this faction sought to win over the people's confidence. The hitherto widely distrusted military would become heroes overnight. ...

The military strategy calling for popular support succeeded in Manila because city dwellers have a relatively lower experience of military repression unlike in the countryside where military operations are a part of everyday life. (Guillermo 1986)

Hindi mahalaga kung tama nga si Guillermo na ginamit lamang ng militar ang mga tao upang ipagpatuloy ang pasismo sa bansa. Ang mahalaga'y iyan ay isang akala, at ang akalang iyan ay taglay ng marami-rami ring mga manunulat, tulad halimbawa ng sumulat ng editoryal ng ikatlong isyu ng *Philippine Currents*:

In this light, this early the new regime finds itself at a crossroad. If it must keep the affection and loyalty of "people power" it should embody the ideals of the struggle for national independence and sovereignty which shall be its reliable instrument for achieving economic liberation and social progress of the Filipino nation. On the other hand, if it should give in to imperialist demands, calling itself "revolutionary" becomes merely a disguise to the ascendancy of a new neocolonial government which will predictably have a future as grim as the Marcos regime's. (Philippine Currents 1986)

Taglay din ang akalang iyan ng maraming istudyante sa ating mga dalubhasaan. Sa Pamantasang De la Salle, halimbawa, kung saan ako nagtuturo ng isang kurso sa makabagong kritisismong pampanitikan (kasama sa kurso ang makalumang istrukturalismo, makabagong istrukturalismo, at makabagong Marxismo), at kung saan masasabing ang mga istudyante'y kung hindi kasapi sa naghaharing-uri ay kasama sa gitnang-uri, hindi mapapagkamalang kasama sa masang Pilipino, sa aking klase sa pamantasang ito'y laganap ang di-pagsang-ayon sa mga salitang "people power." Ayon sa mga istudyante ko, halimbawa, ay hindi masasabing "people power" ang nangyari noong Pebrero dahil nagdala ang mga nasa EDSA ng kung anu-anong mga agimat, tulad ng mga istatwa ng Birheng Maria at ng Santo Niño, ng mga rosaryo, ng mga tuloy-tuloy na mga dasal na kung tutuusi'y pang-eengkanto ng mga mayayaman laban sa demonyong si Marcos. Ano ang pagkakaiba, ayon sa kanila, ng anting-anting ni Ramon Revilla sa kanyang mga pelikula at ng mga rosaryo't bulaklak na hinahawakan ng mga humadlang sa mga tangke?

Minsa'y ipinagawa ko ng mga maiikling talataan ang aking mga istudyante sa kritisismong pampanitikan. Natuklasan ko na karamihan sa kanila'y hindi naniniwala na ang nangyari noong Pebrero ay tunay na rebolusyon. Ayon sa kanila, ang nangyari noong Pebrero'y rebolusyon lamang ng gitnang-uri. Ang ibig sabihin nito'y sa pananaw ng mga kabataang kasapi sa gitnang-uri, ang kanilang uri ang may kagagawan sa nangyari noong Pebrero. Sa akala nila'y sila ang nagtagumpay. Isinipi ko sa artikulong ito, sa apendiks, ang ilan sa mga isinulat na mga pangungusap ng aking mga istudyante. Mula sa mga bibig mismo ng mga naroroon ang mga salitang iyon. Ayon kay Rizal ay nasa kabataan ang pag-asa ng ating bayan. Makikita natin na totoo iyan kung kritisismong pampanitikan ang pag-uusapan natin. Kung ang mga nagsisimula pa lamang sa kritisismo ay ganito na ang naiisip, ano pa kaya ang kanilang matutuklasan kapag lumaki na sila't lumalim na ang kanilang pananaw? Malaki ang aking pag-asa na di maglalaon ay babaguhin ng mga batang kritiko ang larangan ng pagsusuri ng ating kultura't lipunan. Ayon sa makabagong istrukturalismo'y hindi mahalaga kung tama nga sila o mali. Ang mahalaga'y kung ano ang kanilang akala, at iyan ang kanilang akala.

Ang tinalakay ko sa artikulong ito'y iyun lamang mga salitang bumabalot sa mga akala ng ilang tumingin at tumitingin sa mga pangyayari noong Pebrero 22 hanggang 25 ng taong 1986. Sinuri ko ang mga salita at mga akalang ito sa pamamagitan ng dikonstruksiyon na siyang paraan ng kritisismong pampanitikan ng mga makabagong istrukturalista na tulad nina Jacques Lacan, Michel Foucault, at Jacques Derrida. Hindi malayo ang narating ng aking kritisismo, sapagkat hindi malawak ang nasasakop ng makabagong istrukturalismo. Kung nais nating mabuo kahit na kaunti ang ating pagsusuri ay dapat siguro nating gamitan ng mga paraan ng kritisismo na natuklasan ng mga makabagong Marxista na tulad nina Louis Althusser, Pierre Macherey, Terry Eagleton, at Julia Kristeva. Maaari ko na sigurong ipaubaya ang ganitong mas matinding pagsusuri kay Randolph David na maka-Althusser, kay Soledad Reyes na maka-Macherey, kay Edna Manlapaz na balita ko'y maka-Eagleton na, at kay Sonya Silva sa kanyang pagbabalik sa Pilipinas, dahil kasalukuyang pinag-aaralan niya ang mga teoriya ni Kristeva. Sa palagay ko'y matutuklasan ng mga kritikong ito na may gumigitna sa mga pangyayari noong Pebrero at sa mga akalang nababalot sa wika. Ito'y ang tinatawag ng mga makabagong Marxista na "ideolohiya." Malaki ang pagkakaiba ng ganitong "ideolohiya" sa dating paggamit ng salitang iyan ng mga makalumang Marxista na kasalukuyang pinaniniwalaan pa rin ng National Democratic Front. Ngunit ibang paksa na iyan. Bagong akala na iyan. Sa aking palagay, kung inyong mamarapatin, sa pagsusuri ng kung ano man iyong nangyari sa ating bansa noong Pebrero ay tapos na ang aking responsibilidad bilang isang kritikong pampanitikan.

**TALASANGGUNIAN**

*Nais kong kilalanin ang aking utang na loob sa aking mga istudyante sa CONCRIT (Contemporary Literary Criticism) A01, ikatlong trimestre, SY 1985-86, sa Pamantasang De la Salle. Kung hindi sa kanilang pagbibigay ng kuru-kuro sa aking klase'y baka wala akong nasabi sa artikulong ito. Marami sa mga opinyon ko ay nabuo dahil sa aming mga diskusyon sa loob ng klase.*

Abad, Gemino H. 1985. The Space Between. Lungsod ng Quezon: University of the Philippines Press.

Cruz, Isagani R., ed. 1985. Contemporary Literary Criticism. Maynila: De La Salle University.

Daroy, Petronilo Bn. 1986. "Revolution or 'Revolution." *National Midweek*, Marso 19: 3-4.

De Dios, Servillano E., Jr. 1986. "'Twas Awesome." *Business Day*, Marso 21: 33-34.

De Quiros, Conrado. 1986. "People Power: Or, how 'those crazy Filipinos' defied the rules for a noble end." *Sunday Times,* March 16: 4.

Derrida, Jacques. 1971. "The Supplement of Cupola: Philosophy Before Linguistics." Sa: Cruz 1985: 391-393.

Foucault, Michel. 1969. "What is an Author?" Sa: Cruz 1985: 140-155.

Guillermo, Alice G. 1986. "Strategies of populism." *Manila Times*, Marso 23: 4.

KNT News Service. 1986. "Reagan writes new chapter in book on dumping dictators." *Orlando Sentinel,* Pebrero 26: A-12.

Lacan, Jacques. 1956. "Symbol and Language." Sa: Cruz 1985: 385-390.

Rosenblatt, Roger. 1986. "People Power." *Time*, Marso 10: 9.

**APENDIKS**

**Sinulat ng mga Istudyante Ng DLSU**

*TEKSTO 1*

The Crame Revolution was a middle-class revolution. It was the middle class who went to Crame armed with flowers, rosaries and statuettes. They were the ones who distributed food (sandwiches, particularly, are very middle-class), clamored for "snap toilets," donated white shirts, lent flashlights, brought tents, administered medicines and first-aid and turned the event into a picnic of sorts. They were the ones who came in cars with their *barkadas*, toting cameras, binoculars and Betamax recorders. They wore Cory shirts, pins, visors and caps, and fanned themselves with Cory fans. They were the ones who had their jobs to return to regardless of the outcome of the revolt, who would be among the claimants to the monopolies which would be distributed to the people, who would cut newspaper clippings and tape talks at the New TV 4 to send to their middle-class relatives abroad (the same relatives who would later go "balikbayan" to see Malacañang and exchange gossip). They are now the ones keeping watch over the middle-class government which they had cheered on.

## TEKSTO 2

If we clearly analyze the people who've been there, we can clearly tell that they were not farmers or fishermen; they were students, teachers, religious people, businessmen, employees, etc. So maybe from this point, one can say that it was a middle-class revolution; people from the lower stratum of our society were not there and were not represented.

## TEKSTO 3

As we all know Manila is densely populated by middle class citizens who were pushed one stratum down by the dictator and these are most of the people who joined the Crame Revolution. These are now called the new poor which is equivalent to the new rich.

## TEKSTO 4

The middle-class saw this revolution as an opportunity to grow. The ouster of a dictatorship will entail the benefits of freedom which the old regime has selfishly denied them. Under a new administration, the middle-class foresees a horizon full of opportunities to rise above their class.

## TEKSTO 5

Those who were present during the historical affair were mostly students of different schools of Metro Manila. It was very obvious because these people wearing yellow shirts, walking to and fro with banners, yellow ribbons and food of all sorts cannot be mistaken for people who belong to the masses. The reason is quite known to us because the masses cannot afford to purchase yellow shirts and all those stuff that were scattered during the revolution.

## TEKSTO 6

First of all, we should take into consideration the community surrounding Camp Crame where most of its members are bracketed among the middle-class. Villages such as White Plains, St. Ignatius, Blue Ridge, Greenhills and alike house the members of this community.

## TEKSTO 7

Most of the early vigilantes came in cars. The general atmosphere was festive. People manning the barricades did not even constitute five percent of the Philippines' population. Most of all, it was right here in Metro Manila where it broke out, not in the countrysides.

## TEKSTO 8

The economic standing of the middle class enabled them to answer the call for people power.

## TEKSTO 9

It would be a loss of a lot of money if the Cory-Doy ticket would lose since the Marcos Administration had distinguished those businessmen for Marcos and those for Mrs. Aquino. So when that revolution started last Saturday the middle class were the first ones who occupied the Camps as they themselves see this event as the last event that will lead to the ouster of the dictator and in turn preserve their properties.

## TEKSTO 10

The poor couldn't also be very "active" because they have their own lives to support. They do not have extra money to spend for rallies and food to keep them overnight in the streets. When I interviewed vendors, they said that they were there for the business.

## TEKSTO 11

Also, during the 4-day Crame event, it was the middle class who could afford to go to Crame, miss work and bring food.

## TEKSTO 12

First of all, the revolution entailed costs like sandwiches, flowers, etc. to be given away and that is something the masses do not have. Second, the leadership of Mrs. Cory Aquino is identified mainly as middle class because of her degree of intellectual growth, wealth and social position.

## TEKSTO 13

The people from Bulacan and other provinces were more or less middle class (because they could afford to come here).

## TEKSTO 14

Those who could afford to go and share their food were the ones who stayed in Crame. Although a minority of the lower class attended, maybe some took advantage of the food being distributed; vendors took advantage of the crowd, maybe some really went to Crame to participate.

## TEKSTO 15

The surrounding areas of Camp Crame and Camp Aguinaldo are composed of the middle class. They can stay there for 4 days and 3 nights, and have 3 meals a day. They were also the ones that blocked their cars against the incoming tanks.

## TEKSTO 16

In the 4 days that the change happened, the "masa" was there. That's true, but could they have stayed that long and kept vigil if there were not enough food to feed them. These foods were all donated by at least the middle class. If there was not enough food, the people would have just stayed there in the afternoon and gone home eventually at night.

*TEKSTO 17*

What limited the lower class was the way to get there. They can't sacrifice their work to go there. Their family will suffer if they don't work even for just one day. Some can't even afford the fare in going there.

*TEKSTO 18*

[The masses] are just tools of the elite class in such a revolution. The brain of this revolution is actually the upper class or the elite.

*TEKSTO 19*

But if you look closely, the ones who "spearheaded" the revolution, mostly belong to the upper class. For instance, the two military officers — Gen. Ramos and Min. Enrile — are not of middle-class origin.

*TEKSTO 20*

First of all, who started the idea of having a revolution? I think it all started with Ramos and Enrile. Who asked for people power? I think it's Butz Aquino and the ones who were barricading themselves at Camp Crame and Camp Aguinaldo to save the Elite. Like TingTing Cojuangco and the other upper class people — the "bourgeoisie."

*TEKSTO 21*

I refuse to call it a revolution. Why? Because whenever we speak of a revolution, there is a change in political/economic structures in the government system. But what we have here is a handful of "balimbings" and of course a change in personalities.

# REINTEGRATION OF RETURNING OVERSEAS CONTRACT WORKERS: THE CASE OF BARANGAY VERGARA, METRO MANILA

STELLA P. GO

The past decade has seen the unprecedented movement to various parts of the world, particularly the Middle East, of hundreds of thousands of Filipinos in search of better work opportunities. From 1976 to 1982 alone, a total of 1,205,098 Filipino workers were employed abroad, sending home foreign exchange remittances estimated at US$3.45 billion (Institute of Labor and Manpower Studies, 1984:1). Ever since the overseas employment program was instituted as a major government policy in the Philippine Labor Code in 1974 to temporarily solve the problems of unemployment and tight balance of payments of the country, the massive exodus of Filipino workers has continued.

By 1980, the number of jobs in the Middle East rose by a rate of 80.4% (Philippine Overseas Employment Administration, 1984). As a result of the world oil glut which forced some Middle East countries to cut down on their development projects and consequently, to freeze the hiring of foreign manpower, however, employment generation slowed down. The rate declined to 39% in 1981 and 15% in 1982. The Philippine Overseas Employment Administration, however, was of the belief that overseas employment would continue to play a major role in Philippine development, and government statistics showed that in 1983 the rate of increase rose again from 15% in 1982 to 53% in 1983. While the government has focused upon the expansion and maintenance of current international labor markets in its future plans and policies for the overseas employment program (especially with the current economic crisis), it has not adopted policies regarding the absorption and reintegration of return migrants—one area that poses a potential problem for government if not given attention.

Because labor migration to the Middle East is a relatively new phenomenon, little attention has been paid thus far to overseas contract workers (OCWs) who have returned or are returning home. While statistics are not accurate nor complete, it is believed that the number of returnees in the Philippines is steadily growing. In 1985 alone, the POEA reported that a total of 75,573 land-based workers returned as of the end of that year. While this is so, virtually nothing is known of them and the process of adjustment and reintegration which they undergo upon their return. What happens to these workers who leave from and return to their communities of origin? What kinds of adjustment do they and their families have to make? Are they able to find jobs? Are they satisfied with the wage levels in the Philippines after working for higher wages overseas? What do they do with their remittances? These are questions that involve not only economic but social issues as well.

## Objectives of the Study

This paper, therefore, looks into some of the psycho-social and economic aspects of the return migration in Barangay Vergara, one community in Metro Manila. It is based on a pilot study conducted by the Research Center of De La Salle University, Manila, with funding from ESCAP, which looks into the reintegration of returning overseas contract workers in the same community. Specifically, this paper seeks:

1. to determine possible adjustment difficulties at the household and community levels of return migrants;
2. to look into job descriptions and income expectations of return migrants;
3. to determine possible skills acquisition and/or development overseas and their utilization upon return; and
4. to examine the use of remittances especially in relation to investment and consumption expenditures, and possible spill-over effects in the community.

## Methodology

To achieve the objectives of the study, a census of all households with at least one return migrant who had been home for at least one month prior to the census was undertaken in Barangay Vergara. In the case where the return migrant was married, both the migrant and his/her spouse were interviewed. Where the return migrant was single, he/she and either a parent or an adult sibling (18 years old and above) were interviewed. A total of 59 return migrants and 56 spouses and nearest adult kin of the return migrants participated in the study. Data gathering began on May 16, 1985 and ended on June 16, 1985.

## The Setting

Barangay Vergara is a crowded urban community found in the municipality of Mandaluyong in Metro Manila. It is one of 27 barangays in the municipality and occupies an area of 43 hectares. It has a total of about 765 households and an estimated population of 4,991.

Barangay Vergara is surrounded by large factories and industrial plants. Through the years these have attracted urban immigrants in search of better employment opportunities. Community residents have observed that the influx of migrants has caused the population to swell and the number of squatters to increase. As a consequence, the municipal government has occasionally relocated families elsewhere to ease the population pressure on the inadequate basic services of the community. Today, this community is a mixture of various regional groups: Visayans, Pangasinenses, Bikolanos, and Bulakeños.

Many of the Vergara residents are skilled and unskilled laborers employed in nearby industrial and manufacturing companies which recruit from among the ranks of the unemployed. In 1983, an estimated 20% of the total number of households in the community have at least one member who has gone overseas on contract employment. This phenomenon has been perceived by Vergara residents as having gained momentum in the mid-seventies. Engineering Equipment, Incorporated (EEI), one of the country's leading construction companies found in the adjacent *barangay*, has been highly instrumental in the movement of a considerable number of Vergara residents overseas. EEI began recruiting workers for its foreign contracts in the Middle East in the early seventies, and Barangay Vergara was one of the communities from which it drew its manpower.

## Findings

### Profile of Respondents

*Returning Overseas Contract Workers (OCWs).* Table 1 shows that the return migrants are generally males (58 out of 59). They are in their mid-thirties (x = 34.7 years), mostly married (79.7%) and heads of households (78.6%). Like the rest of the Filipino population, a majority belong to the Roman Catholic religion (94.9%).

It is interesting to note that the returnees have a fairly high level of education. The majority (64.3%) have had a complete high school or at least some high school education, while one-fifth (21.4%) have had some college, if not a complete college education.

A fairly substantial proportion of the returnees were unemployed prior to overseas migration (17 out of 59). More than half of these (58.8%), however, were unemployed for only less than a year prior to working overseas. The rest had been unemployed for about two to five years or have not worked at all (Table 1). Whether those who were unemployed for less than a year prior to overseas employment had been so because they had lost their jobs or because they chose to resign from them to apply overseas cannot be ascertained.

On the other hand, their employment history shows that, generally, these returnees have gone to work overseas twice on an average contract length of 18 months (Table 1). A majority (78.0%) have had an opportunity to work in Saudi Arabia, while close to half (45.8%) have worked in other parts of the Middle East (Table 2). During their last overseas job, close to ninety percent (88.2%) worked in the Middle East (Table 3). Most of these workers first left the Philippines to work abroad after the overseas employment program was instituted as a major government policy in 1974 (Table 4). About half of them (52.5%), however, left for abroad for the first time in 1981 and 1982. They started returning to the country in 1979 with the majority (61%) returning only in 1983 and 1984.

*Relatives of Returning Overseas Contract Workers.* The non-OCW respondents, on the other hand, were generally females (94.6%), whose average age was 35.6 years. They were mostly wives of the returning overseas contract workers (78.6%), and like the returning OCWs, a majority of the non-OCW respondents (55.3%) had a complete or at least some high school education, while 25.0 percent had a complete or some college education (Table 5). Most of them were non-gainfully employed as housewives and the like (58.9%); a substantial proportion (37.5%), however, were gainfully employed either as wage and salary earners or as self-employed individuals with an average monthly income of ₱1,238.00 or US$68.70.

*Economic Reintegration*

*Problems Anticipated and Actually Encountered.* While half of the return migrants (52.5%) foresaw no difficulties upon their return to the Philippines, the primary concern of a substantial proportion was economic in nature. They were apprehensive about finding either local or overseas

253

employment (25.4%) and about coping with such economic difficulties as the rising cost of living in the country, low wages locally, and the depletion of their savings (23.7%).

It would seem like the apprehensions of some of the returnees were not without basis. While 47.5% of the 59 returnees encountered no problems when they returned, about a third (30.5%) experienced such difficulties as the rising cost of living and low wages locally. Some also had difficulty finding local and overseas employment (13.6%). Interestingly enough, the non-migrant respondents (mostly wives) also reported the same difficulties encountered by the migrant workers upon their return. While 36.4% replied that they did not experience any problems when their migrant member returned home, a substantial proportion likewise said that finding local and overseas employment was a difficulty (25.5%). Coping with the rising cost of living and the like was another difficulty mentioned by the non-OCW respondents (23.6%). Perhaps, the congruence in the responses between the migrant and his nearest kin may point to the salience of the economic concerns in their lives. The transitory nature of overseas employment aggravated by the economic difficulties of the country has made the overseas contract worker and his family insecure about their economic welfare.

When asked how successfully they coped with these problems, a majority of the returnees who had encountered some problems upon their return replied that they did so with some difficulty (71.4%). While a majority (55.2%) of their spouses and kin replied likewise, a large proportion (37.9%) expressed the opinion that it was with great difficulty that they coped with their problems.

It was not surprising to discover, however, that the returnees who reported that they experienced no difficulties at all when they returned were those who felt a sense of economic security. It was they (18 out of 27) who gave economic-related reasons such as financial stability and assurance of actual employment upon return as accounting for the absence of any problems upon return.

*Local Employment and Income Expectations.* It would seem, therefore, that the economic difficulties currently facing the country as reflected in its high unemployment rate, rising cost of living, and the scarcity of jobs have made the absorption of returning overseas workers difficult. In Metro Manila, which suffered the highest unemployment rate of 22.1% in 1985 (as reported by the National Census and Statistics Office), the problem has become doubly acute.

While a majority of the returnees in Barangay Vergara (61.1%) sought local employment either as wage earners or as self-employed

254

individuals, a substantial proportion (39.0%) did not (Table 6). Among those who sought local wage employment, however, close to half (46.2%) remained unemployed at the time of the survey. Nine (9) out of the 26 returnees who sought local wage employment cited the scarcity of local job opportunities as the main difficulty they encountered. The financial costs of seeking local employment (i.e., transportation) and the low wages in the country relative to the wages they had been used to abroad were among the other difficulties mentioned by a substantial prorportion of return migrants (Table 6). It is interesting to note that, among those who found a job in the Philippines, the shortest time it took them to find one was less than a month while the longest was 2 years. Half of them found their jobs within less than six months, while the other half took over six months to as long as 2 years (Mdn. = 5.5 months).

They landed jobs as craftsmen and production process workers (i.e., tile setters, automobile mechanics, and repairmen), clerical workers, operatives (specifically bus and jeepney drivers) and the like, earning an average monthly income of ₱1,063.00 or US$59.06 (Table 7). These jobs were basically the same types of jobs which most of the 26 returnees who sought or planned to seek local employment said they wanted (Table 8). The average monthly income which they said they would like to earn, however, was ₱1,375.50 or US$76.38, a figure only slightly higher than the salary of those who found local employment. Considering the tight economic situation, it was probably unrealistic to hope for a much higher wage.

When asked why they did not look for a job locally, a majority of the 23 returnees (60.9%) who chose not to look for one in the country replied that they were looking for another contract overseas. While this is so, it is striking to note that almost all of the returnees (56 out of the 59) said they were looking for or planning to look for another job abroad (Table 9). At the time of the census, a majority (83.9%) had already reapplied to various recruitment agencies. Most of them (75.5%) were interested in landing overseas jobs as craftsmen and other related workers (i.e., metal workers, masons, air conditioning mechanics, and repairmen) and as operatives (i.e., truck, tractor, and heavy equipment drivers) at an average monthly salary of US$363.54, an amount six times more than the average monthly income earned by the returnees working locally (Table 9). The exorbitant placement fees, certain unacceptable hiring practices (i.e., the need for "grease money"), the stiff competition locally, and the long process involved in applying for a job overseas, however, were the main difficulties pointed out by the returnees in finding new contracts abroad (Table 10).

*Remittances and Their Use.* All of the migrants sent home monetary remittances to their families while they were working overseas. These were sent mostly to their spouses (71.2%) and their parents (23.7%). On their last jobs prior to their return, the migrants who were mostly in construction-related occupations earned an average of US$386.04 monthly and US$4,632.40 annually. Over the one-year period prior to their return, they were able to send home approximately 50% of their total annual income (US$2286.90). They were also able to save and bring home with them an average of US$1,383.84, an amount equivalent to roughly 30% of their total annual income.

Contrary to the popular notion that most of the remittances of the overseas contract workers are spent on luxury items and big ticket electronic items, the study reveals that among the most important uses of remittances sent home were on basic necessities such as food, clothing, medicine, and the like. This was reported by practically all the return migrants (98.3%) and confirmed by their spouses and nearest kin (100.0%) (see Table 11). A substantial proportion of the migrant respondents likewise reported that the remittances had been spent for the education and training of members of the households (47.5%), paying off debts (33.9%), and for their housing/shelter needs (23.7%). It is striking to note that productive investment is not among the priorities of the migrant and his famiily. Perhaps because the migrants were able to work overseas for only an average of 2 times and for an average duration of 18 months, they may not have accumulated enough savings over and above the priorities they may have for basic necessities, education, and paying off debts for productive investment. It is possible that the more overseas contracts they accumulate, the greater the possibility that part of the remittances may be released for productive investment.

## Skill Acquisition/Upgrading Abroad and Utilization

*Upon return*. Upon return forty-four (44) out of the 59 return migrants reported that they had upgraded at least one of the skills they acquired in the Philippines while working abroad. Construction skills (i.e., carpentry, masonry) ranked first among those reported by the migrants as having been upgraded, followed by skills related to transport, excavating, and lifting equipment operation (generally driving). On the other hand, because their jobs overseas required other skills which they did not possess, the rest (14) reported that they were not able to enhance or to develop the skills they acquired in the Philippines which they brought with them overseas.

While this is so, 20 out of the 59 returnees reported that they were able to acquire new skills in the course of their work experience abroad. Regardless of type of skill, however, respondents generally reported that they were not able to apply what they had learned abroad when they returned (Table 12).

Whether this is simply a function of the fact that only a small proportion of the returnees (14 out of the 59) found jobs locally or because the skills acquired overseas had little or no applicability in the local context is an area that needs further investigation.

## Reintegration into the Family and Community

*Adjustment to the Family.* The adjustment of the returnees back to their families and community seems to be accomplished with little difficulty. When asked what problems they anticipated they would face when they returned home and what problems they actually encountered, not one mentioned anything related to the family. In fact, when asked about possible changes in their relationship with their family members, it was the general perception among the migrants that there had been no change at all in the relationship since they went overseas. In fact, in certain cases their relationships had been enhanced.

Among the married return migrants, a majority (58.06%) were of the opinion that their children had become closer to them and regarded them more highly than before they left (54.84%) (see Table 13). A substantial proportion (43.33%) likewise felt that their children now consulted with them more often than they used to. Hardly anyone said that his relationship with his children in the various aspects mentioned previously had deteriorated since he worked abroad (Table 13). The same pattern emerges for the relationship between the wives and the children indicating that, despite the father's temporary absence, both parents have remained close to their children (Table 14).

Likewise, among the single migrants, there is a general perception that there has been no change in their relationships with their family members (Table 14). The returnees feel that they are as highly regarded by their families (66.67%) and that they have remained as close to their brothers and sisters as before (77.78%). They also feel that their families consult them regarding decisions on family matters as often as they used to before they had gone to work overseas (66.67%). The parents/siblings confirm the migrants' perception (Table 14).

If one looks at the decision-making patterns within the households of the married overseas contract workers before they left for overseas, while they were abroad, and now that they have returned, a very interesting pattern emerges. Level of participation in decision-making for 10 areas of family life was measured on a scale of 1 to 3, with 1, signifying no participation at all in decision-making, 2, joint decision-making, and 3, sole decision-making. Thus, the highest possible score that could be obtained was 30, indicating no participation at all in decision-making regarding any aspect of family life.

The results reveal that there is no significant difference in the perception of the OCWs and their wives of their respective levels of participation on decision-making before the OCW left for abroad (t = .20, df = 37, p .05). The mean composite scores of 22.11 for the OCW and 21.97 for his spouse indicate that each one believes that on the average, his/her decisions are made jointly or in consultation with the spouse and/or with other family members (Table 14).

As expected, while the migrant was overseas, his participation in decision-making within the household decreased (from a mean score of 22.11 to 19.49). On the other hand, because of his absence, and because she now had to take responsibility, the wife's level of participation in decision-making increased (from a mean score of 21.97 to 25.29). The difference in the levels of participation in decision-making between the OCW and his wife while he was away was highly significant (t = 4.75, df = 37, p .001). The mean composite scores indicate a tendency toward more decision-making on her own by the wife (x = 25.29) as compared to the OCW (x = 19.49) who was working overseas. While this is so, when the migrant returned, the pattern reverted once again to approximately the same level as before overseas migration, with the migrant and his spouse sharing jointly in the decision-making (Table 15). It would seem, therefore, that the married OCW falls back into the role he used to play in the family before he left without much difficulty. Whatever changes there are in the roles of the migrant and his spouse as a result of overseas employment are only transitory in nature. Once he returns, the roles easily revert to what they were prior to the migrant's leaving. Perhaps the relatively short length of the absence of the migrant from the household and the fact that the migrant has a chance to visit his family sometime during his stint overseas may explain the ease with which he is able to readjust to his family.

*Adjustment to the Community.* Readjusting to Barangay Vergara also posed little difficulty for the return migrants. Forty-three (43) of the 59 migrants in the study noticed various changes in the community (mostly infrastructure in nature such as the construction of a playground and the installation of water pumps in the community). Among these, a majority (72.1%) liked the changes they saw and had no difficulty in adjusting to them. Moreover, a majority of the migrant respondents whether married or single were of the opinion that their friends and neighbors had not changed at all towards them since they had been away (Table 16).

A majority of the returnees (75.0%) likewise saw many changes in Metro Manila. It was adjusting to Metro Manila, however, that posed some difficulty for the return migrants. A substantial proportion (30.8%) did not like and had difficulty adjusting to the peace and order situation in the country which they perceived had worsened. Moreover, the increasing prices of commodities was a change that some migrants likewise did not like and had difficulty adjusting to.

*Level of Satisfaction.* Overseas employment brought about changes in the level of satisfaction of the overseas contract workers and their nearest kin. In the study, level of satisfaction was measured on a scale of 1 to 10 with 1 indicating great dissatisfaction and 10 indicating great satisfaction. A composite level of satisfaction score was obtained by adding the scores of each of the 7 aspects of life tapped. Thus, the highest possible score was 70, while the lowest possible score was 10. On the whole, there was a significant difference between the overall level of satisfaction of the overseas worker and his nearest kin before migration and after he had returned (t + 4.30 and 4.46, respectively, df = 46, p .001). The mean composite scores indicate that there was an increase in the level of satisfaction of the migrant and his nearest kin after the migrant's return from abroad (Table 17). While this is so, both the migrants and their relatives were only moderately satisfied with their lives at the time of the survey (x = 44.4 and 46.42, respectively). Comparing the married and the single migrants, the data show that the married returnees have a higher level of satisfaction (x = 46.50) than the unmarried (x = 35.56). Because of the very small number of single migrants (9) in the study, however, it is difficult to make any inferences regarding the results.

If one focuses on the married OCWs now that they have returned, one will notice that it is the relationship with their spouse and children that provides them with greatest satisfaction among all of the aspects of their lives (x = 8.44 and 8.35, respectively) (Table 17). Despite the increase, however, the migrants and their spouses are only fairly satisfied with their socio-economic situation. In fact, among the seven aspects of their lives, their socio-economic status provides them with the lowest level of satisfaction. While overseas employment has brought about some improvement in their economic life, the current state of the Philippine economy characterized by rising prices, and high rate of unemployment has minimized the economic impact of overseas employment for the migrant.

## Conclusions and Recommendations

One serious drawback of this pilot study is its small sample size. Because of this, it is difficult to arrive at definitive conclusions about the reintegration process among returning overseas contract workers. The following, however, can be gleaned from the preliminary results:

1. Economic reintegration is probably the major difficulty confronting the returning overseas contract worker. Given the current state of the Philippine economy, it becomes even more imperative for government and the private sector to generate more local employment opportunities. While there is an intensification by government of its efforts to find and to open new markets for Filipino labor abroad, it will only serve as a stop gap measure for a problem that will assume greater magnitude as more and more workers return to the country. Attention to the economic reintegration of returning overseas contract workers is important if the gains of overseas employment for the worker, his family, and Philippine society as a whole are to be sustained and maximized.

2. Workers do acquire new skills overseas; their utility in the local context, however, is an area that needs further investigation.

3. The gains from overseas employment may be of a magnitude that can only adequately meet the basic needs of the worker and his family, particularly those who have had a short overseas employment experience. For the impact of the phenomenon to be felt, a worker may need to work abroad for a longer period of time. Thus, in this study, remittances were used by a substantial proportion of the migrants only for basic necessities such as education and paying off debts. Virtually no one used the remittances for productive investment.

4. Overseas employment does not seem to create problems of readjustment into the family and the community for the overseas contract worker. Perhaps the relatively short duration of the absence of the worker from his family and the limited overseas employment experience of the workers in this study mitigate against problems of this nature. It likewise appears that at this point overseas employment does not seem to have a lasting effect in changing gender roles within the family, particularly in the area of decision-making. It cannot be ascertained by this study, however, whether in the long run the situation will remain the same.

This paper has barely scratched the surface of the reintegration process among returning overseas contract workers. It might be expected that, as the number of Filipino workers returning from their contracts overseas increases, the problems and difficulties they face will become more evident. To gain a better and a more in-depth understanding of the phenomenon, it is suggested that a large-scale study be conducted among return migrants to find out if there are significant differences in the reintegration process from an economic and psycho-social point of view among migrants from different occupational categories, who have worked for varying lengths of time overseas and who have been back for varying lengths of time. By doing such a study, the effects of their overseas experience on their level of skill, productivity, motivation, entrepreneurship, investment intentions, family relationships, and family roles can be assessed with greater certainty.

## REFERENCES

Institute of Labor and Manpower Studies. 1984. Working Abroad. Manila: Institute of Labor and Manpower Studies, Ministry of Labor and Employment.

Philippine Overseas Employment Administration. 1984 statistics.

## APPENDIX

**TABLE 1**    SELECTED  CHARACTERISTICS  OF  RETURNING
OCWs

| SELECTED CHARACTERISTICS | PERCENTAGE | |
|---|---|---|
| Sex: | | |
| Male | 98.3 | |
| Female | 1.7 | 59 |
| Civil Status: | | |
| Single | 20.3 | |
| Married | 79.7 | 59 |
| Religion | | |
| Roman Catholic | 94.9 | |
| Iglesia ni Kristo | 5.1 | 59 |
| Relationship of Returning OCW to Household Head | | |
| Household Head | 78.6 | |
| Son | 19.6 | |
| Brother | 1.8 | 56 |
| Educational Attainment | | |
| Elementary/Some elementary | 12.5 | |
| High School/Some high school | 64.3 | |
| College/Some college | 21.4 | |
| Vocational | 1.8 | 56 |
| Proportion unemployed prior to overseas employment | 28.8 | 17 |
| Proportion unemployed for | | |
| Less than a year | 58.8 | |
| Two to five years | 35.4 | |
| Never employed | 5.8 | 17 |
| Mean Age (in years) | 34.7 | |
| Mean number of times the migrant worked abroad | 2.4 | |
| Mean length of contract of the last overseas job (in months) | 18.8 | |
| Mean duration of last overseas job (in months) | 14.7 | |

**TABLE 2**    PERCENTAGE OF RETURNING OCWs BY COUNTRY EVER WORKED IN

| COUNTRY | % |
| --- | --- |
| I. ASIA | |
|    Middle East | |
|      Iraq | 22.0 |
|      Lebanon | 1.7 |
|      Iran | 1.7 |
|      Kuwait | 5.1 |
|      Bahrain | 1.7 |
|      Saudi Arabia | 78.0 |
|      Qatar | 1.7 |
|      United Arab Emirates | 13.6 |
|    Central Asia | |
|      China | 1.7 |
|    Southeast Asia | |
|      Brunei | 1.7 |
|      Malaysia | 1.7 |
|      Singapore | 5.1 |
| II. WESTERN EUROPE | |
|      Denmark | 1.7 |
| III. AFRICA | |
|      Libya | 8.5 |
| IV. AUSTRALIA, OCEANIA AND THE PACIFIC | |
|      Papua New Guinea | 1.7 |
|      Guam | |
| | 100.1 |
| | (59) |

**TABLE 3**    PERCENTAGE DISTRIBUTION OF RETURNING OCWs BY COUNTRY OF LAST OVERSEAS JOB

| COUNTRY | % |
| --- | --- |
| I. ASIA | |
|    Middle East | 88.2 |
|      Iraq | 15.3 |
|      Lebanon | 1.7 |
|      Kuwait | 5.1 |
|      Saudi Arabia | 61.0 |
|      United Arab Emirates | 5.1 |
|    Central Asia | |
|      China | 1.7 |
|    Southeast Asia | |
|      Singapore | 1.7 |
| II. WESTERN EUROPE | |
|      Denmark | 1.7 |
| III. AFRICA | |
|      Libya | 5.1 |
| IV. AUSTRALIA, OCEANIA AND THE PACIFIC | |
|      Papua New Guinea | 1.7 |
| | 100.1 |
| | (59) |

**TABLE 4**   PERCENTAGE DISTRIBUTION OF RETURNING OCWs BY YEAR OF FIRST DEPARTURE AND BY YEAR OF RETURN FROM LAST OVERSEAS JOB

| YEAR | % DISTRIBUTION OF RETURNING OCWs | |
|---|---|---|
| | FIRST DEPARTURE | RETURN FROM LAST OVERSEAS JOB |
| 1967-1974 | 5.1 | - |
| 1975 | 1.7 | - |
| 1976 | 3.4 | - |
| 1977 | 8.5 | - |
| 1978 | 8.5 | - |
| 1979 | 8.5 | 6.8 |
| 1980 | 5.1 | 1.7 |
| 1981 | 28.8 | 5.1 |
| 1982 | 23.7 | 6.8 |
| 1983 | 3.4 | 28.8 |
| 1984 | 3.4 | 32.2 |
| 1985 | - | 18.6 |
| Total (N = 59) | 100.1 | 100.0 |

**TABLE 5**    SELECTED CHARACTERISTICS OF NON-OCW
RESPONDENTS

| Characteristics | Percentage | Number |
|---|---|---|
| **Sex** | | |
| Total | 100.0 | 56 |
| Male | 5.4 | |
| Female | 94.6 | |
| | | |
| **Relationship to Return Migrant:** | | |
| Total | 100.0 | 56 |
| Spouse | 78.6 | |
| Parent | 12.5 | |
| Sibling | 7.1 | |
| Others (i.e., daughter) | 1.8 | |
| | | |
| **Educational Attainment:** | | |
| Total | 100.0 | 56 |
| Elementary/Some elementary | 19.6 | |
| High School/Some high school | 53.3 | |
| College/Some college | 25.0 | |
| | | |
| **Labor force status** | | |
| Total | 100.0 | 56 |
| Unemployed | 3.6 | |
| Non-gainfully employed | 58.9 | |
| Gainfully employed | 37.5 | |
| | | |
| **Present primary occupation of the gainfully employed:** | | |
| Total | 100.0 | 21 |
| Wage and salary earners | 38.1 | |
| Self-employed | 61.9 | |

| | Average |
|---|---|
| Mean Age (in years) | 35.6 |
| Median monthly income of the gainfully employed | ₱1,238 |

**TABLE 6** MIGRANT'S LOCAL EMPLOYMENT UPON LAST RETURN

| ITEM | PERCENTAGE | NUMBER |
|---|---|---|
| Percentage distribution of returning OCWs who: | | |
| Total | 100.0 | 59 |
| Sought local wage employment | 44.1 | |
| Sought local self employment | 17.0 | |
| Did not seek local employment | 39.0 | |
| Among those who sought local wage employment, percentage who: | | |
| Total | 100.0 | 26 |
| Found local employment | 53.8 | |
| Remained unemployed | 46.2 | |

| | PERIOD |
|---|---|
| Length of time before first local wage employment was found: | |
| Shortest period | less than a month |
| Longest period | 24 months |
| Median period | 5.5 months |

| | PERCENTAGE | NUMBER |
|---|---|---|
| Reasons for not seeking employment: | | |
| Total | 100.0 | 23 |
| Looking for another overseas job | 60.9 | |
| Others (low wages, unacceptable hiring practices, etc.) | 39.1 | |
| Problems encountered in seeking local employment:* | | |
| None | 34.6 | |
| Limited job opportunities/No vacancy | 34.6 | |
| Over-age/Not qualified | 7.7 | |
| Financial costs (i.e., transportation) | 15.4 | |
| Low wage relative to overseas wages | 11.5 | |
| Anomalous or unacceptable recruitment: and hiring practices | 3.8 | |
| Others | 11.5 | |

*The sum of the percentages exceeds 100 because of multiple responses.

**TABLE 7** OCCUPATION AND MEDIAN INCOME OF RETURNING OCWs EMPLOYED FOLLOWING LAST RETURN

| OCCUPATION | NUMBER OF RETURNING OCWs | MEDIAN MONTHLY INCOME (IN PESOS) |
|---|---|---|
| Craftsmen, foremen and kindred workers | 5 | 1,416 |
| Brickmasons, stonemasons and tile setters | | 3,000 |
| Mechanics and repairmen, automobile | 1 | 2,000 |
| Mechanics and repairmen, air-conditioning, heating and refrigeration | 1 | 1,416 |
| Excavating, grading and machinery operations | 1 | 864 |
| Electricians | 1 | 750 |
| Clerical and kindred workers | 2 | 1,852 |
| Clerical and kindred workers (n.e.c.)* | 1 | 3,000 |
| Dispatchers and starters, vehicle | 1 | 704 |
| Operatives and kindred workers | 2 | 1,500 |
| Bus and jeepney drivers, company chauffeurs | 1 | 1,500 |
| Operatives and kindred workers (n.e.c.) | 1 | 1,500 |
| Labourers (n.e.c.) | 1 | 960 |
| Protective service workers | 1 | 650 |
| Accountants and auditors | 1 | 1,750 |
| Total | 12 | |
| Median income | | 1,063 |

*Not elsewhere classified.

267

**TABLE 8** MEDIAN EXPECTED INCOME BY TYPE OF OCCUPATION SOUGHT FOR RETURNING OCWs SEEKING LOCAL EMPLOYMENT FOLLOWING LAST TERM

| TYPE OF OCCUPATION | PERCENTAGE | MEDIAN EXPECTED MONTHLY INCOME |
|---|---|---|
| Craftsmen, foremen and kindred workers (i.e., automobile mechanics, masons) | 63.6 | ₱1,500 |
| Others (i.e., drivers, accountants, auditors, etc.) | 36.4 | ₱1,550 |
| Total | 100.0 | |
| Overall median (N = 22) | | ₱ 1,375.5 |

**TABLE 9** MIGRANTS' PLANNING FOR OVERSEAS EMPLOYMENT FOLLOWING LAST RETURN

| ITEM | PERCENTAGE | NUMBER |
|---|---|---|
| Percentage of returning OCWs looking for or planning to look for overseas employment | 94.9 | 56 |
| Steps taken to find overseas employment | | |
| Total* | 100.0 | 60 |
| Reapplied to recruitment agencies | 78.3 | 47 |
| Looked for referrals or looked in the classified advertisements | 16.7 | 10 |
| Others | 5.0 | 3 |
| Problems encountered in finding overseas employment | | |
| Total | 100.0 | 56 |
| Exorbitant placement fees | 39.3 | 22 |
| Unacceptable hiring practices | 17.9 | 10 |
| Competition/no vacancies | 16.1 | 9 |
| Long process involved in application for overseas employment | 14.3 | 8 |
| Others | 5.4 | 3 |
| No problem reported | 7.1 | 4 |

*Includes multiple responses.

**TABLE 10**  OCCUPATION SOUGHT AND MEDIAN EXPECTED INCOME OF RETURNED OCWs CURRENTLY SEEKING OVERSEAS EMPLOYMENT

| OCCUPATION | PERCENTAGE | MEDIAN EXPECTED MONTHLY INCOME (IN US$) |
|---|---|---|
| Craftsmen, foremen and kindred workers | 47.18 | 390 |
| Foremen (n.e.c.)* | 3.77 | 600 |
| Plumbers and pipe fitters | 1.89 | 600 |
| Mechanics and repairmen (n.e.c.)* | 3.77 | 450 |
| Electricians | 5.66 | 450 |
| Structural metal workers | 7.55 | 425 |
| Mechanics and repairmen, air-conditioning, heating and refrigeration | 1.89 | 390 |
| Cranemen, derrickmen and hoistmen | 1.89 | 370 |
| Mechanics and repairmen, automobile | 3.77 | 365 |
| Carpenters | 1.89 | 360 |
| Brickmasons, stonemasons and tile setters | 13.21 | 301 |
| Painters, construction and maintenance | 1.89 | 300 |
| Operatives and kindred workers | 28.31 | 399: |
| Apprentice or other specified trades | 1.89 | 750 |
| Operatives and kindred workers (n.e.c.) | 3.77 | 400 |
| Oilers and greasers, except auto | 1.89 | 400 |
| Welders and flame cutters | 7.55 | 398 |
| Truck, tractor and heavy equipment drivers | 11.32 | 375 |
| Bus and jeepney drivers, company chauffeurs | 1.89 | 300 |
| Professional, technical and kindred workers | 9.43 | 750 |
| Technicians, electrical and electronic | 1.89 | 850 |
| Accountants and auditors | 3.77 | 750 |
| Industrial radiographer, X-ray operator, maintenance helper | 3.77 | 375 |
| Service workers, except private household | 5.67 | 300 |
| Cooks, except private household | 1.89 | 1,000 |
| Chambermaids and maids except private household | 1.89 | 300 |

| OCCUPATION | PERCENTAGE | MEDIAN INCOME |
|---|---|---|
| Kitchen workers (n.e.c.)* except private household | 1.89 | 250 |
| Labourers, except farm and mine | 5.66 | 350 |
| Warehousemen (n.e.c.)* | 3.77 | 350 |
| Carpenter's helpers, except logging and mining | 1.89 | 350 |
| Clerical and kindred workers | | |
| Stock clerks and storekeepers | 3.77 | 638 |
| Total (N = 53) | 100.2 | |
| Overall median | | 364 |

*Not elsewhere classified.

**TABLE 11**     PERCENTAGE OF RETURNING OCWs AND NON-OCW RESPONDENTS ACCORDING TO REMITTANCE USE

| USE | OCW PERCENTAGE | SPOUSE, PARENT OR SIBLING PERCENTAGE |
|---|---|---|
| Personal consumption or basic necessities including medical expenses | 98.3 | 100.0 |
| Schooling or training cost of household members | 47.5 | 51.8 |
| Paying debts | 33.9 | 19.6 |
| Savings | 15.2 | 23.2 |
| Purchase or development of land | 11.9 | 14.3 |
| Construction, remodelling or purchase of house or rental of dwelling | 23.7 | 23.2 |
| Purchase of furniture or major household appliances | 10.2 | 7.1 |
| Others | 11.9 | 3.6 |

Note: The sum of the percentages exceeds 100 owing to multiple response.

**TABLE 12    SKILLS ACQUIRED OVERSEAS AND WHETHER OR NOT APPLIED LOCALLY**

| SKILLS ACQUIRED OVERSEAS | APPLIED LOCALLY | NOT APPLIED LOCALLY | TOTAL |
|---|---|---|---|
| Toolmaking, welding, fabrication, plating and other related skills | 1 | 4 | 5 |
| Pipe production and processing skills | 3 | 3 | 6 |
| Steel fabrication and other related skills | 1 | 3 | 4 |
| Construction, infra-structure and other related skills (i.e., masonry, painting, glass or aluminum installing or cutting etc.) | 1 | 10 | 11 |
| Transport, excavating, or lifting equipment operation and other related skills (i.e., driving heavy equipment or rigging) | 3 | 10 | 13 |
| Others | 2 | 4 | 6 |
| Total | 11 | 34 | 45 |

Note: The total of 45 skills acquired overseas was reported by 20 individual return migrants.

**TABLE 13**  CHILDREN'S RELATIONSHIP WITH MARRIED RETURNING OCW AND SPOUSE AFTER OCWs RETURN

*(Percentage distribution)*

| ASPECT OF RELATIONSHIP | OCW | | | SPOUSE | | |
|---|---|---|---|---|---|---|
| | DIMINISHED | NOT CHANGED AT ALL | INCREASED | DIMINISHED | NOT CHANGED AT ALL | INCREASED |
| Children's consultations with respondent | 13.33 | 43.33 | 43.33 | 3.33 | 43.33 | 53.33 |
| Children's regard and respect for respondent | 3.23 | 41.94 | 54.84 | 6.67 | 30.00 | 63.33 |
| Children's closeness to respondent | 6.45 | 35.48 | 58.06 | 3.33 | 26.67 | 70.00 |

**TABLE 14**  SINGLE RETURN MIGRANTS' RELATIONSHIP WITH FAMILY MEMBERS FOLLOWING THEIR RETURN

*(Percentage distribution)*

| ASPECT OF RELATIONSHIP | RESPONDENT | | | PARENT OR SIBLING | | |
|---|---|---|---|---|---|---|
| | DIMINISHED | OCW NOT CHANGED AT ALL | INCREASED | DIMINISHED | NOT CHANGED AT ALL | INCREASED |
| Brothers' and sisters' closeness to OCW | 0.0 | 77.78 | 22.22 | 0.0 | 44.44 | 55.56 |
| Frequency of consultations family has with OCW regarding decisions of family matters | 0.0 | 66.67 | 33.33 | 22.22 | 55.56 | 22.22 |
| Family's respect and regard for OCW | 0.0 | 66.67 | 33.33 | 0.0 | 77.78 | 22.22 |

**TABLE 15    MEAN SCORES OF LEVEL OF PARTICIPATION IN DECISION MAKING\* OF RETURNED OCWs BY MARITAL STATUS, AND THEIR NEAREST KIN**

| AREA OF DECISION MAKING | MARRIED OCWs | | | | | |
| --- | --- | --- | --- | --- | --- | --- |
| | OCW | | | SPOUSE | | |
| | BEFORE MIGRATION | WHILE ABROAD | UPON RETURN | BEFORE MIGRATION | WHILE ABROAD | UPON RETURN |
| 1. Marriage plans | 3.00 | 3.00 | 2.50 | 2.00 | 2.50 | 2.00 |
| 2. Family expenses and budgeting | 2.03 | 1.60 | 2.03 | 2.35 | 2.79 | 2.26 |
| 3. Purchase of major household appliances | 2.06 | 1.97 | 2.09 | 2.24 | 2.56 | 2.15 |
| 4. Educational plans of family members | 1.82 | 1.96 | 2.10 | 2.21 | 2.62 | 2.10 |
| 5. Occupation and job selection of family members | 2.41 | 1.83 | 2.27 | 1.68 | 2.05 | 1.63 |
| 6. Disposing of or acquiring family property | 2.09 | 1.89 | 2.09 | 2.22 | 2.44 | 2.13 |
| 7. Choice of residence | 2.33 | 2.00 | 2.27 | 2.10 | 2.42 | 2.13 |
| 8. Construction or repair of house | 2.15 | 1.94 | 2.18 | 2.18 | 2.50 | 2.15 |
| 9. Engaging in family business | 2.08 | 1.91 | 2.12 | 2.09 | 2.43 | 2.17 |
| 10. Political or voting decisions | 2.59 | 2.34 | 2.62 | 2.39 | 2.73 | 2.33 |
| Composite score | 22.11 | 19.49 | 22.00 | 21.97 | 25.29 | 22.31 |
| Before migration and while abroad | $t(34) = 3.73***$ | | | $t(34) = 4.87***$ | | |
| While abroad and upon return | $t(34) = 3.44***$ | | | $t(34) = 2.66**$ | | |

273

| AREA OF DECISION MAKING | SINGLE OCWs | | | | | |
|---|---|---|---|---|---|---|
| | OCW | | | SPOUSE | | |
| | BEFORE MIGRATION | WHILE ABROAD | UPON RETURN | BEFORE MIGRATION | WHILE ABROAD | UPON RETURN |
| 1. Marriage plans | 1.60 | 1.80 | 1.60 | 2.00 | 1.67 | 1.67 |
| 2. Family expenses and budgeting | 1.67 | 1.89 | 1.67 | 1.89 | 2.11 | 1.78 |
| 3. Purchase of major household appliances | 1.89 | 1.67 | 1.56 | 1.89 | 1.89 | 1.89 |
| 4. Educational plans of family members | 2.44 | 1.67 | 1.67 | 1.88 | 1.88 | 1.88 |
| 5. Occupation and job selection of family members | 1.89 | 1.78 | 1.56 | 1.89 | 1.89 | 1.89 |
| 6. Disposing of or acquiring family property | 1.75 | 1.57 | 1.57 | 1.88 | 1.88 | 1.75 |
| 7. Choice of residence | 1.75 | 1.75 | 1.75 | 1.71 | 1.71 | 1.71 |
| 8. Construction or repair of house | 1.89 | 1.89 | 1.89 | 1.89 | 1.89 | 1.89 |
| 9. Engaging in family business | 1.86 | 1.86 | 1.86 | 1.86 | 1.57 | 1.86 |
| 10. Political or voting decisions | 2.67 | 2.67 | 2.44 | 2.00 | 2.22 | 2.33 |
| | | | | | | |
| Composite score | 18.67 | 18.56 | 17.56 | 19.11 | 19.22 | 19.11 |
| Before migration and while abroad | $t(8) = 0.18$ | | | $t(8) = -0.21$ | | |
| While abroad and upon return | $t(8) = 2.12$ | | | $t(8) = 0.16$ | | |

*Returning OCWs and their spouse, parent or sibling were asked to rate their own level of participation in decision making within the households on a scale of 1 to 3, with "1" indicating no participation, "2" joint participation, and "3" sole decision making.

**TABLE 16  RETURN MIGRANTS' RELATIONSHIPS WITH FRIENDS AND NEIGHBOURS FOLLOWING THEIR RETURN**

(Percentage Distribution)

| ASPECT OF RELATIONSHIP | MARRIED OCWs | | | | | | SINGLE OCWs | | | | | |
| --- | --- | --- | --- | --- | --- | --- | --- | --- | --- | --- | --- | --- |
| | OCW | | | SPOUSE | | | OCW | | | PARENT OR SIBLING | | |
| | $-^a$ | $0^b$ | $+^c$ | $-^a$ | $0^b$ | $+^c$ | $-^a$ | $0^b$ | $+^c$ | $-^a$ | $0^b$ | $+^c$ |
| Friends' and neighbours' regard for OCW family | 7.50 | 65.00 | 27.50 | 2.94 | 79.41 | 17.65 | 11.11 | 77.78 | 11.11 | 0.00 | 66.67 | 33.33 |
| Frequency with which friends and neighbours turn to OCW family for financial help | 2.50 | 57.50 | 40.00 | 14.71 | 52.94 | 32.35 | 11.11 | 66.67 | 22.22 | 0.00 | 55.56 | 44.44 |
| Frequency with which friends and neighbours ask OCW family to participate in community activities | 2.50 | 55.00 | 42.50 | 8.82 | 76.47 | 14.71 | 11.11 | 77.78 | 11.11 | 11.11 | 55.56 | 33.33 |
| Frequency with which friends and neighbours invite OCW family to attend parties or get-togethers | 0.00 | 60.00 | 40.00 | 8.82 | 76.47 | 14.71 | 0.00 | 88.89 | 11.11 | 0.00 | 77.78 | 22.22 |
| Frequency with which friends and neighbours ask OCW family to contribute money to community activities | 7.50 | 52.50 | 40.00 | 8.82 | 52.94 | 38.24 | 11.11 | 77.78 | 11.11 | 11.11 | 66.67 | 22.22 |

[a] Diminished.
[b] No change.
[c] Increased.

**TABLE 17** MEAN SATISFACTION SCORES BEFORE OVERSEAS MIGRATION AND UPON RETURN

| ASPECT OF LIFE | MARRIED OCWs | | | | SINGLE OCWs | | | |
| | OCW | | SPOUSE | | OCW | | PARENT OR SIBLING | |
| | BEFORE MIGRATION | UPON RETURN | BEFORE MIGRATION | UPON RETURN | BEFORE MIGRATION | UPON RETURN | BEFORE MIGRATION | UPON RETURN |
|---|---|---|---|---|---|---|---|---|
| 1. Socio-economic situation | 3.40 | 4.95 | 4.05 | 5.76 | 2.78 | 4.44 | 3.11 | 3.89 |
| 2. Individual situation | 3.93 | 5.35 | 4.29 | 5.89 | 3.33 | 4.78 | 4.00 | 4.89 |
| 3. Relationship with spouse | 8.19 | 8.44 | 7.33 | 8.50 | a | a | a | a |
| 4. Relationship with children | 7.97 | 8.35 | 7.97 | 8.38 | a | a | a | a |
| 5. Relationship with friends and neighbours | 6.10 | 6.40 | 6.02 | 6.37 | 5.44 | 5.78 | 6.67 | 6.56 |
| 6. Relationship with relatives | 6.50 | 6.75 | 6.18 | 6.47 | 4.78 | 5.11 | 6.33 | 6.56 |
| 7. Community | 6.68 | 6.93 | 6.08 | 6.39 | 4.67 | 5.11 | 6.33 | 6.22 |
| 8. Relationship with family | a | a | a | a | 4.89 | 5.22 | 5.63 | 6.50 |
| Composed score | 42.77 | 47.17 | 41.92 | 47.76 | 25.89 | 30.44 | 32.07 | 34.62 |
| | t(46) = 4.30*** | | t(46) = 4.46*** | | t(9) = 3.11** | | t(9) = 2.13 | |

a Not asked.
***p < .001
**p < .01

# CITY FICTION:
# MANILA, A WAY OF LIFE AND ART

OPHELIA A. DIMALANTA

The inspiration of this paper is a book on *American City Fiction* by Blanche Housman Gelfant, who sought to introduce a literary genre, the twentieth century American City Novel, touching on certain sociological patterns and recurrent themes in urban fiction as well as giving commentaries on structure, form, technique in relation to urbanism.

Gelfant expounds on the social backgrounds out of which the genre has emerged and upon which it draws its material, tries to discover the basic forms this genre has developed, and considers relationships between a social vision of the city and the aesthetics of modern fiction.

Aware of the city as a distinctive and peculiarly modern way of life that has shaped the writer's vision and influenced his art, I tried to explore the possibilities of using Gelfant's genre-concept of city fiction in relation to local city life, specifically, Manila—Manila, not only as the city of the rich and well-placed in our society, but more importantly, as the city of the hungry and oppressed; not only the city's elegant and impressive suburbia, the city of tall, forbidding buildings of steel, concrete, and glass, but also the city's backlot and back alleys, narrow streets, and cluttered ramshackle apartments and miserable tenement houses.

Needless to say, city life is quite distinctive and offers so much in the form of modern material, which in turn demands literary expression in a modern idiom. The city looms not so much as physical reality as a characteristic and unique way of life that affects the characters moving within the fictional canvas of the author.

To be sure, setting or the locale in contemporary fiction has ceased to be merely a static backdrop against which the characters are made to act. It has become vital and integral to action and characterization. It has become part of the truth of the hero instead of being mere truth to fact or truth to the five senses. The city at times may even be a key actor in a human drama participating in the action not only as a physical place and atmosphere creating a sensuous and emotional, and even psychological, haze affecting the characters' behaviour and frame of mind, but also as a total way of life, a set of values and attitudes, all of which help mold character and destiny.

This is made explicit in a dramatic passage from Robert Herrick's *A Life for a Life:*

"The city was man. And already it was sowing its seed in the heart of the youth this night. It was moulding him as it would the millions after its fashion, warming his blood with desire, the vast, resounding gleaming City!"

Sometimes, the city plays the role of antagonist, serving as obstacle to the fulfillment of the hero's goals. It stands in the way of happiness, creating tensions, conflicts, a sense of alienation that may even eventually lead to the hero's ruin, moral or physical, or both.

This paper is, therefore, not concerned merely with local color urban fiction where the characters are set against a passive and static urban setting which is not a vital and necessary condition for their actions and motivations. Rather, it focuses on that kind of city fiction where urban life is seen as an organic whole, expressed in a total vision of life. The modern city fictionist does not offer an exhortative interpretation or a judgment of the city apart from its influence upon his characters. He does not necessarily attempt to merely record and report what he has seen, felt, experienced about the city, showing what it is and the values it lives by like a roving camera eye with a conscience, but dramatizes its impact upon certain specific lives, objectifying certain felt truths which are not necessarily sociological alone.

Even while city fiction inevitably contains social implications drawn as it is to the surrounding social realities of the times, its intention is never truly exhortatory. It is not problem fiction which presents a particular social evil for the purpose of propaganda. For even as the significant city fictionist's purpose is to express a social vision, his ultimate aim is still to provide aesthetic pleasure by virtue of the form he imposes on his material.

The city fictionist, while drawing upon his own immediate realities for material and inspiration, in the final analysis, comments on a perennial problem of man, urban or rustic, this conflict between his public and private worlds, the outer world against the inner world. This terrible encroachment of the outer world upon the inner world of man as wrought by the pressures of urban life could lead to a transcendence on the part of the character, or a complete submission, and eventually, defeat. Contemporary man cannot just escape the burdens of society by self-willed

278

exile. It is no wonder, then, that city fiction is darkened by much pessimism, preoccupied as it is with themes of dissociation, alienation, frustration, rejection, and loss of faith. Understandably, it is in the city that this death of illusion is most felt: where each one seems to have become a child of sorrow and uncertainty, and each house has become a fragile shack with wolves breeding at the door.

The impact of urbanism as a way of life, the personal implications of materialism, economic inequality and social injustices...all these are supposed to have moved, touched, and inspired the contemporary city-based writer, as he probes human nature in the face of urban victimization. It is in the chaos and clutter of city life that the author's characters move from realism to naturalism and even to existentialism, from being alienated to being completely damned or, happily, to being finally accepted and adjusted.

The main problem of this paper, then, is to interpret the writer's social vision primarily through his art, for in the better writers, the two are really fused as one. The problem of the city fictionist is to give artistic form to the manner of life and the so-called *zeitgeist* or the temper of the times. Needless to say, the sociological and literary interpretations of city life corroborate and complement each other.

## City Fictionists

BRILLANTES. — In "Janis Joplin, the Revolution, and the Melancholy Widow of Gabriela Silang Street," one of the stories of Gregorio Brillantes in his second collection of short stories entitled *The Apollo Centennial*, the locale is the city of Manila from the late 1960's, 1970, 1971, and the years immediately after the imposition of Martial Law, seething pot of ferment and unease, a city of jangled nerves, burning passions, ready angers which lead to sporadic shows of violence. It is virtually a state of dislocation, restlessness where loves and lives come cheap and death becomes as intimate and familiar as the shape, size, and weight of a man's body. And in the midst of such wrenching social upheavals dramatized poignantly in the city at a time when the face of the country hangs in the balance, Crisostomo Hidalgo, writer turned executive, continues to retreat into his own private world, "enduring amidst all that fury," pursuing his individual life and, in the process, has his own dramatic encounters with his own personal fate and destiny in a motel at Pasay City or in an air-conditioned house at Magallanes.

It is a city of stalking hunger, hold-ups, typhoons, Metrocom raids, incessant hunts for top leaders of outlawed organizations, sudden deaths, sudden loves, and long hours of loneliness and solitude. So much is happening in the city of these particular times that try men's sanity, but the writer Hidalgo, central character of the story, maintains a detached post of observation, through an apparently slanted non-partisanship, withdrawing from the prevailing belligerent and aggressive stances of the moment. The truth is that this one writer, apparently, has not been touched by the city too profoundly—like a Zhivago who regards his inner life as sacrosanct, inviolate, that part of man which must remain steadfast, constant, firm against external encroachments.

As city fiction then, the story presents an urbanism that does not significantly affect the protagonist, hardly responding as he is to the pressures surrounding him. The hero, then, transcends the time simply by putting on an armor of indifference. And yet, in the passage of time, impaled as he is in a particular space in this city where many happenings take place or threaten to erupt, he inevitably makes his own responses to the outer world, discovering his own vulnerabilities and his own identity. Never really having been victimized by the city, he never truly repudiates it. He is still, after all, very much a part of this city of demonstrations and sporadic violences, of plush buildings and glass-panelled cubicles with their fantastic view of sunlit Manila and the bay and the distant mountains.

In "Excerpts from the Autobiography of a Middle-aged Ghostwriter With Insomnia," urbanism is not just the physical locale of the story; it is the psychological center informing a long, rambling view of a kind of life that unfolds from the past, nudges into the present in the form of solidly subjective-narrative rendering of action, or rather, more aptly, inaction. It starts from the boyhood town of the author, San Bartolome, Pangasinan, and on to Manila, from the narrator's college days at the old university campus of U.P. at Padre Faura, and on to the house at McKinley Village where he finally settles down with his wife and children, moderately *burgis*, and luxuriating in the minor vices and lassitude of an aging (surprisingly) writer ... surprisingly, I say, because in this country "a writer is supposed to remain malnourished and poverty stricken, and to have a swimming pool is quite an anomalous acquisition." Unless of course one is a ghostwriter. And it also depends on the person one is ghostwriting for.

Structurally, the story is built upon a welter of details and incidents, mostly city-based and city-motivated which impresses upon the hero and the reader for that matter, certain sociological implications. For it is, on the whole, a low-keyed soporific satire on city life as well as on the writer himself, a terrible sense of being adrift in a stream of events, terribly bored and alienated, and sleepless. He does not grapple with the city; he allows the city's poison to seep into his system, allowing it to carry him painfully in its lethargic-lethal wake.

JOSE. – F. Sionil Jose's *Two Filipino Women* is city fiction where city life is revealed in relation to its impact on a protagonist whose personal defeat becomes a register of and a judgment upon urbanism as a way of life. For instance, *Obsession*, one of the novellas in the collection, is about Ermi Rojo, a prostitute. No ordinary prostitute here, but a *dies mil* belle, ten thousand pesos a night. Rolando Cruz, the middle-aged first-person narrator, historian, ghostwriter, media man, bum husband, is another prostitute in the story, in the more obscene sense. What he sells is not only himself, but also his own country, pimping for the gnomes of Wall Street. His obscenities are spread on more thickly and messily in the story, as he ends up being a near cop-out, swearing prostitution is "not a social condition but a matter of integrity," this time referring to Ermi's kind of prostitution. In fact, the obscenities in the book are everything else except Ermi's kind, like ... poverty, social anomalies, the palaces of the rich, the new hotels erected at the expense of people, the hospitals where the poor die and the sick get worse because of the high cost of being sick, corruption among the government officials ... the only honest thing is sex! Manila's Ermita or more specifically, Ermita's Camarin, favorite watering hole of the jaded lechers of the city in their search for short-lived sybaritic pleasures, has become both a social and moral environment. The hero's obsession for the prostitute Ermi is symbolic of the hero's almost insane attachment to a city's dissolute ways:

"Mabini is itself swept clean for the tourists as with all of Manila's major avenues, but the narrow sidestreets are awash with the stench of uncollected garbage and human waste oozing out of clogged sewers."

In the end, it is not Ermi the prostitute who destroys him. It is the city, a dissolute personality in itself, the antagonist, its flagrant materialism, perversions, sensations, and worst, its indifference, its social injustices, its failure to hold on to the old traditional values. The story as city fiction explores a pathological case intrinsic in a sick society, a sick hero, social pressures destroying the individual and the individual himself causing a social void. Sadly, the author does not offer the consolation of an affirmative note, especially where the protagonist is concerned. If ever there is any positive note at all, it is in making the readers look at the likes of Ermi in a new light, realizing that her kind of prostitution is not necessarily the worst that there is.

Jose's characters are usually the sensitive middle-class intellectuals who have become dissociated, frustrated, and emotionally drained on account of pressures exerted by the milieu. Being weak, they easily succumb to such pressures, eventually incorporating into their own lives the very disorder they are supposed to protest against, the exploitation of man by man, the social injustices that foster unrest and allow for tensions and shallow relationships, indiscretions, and finally, perdition. Even love takes on the form of an obsessive passion that debilitates more than ennobles. Jose's characters in this particular collection of novellas are really part of the complex aesthetic design of his vast fictional canvas which continues to evolve from story to story, from novel to novel, expressing the social and moral structure of the times as well as the social and moral vision of the author.

REYES. — The only city fiction in Pilipino chosen for study is *Utos Ng Hari at iba pang kuwento*, which covers a writing time stretch of almost a decade in the life of young writer Jun Cruz Reyes, a collection of Palanca-winning stories the setting of which is Looban, which could be any forsaken Skid Row world of petty thieves, punks, muggers, prostitutes, the *tambays* of any streetcorner, the city's backyard, the city's lower depths, the stinking alleys of garbage, and heaps and heaps of discarded unfulfilled dreams.

Using the restricted first-person point of view as strategy of socio-psychological revelation, Reyes pursues his subject: the effect of environment upon the characters. The portrayal of Looban becomes a portrayal of more than just a social group living within a specific vicinity but a portrayal of *inner experience*. The reader is made to see the outer world through the consciousness of youngsters who complain but never really rage.

Each story mirrors, exacerbates the hurt in empty, meaningless banter hurled at each other over endless rounds of beer and banalities, all of which emphasize rather than banish disparities. And the days pass for these characters in an endlessly monotonous pattern of need, momentary submission, regret, unbroken neither by the intervention and guidance of authorities (teachers, elders) who have become too ineffectual, too weak and weakened to exercise control; nor by individual will, also rendered weak with an almost frightening finality. Each story ends in a note of bafflement:

"Ang ambisyong yumaman, kung walang mangyayari ay parati kang mangangarap ng dilat. Ang lakas makaloko!"

And for the young, growing up and wiser is going against the staid conventions of the old and jaded, like one's teachers:

"Yung teacher ko sa English, walang pakialam sa mundo. Basta't magamit lang niya yung nalalaman niya sa voice and diction, maligaya na siya sa buhay. Basta kami ang papel namin lang ay ang tagapakinig sa kaniyang mga asides."

"Magrereklamo rin ako sa pader kung kailangan, hanggang may makabasa at makarinig sa aking mga sumbong. Pero sa ngayon, iji-jingle ko na lang muna ang sama ko ng loob."

Reyes' *Utos ng Hari* proves that sociological and literary interpretations indeed enhance each other's significance, and an awareness of urban sociology helps to explain and expound upon the basic persuasions and orientation of most of the 20th-century fiction in Pilipino.

The book follows the ecological pattern of focusing on a small spatial unit, a localized area, that of the city's squatters. The protagonist of this kind of city fiction is usually not a single person but a spatial unit, allowing the reader a peek into this breakdown of the city into small, self-contained social worlds, thus intensifying the expression of this sense of isolation from and disenchantment with the whole system.

Despite the element of personal defeat and even self-pity, the collection is not bleakly dispiriting, as is most city fiction. In fact it ends with a story which is as open-ended as life itself. For Reyes' fiction is rooted on a faith in man's desire for truth, for the meaning of life, through the shambles of an urbane faith in the better things in man and in life. It ends in an eventual shaking, the possibility of one, at least, an upheaval (*pagbabalikwas*) even as the author seeks answers to unanswered questions in the book, in every face he meets, in every *tambay* he bumps into, in the blind alleys and condemned streetcorners of experience.

APRIETO/CRUZ. — Though related to the so-called proletariat writing of the 30's, the stories of Pacifico Aprieto and Andres Cristobal Cruz in *Tondo by Two* are told in stronger accents, and louder voices, with a pervasive tone of tenderness whose "roots dig deep into the very soul of poverty," quoting N.V.M. Gonzalez.

Cruz' "White Wall" revolves around the esteros of Tondo, the termite-inhabited posts of the squalid-looking *accesorias* here in the seamier side of the city. It is the story of unspoken love set against an atmosphere of scum and garbage alternating with the linking shadow and reality of the white wall. The white wall is contrasted with the blackness and squalor of the estero, and it stands for everything that Tondo denizens like Cris and Magdalena look up or forward to, past the sordid and immediate contingencies of their Tondo-centered actualities — the violent quarrels of the occupants, the shrieking of children, already filthy-mouthed at an early age, the bumping of urinals against the parapet, the smell of garbage refuse, the reek of all kinds of objects thrown into the

283

estero's murk.

Cruz writes with such brutal graphicness: the foot of the bridge of Pritil where Tayuman starts off from Juan Luna promising fresher air, the camera panning towards the army bands in Luneta's sunset concerts, and then shifting to the Cine Esa down Herbosa, inevitably settling at the L-shaped accesoria and the cornerstores of the hero's adolescent days.

Cruz' characters do not succumb easily to the forces acting upon them, doing so only after a gigantic struggle. There is no outright condemnation of this urban society he paints with such painstaking eye for details. His protagonists who yearn and love past the smelly waters of the estero are still part of the bigger unit they cannot condemn, their own miserable section of Manila having no autonomous life of its own that can improve and change itself. And for all the sordid, almost naturalistic details, there are still romantic undertows rippling below the murky surface of the esteros of Tondo. Quoting Cruz, "here, dwarfs still come and go taking us with them to their wonderful and ever-happy world of the secret cities of the earth."

Aprieto's stories are most of the time nothing more than introspective or descriptive sketches with the characters acting or merely feeling and thinking against a static urban setting which is, however, a vital and necessary condition to their acts and thoughts. Aprieto's sense of detail is, like Cruz', sharply physical—three men staggering inside a cafe near the corner of Herbosa and Juan Luna, one of them suddenly urinating right on the concrete floor, protagonist and friend feeling terribly nauseated and depressed as they leave the cafe walking towards the small bridge spanning Canal de la Reina, their steps sounding flat and empty.

And then, there is that barbershop in a story entitled "Haircut," converging scene of all of Tondo's grim morbidities and obscenities, like that report on somebody dying not with his pants on in the act of love, his guts strewn all over the dirty floor of a monte house in Angustia, etc.

Cruz and Aprieto not only express an impression of reality but also a concrete sense of physical actualities through a vivid cataloguing of palpable details fundamental to their creation of character and personal as well as social relationship. *Tondo by Two* is not the city fiction of city glitter, skyscrapers and skyscapes, the city with all its gaudy show. Rather it is one that closes in on a bleak section of the city where poverty and squalor is familiar sight and experience. But unlike other city fiction which treats of the allusions to frustration, anguish, and dislocation, this slim volume does not dwell too lovingly or lengthily on the city's nerve-racking pace, the jagged tempo of city life, the structures of futility and undercurrents of social tensions commonly associated with the city's milieu, especially in naturalistic city fiction. The characters are sensitive, brooding, intelligent, and even romantic, managing to train their eyes above the esteros of their childhood. Both Aprieto and Cruz live away from Tondo now. Their houses in the suburbs may be worlds away from the esteros and lean-to makeshift stores and dreary corners of their childhood haunts. The authors' romanticism prevails. Tondo, however, remains a presence made romantic by time and distance, and this volume sums up the memory, a little bitter, a little sad, but always with tenderness, never with rejection and contempt.

GUERRERO. — In the foreword to the collection, *Children of the City*, Pete Daroy writes: "No other writer, it seems, has rendered the haunting edges of Manila's pavements by night more hauntingly than Amadis Ma. Guerrero."

In "The Children of the City," title story of this volume, the author tries to recreate the atmosphere of Manila, specifically around the vicinities of Intramuros, now and then shifting to the seedy and ominous waterfront where the father of Vic, the young protagonist, works. His father dies in a violent encounter between the picketeers and the dock goons. Thus begins Vic's initiation into the evils of the city which have not spared youngsters like him. He roams the streets, the byways, and darkened alleys of the teeming district, passing by children his age scrounging around trash cans. His first whiff of a cigarette is his inevitable acceptance of the bewildering swirl of the city's environs, "this city where workers were made to sign statements certifying they received the minimum wage, where the millionaire politicians received Holy Communion every Sunday, where mothers taught their sons and daughters the art of begging, where orphans and children from broken homes slept on the pavements and under darkened bridges, and where the best of friends fell out and betrayed each other."

This typical Guerrero description of the city underscores the themes of urban victimization especially of the young and defenseless. Many of the heroes of city fiction submit to contemporary modes of moral humiliations, and somehow, their submission, for writers like Guerrero, becomes an indirect indictment of society. Stalking the city's dark pavements, the young victims in Guerrero's fiction must be prepared to face whatever there is to face and meet in the stealthy corners, ready to melt into and be one with the shadows themselves, in abject fear and desire to be invisible in the night's dark.

Incidentally, the city's dark streets and street corners also become the sites for discoveries of disparities and kinships among men.

In another story, "Clock Watchers," the hero is a teletype operator who works eight hours a day and six days a week in front of a machine that hums twenty hours a day, "like a first-class train speeding surely towards its destination, except that the destination seems never to be in sight ..." He has become a machine, or rather, a cog in a machine and as such he cannot afford to break down, lest the whole machinery of this damned society made up of mechanized humans like him goes to pot. For Guerrero, then, more tragic than a life of debaucheries within the city's seamier sides as in Jose's Ermita, is a life of emotional deadness where one is rendered numbed by the constant tinkering with machines in his city-struggle to keep body and soul glued.

In another story, "Click of the Camera," the hero as photographer scrambles for the most interesting situation, meaning, the goriest, bloodiest, like a knifed jeepney driver clutching his bleeding stomach and doubling up in agony as his assailant is caught on film as he is fleeing the scene. A matter of luck, really. The photographer with the goriest visual treat recorded for posterity is the envy of the press club. The recognition is tantamount to its correspondence in terms of an increase in his month's pay. And so, the hero as city photographer stalks the streets for violence, for money. Guerrero describes the city itinerant's daily fare: massed pedestrians, broken sidewalks, cheerless two-story residences and littered canals juxtaposed with a picture of Dewey Boulevard with its rows of nightclubs, waving palms, and blazing sunsets. For Javier, the photographer-hero of the story, luck comes in terms of one click of his camera, "that violent impact of flesh and metal."

Guerrero's characters are all entangled in the city's web, and in making his characters readily submit to the forces bearing down on them, he minimizes the two vital forces of human choice and human struggle. He raises questions, though. What place can man make for himself in such a materialistic environment? What hope is there except to be a machine in such a money-obsessed, machine-run world? What hope is there for beauty, for a sense of individuality, for privacy and serenity? Man has become the machine, and a badly driven one at that.

**The City As Subject**

Wirth, in his *Urbanism As A Way of Life*, speaks of three characteristics of an urban population:

1.	its numerical size (which leads to a weakening of social ties resulting in impersonality, superficial and segmental relationships);

2. its density (which could lead to hostilities, tensions, alienation and even violence); and
3. its heterogeneity (which leads to social inequalities, conflicting traditions and moral codes, instability, social disintegration).

Add to this the onset of modern technology which has led to flagrant materialism, economic instability leading to aloneness, anonymity, predatoriness, cut-throat competition, leading to a general breakdown of values and established mores.

For Jose the city is antagonist, the villain with its crass materialism, perversions, debaucheries, one-night stands. His major characters are usually weak, badly driven machines, like Guerrero's.

Greg Brillantes' characters are never really badly victimized because of their protective devices. A part of them submits, yes, but a part of them still holds out in a city they have never really rejected.

Reyes' fiction is, on the other hand, an outright defiance of what the city with its stinking alleys has made of most of the young, impaled as they are in a small spatial unit where poverty is rife and where, just a curse away, can be seen some fish magnate's air-conditioned mansion, impervious to the reek and stench of the whole place.

The social protests are never really loud-mouthed, not even in Amadis Guerrero's *Children of the City*, where the children are the hapless victims. His adult characters, on the other hand, have become dehumanized, emotionally drained, transformed from artisans to mere machine hands.

Cruz and Aprieto's Tondo is not really all that hostile and malign. In fact, at times, it becomes almost an elusive ghost of the past intruding nostalgically into the present. For all its unprepossessingness, it is still capable of evoking romantic yearnings and idealism in the characters who make love, dream, and eventually die within breathing range of the estero, the fictional constant in the collection.

At this point, allow me to touch on some other city fictionists whom I have not discussed and who have already been written about almost dry. Even in Bienvenido Santos' Sulucan stories (from *Brother, My Brother*) and Nick Joaquin's "Order of Melkizedek" and "Candido's Apocalypse," dislocation and inauthenticity become a pervasive city ailment. In Nick Joaquin as in Greg Brillantes (even in his first collection, *The Distance to Andromeda*), there looms that appalling contrast between the haves and have-nots. While the acquisition of wealth gives one a greater sense of belonging where money is of the essence, the process of its acquisition may in itself lead to social disunity and spiritual unrest, and a total disintegration of the person.

While some claim the legendary nature of the city as a center of culture, epitome of modern progress, it remains to most modern fictionists an expression of this collapse of traditions, family ties and relationships, and the frightening desert places within man.

The greatest travesty that the city has inflicted on man is the invasion of and encroachment on self. What is this self? T. S. Eliot aptly portrays it in *The Waste Land* as crossing the bridge in a great modern city not knowing that death has already undone him. For all our countrymen's propensities for romanticism and whitewashing, our writers have never really portrayed the city as a fabled land of milk and honey, never a dream world of surging crowds, exciting plush restaurants, stretches of streets lined with awesome buildings, spectacle of wealth and glamour as most of the time portrayed by American city fictionists. In the first place, Manila is never really like that, not even in our wildest romantic dreams.

On the whole, the handling of themes of city fiction by the short story writers taken up expresses a particular brand of tragic vision or tragic view of life which is distinctly Filipino. It is unmistakably Filipino expressed by one imbibing these particular realities, breathing in this polluted air, this particular dust-soaked atmosphere, living in this specific corner of this so-called city of man and manholes.

Our writers' deeply-rooted romanticism rules out cold-blooded naturalism, their basic pieties preventing them from falling into moral ruts and out-and-out pessimism. Their brand of pessimism is that view of the hurt person who has perceived his own potentials for pain within himself and also around himself in the contortions of city living. It is a kind of pessimism informed by a life-drive, a sense of life-validity, carrying with it some notions (no matter how faint at times) of the vastness of the human potential. The other fellow is still a brother even as they tangle, whether bumped into in the city's dark corners, or engaged in empty prattle, in meaningless cocktails or gripe sessions, in pain, in hope. No matter how confused, how alone he is, he has his sudden short moments of lucidity, as he takes time out from the most hectic, killing pace of fast city living, for a soul-searching or self-appraisal.

Although the local city fictionists have not been spared from the so-called modern malaise so typical of the contemporary sensibility, they have not lost their aesthetic composure, and in spite of their tendency to wallow in self-pity, they get up, vision clarified, faith reaffirmed. There is really not much of the truly heroic, truly tragic and sublime in the pages of their fiction; the very nature of the genre chosen by them excludes such possibility. Local city fiction usually deals with ordinary people with ordinary problems and even ordinary dreams, and therefore does not go beyond mere pathos, with hardly any peeks into tragedy in the grand and ennobling sense.

The sufferings presented by the writers are not really all that great, and they do not necessarily stem from *hamartia*, or a tragic flaw within the characters, nullifying the virtues of otherwise noble souls possessing such infinite capacity for pain and sorrow. Their sufferings come from maladjustments with their own selves, the environment or from conflicts of interests in small groups of individuals upon no one of whom is the special guilt to be pinned.

Some would claim that there is still a kind of romantic whitewashing here. Except instead of the word whitewashing (and everything the word connotes), I would rather say a refining of or glossing over the more lurid details, in the service of art. For art, according to Henry James, must remind us of life, but not too much.

Perhaps, some critics would even claim that it remains for our younger, more impassioned writers (especially those writing in Pilipino) today to sound off louder and more vehement denunciations of the city's jungles and man's slow dehumanization, man's cruelty to man, men preying upon each other. It is interesting to note that none of the five Manila fictionists taken up are blatantly political. This is, of course, just a view of Manila, one face of Manila about a decade ago, or even earlier. Other younger writers could be more blatantly political, more embittered, dipping their pens not only in acid but in blood, and a study of their kind of city fiction could constitute the subject for another paper. The danger lies in these young writers' turning out manifestoes, not art. Our writers, young and old, serene or frenzied in their anger, must define their special loyalties and their special missions.

# THE CANON OF PHILIPPINE LITERATURE ACCORDING TO TEACHERS OF METRO MANILA

ESTRELLITA V. GRUENBERG

In canon-formation, the professors, the scholars, and the critics are the arbiters of taste. They are the ones who can create anthologies that can reflect, expand, or redirect the canon of a period. To determine the canon of Philippine Literature according to teachers of Metro Manila, I sent a questionnaire to tertiary level teachers of Philippine Literature in 30 representative schools in Metro Manila. Only 50 teachers from the following 18 schools (10 universities and 8 colleges), however, returned the questionnaire: Adamson University, Ateneo de Manila University, Centro Escolar University, De La Salle University, Far Eastern University, Feati University, Pamantasan ng Lungsod ng Maynila, Philippine Christian University, University of the Philippines, University of Sto. Tomas, Assumption College, Chinese General School of Nursing, College of the Holy Spirit, Lyceum of the Philippines, Maryknoll College, Siena College, St. Joseph's College, and St. Scholastica's College.

The cover letter of the questionnaire asked the respondents to name which Philippine writers and which Philippine works they consider best in six literary genres, i.e., novelists/novels, short story writers/short stories, poets/poems, essayists/essays, playwrights/plays, and critics/literary criticism from the Spanish period to the present in any language, published in the Philippines or abroad. The respondents were asked to name in descending order the ten best writers in each of the six literary genres with number one as best and most important. They were also asked to indicate the textbooks and references they use in their Philippine Literature classes. The data gathered from the teachers were tabulated and ranked from first to tenth in descending order, but due to ties in some numbers, several of the originally planned Top Ten Lists contain more than 10 names or works.

**Table 1**: Teachers' Choice of Novelists

| Rank | Name | Frequency |
|------|------|-----------|
| 1 | Nick Joaquin | 45 |
| 2 | N.V.M. Gonzalez | 40 |
| 3 | F. Sionil Jose | 35 |
| 4-5 | Kerima P. Tuvera | 29 |
| 4-5 | Stevan Javellana | 29 |
| 6 | Bienvenido N. Santos | 28 |
| 7 | Edilberto Tiempo | 25 |
| 8 | Jose P. Rizal | 21 |
| 9 | Juan C. Laya | 15 |
| 10 | Celso Carunungan | 10 |

Nine out of the top ten novelists write or have written in English and only one writes in Spanish (Rizal). One writer in Filipino almost made it to the Top Ten List: Lope K. Santos, who was cited eight times.

**Table 2**: Teachers' Choice of Novels

| Rank | Title | Frequency |
|------|-------|-----------|
| 1 | *The Woman Who Had Two Navels* (by Nick Joaquin) | 43 |
| 2 | *Without Seeing the Dawn* (by Stevan Javellana) | 38 |
| 3 | *The Bamboo Dancers* (by N.V.M. Gonzalez) | 31 |
| 4-5 | *The Hand of the Enemy* (by Kerima P. Tuvera) | 26 |
| 4-5 | *The Pretenders* (by F. Sionil Jose) | 26 |
| 6 | *Noli Me Tangere* (by Jose P. Rizal) | 25 |
| 7 | *El Filibusterismo* (by Jose P. Rizal) | 19 |
| 8 | *A Season of Grace* (by N. V. M. Gonzalez) | 16 |
| 9 | *To Be Free* (by Edilberto Tiempo) | 12 |

| | | |
|---|---|---|
| 10-12 | *His Native Soil* | |
| | (by Juan C. Laya) | 10 |
| 10-12 | *Villa Magdalena* | |
| | (by Bienvenido Santos) | 10 |
| 10-12 | *The Peninsulars* | |
| | (by Linda Ty-Casper) | 10 |

More than ten novels appear in the list because three tied for the tenth place. Of the twelve, ten are written in English, two in Spanish, and none in Filipino. Lope K. Santos' *Banaag at Sikat* was cited only five times, already the highest received by a novel in Filipino.

From the survey, Nick Joaquin is considered by the teachers as the foremost Filipino novelist, and his novel *The Woman Who Had Two Navels* as the foremost Filipino novel. The reputation of Joaquin is established solely by this novel which was cited by 43 of the 50 teachers who answered the questionnaire. N. V. M. Gonzalez occupies second place among the novelists, but his novel *The Bamboo Dancers* is only third in the list of top novels. F. Sionil Jose is third among the novelists, but his novel *The Pretenders* ties for 4th-5th place with *The Hand of the Enemy* by Kerima P. Tuvera, who occupies 4th-5th place with Stevan Javellana. Javellana, who occupies 4th-5th place, has his novel *Without Seeing the Dawn* second among the novels. Bienvenido N. Santos is in sixth place, and his *Villa Magdalena* ties with Juan C. Laya's *His Native Soil* and Linda Casper's *The Peninsulars* for 10th-12th place. Edilberto Tiempo is seventh among the novelists, but his novel *To Be Free* ranks only ninth. Jose P. Rizal is only in eighth place among the novelists, but his *Noli Me Tangere* and *El Filibusterismo* occupy sixth and seventh places respectively among the works. Juan C. Laya is ninth, and his novel, *His Native Soil*, ties with two other novels for 10th-12th place. Celso Carunungan, who is tenth among the novelists, has no novel in the list. His *Like A Big Brave Man* which ranks 14th-15th place was cited only seven times.

**Table 3**: Teachers' Choice of Short Story Writers

| Rank | Name | Frequency |
|---|---|---|
| 1 | Nick Joaquin | 39 |
| 2-3 | N.V.M. Gonzalez | 32 |
| 2-3 | Gregorio Brillantes | 32 |
| 4 | Manuel Arguilla | 31 |
| 5 | Bienvenido N. Santos | 26 |

| 6 | Gilda Cordero-Fernando | 22 |
| 7 | Francisco Arcellana | 20 |
| 8 | Kerima P. Tuvera | 19 |
| 9 | F. Sionil Jose | 16 |
| 10 | Edith Tiempo | 14 |

Unlike in the case of the novelists who write in English and Spanish, all the short story writers use English as medium.

## Table 4: Teachers' Choice of Short Stories

| Rank | Title | Frequency |
|------|-------|-----------|
| 1 | "How My Brother Leon Brought Home a Wife" (by Manuel Arguilla) | 19 |
| 2 | "May Day Eve" (by Nick Joaquin) | 18 |
| 3 | "Scent of Apples" (by Bienvenido Santos) | 16 |
| 4 | "Faith, Love, Time, and Dr. Lazaro" (by Gregorio Brillantes) | 15 |
| 5 | "The Distance to Andromeda" (by Gregorio Brillantes) | 14 |
| 6-7 | "Foonote to Youth" (by Jose Garcia Villa) | 13 |
| 6-7 | "The God Stealer" (by F. Sionil Jose) | 13 |
| 8 | "The Day the Dancers Came" (by Bienvenido Santos) | 12 |
| 9 | "The Visitation of the Gods" (by Gilda Cordero Fernando) | 11 |
| 10-11 | "Dead Stars" (by Paz M. Benitez) | 10 |
| 10-11 | "Divide by Two" (by Francisco Arcellana) | 10 |

There are eleven short stories in all because of a tie in the tenth place. All these short stories are written in English.

Nick Joaquin again tops the short story writers according to the teachers who answered the questionnaire, but his short story "May Day

Eve" is only in second place. N.V.M. Gonzalez and Gregorio Brillantes tie for the 2nd-3rd place and yet none of Gonzalez' short stories made the top ten; his "Children of the Ash-Covered Loam" is only 19th-21st in the tally sheet. Brillantes' short stories, "Faith, Love, Time and Dr. Lazaro" and "The Distance to Andromeda" made fourth and fifth places, respectively. Although Manuel Arguilla is only fourth in the line-up of short story writers, his "How My Brother Leon Brought Home A Wife" is first among the short stories. Bienvenido Santos is fifth; two of his short stories made it to the top ten list: "Scent of Apples" is third place, and "The Day the Dancers Came" is eighth place. Gilda Cordero-Fernando got sixth place; her "The Visitation of the Gods," however, is only in ninth place. Francisco Arcellana is seventh in the list, but his "Divide by Two" is only in 10th-11th place. Kerima P. Tuvera is the eighth placer, but none of her short stories made the top ten list. F. Sionil Jose is only ninth place among short story writers, but his "The God Stealer" ties for 6th-7th place. Edith Tiempo is in tenth place, but like Tuvera, none of her short stories appear in the top ten list.

Two short stories, "Footnote to Youth" by Jose Garcia Villa, and "Dead Stars" by Paz M. Benitez, made it to the top ten list (6th-7th and 10th-11th respectively), yet their authors do not appear among the top ten short story writers.

### Table 5: Teachers' Choice of Poets

| Rank | Name | Frequency |
|------|------|-----------|
| 1 | Jose Garcia Villa | 38 |
| 2 | Cirilo F. Bautista | 26 |
| 3-4 | Emmanuel Torres | 22 |
| 3-4 | Ophelia A. Dimalanta | 22 |
| 5 | Virginia Moreno | 21 |
| 6 | Ricaredo Demetillo | 18 |
| 7 | Nick Joaquin | 16 |
| 8 | Edith Tiempo | 15 |
| 9-10 | Carlos Angeles | 12 |
| 9-10 | R. Zulueta da Costa | 12 |

All the above poets write in English, although Cirilo F. Bautista also writes in Filipino, and R. Zulueta da Costa in Spanish.

**Table 6**: Teachers' Choice of Poems

| Rank | Title | Frequency |
|------|-------|-----------|
| 1 | "Montage" (by Ophelia A. Dimalanta) | 14 |
| 2 | "Like the Molave" (by R. Zulueta da Costa) | 13 |
| 3 | "Order for Masks" (by Virginia Moreno) | 8 |
| 4-6 | "The Flaming Lyre" (by Amador Daguio) | 7 |
| 4-6 | "Gabu" (by Carlos Angeles) | 7 |
| 4-6 | "Batik Maker" (by Virginia Moreno) | 7 |
| 7-9 | "God Said: I Made A Man" (by Jose Garcia Villa) | 6 |
| 7-9 | "Verde Yo Te Quiero Verde" (by Nick Joaquin) | 6 |
| 7-9 | "Mi Ultimo Adios" (by Jose P. Rizal) | 6 |
| 10-13 | "Isang Dipang Langit" (by Amado Hernandez) | 5 |
| 10-13 | "If You Want to Know Who We Are" (by Carlos Bulosan) | 5 |
| 10-13 | "The Return" (by Edith Tiempo) | 5 |
| 10-13 | "Florante at Laura" (by Francisco Baltazar) | 5 |

Due to ties for the 4th-6th, 7th-9th and 10th-13th positions, there are 13 poems in all in the list. Unlike the poets cited above, the poems that made the top ten list are not all written in English. Two are written in Filipino, "Isang Dipang Langit" and "Florante at Laura," and one in Spanish, "Mi Ultimo Adios."

Jose Garcia Villa is number one among the poets, far ahead in frequency count than the second placer, and yet his poem, "God Said: I Made A Man," is only in 7th-9th position. Similarly, Cirilo Bautista occupies second place, but none of his poems made it among the top ten poems; his poems "The Archipelago" and "The Cave," however, were cited three times in the survey. Emmanuel Torres and Ophelia A. Dimalanta tie for 3rd-4th place, but none of Torres' poems appear in the top list, while Dimalanta's poem "Montage" tops the list. Virginia Moreno is number five, and her poem "Order for Masks" is number three. Ricaredo Demetillo landed in sixth place, but no poem of his is included in the list of top ten poems. His "Barter in Panay" was cited only three times. Nick Joaquin placed seventh, and his "Verde Yo Te Quiero Verde" is also 7th-9th place. Edith Tiempo is in eighth position, and her poem "The Return" is tied for 10th-13th position. Carlos Angeles is 9th placer, and his "Gabu" tied for 4th-6th position. Also 9th-10th placer is R. Zulueta da Costa, yet his poem "Like the Molave" is in second position.

The authors of five poems that appear in the thirteen best poems do not figure in the list of top ten poets. They are: Amador Daguio ("The Flaming Lyre," 4th-6th place), Jose Rizal, ("Mi Ultimo Adios," 7th-9th place), Amado Hernandez ("Isang Dipang Langit", 10th-13th place), Carlos Bulosan ("If You Want to Know Who We Are," 10th-13th place), and Francisco Baltazar ("Florante at Laura," 10th-13th place). Amador Daguio was cited 11 times, Jose Rizal 6 times, Carlos Bulosan 9 times, Amado Hernandez 9 times, and Francisco Baltazar 8 times.

### Table 7: Teachers' Choice of Essayists

| Rank | Name | Frequency |
| --- | --- | --- |
| 1 | Salvador Lopez | 29 |
| 2 | Carmen Guerrero-Nakpil | 26 |
| 3 | Carlos P. Romulo | 24 |
| 4 | Leon Ma. Guerrero | 18 |
| 5 | I. V. Mallari | 17 |
| 6 | Nick Joaquin | 15 |
| 7-8 | Claro M. Recto | 14 |
| 7-8 | Pura S. Castrence | 14 |
| 9 | Francisco Icasiano | 13 |
| 10 | Horacio de la Costa | 12 |

Except for Claro M. Recto who also wrote in Spanish, all the top essayists write in English.

**Table 8**: Teachers' Choice of Essays

| Rank | Title | Frequency |
|------|-------|-----------|
| 1 | "What are Filipinos Like?" (by Leon Ma. Guerrero) | 15 |
| 2 | "Literature and Society" (by Salvador P. Lopez) | 14 |
| 3 | "The Will of a River" (by Alfredo Gonzales) | 10 |
| 4 | "Baroque: The Filipino Obsession" (by Rodrigo Perez III) | 8 |
| 5-7 | "What is an Educated Filipino?" (by Francisco Benitez) | 5 |
| 5-7 | "Rediscovery of our Past" (by Horacio de la Costa) | 5 |
| 5-7 | "Return to the Primitive" (by Salvador P. Lopez) | 5 |
| 8-10 | "Art and You" (by I.V. Mallari) | 4 |
| 8-10 | "The Miseducation of the Filipino" (by Renato Constantino) | 4 |
| 8-10 | "I Saw the Fall of the Philippines" (by Carlos P. Romulo) | 4 |

All the essays are written in English.

While Salvador Lopez is number one among the essayists, his "Literature and Society" is number two and "Return to the Primitive" is 5th-7th among the essays. Carmen Guerrero-Nakpil is listed second, but none of her works appear in the list of top ten essays. Her "Filipino Woman" was cited three times. Carlos P. Romulo is third placer among the essayists, but his "I Saw the Fall of the Philippines" is only in 8th-10th position. Leon Ma. Guerrero is only fourth placer, and yet his "What are Filipinos Like?" is in first place among the essays. I. V. Mallari placed fifth, but "Art and You" is tied at 8th-12th place. Nick Joaquin took seventh place, but none of the essays in the list was authored by him. Claro M. Recto and Pura S. Castrence occupy 7th-8th position, and yet no essay of theirs made it to the top ten list. The same applies to Francisco Icasiano, who landed in ninth position, but has no essay among the top ten. On the other hand, Horacio de la Costa is only tenth placer, but his "Rediscovering Our Past" is in 5th-7th place.

Four of the top ten essays do not have their authors in the top ten list of essayists: Alfredo Gonzales ("The Will of a River," 3rd place), Rodrigo Perez III ("Baroque: The Filipino Obsession," 4th place), Francisco Benitez ("What is an Educated Filipino?," 5th-7th place), and Renato Constantino ("The Miseducation of the Filipino," 8th-10th place).

### Table 9: Teachers' Choice of Playwrights

| Rank | Name | Frequency |
|------|------|-----------|
| 1 | Alberto Florentino | 34 |
| 2 | Nick Joaquin | 31 |
| 3 | Wilfrido Ma. Guerrero | 29 |
| 4 | Wilfrido Nolledo | 27 |
| 5 | Severino Montano | 19 |
| 6 | Jesus Peralta | 14 |
| 7-8 | Virginia Moreno | 11 |
| 7-8 | Rolando Tinio | 11 |
| 9 | Aurelio Tolentino | 10 |
| 10 | Amelia Lapeña-Bonifacio | 9 |

It is interesting to note that among the playwrights, two write in languages other than English. Severino Reyes wrote in Filipino and Aurelio Tolentino wrote in both Filipino and Pampango. The rest wrote in English. Tinio, Florentino, Bonifacio also wrote in Filipino; Guerrero is sometimes presented in Filipino.

### Table 10: Teachers' Choice of Plays

| Rank | Title | Frequency |
|------|-------|-----------|
| 1 | "The World is an Apple" (by Alberto Florentino) | 27 |
| 2 | "A Portrait of the Artist as Filipino" (by Nick Joaquin) | 21 |
| 3 | "New Yorker in Tondo" (by Marcelino Agana) | 14 |
| 4 | "Turn Red the Sea" (by Wilfrido Nolledo) | 10 |
| 5-8 | "Walang Sugat" (by Severino Reyes) | 8 |

| | | |
|---|---|---|
| 5-8 | "Kahapon, Ngayon at Bukas" | |
| | (by Aurelio Tolentino) | 8 |
| 5-8 | "Ang Paglilitis ni Mang Serapio" | |
| | (by Paul Dumol) | 8 |
| 5-8 | "Sabina" | |
| | (by Severino Montano) | 8 |
| 9 | "Forever" | |
| | (by Wilfrido Ma. Guerrero) | 7 |
| 10 | "A Life in the Slums" | |
| | (by Rolando Tinio) | 6 |

Of the ten plays three are in Filipino and seven in English.

Alberto Florentino is the top playwright and his play, "The World is an Apple" also topped the list of plays. Nick Joaquin is number two, and his "A Portrait of the Artist as Filipino" is also number two. Wilfrido Ma. Guerrero is third placer, but his play "Forever" is only in ninth position. Wilfrido Nolledo and his play "Turn Red the Sea" are both in fourth position. Severino Montano is in fifth place, and his play is also in 5th-8th place. Jesus Peralta, however, is in sixth position, but his plays did not make the top ten list. Virginia Moreno and Rolando Tinio tied for 7th-8th position, but none of Moreno's plays were chosen, while Tinio's "A Life in the Slums" made tenth place. Aurelio Tolentino is in ninth place but his play placed higher (5th-8th). Amelia Lapeña-Bonifacio is tenth placer, but no Bonifacio play is in the line-up.

Two young playwrights did not make it to the top ten list, but their plays did: Marcelino Agana's "New Yorker in Tondo" is third, and Paul Dumol's "Ang Paglilitis ni Mang Serapio" is 5th-8th.

So far, only the division of playwrights gives an almost clear correspondence between the playwright and the play. Also, only in this division are three works in Filipino found.

### Table 11: Teachers' Choice of Critics

| Rank | Name | Frequency |
|---|---|---|
| 1 | Isagani R. Cruz | 28 |
| 2 | Miguel Bernad | 22 |
| 3 | Bienvenido Lumbera | 17 |
| 4 | Salvador Lopez | 13 |
| 5 | Manuel Viray | 12 |
| 6-9 | Ophelia A. Dimalanta | 10 |

299

| 6-9 | Josefina Constantino | 10 |
| 6-9 | Ricaredo Demetillo | 10 |
| 6-9 | Epifanio San Juan, Jr. | 10 |
| 10-13 | Gemino Abad | 7 |
| 10-13 | Joseph Galdon | 7 |
| 10-13 | Alfrredo Navarro Salanga | 7 |
| 10-13 | Leopoldo Yabes | 7 |

Due to ties in the 8th-9th and 10th-13th positions, thirteen critics are listed. Of the thirteen, Isagani Cruz, Epifanio San Juan, and Bienvenido Lumbera write in both English and Filipino; the rest write only in English.

**Table 12**: Teachers' Choice of Literary Criticism

| Rank | Name | Frequency |
|---|---|---|
| 1 | "Philippine Literature: Perpetually Inchoate" (by Miguel Bernad) | 11 |
| 2 | *Carlos Bulosan and the Imagination of Class Struggle* (by Epifanio San Juan, Jr.) | 8 |
| 3 | "Mandarins on Native Grounds" (by Aurelio Calderon) | 6 |
| 4-5 | *Literature and Society* (by Salvador P. Lopez) | 5 |
| 4-5 | "Joaquin: The Woman Who Had Two Navels" (by Josefina Constantino) | 5 |
| 6-9 | *Bamboo and the Greenwood Tree* (by Miguel Bernad) | 4 |
| 6-9 | *Philippine Fiction: Essays from Philippine Studies 1953-1972* (by Joseph Galdon) | 4 |
| 6-9 | *Pasyon and Revolution: Popular Movements in the Philippines, 1840-1910* (by Reynaldo Ileto) | 4 |
| 6-9 | *Ang Makata sa Panahon ng Makina* (by Virgilio S. Almario) | 4 |

Fifteen works of literary criticism are listed because of ties for the 4th-5th, 6th-9th, and 10th-15th places. Among the fifteen works, thirteen are in English and only two in Filipino: Virgilio Almario's *Ang Makata sa Panahon ng Makina* and Soledad S. Reyes' *Ang Nobelang Tagalog.*

Isagani R. Cruz, who was cited twenty-eight times, tops the teachers' list; his recent book *Beyond Futility: The Filipino as Critic*, however, placed only 10th-15th place. Miguel Bernad ranks number two, while his work "Philippine Literature: Perpetually Inchoate" ranks number one. Bienvenido Lumbera took third place, but none of his works appeared in the top ten list. Salvador Lopez is fourth in rank, and his *Literature and Society* correspondingly took number 4-5. Manuel Viray, the fifth placer, was cited 13 times, while his work which was cited only three times took only 10th-15th. Four critics tie for the 6th-9th place: Ricaredo Demetillo (*The Authentic Voice of Poetry*) ranks a 10th-15th; Josefina Constantino ("Joaquin: The Woman Who Had Two Navels") ranks 4th-5th; Epifanio San Juan (*Carlos Bulosan and the Imagination of the Class Struggle*) took second place and Ophelia A. Dimalanta ("The Poetic Image in Philippine Literature") ranks 10th-15th. Among those who tied for the 10th-13th place, only Joseph Galdon has a work in the top ten list—*Philippine Fiction: Essays from Philippine Studies 1953-1972.* The works of Gemino H. Abad, Alfrredo N. Salanga, and Leopoldo Yabes did not make it in the popular listing.

It should be noted that, although Reynaldo Ileto's *Pasyon and Revolution: Popular Movements in the Philippines, 1840-1910*, Aurelio Calderon's "Mandarins on Native Grounds," Soledad Reyes' *Ang*

*Nobelang Tagalog,* and Antonio Manuud's *Brown Heritage: Essays on Philippine Cultural Tradition and Literature* made it to the top ten list of literary criticism, their respective authors/editors are not included in the list of top literary critics.

# MANILA AS A SETTING
# FOR TAGLISH ROMANCE NOVELS

ROSARIO CRUZ LUCERO

The publication of Taglish romance pocketbooks started in February, 1984, when the business sector was reeling from the impact of capital flight that resulted from the Aquino assassination six months before. This was a time when no new enterprises were being established, businesses were closing down, and mass unemployment worsened even more with the lay-off of thousands of heretofore securely employed professionals. Print media suffered like every other business in the country: *Who* and *Celebrity* magazines folded up; *Mr. & Ms.* barely survived and would have gone under, if not for the brilliant idea of the *Mr. & Ms. Special Edition*. However, the Atlas Publishing Co., the same company which publishes the most popular Filipino comic magazines in the country, boldly put out 5,000 copies of each of ten romance titles. As of August, 1985 (one and a half years later), all titles had been sold out, and new titles were constantly being produced.

It may therefore be of significance that the literature that exists solely for "passive consumption, entertainment, and leisure" (Goldmann, 1978, p. 169), such as the romance novel, should come at a time when people are hounded by political and economic anxieties of the magnitude that we are still presently experiencing. While the reader's primary reason for reading the romance may be that of escape, there is also contained in these stories the "negativity of culture" with which at no other time have they perhaps been more familiar. Poverty is a reality that people of all classes suddenly have to fear, as even Negros sugar planters (once the most affluent people this side of earth) — and now even an infamous couple in Hawaii — have suddenly been faced with bankruptcy. Economic insecurity constantly hounds the middle class wage earner.

While comic magazines and *Liwayway* are primarily intended for the lower class, the target audience of romance novels is the professional, white-collar wage earner, ranging from the middle executive to the office clerk and teachers of all academic levels. Hence, the attempt to "legitimize" it for the middle class is evidenced by its physical format (pocketbook), the fictional characters' socio-economic class (high to middle class, with a few exceptions), and the arrangement and position of these books in the bookstore (side by side with the English-language Mills & Boon pocketbooks).

In the world of the romance novel, the office culture is reassuringly intact and whole, and despite the near anarchy that one faces after 5:00, these romances assure the reader that there is still a "unified culture" as manifested by the similarities between the romance world and the real world of her office.

Like the American and British romances, the titles are apparently classified under various lines: Gemini, Twin Hearts, Sweet Romance, etc. However, the difference between these Philippine books, even more than the British and American, is illusory. One category follows a formula no different from the other. In the American and British romances, there are at least formulas that serve as the bases for their classification (See Appendix). In the Philippines, the labels may only deceive one into thinking that there may be a difference in content and style. The effect is that such labelling serves only "to perpetuate the semblance of competition and range of choice" (Horkheimer and Adorno, 1972, p. 123).

For the Taglish romances there is only one formula: that the heroine is a "liberated" woman, preferably a working woman, that the style may be erotic but not pornographic ("hindi malaswa"), and that the storyline be fresh and modern ("makabago"), suitable for the contemporary working woman. (There is much to say about the question of whether the heroine is truly liberated or just pseudo-male, but that would be a topic for another paper.)

Perhaps because of its formula—i.e., that the heroine should be "liberated"—the setting for these romance plots is invariably Manila. True, the editors have informed me that there have been attempts by some writers living in the provinces (e.g. Samar, Baguio) to have their romance manuscripts break into print, but these have been rejected mainly because they were "makaluma" (old-fashioned).

Using Barthes' method of novel analysis by dividing the work into narrative units, we may categorize setting under what Barthes calls Indices. There are two kinds of Indices: the Indices Proper and Informants. The Indices Proper involve an activity of deciphering. For example, the description of the setting contributes to atmosphere, characterization, etc. Informants, on the other hand, serve "to authenticate the reality of the referent, to embed fiction in the real world"

(Barthes, 1979, p. 223). For example, to say in a story that the characters had dinner at Cafe Adriatico and then took a stroll at Luneta Park authenticates the reality of the story.

Because these Taglish romances must go against the grain of the traditional, melodramatic formula that Tagalog romance is always associated with, the writers make a conscious effort to fill their stories with realistic details, and this they do by painstakingly describing particular spots in Manila as the setting of their romance plots. As an Index Proper, the setting may be used to contribute to characterization. For example, in a rich-boy-poor-girl story by Lualhati Bautista (*Isang Milyong Pisong Babae*), the places that the couple go to serve to show how naive the heroine is because of her poverty, and this naivete is what makes the hero fall in love with her:

Nakarating sila sa Wild Life, sa Nayong Pilipino. Nata-touched siya sa kasimplehan ng mga pangangailangan ng isang gaya ni Evelyn para lumigaya. Color picture. Telescope sa Tagaytay. Kamerang may zoom in at zoom out. Video games. Bump car. Mga bagay na pinagsawaan na niya noong kamusmusan niya pero ngayon pa lang nagbubukas dito ng bagong kaalaman at bagong karanasan.

Or in another story by Emelita Perez Baes (*Ano nga ba ang Pag-ibig?*), two male characters vying for the hand of the heroine are contrasted by showing what places they bring the girl to on a date. Efren, the old-fashioned one, takes her to a Chinese restaurant and to a movie, and then they take a stroll at Luneta Park. Conrad, the more modern one, who lives in a condominium unit, brings her to Cafe Makati on a date where they eat Italian steak.

On the other hand, as Informants, the spots mentioned may give the reader a thrill of pleasure at their familiarity. In Bautista's novel, the lovers meet in front of National Bookstore, eat at McDonald's and then the hero buys her a Sanrio Doll at Gift Gate. The reader can readily guess that these spots are located along Quezon Boulevard, a block away from a now famous house on Times Street.

The hero and heroine live in village subdivisions, which gives the writer an opportunity to describe the suburban culture. In one novel, there is a description of a garage as having two to three cars, the security guard ritual at the village gate (surrendering the ID, giving the name and address of the resident one intends to visit), and pet dogs with glamorous English names that obey commands given only in English. All these details are therefore meant to render a pictorial effect and to create the ambience of a higher middle-class life.

How does Manila, as a setting, figure in the romance plot? There is, of course, the usual theme of the corruption of the city. In one novel by Gilda Olvidado (*Ano ang Bulong ng Puso?*), the heroine wants to become a nun because she wants to get away from the chaos of worldly life, which is represented by Manila. The man she falls in love with is a demon lover, a cynical young man who delights in alternately tormenting her and attempting to seduce her because of his disillusionment with life, as represented by Manila. Of course, in the end, the couple realizes that this city of corruption and sin is life and fate, and together they can stand strong and live happily ever after.

The ideology of the romance novel, as part of the culture industry, is made apparent here—to render this present life meaningful in order to make it bearable. Such an ideology of the culture industry serves to preserve the status quo, for it presents society's conditions as life; thus, as the "embodiment of authoritative pronouncements," the romance novel becomes the "irrefutable prophet of the prevailing order" (Horkheimer & Adorno, pp. 148-149).

What is criticized as a flawed society becomes, in the end, the only acceptable one. Barthes (1979) would call this the "inoculation," a device by which a capitalist system perpetuates the myth that a "contingent evil" exists in the system in order "to prevent or cure an essential one." The novel criticizes the system by exposing its petty blemishes, and yet, in the end, saves it by showing that love conquers all.

Significantly, because of the formula of the liberated heroine, she is almost always a working woman—which means she is an office girl in Makati—with, of course, the boss as the hero. It would be interesting to see, therefore, what kind of work the heroine does, what her attitude toward work is, or what the office culture is.

In the romance novel the office is not a place of work, although there is the atmosphere of work lurking vaguely in the background. There is never any hint as to what kind of work the characters do in the office, which is a place merely where romance can bloom, thrive, falter and live again. It is a good place to prove the heroine to be a liberated woman, because it proves that she is a working woman. The office is a place bustling with social activity—flirtation, a lovers' quarrel, gossip. (The description of girls gossiping together in the office is the modern equivalent of the rural womenfolk gathering around the waterpump or river to gossip while doing the laundry.) The office is merely a place where the characters can bump into one another, and from where the author gets a motley of characters to contribute to each plot complication. It is where the heroine is either waiting for the hero to arrive or where the hero is asking her to work overtime so they have an excuse to have dinner together.

The characters refer to work verbally, and when they do, they reveal a feudal view of it. Loyalty to the company is stressed as the employee's best virtue, because from it will spring the virtues of industriousness and diligence. This, says the heroine in Paez Baes' *Ano nga ba ang Pag-ibig?* is the employee's capital:

"Kapag umunlad ang kompanya dahil sa sipag, tiyaga at loyalty na puhunan ng bawat kawani, kasama ring uunlad ang indibidwal na manggagawa ng kompanyang kinabibilangan niya. .... Pa'no kapag dedikado ka, ang impresyon, may pagmamahal ka sa kompanyang pinaglilingkuran mo. Bihira na 'yang ganyan ngayon. Kasi, kailangang sulit lamang ang trabahong katumbas ng salaping kinikita sa kompanya. Nawawala ang loyalty, at nagiging makasarili."

Such a notion of work illustrates the ideology that the dominant (capitalist) class wishes to perpetuate: that the work force find self-fulfillment in loyalty to the dominant class, that while the dominant class' capital is money, of which it must have an abundant supply in order to build up an enterprise, the work force is consoled with the thought that though penniless, it has "capital," which is "sipag, tiyaga at loyalty." It is in this sense that Althusser defines ideology: ". . . the reproduction of the ensemble of habits, moralities, opinions which ensure that the workforce . . . are maintained in their subordination to the dominant class" (Laing, 1978, p. 91).

Consonant with this romanticized concept of work is the failure to see, or the deliberate ignorance of, the problem of unemployment prevailing in the city. The heroine wants to migrate to the U.S. or Canada as a solution to her romantic dilemma; thus the novel ignores the social realities that have given rise to the immigration trend. Or when the heroine persuades a male fellow employee to flirt with her in order to arouse the boss' jealousy, she promises him another, even better job, if the boss fires him.

If the story uses the rich-boy-poor-girl formula, the two can only meet under accidental circumstances. In fact, the accidental meeting between rich boy and poor girl is a standard device for initiating romantic plots. While this may go against the sensibilities of a literary student trained in Aristotelian rules of organic unity, we can understand the logic of this formula. In the city, society is a rigid system of class stratification and opportunities for any sort of social mix would be extremely limited. So, while the literary student may be critical of the use of accident, or *deus ex machina*, such a device may actually follow society's rules of logic, because rich boy and poor girl can, in reality, only meet accidentally. As one character puts it: "'Yang mayaman at mahirap, mahirap pagtapatin 'yan. Sa komiks lang nagkakaibigan yan. Sa sine lang. Pero sa totoong buhay. . ." Their social circles and territories are mutually exclusive and this fact is what gives rise to the plot conflict.

Yet the odds against such fortunate accidental meetings and unions actually happening are great, and, even while rich-boy-poor-girl romance plots are commonplace, they happen so rarely in real life they make news when they do happen (e.g. Rockefeller and the Swedish maid; the Filipina immigrant who found herself a millionaire husband in America). This is the culture industry's way of assuring the common people that equality in this society does exist, and that one does have the freedom to transcend the boundaries of his social class. However, such opportunities for equality, because they are so few and far between, only emphasize the "insurmountable separation" of the social classes. The freedom that it implies consists in the "arbitrary selection of average individuals"; hence, statistically, the chance of it actually happening to anyone is so infinitesimal that one also becomes conditioned into "rejoicing in the other's success, which might just as well have been hers, and somehow never is. Whenever the culture industry still issues an invitation naively to identify, it is immediately withdrawn" (Horkheimer & Adorno, p. 145). The result is that the heroine of the romance novel is "the ideal type of the new dependent average."

In summary, Manila as a setting has produced the following conventions in the Taglish romance novels:

1. the higher middle class ambience;
2. the pictorial effect by means of detailed descriptions of familiar spots in Manila;
3. the affirmation that corruption in Manila is life and made meaningful by love;
4. the notion of work, not as a socio-economic reality, but as an opportunity for romance with the boss; therefore, it is identical to loyalty to the company or employer; and
5. accidental meetings between rich boy and poor girl become logically acceptable because there is really no logical opportunity for social interaction between the rich and the poor in the city.

## REFERENCES

Barthes, Roland. 1979. *Myth Today.* London: Granada Publishing Limited.

Goldmann, Lucien. 1975. *Towards a Sociology of the Novel.* London: Tavistock Publications, Ltd.

Horkheimer, Max and Theodor W. Adorno. 1972. *Dialectic of Enlightenment.* English trans. New York: Seabury Press.

Laing, David. 1978. *The Marxist Theory of Art.* New Jersey: Humanities Press.

## APPENDIX

Falk, Kathryn. 1983. *How to Write a Romance and Get it Published.* New York: Signet, p. 12.

### Types of Category Romances

The current series of category romance are becoming more confined to two kinds of stories:

1. Fun, light, charming, and sensuous.
2. Hot, steamy, and perhaps issue-oriented.

A more exact breakdown is impossible because changes constantly occur.

Two considerations are certain: (A) Sex is either (1) virginal or sweet, (2) spicy (some sensual action above the waist), or (3) steamy (no holds barred, sexually). (B) Manuscript lengths are either (1) short, 50,000-60,000 words (around 200-225 typed manuscript pages), or (2) longer, 70,000-10,000 words (250-300 manuscript pages).

Here is a very general look at the current types of romances. Lines may subtly change from season to season regarding plot points or word lengths.

*Short Category Romances* (50,000-60,000 words)

Candlelight Ecstasy — steamy
Harlequin Presents — spicy
Harlequin Romances — sweet
Loveswept — sensual and/or steamy
Rapture — spicy or steamy
Second Chance at Love — spicy or steamy
Silhouette Desire — steamy
Silhouette Romance — sweet

*Longer Category Romances* (70,000-100,000 words)

Harlequin American Romance — sensual, mainstream fiction
Harlequin Temptation — steamy
Silhouette Special Edition — spicy or sensual, issue-oriented
Silhouette Intimate Moments — steamy
Superromance — spicy

# ANG LUNSOD SA NOBELA:
# MADILIM NA PANGITAIN

SOLEDAD S. REYES

Bago ko talakayin ang larawan ng Maynila sa nobelang Pilipino, nais ko munang ibigay ang ilang batayang konseptuwal ng sanaysay. Mahalaga ito upang mapalinaw ang limitasyon ng sanaysay.

Una, dapat mapalinaw na bagamat may kaugnayan ang panitikan at lipunan, ito ay hindi tahasan, simplistiko at *causal*. Hindi makatuwirang ituring ang panitikan bilang malinaw na larawan/salamin o representasyon ng buhay at ng mga karanasang dito'y bumubuo. Sa pagitan ng isang akda at ang hilaw o aktuwal na karanasan ay malaking bilang ng tagapamagitan o *mediations* na nagtutulong-tulong sa pagbibigay-hugis sa nobela, tula o dula. Mga puwersang pangkasaysayan at kultural ang umiiral upang mabigyang-daan ang pagbuo ng isang likha. Kabilang sa mga puwersang ito ang impluwensiya ng lipunan at kasaysayan — pangkalahatang pangkabuhayan ng mamamayan, ang pananaw sa buhay, ang mga ideolohiya, ang mga paraan ng pagtanggap sa panitikan — at mga impluwensiyang halaw sa kultura at estetika — mga tradisyong pampanitikan, ang sistema ng wika, ang uri ng mambabasa, ang posisyon ng manunulat sa kanyang lipunan.

Ikalawa, ang nobela ay isang likha/produkto o *construct* at sa loob nito ay matatagpuan ang isa pang *construct*, ang mga imahen o larawan ng lunsod. Maraming puwersa ang nagtulung-tulong upang makabuo ng mga masasalimuot na larawan ng Maynila, at ang mga puwersang ito ay nakaugat din sa mga impluwensiyang historikal, kultural at personal. Samakatuwid, ang larawan ng lunsod sa mga nobela ay ilang hakbang ang layo sa aktuwal na Maynila bilang isang aktuwal na karanasan batay sa pananaw na empirikal.

Panghuli, bagamat malinaw na ang nobela ay isang likhang-isip, na may sariling mga batas, malakas din ang naging impluwensiya ng realismo. Sa gayon, maaaring suriin ang mga nobela bilang tekstong mapagkukunan ng mga persepsiyon ng mga manunulat hinggil sa lunsod ng Maynila. Sa

311

kasaysayan ng nobelang Tagalog, nabuo at nabigyan ng maraming interpretasyon ang larawan ng Maynila na pinagitaw sa mga akda sa iba't ibang paraan. Kung gagamitin ang realistikong pananaw, maaaring makapagtatag ng istruktura na nagbigay-hugis sa larawan ng lunsod sa nobela sa loob ng walumpung taon, 1905-1985.

Upang malinaw na maihayag ang mga larawan at imahen ng Maynila, makabubuting bigyang-pansin ang mga manunulat na siyang pinagmulan ng mga persepsiyon at ang kontekstong historikal na pinag-ugatan ng mga akda.

### Ang Nobela, 1900-1920: Ang Pasimula

Kabilang sa mga nobelistang unang nagsulat ng nobela sina Lope K. Santos, Faustino Aguilar, Roman Reyes, Valeriano Hernandez Peña, Iñigo Ed. Regalado, Patricio Mariano at marami pang iba na magsusulat hanggang sa susunod na mga dekada. Karamihan sa kanila ay ipinanganak sa huling dekada ng panahon ng Kastila kundi sa Maynila ay sa mga lalawigang kalapit ng Maynila tulad ng Bulakan at Pampanga. Lumaki sila at nagkaisip sa panahong puno ng makukulay na pangyayari sa kasaysayan—ang Rebolusyon at ang pagdating ng bagong mananakop sa katauhan ng Amerika. Nabibilang sila sa gitnang uri, may sapat na pinag-aralan at naniniwala sa kapangyarihan ng isipan upang lumikha ng pagbabago.

Dumating ang mga Amerikano at taglay nila ang mga nakandidilat-ng-matang pangako ng isang bagong kultura. Sa kanilang pagdating maraming materyal na pagbabagong naganap sa buhay ng mga mamamayan, lalo na yaong nakatira sa Kamaynilaan. Nagbago ang kapaligiran—dumating ang mga trambia, mga *restaurant*, *soda fountains*, mga kabaret, mga sinehan. Nagkaroon ng di-maiiwasang pagbabago sa mga kaugalian, sa pananaw sa buhay, mga kostumbre, at mga aktitud na bunga ng pagpasok ng mga banyagang institusyon.

Matatagpuan ang mga unang larawan ng Maynila doon sa mga nobelang inilathala sa unang dekada, katulad na ng mga isinulat nina Roman Reyes at Valeriano Hernandez Peña. Sa triolohiya ni Roman Reyes, halimbawa na, makikita ang nabubuong larawan ng Maynila—magulo, masalimuot, nakasisilaw sa paningin dahil sa makulay na kapaligiran. Marami ditong pagkakataong pagbutihan ang kalagayan ng sarili sapagkat dito maaaring makapag-aral sa kolehiyo at makapaghanap-buhay. Ang ganitong kaisipan ay pinag-ikutan ng *Pusong Walang Pag-ibig* (1910) at *Bagong Dalaga* (1910). Sa mga akda nina Reyes at Peña, hindi nakatatakot ang Maynila bilang bangin ng dusa at kasamaan. Dapat pansinin na kapwa taga-Bulakan sina Reyes at Peña, at maaaring ang kanilang persepsiyon sa lunsod ay bunga ng malaking interes sa isang di-kinamihasnang daigdig.

Subalit sa malaking bilang ng mga nobelang isinulat ng mga taal na taga-Maynila, naiiba na ang inihayag na larawan. Binigyang-hugis ng matalas na isipan ni Faustino Aguilar ang nobelang *Pinaglahuan* (1907) na kung saan ang Maynila ay inilarawan bilang tagpuan ng isang masalimuot na kuwento ng paniniil at pang-aapi. Inapi si Luis Gatbuhay at itinuring na yagit ng mga dayuhang negosyante, ng kanilang kasabwat na Pilipino, mga limatik sa pamahalaan. Naganap ang lahat ng ito sa pusod ng Maynila. Kung kaya't sa pagwawakas ng nobela, ang huling larawan sa naglalahong paningin ni Luis ay ang Kamaynilaang tinutupok ng malaking sunog. Sa *Busabos ng Palad* (1909), pinasimulan ang paggamit ng tema ng "masamang babae na may ginintuang puso." Pinainog ang kuwento sa kapalaran ng isang dalagang inilugso ang puri at pagkatapos ay itinapon sa bahay na pula sa isang pook sa Maynila. Iba't ibang uring ng karahasan ang malinaw na inilarawan at ang mga ito ay naganap sa lunsod na puno ng mga institusyong mapaniil.

Sa mga nobela naman ni Iñigo Ed. Regalado tulad ng *Sampagitang Walang Bango* (1918), *May Pagsinta'y Walang Puso* (1921) at maging sa *Madaling-Araw* (1909), ang mga galaw at gawi sa buhay ng mga taga-Maynila—mga negosyante, usurero, alta-sosyedad, mga makata at manunulat, mag-aaral, at mga kalunya at mananayaw sa kabaret—ang baha-bahaging inilalarawan. Sa mga nobela ni Regalado at sa iba pang mga akda, mga pangunahing tauhan ang mga babaeng pinagsamantalahan hindi ng tadhana kundi ng mga lalaking walang puso. Naging tagpuan sa mga karanasan ang mga pook na pamilyar sa publiko sa panahong ito—sa Manila Hotel, sa Sta. Ana Cabaret, sa mga chalet sa Ermita, sa mga bahay na pula sa Culi-Culi at Pasay.

Ilan pang larawan ng lunsod ang pinagitaw sa marami pang nobela nina Patricio Mariano, Juan Arsciwals at Isabelo de los Reyes. Para sa pangunahing tauhan sa akda ni Mariano, *Tala sa Paghulo* (1913), ang Maynila ang pinag-ugatan ng kapalaluan, at paghamak sa mga mahihirap. Para kay Arsciwals, sa kabilang dako, maraming mukha ang Kamaynilaan—isa itong patibong, isang bitag, isang pook ng bisyo. Sa *Singsing ng Dalagang Marmol* (1914) ni Isabelo de los Reyes, isang tauhang Amerikano ang pinagsalita hinggil sa mga biyayang dulot ng Amerikanisasyon.

Subalit sa karamihan ng mga nobela sa panahong ito, waring iisang tinig ang mga nobelista sa pagtingin sa Maynila bilang produkto ng Amerikanisasyon, isang lugar na pinamamayanihan ng mga mananakop.

At sa kanilang paglalarawan ng Maynila bilang pook at bilang isang sistema ng buhay, waring nagugulumihanan ang mga nobelista sapagkat hindi na ito ang Maynila ng kanilang nakaraan. Ang Maynila sa nobela ay isang masalimuot na daigdig na ginagalaw ng ganid na mangangalakal, politikong mandaraya, mga mapaglilong babae at lalaki, mga walang galang na mga anak, mga dalagang hindi marunong magmahal, at mga tauhang galing sa baryo na pagdating sa Maynila ay naging biktima ng marahas na sistema.

Ang ganitong pangkalahatang pananaw ay maaaring bunga ng pagkakatiwalag ng unang henerasyon ng nobelista sa kasalukuyan na sinasagisag ng Maynila. Pawang nanggagaling sila sa nakaraan, isang daigdig na kanilang kinamihasnan. Hindi nila matanggap ang mga pagbabago sa lunsod sapagkat nanatili ang mga ito bilang di-pamilyar at samakatuwid ay di-maunawaang penomena. Higit na makabuluhan ang nakaraan (na sinasagisag ng nayon o mga pook na hindi nalahiran ng Amerikanisasyon) at ang pananaw sa buhay na nagbukal sa nakaraan.

Ang kalipunan ng nobela sa panahong ito ay hindi lamang nagbigay ng larawan ng buhay; ang pagsulat ay isang aksiyong politikal – isang paglaban sa mga pagbabagong nagaganap, sa mga bunga ng imperyalismo. Makikita ang ganitong pananaw sa malaking bilang ng nobela sa unang dalawang dekada, lalo na sa paglalarawan ng mga klase ng tauhan. Ang makabagong tauhan na karaniwang palalo, mapangmata, sukaban ay produkto ng Amerikanisasyon; siya ay karaniwang taga-Maynila. Sa kabilang dako, ang tauhang may ginintuang kalooban, marunong lumingon sa pinanggalingan, at mapagpakasakit ay karaniwang taga-baryo. Malinaw na sa panahong ito, nabuo na ang isang matatag na *construct* ng Maynila, isang kombensiyunal na pananaw sa lunsod.

## Ang Nobela, 1920-1940: Ang Paglalim ng Impluwensiya

Sa pagsisimula ng ikatlong dekada, marami nang pagbabagong naganap sa kultura ng mga Pilipino. Isang resulta nito ang paglikha ng henerasyon ng mga nobelista na ang kaisipan ay hinubog na ng edukasyong kolonyal. Bukod dito, higit na ang kalayuan nila sa mga pangyayaring naganap nuong simula ng ikadalawampung siglo. Ilan sa mga popular na nobelista sa panahong ito sina Fausto Galauran, Antonio Sempio, Simplicio Flores, Gregorio Coching at iba pang manunulat.

Subalit malinaw na ang larawang nabuo tungkol sa Maynila ay patuloy na nakabaon sa kamalayan ng mga nobelista. Bagamat nagbago na ang pangalan ng mga tauhan at mga pamagat ng nobela, namayani pa rin ang pundamental na sitwasyon na ginamit sa naunang mga nobela. Higit na marami ang mga tauhang nalahiran ng mga impluwensiyang kanluranin—hindi lamang sa pagdadamit (hindi na baro't saya at camisa chino kundi mga suot ng idolo ng *flapper era* at *Americana cerrada*), sa panlabas na anyo (maikling buhok a la Valentino; mapulang kuko, manipis na kilay a la Garbo), sa pagdami ng mga nag-aaral sa unibersidad—kundi sa mga bagay na kultural—sa paggamit ng Ingles at sa pagsamba sa mga bagay na kanluranin, mga pagbabago tungkol sa paniniwala hinggil sa pag-ibig, pag-aasawa, indibiduwalismo at iba pang aktitud. Makikita ang ganitong makukulay na transpormasyon sa ilang akda tulad ng *Kundangan* (1927), *Punyal na Ginto* (1933), at *Bulaklak ng Kabaret* (1930).

Para sa mga naunang nobelista, ang Maynila ay isang bangin ng hirap at kanilang inihayag ang mensahe sa isang seryoso at moralistikong paraan; katulad sila ng mga propeta sa Bibliya na nagbabala ng malagim na wakas doon sa mga taong nagugumon sa mga bagong bisyo na dala ng mga Amerikano. Subalit para sa kabataang nobelista, wala na ang tono ng propeta. Bukal ang lunsod ng kasamaan sapagkat malaking bilang ng tauhan ang dinihagi sa lunsod subalit waring tinatanggap na ito ng mga manunulat bilang di-maiwasang epekto ng kolonisasyon.

Anuman ang mga di-pampanitikang dahilan (historikal, kultural, o awtobiograpikal), sa pagsapit ng ikatlo at ikaapat na dekada, nakalikha ng ilang larawan ng Maynila sa isipan ng libu-libong mambabasa ng *Liwayway* at *Sampagita*. Pinalabas ang Maynila bilang isang daigdig na nakahahalina, lubhang nakababaliw, nakalalango, pook ng tagumpay, salapi at katanyagan. Ito ang Makiring Maynila. Subalit isa pang kaalinsabay na larawan ay kakikitaan ng lunsod bilang isang bilangguang mahirap takasan, hindi katatagpuan ng tunay na kaligayahan, namamanginoon sa malalakas at mayayaman. Sa panahong ito, lalong pinatindi ang pananaw tungkol sa Maynila bilang sagisag ng pagbabalat-kayo, samantalang patuloy na positibo ang pagtingin sa nayon bilang bukal ng katotohanan.

### Ang Nobela, 1940-80: Madilim ang Kalangitan sa Lunsod

Naging biktima ang Pilipinas, lalong lalo na ang Kamaynilaan nang sumiklab ang Ikalawang Digmaang Pandaigdig. Malilinaw na detalye ng kamatayan, paniniil, pagsasamantala, *buy and sell*, ng mga *kempeitai* at gerilyero, ng kanstanyog at *chocolate bars* ang pumuno sa mga nobelang nasulat sa pagitan ng 1945 at 1950. Waring pinagtuunan sa mga nobelang *Fort Santiago* (1946), *Erlinda ng Bataan Mutyang Taga-Ilog* (1948) ang mga karanasang pamilyar sa mga mamamayan—paghihiwalay ng mga pamilya, pagdami ng mga *squatters*, pagdami ng mandurukot, mamamatay-tao at masasamang babae; walang buhay at sigla ang Maynila sa panahong ito.

Sa pagdaraan ng panahon — sa ikaanim hanggang sa ikawalong dekada — pumasok ang mga batang manunulat. Pinagpakuan nila ng masusing pansin ang isang pook sa Maynila — ang Tundo. Nuong nakalipas na mga dekada, ginawang tagpuan ang mga bungalow sa Singalong, ang Mehan Garden, Tom's Restaurant, Lyric, Clover Theater, Manila Grand Opera House, ang mga distrito ng Quiapo at Sta. Cruz — mga pook na pamilyar sa mayayaman at mahihirap. Subalit sa kamay nina Pedro Ricarte, Rosario Lingat, Efren Abueg, Edgardo Reyes, Mercedes Jose, at Andres Cristobal Cruz, waring higit na pinabigat ang papel ng Tundo — isang sagisag ng kawalan sa maraming akda. Sa paggamit ng teknik ng realismo at maging naturalismo, ipinakita sa mga nobelang tulad ng *Sa Mga Kuko ng Liwanag* (1967), *Dilim sa Umaga* (1968), *Madilim ang Langit sa Bayan Ko* (1970), *Kagubatan ng Lunsod* (1964), *Pagtakas sa Estero* (1969), *Halik sa Alabok* (1967), *Apoy sa Madaling Araw* (1964) ang paglikha ng mga nobelista ng isang pangit na daigdig ng karahasan at kawalan ng katarungan.

Bagamat sa unang tanaw ay magkawangis ang larawan ng lunsod sa makabagong nobela at doon sa mga naunang nobela nina Regalado at Galauran, lalabas ang malaking pagkakaiba sa isang malalim na pagsusuri. Sa unang hati ng kasalukuyang dantaon, ang Maynila ay isang konsepto na itinapat sa konsepto ng nayon at bukirin; ang dalawang pook sa sagisag ng magkaibang realidad, ng dalawang bisyon ng buhay. Ang lunsod ay hindi lamang isang partikular na pook kundi isang abstraktong konsepto na binigyan ng laman at isinangkap sa mga nobela nina Aguilar at Sempio. Sa ikatlong dekada, ipinagpatuloy ang paggamit ng lunsod bilang tagpuan at sagisag ng oposisyon ng nakaraan (tradisyon) at kasalukuyan (Amerikanisasyon). Papalingon ang tanaw ng mga nobelista. Malinaw na kung hindi man nila kinasusuklaman ang lunsod at ang mga institusyong dito'y nagkalat, higit nilang nanaisin na pabalikin ang mga tauhan sa lalawigang pinagmulan.

Subalit sa ikapito at ikawalong dekada, sa gitna ng maramihan at malawakang pagbabago ng buhay ng mga tao sa Maynila, nag-iba ang larawan ng lunsod bilang *construct*. Ang romantikong papanawang naunang mga nobelista na nag-ugat sa konserbatismo (ang anumang pagbabago ay kailangang labanan sapagkat nagbibigay-daan ang mga ito sa pagtalikod sa nakaraan) ay nagbigay-daan sa isang higit na realistikong pagtingin sa Maynila, sa mga pook tulad ng Tundo — ng mga libu-libong barong-barong, mababahong estero, makikipot na kalsada, na pinanahanan ng libu-libong mahihirap at mga biktima ng puwersang nag-uugat sa panlipunang institusyon.

Maaaring batay ang ganitong pananaw sa aktuwal na buhay at

karanasan ng mga nobelista na karamiha'y nabibilang sa mahirap na uri. Subalit maaari din naman bunga ang ganitong pananaw ng pagsisikap nilang sumulat ng panitikang katulad ng mga nobela nina Steinbeck at dos Passos sa Amerika. Sa madaling salita, may ilang dahilang nagtulak sa mga nobelista upang pagpakuan ng ekslusibong pansin hindi ang Luneta kundi Estero Sunog-Apog.

Isang resulta ng ganitong pagbabago ng oryentasyon ang pagpapalit ng tono sa mga nobela. Napalitan ang moralistikong tono ng naunang nobelista ng higit na obhetibong tono ng mga batang nobelista. Ang nobela ay nagmistulang dokumentaryo ng kahirapan at karahasan. Ang Maynila ay hindi tagpuan o konsepto lamang na katulad ng pagkagamit ng naunang nobelista. Ang Tundo ay isang metapora ng pangkalahatang sistema na kung saan ang mga tauhan ay lumalabas bilang biktima.

Ang nobelang *Sa Mga Kuko ng Liwanag* ni Edgardo Reyes ay isang malinaw na halimbawa. Pinaikot ang akda sa naunsiyaming pag-ibigan nina Ligaya Pariso at Julio Madiaga. Maraming dinanas si Julio sa kanyang paghahanap sa dalaga; naroroong naging piyon siya, napilitang pumatay ng tao, nakisama sa kapwa-mahirap. Natagpuan ni Julio si Ligaya na isa nang babaeng kinakasama ni Ah Tek. Binalak nilang tumakas subalit hindi sila nagtagumpay. Nang mabatid ni Julio na patay na si Ligaya, naghiganti siya sa pamamagitan ng pagpatay sa Intsik.

Batay ang nobela sa isang balita sa pahayagan. Subalit malinaw na ginamit ang balita upang ilarawan ang Maynila bilang isang kagubatan, at ang mga tauhan bilang biktima ng matatalim na kuko ng kasaysayan at lipunan. Sa nobela ang naglalakihang mga gusali, ang mga eskinita sa Quiapo ay wala nang sangkap ng romantisismo. Winasak ng nobelista ang birang ng ilusyon upang ipakita ang mapait na katotohanan tungkol sa lunsod.

Mga pamilyar na tema ng pag-iibigan ng dalawang nilalang, na malaon nang kinagigiliwan ng publiko, ay nabigyan ng siyentipikong analisi. Ang *Pagtakas sa Estero* ni Pedro Ricarte at *Madilim ang Langit sa Bayan Ko* ni Mercedes Jose ay dalawang halimbawa ng ganitong uri ng nobela na pinagalaw sa tagpuang pamilyar sa mambabasa.

Sa pagwawakas ng ikapitong dekada at sa pagsisimula ng ikawalong dekada, sa paglalim ng antas ng kamalayan ng mga nobelista, nagkaroon ng malaking bilang ng mga nobelang nagtaglay ng sosyal at politikal na dimensiyon. Naglabas ang mga manunulat tulad nina Celso Carunungan, Liwayway Arceo, Clodualdo del Mundo, Fausto Galauran ng mga akdang tumalakay sa panlipunang realidad na pinaikot sa pagtatagisan ng lakas sa lipunan. Maynila pa rin ang tagpuan ng mga kuwentong ito na karaniwang atake sa uri ng namamayaning sistema. Ang *Canal de la Reina* ni

Liwayway Arceo ay isang paglalarawan ng mga paraan kung paanong nagiging biktima ng lakas at kayamanan ang maraming pamilya sa Tundo. Sa kabilang dako, ang *Ano Ngayon, Ricky?* ay tumurol sa pakikisangkot ng isang kabataan aktibista sa madudugong pangyayari nuong unang sigwa, at ang kanyang pagharap sa katotohanang ang lipunan ay isang walang katapusang paggamit sa mga maliliit na tao.

Sa mga nobelang nasulat sa ikawalo at ikasiyam na dekada tulad ng *Ginto ang Kayumangging Lupa* (1975) ni Dominador Mirasol at *Dekada '70* (1984) ni Lualhati Bautista, patuloy ang paglalarawan sa lunsod bilang tagpuan at sagisag. Ang pagbabago ay makikita sa pagkakaroon ng kamalayang politikal ng mga tauhan. Ang kaawa-awang biktima ay hinahalinhan ng isang babae o lalaking handang lumaban sa sistema katulad, halimbawa na, ng tauhan sa *Dekada '70.*

May isa pang uri ng nobela na nagpakita ng pagbabago sa larawan ng Maynila. Tinutukoy dito ang tinatawag na *sex novels* nina Benjamin Pascual at Efren Abueg. Sa mga akdang tulad ng *Kumusta ka, Peter?* o *May Lalaki sa Ilalim ng Kama Ko,* na naging popular nuong ikawalong dekada, tagpuan ang Maynila hindi bilang isang pook ng kahirapan kundi lugar ng walang katapusang tuksuhan ng mga babae at lalaki. Ang lunsod ay tinanggap na bilang isang pook ng oportunidad lalo na para sa mga tauhang nabibilang sa gitnang uri sa kanilang paghahanap ng panandaliang libangan.

## Mga Papel ng Lunsod sa Nobela

Sa loob ng siyam na dekada, nagkaroon ang nobela ng pagkakataong gamitin ang lunsod sa iba't ibang paraan.

Unang-una, sa superpisyal na pananaw, ang lunsod ay inilarawan bilang isang tagpuan o konteksto ng mga pangyayari. Sa ganoon, ang lunsod ay ipinaloob sa isa pang akda bilang dokumentaryo ng nagbabagong realidad sa Kamaynilaan. Isang saksi ang nobela sa mga transpormasyon ng lipunan mula sa panahon ng Amerikano hanggang sa kasalukuyang panahon. Sa ganitong pananaw, ang paglalarawan ng lunsod ay mapagkukunan ng salamin ng nagbabagong kaugalian at gawi ng mga mamamayan.

Pangalawa, ginamit ang larawan ng lunsod hindi lamang tagpuan na kasasalaminan ng mga pagbabago kundi bilang instrumento ng protesta. Sa malaking bilang ng nobela, lumikha ang mga manunulat ng larawan ng lunsod bilang isang daigdig na nakaririmarim, isang lugar na may taglay na kapangyarihang wasakin ang isang tauhan. Sa pamamagitan ng pagpapakita ng mga negatibong katangian ng lunsod, nagamit ng mga tradisyunal na nobelista ang kanilang sining upang ihayag ang kanilang mariing protesta laban sa nagaganap na imperyalismong kultural. Makikita ang ganitong oryentasyon mula kay Regalado hanggang kay Galauran at maging kay Edgardo Reyes. Hindi isang matulaing pangarap ang lunsod kundi isang madilim na pangitain. Isa itong malinaw na larawan ng lunsod sa nobela, nilikha at pinalakas sa pagdaraan ng taon ng maraming nobelista dahil sa mga dahilang historikal, kultural at marahil ay personal.

Malawak ang sinakop ng ganitong pananaw — mula sa pinakaromantiko (isang pagpupuri sa nayon at pagtalikod sa lunsod) hanggang sa pinakarealistiko (ang obhetibong paglalarawan ng mga karanasan sa mga pook ng Maynila). Subalit nagkaisa sila sa pagtukoy sa lunsod bilang isang madawag na kagubatang dapat iwasan ng mga mamamayan.

Panghuli, sa unang dalawang papel, itinuturo tayo ng larawan ng lunsod sa tunay na Maynila, ang aktuwal na pook ng ating karanasan. Subalit sa pangatlong papel ng larawan ng lunsod, hindi na tayo itinuturo sa panlabas na realidad. Sa mga larawang matatagpuan sa iba't ibang nobela, bumuo ang mga nobelista ng mga imahen ng lunsod na may sariling kakanyahan at hindi na nangangailangan ng paghahanap ng *correspondences*. Binabasa ang mga nobela, at ang mga larawan ng lunsod na dito'y nakapaloob, bilang likhang-isip, bilang produkto ng isang proseso ng paggawa na pinaggamitan ng maraming konsepto at imahen. Maaaring malaki ang pagkakahawig sa tunay na lunsod ng mga larawang ito. Subalit ang pagtanggap sa mga larawan ng lunsod ng ating kamalayan ay isang proseso ng pagtanggap sa isang *construct* at hindi ng datang empirikal.

Sa madaling salita, maaaring tingnan ang nobela tungkol sa Maynila bilang salamin at dokumento. Subalit kung susuriin ito bilang panitikan, kinakailangang higit na pag-aralan kung paanong nalilikha ang larawan sa nobela at kung paanong tinatanggap ng kamalayan ng mambabasa ang ganitong nabuong realidad, at kung paanong nagbubunga ang ganitong pagtanggap sa sarili niyang isipan at damdamin.

Ang pagsusuri sa mga ganitong problematiko ay magagamit na materyal para sa iba pang sanaysay tungkol sa mga nagbabagong larawan ng Maynila — ang Lunsod ng Tao na isang pariralang pulos anyo at walang tunay na nilalaman sa ilalim ng nakaraang pamahalaan.

Sa sanaysay na ito, sinikap kong suriin ang iba't ibang larawan at imahen ng lunsod na nilikha at ginamit na modelo ng maraming nobelista sa kanilang pagtatangkang bumuo ng mga realidad sa panitikan. Waring ang pangkalahatang larawan ng Maynila ay madilim at puno ng panganib. Ilang magkakaugnay na dahilan na nakaugat sa kasaysayan at lipunan ang pahapyaw na natalakay sa pagsusuri.

Lubhang malawak ang larangan ng pag-aaral ng kaugnayan ng larawan/imahen ng lunsod, ng panitikan at kasaysayan. Maraming puwang at pagitan sa mga kaisipang bumuo sa pangkalahatang argumento ng sanaysay. Marami pang dapat gawin upang mapalitaw ang higit na malinaw na larawan ng Maynila mula sa iba't ibang pananaw. Magandang isipin na ang papel na ito ay isang maliit na hakbang sa pagpapalalim ng ating pang-unawa sa angking kakanyahan ng lunsod ng Maynila.

# ANOTHER LOOK AT PHILIPPINE VALUES

JAIME C. BULATAO, S.J.

## Introduction

At the beginning of a new era of Philippine political history it is time to take another look at the values of the Filipino. A quarter of a century ago, when the Psychological Association of the Philippines was just being founded, the study of Philippine values was one of the first main areas of research to which the psychologists turned their attention and their newly discovered research tools. It was at that time that the present writer wrote the article "The Manileños Mainsprings" (IPC, 1962), which has since become (fortunately or unfortunately) obligatory reading for many a struggling college freshman. The tools then used were various: a Filipino version of the Thematic Apperception Test, a test on Filipino annoyances, participant observation in people's groups, group discussion with Peace Corps volunteers fresh from a first encounter with Philippine culture, an analysis of consciousness, a phenomenological collection of key stories and events, and straight, simple observation.

## Summary of Philippine Values Research

At that time, I summed up the Philippine system of social values under three headings: Personalism, Authoritarianism, and small Group Centredness. That is to say that the great values of Philippine culture have to do with preserving a system of personal relationships where the key unit of the system is the family. Within this society the powerful ones exert an influence very much like parental authority, at once personal and inviolable. Within the family and with parent-like support from authority figures, one is at peace with one's conscience and with God.

From these inter-matting values of family-life relationships one can derive the more specific values in everyday Philippine life:

*Hiya* for instance typically occurs when one has to perform outside of one's circle of close acquaintances. It is the fear of being treated like an object, of being analyzed or criticized and being found wanting by outsiders.

*Pakikisama* means going along with the demands of powerful individuals. One is also afraid of being left alone without a sustaining group, hence one "goes along."

*Utang na loob* is a debt to someone who in the past took over the sustaining role of parent in a time of crisis. And who can go against one's parents? You have an *utang na loob* to the one who gives you a job even if it is a government job.

*Pakikipagkapwa-tao* is the rare virtue of the great and the powerful who have risen above their own small group and are willing to treat others as though they belong to their family.

*Smooth interpersonal relationship* means avoiding confrontation with outsiders. As Amang Rodriguez said: "Politics in addition."

At the time also when these values were being discussed, accepted or criticized, I wrote a little pamphlet entitled "Split-Level Christianity" (Ateneo University Press, 1965), wherein I suggested that in many (if not most) Filipinos there exist simultaneously two systems of values, more or less unconsciously dissociated from one another. On the level (which one may now term "level X") there exists the value system as described above. These are the values that one absorbs with one's mother's milk. They are gut-feeling values that are so "natural" that one does not even think about them but takes them for granted as right. But there is another system of values (which we may now term "level Y") which was probably learned in school or in church and which are more easily expressed in words or concepts. Such concepts are: democracy, nationalism, monogamy, theology, traffic signs, financial accountability, human rights, etc., etc. As one can see level X has to do with relationships in the here and now, level Y has to do with the abstract and the distant. And the split-level phenomenon keeps these two levels apart almost as if one level is the real and the other the theoretical. It is interesting to recall that Freddie Aguilar's song, "Anak," was panned by the critics but became an outstanding song-hit for the masses. The father-son relationship was what was real on level X.

This is, thus far, the system of Philippine values as we saw them a quarter of a century ago. But since then this easy-going Filipino, happy with his children and his saints, has had to go through the experience of martial law and revolution. Great national crises, they say, make or at

322

least manifest a people's values. Can we learn something about our values as we cast another look on them in the light of these recent experiences?

## Martial Law and the EDSA Revolution

Ferdinand Marcos, so said his ministry of information, was the "quintessence of the Filipino." And so indeed he was. He used all the values that the Filipinos hold dear and succeeded in manipulating them to his own ends.

The small group around him, his cronies, was personally faithful to him by the ties of reciprocity (the term was Mary Hollnsteiner's). The *pakikisama* was rewarded by a return of favors.

The military around him were faithful to him from family ties or the equivalent *compadrazco* through the sacrament of baptism or matrimony. His presidential security command, almost to a man including the chaplains, were Ilocanos. The generals in regional commands were either Ilocanos or were tied by *utang na loob* for their appointments.

The members of the Supreme Court were his U.P. classmates or fraternity brothers. (His greatest enemy in the Supreme Court was an Atenean.)

He aimed his largesse at local authority figures binding them personally to himself. He knew that they in turn would use the authority vested in them to deliver the votes. Some of the most zealous and active supporters of Marcos who exerted pressure on their constituents and brought them in buses and *fieras* to rallies were the barangay captains.

His insistence on presenting an image of health came from an inmost belief that the Filipino would follow the *malakas*. One of his most effective attacks upon his opponent in the presidential elections was that she was "*walang alam*."

But in all these, the mass of Filipinos responded according to traditional values of personalism, authority, and small group centredness. They followed the barangay boss (personal, authoritarian). They accepted money which they needed for their families. They were in great part unable to see the national harm being done by the people in power. One can see a mentality such as of the one who built the stone face of Marcos: reverence for the strong person who can be beneficient unto those who reverence him. In sum, what is distant in space and time is not important. The abstract and the distant are rational concepts. The concrete is what is present. The present feeling is what is important and one reacts to what is personal and personally influential. Between Marcos and the masses there was a certain cultural symbiosis. He used their values and manipulated them very intelligently to obtain his own ends.

Furthermore, during all this time Marcos' "Ideology for the Filipinos" could not be said to have been rejected. This ideology, together with all that was said in the Constitution and the laws on freedom, justice, rights, responsibilities, democracy—all these were true, if abstract, values of the people and even of the KBL. But these values formed a system apart and were on another level from the concrete feelings, the dominant set of cultural values, almost as if head and heart were separate and one chose to follow the heart. The situation was very much like those who say that they believe in monogamy but "as a matter of fact, men are by nature polygamous," or "I don't believe in ghosts, but still I am afraid of them." It was the old split-level mechanism at work.

Then came the revolution. It was a yellow revolution, not red, and all accounts both local and foreign, highlighted the fact that it was primarily a revolution of the middle class, led by professionals and managers and by formal religious leaders. One had only to walk up and down EDSA on the fateful Sunday, Monday, and Tuesday to see that this was a different crowd from the typically political one that had been transported (*hakot*) to the Luneta by the KBL two weeks before. Workers, too, were present at EDSA, but their banners indicated that they were cause-oriented or that they came from such and such a parish in pursuit of justice. These revolutionaries at EDSA were pretty much the same people who only two weeks before had fought to preserve the sanctity of the ballot and the will of the people at the polls.

One could not say that the revolutionaries had altogether different value systems from the rest of the population. In fact, the EDSA atmosphere was that of a town fiesta with people parading and greeting each other, with food being shared as in a picnic. In moments of stress in front of the tanks there was an appeal to the group solidarity with the chant, *"Walang aalis, walang aalis!"* And through it all there was the personal participation of the Sto. Niño or the Blessed Mother leading the processions. It was all very Filipino.

But from the point of view of values development there was now something new. There now was:

1. a willingness to confront, not just smooth-over interpersonal relations.
2. a willingness to confront authority, not only civil authority but even military.
3. a willingness to fight for an abstract ideal, justice and democracy.

4. an ability to see the national picture, not just the good of one's primary group.
5. a value for morality as something more basic then legality.

The revolution revealed values in the Filipino indicating that his identity, his *ako* (self), extended beyond his family, beyond his region. Maybe it took the assassination of Ninoy Aquino to access these values and to give them a prominence in the hierarchy of values that they formally lacked. In any case, the revolution was not only political, a change of rulers. It was also an indication of change and development within persons, at least persons within a social class.

It may be naive to think that there has been a deep change in the value of the lower class or the mass of the Filipinos. Even in the upper classes the old personalistic values remain very much of a reality, at odds with the newer values of the cutting edge of the culture. In the post revolutionary situation one can see these personalistic and authoritarian values at work in the squabbling over government posts where one has to *personally* appeal to a top *authority* to make a decision, implying that decisions are made on personalistic, paternalistic or maternalistic lines, like a father or mother settling the "gimme this" and "gimme that" of their children. Regarding the cultural inability of individuals to cooperate on a horizontal level by themselves with each other, such as in the example of a Japanese and one Filipino in opposition against each other, the Filipino stands a fifty-fifty chance of winning. But in a fight between two Japanese against two Filipinos, the Japanese were sure of winning because the Filipinos would not be able to cooperate with each other.

It is exemplary of the cultural pattern of small groups and their inability to reach an agreement unless the authority figure steps in to make them agree. The post revolution situation misses the Marcos style of authority figure making all the decisions. It will take time for the nation to learn new skills of compromise and group decision-making that go with the new presidential style of management and with the values of freedom and large group consciousness.

To see the old values continue working in the concrete side by side with the new values, one can listen to an interview with the mayor of San Juan (*Sunday Inquirer Magazine*, 6 April 1986, pp. 14-15):

Q: What did you give Marcos in exchange ... Did you give him your soul?

A: No, *naman.* I owed him my debt of gratitude. You see, if you're the head of the family and you see your

Q: children dying of hunger, you'll be forced to do anything, even steal, just so your children will live....

Q: I mean, did Marcos ask you to do anything which was against your conscience?

A: I wouldn't say that he told me directly. Well, in the 1978 election, I was with him already. LABAN won 11 seats and KBL won 10. But in the final results, KBL won all 21.

Q: With all the revelations coming out about the Marcoses now, would you still be loyal to him?

A: They would not change the fact that I owe him a debt of gratitude. I would still be honor-bound to pay him my *utang-na-loob*.

Q: Would you not feel concerned about human rights violations, corruption, etc. so long as you got benefits for your municipality?

A: If I were a national leader, I might perhaps fight Marcos. But since I was only elected town mayor and my sworn duty is to protect the interest of the people of San Juan, that's what I would be concerned about. So whatever Marcos does nationally, I have nothing to do with it. Those in national positions are the ones to do that — fight Marcos. For instance, if I were in the Batasan, I wouldn't permit all these things to happen to the country. I am shocked by the amount stolen from our coffers.

Q: So would you still support him now?

A: I would still pay my debt of gratitude.

Comment: A personal debt of gratitude for favors personally given by an authority figure outweighs the national good. One identifies with one's barangay, San Juan. There is some shock from dishonesty. There is only personalism, authoritarianism, and small group centredness, including a shocked awareness of violated values in the abstract. National concerns are seen as too far away, beyond one's area of duty — "I have nothing to do with it"

## Conceptualization

How then does one now conceptualize the value of the Filipino? Is there a gradual integration of levels X and Y, a fusing of spontaneous, indigenous values with the conceptually learned, abstract values? Is there a growing prominence of the left brain over the right brain? Are we seeing a social class phenomenon indicating a difference in cognitive styles according to one's social class experience? Undoubtedly a great deal more research will have to be done to pinpoint what is basically happening in the Filipino psyche. Allow me here to give a hypothetical scheme of what to my eyes seems to be happening.

One starts off by stating that cultural values are relics of a people's experiences. They are the imperatives implanted in a growing child by his environment, which will serve to guide him to attain the goals of his society. In a society such as that of the pre-Spanish Filipino, the existence of small, autonomous barangays bred into the individual a trust in and a dependence upon his own small group and a carefulness in his dealings with those not of his barangay. Thus, the need for smooth interpersonal relations with those outside of one's family.

During the Spanish times he accepted Roman Catholicism whose saints fused beautifully with his beliefs in a spirit world, whose religious practices became his own processions, novenas and *penitencias,* but whose theology and thought-system remained "unindigenized," forming as it were a level split off from his own experientially learned thought and ethical system. So too during the early American occupation, ideals of democracy taught through words could only have as much effect as Marcos's ideology for the Filipino, something learned from schoolbooks.

Until the time of the Japanese war there really was not much opportunity for travel for a broadening of experiences. There was little experience outside the small town. As the Tagalog writer Macario Pineda put it in "Talambuhay ng Aming Nayon":

> Sa silangan daw ay kabuhayan....
> sa kanluran daw ay kamatayan....
> at sa pagitan nito ang aming nayon
> Dito kami pinanganak,
> dito kami nabubuhay,
> dito kami namamatay....
> at dito kami muling mabubuhay.

Thus, it was not to be wondered at that values centered around the family.

But the aftermath of the Japanese war brought a lot of movement, not only within the country but also to the outside, not only to the United

States and Europe but also to the Middle East, to Southeast Asia and Australia. Suddenly, Filipinos were all over the world and provided links with other cultures. Furthermore, television brought at least to urban Filipinos the possibility of experience never possible before.

While the life experiences of the lower classes have remained relatively the same, those of the middle and upper classes have changed qualitatively from those before the war. Social and economic expectancies have grown. Whereas people used to be satisfied keeping their way of life, earning some money through the year, spending it all at fiesta time and taking up from there again, the new Filipino learned to plan ahead in order to acquire a house in a better neighborhood, a car, TV, education for the children, maybe a graduate degree, etc. A new value seems to have developed: *Makaangat*, which may roughly be translated as "socio-economic development." And this socio-economic advance is seen as linked with education, which by itself brings awareness of the larger group, the nation.

I suggest that it was the frustration of this value that led to the yellow revolution of February 1986. Martial law with all its violations of justice and human rights in the 1970's was bad enough, yet the people did not rise. It took the economic disaster of the 1980's, clearly rising from the mismanagement and corruption of the regime in power, all these climaxed by the Ninoy Aquino assassination, that led to the shouts of *"Tama na. Sobra na. Palitan na!"*

These shouts, from the framework of the value system meant that there were limits to personal authoritarianism and small group thinking. At least the middle class, with its exposure to the West, has broadened its area of identification seemingly to include the nation. At least one can say that large group values are now in competition with small group values. The mentality that one is justified in blindly following the politician to whom one owes a debt of gratitude, in selling one's vote to help support one's family, in backing whoever is politically strong—this mentality is counter-balanced by the value of being identified with the bigger group and seeing one's good or one's evil as part of it. Thus, when certain roughnecks were looting Malacañang on the fateful night of February 25, voices from the crowd itself cautioned the looters that what they were taking or destroying was not Marcos' but was now the nation's. So too the same value expressed itself in returning *balikbayans* who proudly wore lapel buttons, "I am a Filipino."

It may be too much to say that there has been a conversion of the Filipino people. More accurately one can say that a middle class has developed, exposed as it is to Western values, and it is this sector of society that has taken on a value of socio-economic growth in a nationalistic framework. Justice plays an important part in this new value system, a justice that goes beyond the legalism of the old.

The presence of this particular value does not eliminate the traditional personalistic values found in the deep recesses of the Filipino soul. It will be most interesting to watch how, in the process of rebuilding and in the appointment of officers in charge, traditional lines of influence will continue to be followed. For a Filipino to fall back in time of need upon family and relatives is as "natural" as for Marcos even in exile to seek a home among Hawaiian Ilocanos.

## Theory Change

In the overall attempt to study Filipino values and value changes, it may be best to clarify our own concepts of what values are and the part they play in human nature. The human being is not a mechanical toy that must do what its internal machines tell it to do. Neither is it a rat in a maze that is programmed by external programming agents to follow an objectively "best" path. Rather he/she is a free agent, free in regard to choices. One chooses which value will prevail. The choices are set alternatives like crossroads, limited in number of choices, determined as to their number by past experiences. The choice as to which crossroads to turn to is the car driver's choice.

A man or woman of narrow experience has few alternatives to choose from. Thus, those who live on the brink of hunger from day to day have few alternatives to choose from because the values of their social experience have taught them few choices between values. On the other hand, the man/woman who in his/her growing years has a broad experience ends up with many values to choose from. These values may be contradictory choices between many values. The choice of a value at a particular time increases future freedom to choose that same value, without removing the possibility of choosing its opposite. At EDSA the people chose freedom and justice, allowing these values to prevail over values of conformity, security, and smooth interpersonal relations.

If the free world rejoiced with the Filipinos because of their choice of freedom above a manipulating dictatorship, it was because of the free world's own values of freedom. The Filipinos could have chosen a personalistic authoritarianism, but the choice of freedom seems to have added to the supply of this valued commodity on earth.

## Conclusion

To sum up, as the Filipino nation makes its way up the super highway of history, it acquires a full load of experiences from which it chooses what things are most *valuable* in its present stage of journey. In the past stages, Filipinos have developed a particular value and skill in personalistic relationships modeled after family ties. The lower classes and the people of the countryside have kept this value. That forms the rear half of the convoy. But the front half of the convoy, being exposed to the rapidly developing scenery of a twentieth century world, has developed new values, new tastes of life as it were. And these may be the values of human development, of freedom, and of justice. It may console us to think that the whole convoy is moving forward, though slowly, like a turtle. They say that a turtle does not make progress until it sticks its neck out. Fortunately, we stuck our necks out and we are now moving forward.

# FOLK CATHOLICISM IN MANILA: SECTS IN THE MAKING

BASILIO P. BALAJADIA

This paper is about five cases of spirit possession groups in Metro Manila. They are being discussed under the heading of folk Catholicism in Manila in as much as these groups are deeply rooted in Filipino folk religious traditions. The purpose of the paper is to show that these groups exhibit characteristics of sects in the making.

## Review of Related Literature

One innovation of the Second Vatican Council that has far-reaching consequences in Catholic life today is the concept of the Church as the People of God (Lumen Gentium), that the Church is not just the priests, bishops, cardinals and the Pope, but the people who make up the community of believers. The idea led the Catholic Church to take a hard look at folk religion, or folk religiosity, especially in those regions where the Church has been established for centuries and where she is in the course of becoming established. This popular expression, as Pope Paul VI put it, was regarded as less pure and was sometimes despised, but today, is almost everywhere being rediscovered (Evangelii Nuntianti p. 48).

Predicated on the theological principle that Jesus is Savior of man "as he is and where he is," impetus and efforts to inculturate the faith in the Filipino life were undertaken in the Philippines during the decades following the Second Vatican Council (*Philippiniana Sacra*, 1979).

Much has been said about the positive aspects of folk Catholicism in the Philippines, its riches and possibilities for evangelization. The traditional values of *pakikisama, damayan, bayanihan, hiya, utang na loob, bahala na*, among others, could serve as the basis for the development of genuine Christian virtues. The Filipino religious belief system, which includes a deep sense of God, recognition of the presence of various spirits, fatalistic submission to the *gulong ng palad* and *tadhana*, the

331

veneration of dead ancestors, and the devotion to the Blessed Virgin Mary, Santo Niño and the saints, could form a suitable jumping board for Cathechesis. (ECERI, 1982 pp. 5-9)

Notwithstanding the positive aspects of folk Catholicism, it also has its limitations which can make it quite vulnerable. As Evangelii Nuntianti notes: "Popular religiosity is often subject to penetration by many distortions of religion and even of superstitions. It frequently remains at the level of forms of worship not involving a true acceptance by faith. It can even lead to the creation of sects and endanger the true ecclesiastical community (p. 48)."

This paper will focus on this aspect of the creation of sects, specifically spirit possession groups, from among groups of folk Catholics in Manila.

What is a sect? Sociologists of religion (Vernon 1962, Troeltsch 1930, Hunt 1977, Nottingham 1971) would generally describe it as a type of religious organization which is in opposition to the *ecclesia*, or church, the religion of the majority. It was Troeltsch who started this distinction when he traced the development of Christianity from the small groups of Jesus' followers to the highly complex institution of the present-day church. Later, scholars would elaborate on this church-sect typology and introduce subtypes like denominations and cults. Still others would come up with alternative ways of categorizing religious groups (Wilson 1973, pp. 16-30). From these various studies, the following characteristics of a sect could be gleaned:

1.  It is a small organization composed of individuals who are led by a charismatic leader.
2.  The group regards the majority religion as no longer embodying the genuine message and spirit of the original religion. Consequently, it considers itself a religious elite that will faithfully live the spirit of the original religion and;
4.  Its rise is usually occasioned by crisis, particularly economic crisis, although any other crisis can precipitate the formation of one. In urban areas, it thrives in relative anonymity and can often end up corrupt.

Among the studies on religious groups in the Philippines are those about Iglesia ni Kristo (Elesterio, 1977), Aglipayan Church (Achutegui and Bernad, 1960) and Iglesia Watawat ng Lahi Rizalist Cults (Foronda). Although studies have been made on spirit possession groups (Marasigan 1975, 1979; Tejido, 1979), these have been mostly theological and pastoral.

There is a need therefore for the present study of spirit possession groups from a sociological perspective.

## Scope and Limitation

This study is basically sociological. It does not attempt to prove or disprove the claims of these spirit possession groups nor criticize the theological aspects of their beliefs and practices. Instead, it limits itself to the description of the various spirit possession groups in relation to their development as sects.

## Methodology

The methodologies employed in the study are participant observation and informal interviews with members and leaders of the five spirit possession groups. The groups can be found in various parts of Metro Manila, namely, Makati, Malate, Tondo, Marikina and Mandaluyong.

## Manner of Presentation

A typical case of spirit possession will be presented. This will be followed by an analysis of the various groups using the characteristics of a sect given earlier, after which some conclusions will be given.

The following is a typical case of spirit possession in Metro Manila. Although the other cases could differ from it in certain degrees and respects, they all reflect the basic structure and development.

## Simbahan ng Diyos Ama (Church of God the Father)

The group called *Simbahan ng Diyos Ama* can be found in a populous barangay in Makati. It has been in existence for more than a decade now. It is based in the house of its leader. The house includes a chapel which serves not only as a place for prayer but also for healing.

The *Simbahan ng Diyos Ama* started as a small group of folk Catholics who would gather for prayers and healing at the chapel and to assist their leader, Sister Fely, during her trances. Sister Fely is believed to be possessed by the spirits during her trances. God the Father is said to be the most frequent possessor of Sister Fely because she speaks in an authoritative manly voice during her trance. The other spirits who also possess Sister Fely are the Blessed Virgin Mary, Jesus Christ, St. Joseph

333

and a host of other saintly spirits. They are identified by voice, gesture, facial expression, and other things associated with the spirits. It is this close relationship with the spirits that is said to give Sister Fely extraordinary powers like healing, prophecy, exorcism, mind-reading and astral travelling.

The group members spend their time making the traditional novenas every Friday evening, pilgrimages to the mountains of Montalban every Saturday evening. They also set up healing centers in various parts of Manila, and raise funds for a complex of church, hospital, orphanage, home for the aged and social welfare buildings, which they plan to put up in the mountains of Montalban.

Although quite informal at the start, the group later tried to make the organization formal by registering it with the Securities and Exchange Commission under the name of "Church of God the Father," with Sister Fely as supreme head. It had hoped for a setup similar to the *Iglesia ni Kristo* but found it difficult to require members to regularly contribute part of their income. Even if members are aware that theirs is becoming a religious group independent of the Catholic Church, they seem rather indifferent to the implication of such a position.

## Analysis of the Five Cases of Spirit Possession Groups

The analysis of the five cases will be based on the conception of sect a derived from the studies of sociologists of religion given earlier, namely:

1) it is a splinter group from the larger organization led by a charismatic leader;

2) it regards the larger group as no longer embodying the genuine message and spirit of the original religion. Consequently, it considers itself a religious elite that will live faithfully the spirit of the original religion; and

3) its rise is usually occasioned by crisis, particularly economic crisis, although any other crisis can precipitate the formation of one. In urban areas, it thrives in relative anonymity and can often end up corrupt.

## A Splinter group from the larger religion led by a charismatic leader

All the groups considered can be said to be members of the Catholic Church although they could be better classified under the folk Catholicism category. This could be seen from what Evangelii Nuntianti said about the characteristics of folk religiosity which apply very well to the various groups:

"It manifests a thirst for God which only the simple and poor can know. It makes people capable of generosity and sacrifice even to the point of heroism, when it is a question of manifesting belief. It involves an acute awareness of profound attributes of God: fatherhood, providence, loving and constant presence. It engenders interior attitudes rarely observed to the same degree elsewhere: patience, the sense of the Cross in daily life, detachment, openness to others, devotion." (p. 48)

Their predilection for certain devotions like novenas, processions, pilgrimages, vigils, vows and others also shows that these groups are very much rooted in the traditions and life of the people. Their conception, in fact, of the spirits and saints as well as their titles reflects the traditional patterns. The spirits who possess the mediums are described as having Castilian features and are given spiritual traditional names as *Dios Ama, Nazareno, Santo Niño, Mahal na Ina Fatima, San Antonio* or *San Jose.*

Although members acknowledge that they are Catholics, they seem to be quite aloof and wary of the officials of the Church. The reason could be that most priests generally refuse to join them or say mass in their chapels. Priests are fearful perhaps of the scandal it would cause among Catholics who are skeptical of these mediums and look down on the groups as simple-minded people or even outright lunatics. The presence of priest in the group could no doubt lend legitimacy to these activities and as such be taken as an act of approval or an acknowledgement of the validity of their claims.

Consequently, these groups resort to devising their own rituals and worship which are crude imitations of those of the Catholic Church. The leaders themselves assume functions associated with the priesthood such as in the case of the medium in Tondo who would, during her trances, don what resembles a priestly garment while seemingly dramatizing some scenes in the passion of Christ. All the mediums also bless water, oil, candles and other objects which only priests would do. The medium also acts as a preacher and teacher of doctrines. And they do so authoritatively inasmuch as it is understood that the spirits are their immediate sources. Sometimes, the line dividing the spirits and the mediums is no longer clear, such as when worship is directly addressed to the mediums. The followers kneel before them, kiss their feet, and direct their prayers to them. Ascribing supernatural powers to the mediums such as being all-present, all-knowing, and almighty comes quite naturally. This supposedly direct religious contact with God, which is not present in the official Catholic religion, seems to be an important factor in the rise and development of

335

these spirit possession groups.

## Charismatic Leaders

The various spirit possession groups cannot survive at the moment without their leaders, the mediums whom they believe to be visible manifestations of God on earth. They are believed to be possessed by God whenever they fall into a trance. It is also believed that the spirits who enter their bodies could be no less than God the Father Himself, Jesus Christ, the Holy Spirit, or all of them together; the Blessed Virgin Mary in her various titles and manifestations such as Fatima, Lourdes, Immaculate Conception, the Rosary or, the saints like St. Joseph, St. Martin de Porres, St. Francis of Assisi, or St. Michael. These spirits are identified by the members according to the voice, gestures, facial expression of the medium during his/her trance, or through the message given. The constant physical movements and monologues of the medium hold the audience enthralled and in suspense during a trance. The viewers, who are expected to regard the experience as a miraculous coming of the Spirit, generally react with overwhelming emotion and by professing faith in the medium.

As a result of this intimate relationship existing between the mediums and the spirits supposedly possessing them, the mediums are perceived to have tremendous spiritual and natural powers. Some of these powers are: direct intercession to God, the capacity to influence nature and events including the healing of all kinds of diseases, prophecy, clairvoyance, and the ability to read the past, the future, and the innermost thoughts of anyone. Consequently, the leader has divine authority to determine the will of the spirit, the most effective prayers to be said, the right doctrine, a sense of good and evil, the rituals to be observed and in general, how to run one's life.

## An Elite Group

The group considers itself especially privileged by God to be allowed to hear Him speak directly. Many are called but few are chosen! Other people would refuse to believe even if they have witnessed what believers have claimed to have happened. Most of the members attest to having seen visions related to the medium. Consequently, they have resolved to serve the spirit that possesses the medium. This commitment is manifested by their frequent visits to the chapel and their cooperation in the projects of the group. Although they do not condemn the whole world, they generally say that the present world is being misled by Satan through materialism and godlessness. In fact, they believe that it is this sad development that makes the spirit possess the medium. The world must be reminded of its obligation to acknowledge God. Reference to priests who forget the nature of their calling and have become themselves worldly is often made. Consequently, much prayer is being asked from members. They could help save the world! Novenas, prayer, vigils, pilgrimages and other forms of sacrifices thus become unending activities for the group.

### Crisis and Relative Anonymity

Although there are many factors that could give rise to a sect, this writer feels that the grave economic crisis during the decade of the seventies to the present, as well as the political, social and religious developments not only in the Philippines but the whole world over could have influenced the rise of these groups. It can be observed that these groups became markedly numerous specifically during the said period.

All the various groups started and thrived in relative anonymity in different parts of Metro Manila. Although they could all be found in the more populous areas of Tondo, Marikina, Makati and Mandaluyong, most people came to know about them only by hearsay. People in the neighborhood did not give the mediums and their groups much importance and perhaps even ignored them completely. However, they became instant celebrities when some journalist wrote about them as objects of curiosity particularly during the Lenten season.

What Nottingham noted about the possibility and likelihood of corruption among these groups due to their relative anonymity (p. 233) could have an application here although much time and effort would be needed to substantiate and prove this. Suffice it to say here that the author feels that there are some grounds to suspect that corruption could be happening among these groups in varying degrees.

### Conclusion

From the study, the following conclusions may be suggested:

1. Further study on Filipino folk Catholic beliefs and practices should be undertaken with the end view of discovering the dynamics of folk religiosity. This could serve as the meeting point for genuine dialogue between the agents and subjects of religious change. The formation of sects indicate that there are certain religious needs in the community that are not being adequately

337

met by the official religious group. The predominance, for example, of women in the leadership of the spirit possession groups could point out how women are not generally afforded participation in the leadership of the official Catholic religion.

2. A vigorous educational campaign should be initiated by the Church authorities so that the masses of the Filipino Catholics could catch up with the developments in the Church. In this connection, the lay leaders' participation could be of great help considering the lack of priests and religious personnel in the country.

3. A holistic approach to the phenomenon of spirit possession groups is demanded inasmuch as the formation and rise of these groups could be attributed to various factors, not excluding economic, political, and social ones. A case in point is the exhorbitant price of medicines as well as excessive fees that doctors and hospitals charge which put medical services beyond the reach of the masses. Hence, the proliferation of native healers and the open invitation to fake healers.

4. The print and broadcast media should help in the religious education of the masses through objective reports and discussions rather than sensationalizing reported supernatural happenings which only play inordinately on the superstitious imagination of the population.

## REFERENCES

Achutegui, Pedro S. and Bernad, Miguel. 1960. *Religious Revolution in the Philippines*, Quezon City: Ateneo de Manila Press.

ECERI. 1982. *Maturing in Christian Faith*, National Catechetical Directory for the Philippines.

Covar, Prospero. 1977. "Leadership in the Iglesia Watawat ng Lahi" in *Filipino Religious Psychology*, ed. by Mercado, L., Tacloban City: Divine Word Publications, pp. 109-126.

Elesterio, Fernando. 1977. *The Iglesia ni Kristo*, Quezon City: Cardinal Bea Institute.

Evangelii Nuntianti. 1975. *Apostolic Exhortation of His Holiness Pope Paul VI on Evangelization in the Modern World.*

Hunt, Chester. 1977. "Religion and Society," *Sociology in the New Philippine Setting*, ed. by Espiritu, S., Hollnsteiner, M., et al. Quezon City: Alemar Phoenix Publishing House, pp. 192-195.

*Lumen Gentium, Vatican Council II document.* 1964.

Marasigan, Vicente. 1975. "Grassroots Pentecostalism." In *Philippine Priests' Forum,* September, pp. 61-65.

Marasigan, Vicente. 1979. "Rituals in Manila's Catacombs" in *Philippine Studies* 27, pp. 74-81.

Nottingham, Elizabeth. 1971. *Religion: A Sociological View.* New York: Random House.

*Philippiniana,* Sacra. 1979. "Special Issues on Contextual Theology," 14.40

Tejido, Manuel. 1979. "The Ingkong Phenomenon in the Banal na Pag-aaral." In *Filipino Theology Today.* Budhi Papers 3, Quezon City: Ateneo de Manila University, pp. 25-44.

Troeltsch, Ernst. 1930. *The Social Teachings of the Christian Churches,* New York: The MacMillan Co., pp. 331-342.

Vernon, Glenn. 1962. *Sociology of Religion,* New York: McGraw-Hill Book Co., pp. 160-180.

# THE K.A.L.K.:
# A RIZALIST CULT IN METRO MANILA

MARCELINO A. FORONDA, JR.

## Introduction

Cults honoring Rizal as a god or at least as an extraordinary being bordering on the divine have been established in various parts of the country.[1]

Some of these Rizalist cults like the *Sambahang Rizal*, established in Cupao, Nueva Ecija in 1918, for instance, are now extinct. A few like the Bathalaismo, *Inang Mahiwaga,* organized in San Leonardo, Nueva Ecija earlier but registered with the Securities and Exchange Commission on November 25, 1948, have merged with others. Other cults like the *Watawat ng Lahi,* founded in Masbate in 1914, have survived and may even be said to have flourished in certain parts of the country.

Other Rizalist cults have been established in more recent years.

Among these is the Metro Manila-based K.A.L.K. (*Kataastaasang Ama ng Lupa, Kalangitan: Templo Rizal*) (The Highest Father on Earth and in Heaven, the Rizal Temple).[2]

Not much is known about the origins or the founder of K.A.L.K.. Nor is the belief system or its membership known to outsiders. This is due to the fact that no materials have been written, much less published about the K.A.L.K.. To my knowledge, this paper is the very first known notice about the cult.

To be sure, a study of K.A.L.K. should prove interesting to the student of Philippine indigenous religious cults.

This study thus examines the beginnings of the K.A.L.K., the principles and aims that led to its establishment, its structure and leadership, rites, rituals, belief, system, and membership.

My interest in the cult was aroused when, coming from a meeting at the University of the Philippines in February, 1980, I chanced upon young women dressed in white, flowing ankle-length, long-sleeved robes walking not too far from what appeared to be a decrepit, somewhat makeshift building in G.S.I.S. Village in Quezon City, Metro Manila.

I guessed that these young women were some kind of priestesses. As I found out later, they were actually priestesses of a religious group in whose worship Rizal occupied a special place.

I wanted to know more about the group, for which I structured an oral history project, and enlisted the help of some of my history students at De La Salle University to gather data about the K.A.L.K.[3]

I prepared the interview questions, briefed these students about the project, and sent them to interview the leaders and members of the K.A.L.K.[4]

Insofar as could be ascertained, Angel Lorenzo founded the K.A.L.K. Hardly anything is known about Lorenzo, or about the circumstances that led to the establishment of the K.A.L.K.

This is due, as has been pointed out, to the lack of published or unpublished materials about the cult and to the interviewees' general lack of knowledge about their founder and the early beginnings of their church.

Nevertheless, one can piece together some facts about the church. For instance, a member ventured the information that K.A.L.K. was established sometime in 1934. The aims of the cult, briefly stated, were based on divine, humane and nationalistic principles (*simulaing makadiyos, makatao at makabansa*). Although these principles were not specifically articulated by the interviewees, they will become apparent as we continue with this narrative.

## Founding

The remote origins of the K.A.L.K., according to one of our interviewees, may be traced to long before the year 1934. Indeed, such origins can be traced to the remote past, when few foreigners lived in the country, and therefore no church or religion had yet been established by them here.

It is claimed that in the past, many people perceived the likeness and representation of God in Rizal (*pinakalarawan ng Diyos*). This faith was called K.A.L.K. When foreigners, however, came to this country to spread their own religion and their own beliefs, those who believed in the K.A.L.K. were practically wiped out. Those who remained fled to the caves and to the distant hills, where they continued to profess their belief in the K.A.L.K.

The K.A.L.K. thus survived the onslaught of the foreigners' persecution, and, in fact, has continued to spread even in recent years.

Those who formally established this following spread it throughout the whole archipelago (*"yong nagtatag nito pinalaganap na sa kapuluang Filipinas na sa bawat dako"*).

## Leadership

The K.A.L.K. was registered with the Securities and Exchange Commission on April 14, 1934. The present head of the cult, Mrs. Salud Nuevo, replaced the original founder and head, Angel Lorenzo, when Lorenzo died.

Interviewees, however, were not clear about how Mrs. Nuevo was chosen to become the head of the K.A.L.K.. Requests for interviews with Mrs. Nuevo proved fruitless; she was always on some mission to the other branches of the sect. Nevertheless, the interviewees volunteered the information that Nuevo was elected by the members, and was never replaced (*...hindi nagpapalitan. Yan din ang pinipili*).

## Membership

The actual number of members has not been determined; no records are kept of the actual membership of the K.A.L.K.. But members of the cult generally belong to the masses and, as the interviewees pointed out, can be found in Metro Manila; in the provinces of Quezon, Laguna, Pangasinan, and Tarlac; in Bicol; the Visayas; and Mindanao. These members worship in the various chapels called *Templo Rizal* that have been established.

## Templo Rizal

If the cults' *Templo Rizal* in Quezon City is typical, then one can say that a *Templo Rizal* is not an independent unit in itself but attached to a home. The Quezon City temple is actually the ground floor of a two-story structure, and the living quarters of some members of the cult.

To enter the chapel one goes through a shabby, adobe and wooden structure roofed with GI sheets.

The major portion of the cemented first floor serves as a chapel, beside which is a small room partitioned off by a green curtain, which Salud Nuevo occupies when she is in town. Close by but smaller in size is storage space, which may be converted into a room where members from other places visiting in Quezon City may stay.

A single table covered with a crocheted runner serves as the altar.

Above the table on the wall is a framed lithograph of Jose Rizal, above which, painted on the wall, is the "All-Seeing-Eye." The "All-Seeing-Eye," the interviewees point out, is a representation of Father Sun who gives us light. He is adored for it is He who explains the answers to questions (...*yung iisang mata yung ang larawan ng amamg araw na siya ang lumiliwanag sa atin. Siya ang dinadalangin dahil siya'y magpaliwanag sa magtatanong*). The "All-Seeing-Eye," is thus, the symbol of the K.A.L.K.

Below the altar are two vases of multi-colored plastic flowers bordered by two candles on either side. Another picture of Rizal adorns the table. Sometimes, a white plastic bust of Rizal is also placed below his portrait on the table, but this bust is removed when not needed.

Facing the altar are wooden pews separated by a center aisle. During religious ceremonies, men occupy the pews on one side, and the women, the pews on the other side. This is done, our interviewees say, to maintain good order (*para maayos*).

Inscribed on the walls behind the pews are the following quotation in Tagalog:

*Ang Inang Lupang Tinubuan/ang dili ibat ang Pilipinas ay napa/kahalaga pagkat ito ang ban/sang ipinag/kaloob sa atin ng ka/ taastaasang ama ng lupa at kalangitan*

(Our Mother Native Land/ is nothing but the Philippines which is/ most important because this is/ the country which was given us/ by the Father Most high of the earth and heaven)

The temple in Quezon City was the very first church built by the K.A.L.K.. It was the founder who built it there for no other reason but that the lot was donated to the sect on condition that a church be built there.

### Rites, Rituals and Ceremonies

Certain rites, rituals and ceremonies are performed in the Quezon City church. At the end of each month, a mass is held in the Quezon City church, which members from the other branches of the sect, aside from those who belong to the Quezon City church, attend.

Other rites include those of baptism (*binyag*) during which water is used in a ritual cleansing. Members are also subjected to the rite of confirmation (*kumpil*). They have no rites similar to communion. Nor do they have ritual confession. (*Ang pagsisisi diyan, halimbawang*

343

*nangungumpisal, nasa sarili mo na.*)

K.A.L.K., however, has a special ceremony called the *pagpapasalamat* (thanksgiving), during which members of the K.A.L.K., not only from Quezon City but also from other branches, come to the Quezon City church to make their offering to God. This is done at least once a month. In the Quezon City church this is held at the end of the month because their leader, Salud Nuevo, schedules her visits to the other branches on the other days, in the so-called *recorrida*. During this *pagpapasalamat* ceremony the leader of the sect leads in the prayers of thanksgiving. She stands before the altar facing the people. Seven priestesses also stand in front of the altar. These priestesses, clothed in long flowing robes, are called the *obispo apostoladas* (i.e. bishop-apostles), but "priestesses" is the better term designated to them inasmuch as they have no administrative functions (as in the case of a bishop) within the church, and therefore, perform only the duties of priests.

The ceremony is as follows:
Leader: The Lord be upon us (*Ang Diyos ay sumasaatin*).

People: And may He bless us (*Pagpalain tayo*).

Then both the leader and the people recite the following prayer:

Almighty God, we beseech You to grant perfect peace and tranquility over all mankind.

Deliver us from all troubles and dangers and imbue us with sincere love and affection, good companionship and camaraderie thus bringing paradise to people here on earth.

Cleanse our consciences, make our souls holy that we may never deviate from Your holy commands and teachings.

Guide us to act at all times according to Your Holy will and rid us of all the evil inclinations of the flesh.

Our Father, may we always remain within Your Holy protection. Do not bring us to the test, but deliver us from evil, now and forever.

(*Amang Makapangyarihan, kami ay nagmamakaawa at humihiling na nawa'y umiral na ang ganap na kapayapaan at katahimikan ng mga mamamayan.*

*Huwag na pong pahintulutan na magkaroon ng ligalig ang aming mga kalagayan at pakitawasayin mo na po ang aming matapat na pag-iibigan at pagmamahalan, mabuting pagsusunuran at pagsasamahan ang siyang paraiso ng mga tao dito sa lupa.*

*Pakilinisin mo po ang aming mga budhi, pakibanalin mo na po ang aming mga kaluluwa upang kami ay hindi malihis sa mga banal mong utos at aral.*

*Patnubayan mo po ang aming pagkilos sa lahat ng pagkakataon at iwaksi ang masasamang hilig ng aming katawan.*

*Ama namin, nawa'y kami'y lumagi sa iyong banal na pakukupkop at layo sa kasakiman at tukso, iadya mo po kami sa dilang masasama, ngayon at magpakailan man.)*

These rites, rituals and ceremonies may be said to be their creed or the externalization of their belief system.

## Beliefs

What then are the beliefs of the K.A.L.K.?

To begin with, they believe in a loving, all-merciful God, who is the all-powerful and almighty K.A.L.K., the highest Father of the earth and heaven.

They also believe that Rizal has a very special place in the hierarchy of their beliefs. Rizal, in the belief of the K.A.L.K., is not a god. (The *Watawat ng Lahi*, on the other hand, adores him as a god.) Even so, the K.A.L.K. members profess the belief that Rizal is the Christ of the Philippines, in the same way that Christ is prophet among his own Jewish people. Thus, the K.A.L.K. members do not believe in Christ, but they do believe in Rizal. They believe that the sacrifices that Rizal made are very precious for his country and for his people.

The K.A.L.K. members have no saints in contrast to Catholics who, for instance, venerate the Virgin Mary and the other saints. K.A.L.K. members consider it more worthwhile to venerate their own Filipino heroes who after all, they say, dedicated their lives to their country. Foremost among them is Rizal, the Filipino Christ.

Even though Rizal is a mere man, he did much, much more than any other individual for his country. It is thus that Rizal is venerated on the altars of the K.A.L.K. — to give him the importance that he deserves, and to express the members' gratitude to him.

Members of the K.A.L.K. believe in God who created everything. But they also believe that Rizal is God's prophet, or, viewed in a different light, Rizal is the very first saint of the K.A.L.K. (*pinakaunang santo*).

Indeed, God made Rizal a man. God gave Rizal a body. Like Christ, Rizal came to the world as a son of God. Like Christ, Rizal is known all over the world. But as man, Rizal did commit mistakes.

While Catholics believe that Christ is God, the K.A.L.K. members do not profess the same belief (*sadyang hindi kami naniniwala sa bagay na iyon*). This is because they believe there is a God who created Rizal, meaning that there is only one God who created us all. Christ saved his own country and his own people, which, in a similar way, is what Rizal did for his own people in his role as prophet of the Philippines. (*Lamang, yung nagawa ni Hesukristo sa kanyang bayan—naging manunubos siya ng kanyang bansa, at yung nagawa ni Gat. Dr. Jose Rizal, yung pinagkaloob rin sa kanya bilang sugo*).

In the same manner that Rizal is the great prophet of the Philippines, so also is Jesus Christ the great prophet of the Jewish nation. And so it is that K.A.L.K. members, as Rizal's countrymen, recognize Rizal as the greatest hero and the greatest martyr of their own race, as the most heroic prophet of all (*pinakamartir at pinakabayani na sugo*).

Although K.A.L.K. members do not believe that Christ is God, they respect those who profess this belief in order to maintain peace and to prevent feuds or bickering among the citizens.

The K.A.L.K., according to its members, contains no foreign influences. Everything is purely Filipino. (*Walang dayuhan kami. Basta lahat Pilipino*). Christianity, on the other hand, is "foreign" to Filipinos. Unlike Rizal who spoke many languages, Christ did not speak Tagalog; indeed, Christ spoke only one language. In addition, K.A.L.K. members say, Christ himself never came to the Philippines, and thus, remains a total foreigner here.

There is, thus, the implication that Filipinos should profess belief in their own rather than believe in someone or something which is foreign to them. To prove their point, they quote a Tagalog proverb which says, "Mix together a red ant with a black ant, and they will go their separate ways." (*Ang langgam na pula at ang langgam na itim; pagsamahin mo man, maghihiwalay din*). K.A.L.K. members ask a rhetorical question, whose answer, nevertheless, is clear: Who should rule the Philippines: the Filipino or the foreigner? In answer to that, they give a meaningful saying: Rome is Rome, and ours is ours.

How does the K.A.L.K. view the other Rizalist cults, like those found in places such as in Mount Banahaw and in Lecheria Hill in Calamba, Laguna? Members of the K.A.L.K. maintain no relationship with them. But they are quick to point out that their Rizalist cult—K.A.L.K.—is uniquely and genuinely Filipino with no foreign influence whatsoever (*walang dayuhan kami; basta lahat pang-Pilipino*), implying that the other Rizalist sects are foreign-influenced.

They do, however, plan to spread their own faith and their beliefs. As of now, membership is confined to only a few places in the archipelago. They hope to spread their religion throughout the country. They plan to organize meetings during which they will expound on the tenets of their faith.

## Problems

A pressing problem of the K.A.L.K. is funding for its activities. The K.A.L.K. charges no fees for their rites, rituals or ceremonies. It is entirely dependent on the voluntary contributions of their members, and aid given by the different branches of the sect (*abuloy ng mga ibang sangay*).

Problems and difficulties, mainly financial, will certainly remain with the K.A.L.K. But these are not so hopeless that they cannot be solved through prayer. Indeed, K.A.L.K. members believe that man proposes but that God disposes (*Nasa Diyos ang awa, nasa tao ang gawa*).

## Conclusion

Even with the meager data at hand, aspects of the K.A.L.K., a Rizalist cult in Metro Manila, its early beginnings, its belief system, sacraments, rites and rituals, its leaders and membership, and, significantly, the place of Rizal in the cult can be pieced together.

Inevitably, Rizal is compared with Christ, and, as expected, the comparison tilts in favor of Rizal who after all is not a *dayuhan* (foreigner), but is indeed a fellow Filipino. K.A.L.K. members believe that Rizal is much more worthy of veneration by Filipinos than Christ, who after all did not speak Tagalog, and had never been to the Philippines.

Wittingly or unwittingly, the K.A.L.K. thus preaches nationalism, pride in being a Filipino, and pride to the race that produced a Rizal.

K.A.L.K. members proudly use the terms "Filipino Christ," "the greatest prophet of the Filipino people," and "the most martyred and the most heroic Filipino" when referring to Rizal.

Aside from these nationalistic sentiments that Rizal has engendered among the K.A.L.K. members it seems clear that this cult has also brought about other-worldly values, what may be termed as the religious values of the members.

To be able to find out what these religious values are and how deeply they have penetrated and, therefore, influenced the moral lives of members would take more than a mere cursory look at the principles,

347

aims, belief system, rites, rituals and ceremonies of the church. But this is beyond the scope of this present study.

## NOTES

1. For a seminal work on the Rizalist cults, see my own monograph, *Cults Honoring Rizal.* Manila, R.P. Garcia, 1961.
2. Henceforth, this Rizalist cult will be cited as K.A.L.K. for convenience.
3. I would like to acknowledge the help of my students Aresa M. Cochico, Ilene Y. Lopez, Regina M. Santos, Lucille Villaruz and Hector C. Maniquiz, Jr. for help in gathering data used in this paper. This data is contained in a group paper entitled "An Interview with K.A.L.K., Templo Rizal", prepared under my guidance and supervision. This was further augmented by my own interviews with some members of the K.A.L.K.
4. In this paper no informant will be cited individually to make for an easier flow of the narrative.

A grant from the De La Salle University Research Center made the preparation and writing of this paper possible.

# CULTURAL RESOURCES IN DEVELOPMENT: THE CASE OF INTRAMUROS

CANDIDO P. FILIO

The Most Noble and Ever Loyal City of Manila, which served as the capital of Hispanic Philippines and the bastion of Spanish colonial power in the Far East for more than 300 years up to the close of the 19th century, was contained in a 61-hectare Walled City called Intramuros. Considered one of the finest cities of the Orient—with its complex of civil, religious, military, educational, commercial, residential, and other urban structures, networks, and spaces—the Walled City of Manila could indeed be a priceless heritage of the Filipino people and society.

This legacy of Spanish colonization could have been enriched by the subsequent American and Japanese occupations, not to mention the Chinese and other foreign influences. Yet, this important artifact almost disappeared from the face of the earth, while efforts at historical reconstruction over the past two decades have not done much to recoup the cultural value of Intramuros to the larger Philippine society and Southeast Asian countries.

What is, therefore, needed now is a paper conceptualization of cultural resources, and making it the basis for development policy, planning, and management decisions. Without such a concept and the corresponding political will, the historical reconstruction of the Walled City could always lose out in the competition for scarce resources using conventional allocation tools. This paper shows how a culture-based innovation in the development process could ensure the conservation of a historic resource for future generations.

## Background of the Paper

This paper was originally prepared for the International Conference on Heritage and Conservation last March 16-20, 1986, hosted by the Municipality of Jerusalem and jointly sponsored by some 13 international organizations and Israeli institutions led by the Conservation Foundation of Washington, D.C. It should have been presented on March 18 at the Laromme Hotel in Jerusalem in a workshop chaired by Prof. Jehoshua Ben Aryeh. Unfortunately, I was too occupied with "revolutionary" activities to make the trip to the Holy Land during the Lenten season.

Addressing an international audience, my Jerusalem paper contained a lot of historical as well as contemporary backgrounds on the Walled City of Manila. But since our venue is right here in the heart of Intramuros itself, and some participants are presumably knowledgeable of its history and current developments, I have deleted those backgrounders.

Aside from the prospect of visiting Jerusalem, my interest in writing this paper stemmed from two of my previous studies. In 1981, I prepared a case study on Intramuros, specifically on the planning of its historical reconstruction, which was among the 14 case studies selected for presentation at the 17th Congress of the International Society of City and Regional Planners on the theme, "Renaissance of the City," on August 5-11 in Stockholm, Sweden.[1] In this regard, a term paper on Intramuros prepared by a student of De La Salle University for our course in Development Planning has been very valuable.[2]

From this early work, I learned that the proper nomenclature for the current efforts in Intramuros is "historical reconstruction," rather than "conservation" or "restoration." I also learned of the low level of priority given by the government to the "restoration project," if such commitment is to be measured in terms of the adequacy of the development resources actually allocated to it, rather than to the laws, ordinances, and decrees promulgated for it, or to the efforts of concerned groups and individuals, notably the Zonta Club ladies and then Minister Jaime C. Laya. Moreover, Philippine authorities had very little appreciation of the significance of Intramuros, and it took the study of a Spanish citizen, Don Pedro Ortiz Armengol, to arouse the interest of the Filipinos.[3]

The other work is a paper entitled "Productivity of Natural Resource-Based Industries," which I prepared for a symposium on Wages and Productivity last December 1982 at the Mirador Hotel in Manila, sponsored by, among others, the International Labor Organization.[4] In this study, I learned that natural resource-based industries, notably forestry and fishery, have very peculiar natures. For instance, unlike agriculture, they do not entail preparation, seeding, planting, and growing costs — only harvesting, transport, and processing costs; this is true even of non-renewable resources, like mining. Also, in the case of renewable resources, as long as harvest flows are kept within sustainable-yield levels — i.e., within allowable cut or catch — their stocks are never depleted. Natural resource-based industries are thus very susceptible to supra-normal profits, unearned by the entrepreneurs, which have to be taxed away for the benefit of the rest of society.

Now, if natural resource-based industries are to be treated differently from ordinary economic activities — which has, of course, never been observed in the Philippines — how about cultural resource-based activities, like the Intramuros project? Don't they have their own peculiarities to warrant special treatment?

## Integrated Framework of Development

Before answering these questions, it would be useful to establish first an integrated framework of development to place the discussion in its proper perspective.[5] This framework will also be followed in carrying out a development planning exercise recommended for Intramuros.

*Concept of development.* Development may be considered as a set of goals to be achieved by a society. These goals may also be structural — physical, economic, social and political.

Alternatively, development may be considered as process — viz., the process of improving all human lives and the quality of their environment, as well as the process of attaining societal goals. This approach involves a value judgment as it is premised on the notion of what is good. It is, however, more realistic because it does not assume an end state when development goals have already been achieved.

*Coordinate decision-making functions.* The concept of development as process implies that decisions are being made and actions are being taken at three functional levels — policy, planning, and management (See the diagram at the end of this paper). These three functions are coordinate — i.e., no one is subordinated to another — in the sense that they are concerned with different decisions in time, as well as in space, and their processes or systems have different outputs and inputs and require different decision-making tools and techniques.

The policy system is concerned with the ends of development. It is here where the philosophy of development is formulated, starting with the welfare function, a statement of what is good for the society — the commonweal. This system generates the social values which inform the formulation of societal goals and specifies the criteria which constitute the broad guidelines for pursuing such goals, including those which measure the degree of their attainment. Policy perspectives must be futuristic — i.e., they must reflect the people's vision of and aspiration for a good life in the

351

future. They must have global dimensions in that they do not only take an aggregative or a holistic view of society, but they also consider its relationships with other entities in the universe. Finally, they must be critical in the sense of being selective—i.e., they must zero in first on the most crucial problems affecting the society at any given time, like security. This last aspect calls for a scheme of priorities.

The development planning system consists of the strategy and process, as well as the organization, for generating the programs, projects, and activities—together with their implementing and operational structures—i.e., the means for attaining societal ends. Planning is, therefore, concerned with major investment decisions required to create productive capacity. Thus, resource allocation is the heart of the planning system.

The third component of the development process—the management system—takes off from an assumption that decisions have already been made as to the kinds of programs, projects, and activities required to produce the goods and services desired by society. In other words, it is already known what productive capacity to build and what remains to be done is the actual building of that capacity to generate the products of development effectively and efficiently. Thus, the management function is concerned with plan implementation, operation, maintenance, control, monitoring, and evaluation.

*Functional integration of development.* Integrated planning requires both sectoral, disciplinal, or vertical integration, where the subject is the integrating element, and areal, territorial element—as well as the reconciliation between sectoral and areal integration. It also requires temporal integration which can be achieved by harmonizing both the decision-making functions of development and the components of the planning system. This functional integration of development would ensure doing right (i.e., effectively and efficiently in management) the right things (i.e., the programs, projects, and activities generated in planning) for the right reasons (i.e., in accordance with the values, goals, and criteria generated by policy), of, for, and by the right people (i.e., with the proper structures). In other words, adequate management has to be based on valid planning, which is, in turn, premised on sound policy.

This functional integration of development over the decision space, with its time dimension, would lead to the temporal integration of planning. Then development can be seen as one continuous flow from ends (policy) through means (planning) to products (management), with appropriate feedback at each level. This concept of functional integration could also be enhanced by the recognition that development does not take

352

place in a vacuum and its participants work in a common environment.

*Environment of development.* In the development of a particular society, it is important to consider the relevant environments that impinge on its performance. Two environments may be recognized: an internal environment consisting of ideological elements, problem sets, and resource endowments; and an external environment consisting of factors outside of but affecting the given society—e.g., international economics and politics.

The topmost position of the development model is occupied by the ideology of the society. The term "ideology" simply refers to the system of beliefs, or the internally-consistent set of values shared by the people, which could serve as guides for development decision-making. Such values are rooted in the moral, cultural, and political traditions of the people. Without such an ideological framework, policies could be self-defeating.

Development problems may be defined, in general, as obstacles to the attainments of the "good life" for a given society. They result in the deficiencies—both qualitative and quantitative—in the goods and services available to the people. These problems may be categorized as: social, having to do with the human condition and the relationships among people; environmental, having to do with the physical factors for living; and economic, having to do with levels of production and consumption.

Resources constitute the basic ingredients of development. They may be grouped under three broad categories—natural, human, and financial—corresponding, respectively, to the three traditional factors of production—land, labor, and capital. Development is then the process of using these resources, according to a certain technology, to produce the goods and services desired by the people—the quality and quantity of such products being a function of the quality and quantity of such resources and the level of technology. Mal- or mis-development is bound to happen whenever such use is not properly harmonized. One may note the difficulties experienced by some oil-producing countries that may have all the financial resources they need from oil, but without the corresponding human and natural resources, apart from oil.

The primary resources are the natural resources—which include the physical factors of production, like lands and soils, forests and wildlife, minerals, and water—as distinguished from man-made physical structures. Human resources may also be considered primary, but because of their autonomous nature, they may even be considered exogenous to the system. Financial resources are derived resources in that they may be created through institutional arrangements.

The external environment relevant to the development of a given

353

country refers to the supranational-regional, international, and global development systems. In an increasingly interdependent world, the external environment becomes very important. Thus, geopolitical, diplomatic, and other external factors come to the fore in development decision-making.

## Cultural Resources and Development

With natural, human, and financial as the three broad categories of resources for development, there is a fourth category that is gaining currency—viz., cultural resources. Traditionally, the term "cultural resources" has been used to refer to archaeological and historical structures.[6] These are, therefore, physical artifacts that have archaeological and historical values. In the Philippines, the Walled City, or Intramuros, of Manila—as well as its walls—would be a very good example of a cultural resource.

There is, however, a move to expand this narrow definition of cultural resources to include social groups and folk traditions—i.e., to cover the cultures of living peoples, like cultural minorities. Thus, the Mangyans of Mindoro and the Tagbanuas of Palawan are not just special human resources, but they are also cultural resources for development.

The reasons for designating cultural resources as a separate category in development is that in evaluating cultural resource-based programs, projects, and activities, the traditional economic tools—e.g, cost-benefit analysis—would no longer suffice in determining their viability. Project designers or proponents would, instead, undertake the necessary cultural-impact assessment, and include in their proposals the corresponding cultural-impact statement.

But the main idea here is for removing cultural resource-based programs, projects, and activities from the traditional economic framework or the ordinary commerce of man. They should not be made to compete with other programs, projects, and activities for scarce development resources according to the allocation principle of efficiency vis-a-vis equity. Allocation of resources to cultural resource-based projects should not be made at the planning level, but higher at the policy level according to the simple criterion of affordability.

The assumption behind all this is that archaeological and historical values—cultural values, in general—are by themselves desirable for society. To be sure, this is not debatable, since such values foster national identity, which is a *sine qua non* of true development. But once the relative degree of such desirability has been determined and established, a

354

reasonable level constituting a "critical mass" of resources has to be committed right away.

In answer, therefore, to the set of questions raised earlier, it can now be stated that like natural resource-based industries, cultural resource-based programs, projects, and activities deserve special treatment.

The proposal where resource-allocation decisions involving cultural resource-based projects are made at the policy level, is actually the practice in many of the more civilized countries of the world. One can imagine this to be the natural arrangement in socialist countries. In China, there is a real effort to balance the demands of ideology, security, politics, economics, society, culture, and other developmental aspects at the highest level of decision-making. Thus, there is a clear-cut policy on cultural developments; for instance, as to how many of the Ming tombs to dig up, when to excavate, at what cost, or whether to dig up at all.

The same is true in such diverse countries as Yugoslavia and France. But even in the United States, there is, at least on paper, a clear policy on cultural resource development, as in the National Environmental Policy Act.

## Implications for Intramuros

The ongoing historical reconstruction of Intramuros is fraught with many problems which have been aggravated by the neglect of decades. These include technical difficulties, the private ownership of the land, and the incompatibility of its existing uses.

But the most pressing problem of the Intramuros project, as seen by its administrators, is the inadequacy of financial resources—its low levels and improper timing—i.e., not only "too little and too late," but especially its uncertainty of availability. How can project activities be scheduled if the availability of funds cannot even be assured? This is very crucial in the Philippines and especially, in Manila, because of its unpredictable climate and weather conditions.

As to financial and financing problems, this is indeed very hard to accept. Ten years ago, whenever such problems were raised, people would inventory funds wasted in wrong, improperly designed, or aborted programs, projects, and activities—like "white elephants"—and the problems would immediately assume other forms.

Now, however, there are strong arguments against accepting the lack-of-funds syndrome. People merely point to the financial resources squandered or stolen by the Marcoses. If, as reported, the former First

Lady, could spend ₱ 84 million for her facelift, why could she not spend half of that amount for the facelifting of the historic Walled City?

The problems of Intramuros are certainly much more basic than those in planning. They include graft and corruption, power and politics, and distorted priorities.

This paper, however, would like to focus only on the problems of improper development — from policy through planning to management — starting with conceptualization. Following the monumental work of Ambassador Armengol, the Ministry of Human Settlements formulated the Intramuros mission in terms of tourism — in fact, one wonders what the Ministry of Tourism had to do with it, if any. But as Intramuros Administrator Laya said: "Intramuros is valuable real estate, a large tract of undeveloped land in the center of Manila. It is bound to yield to the pressure of land use and development."[7]

What is, therefore, clear, is the need to reformulate the problem from economic to cultural. Then a totally different development would be seen — from policy through planning to management. This would also call for a reorientation of the process from one that is centralized, manipulative, closed, technocratic, etc., to one that is decentralized, participative, open, humanistic, etc. The latter process could then be operationally designed and implemented as a joint effort of the people, planners, and politicians in a viable, integrative and continuous development planning exercise.

# NOTES

1. Candido P. Filio, "Planning the Historical Reconstruction of Intramuros" (Case study prepared for the 17th Congress of the International Society of City and Regional Planners on the theme, "Renaissance of the City" on August 5-11, 1981, in Stockholm, Sweden.)
2. Ms. Pia Mapua Lim, AB-BSC, whose valuable contribution is hereby acknowledged with appreciation and gratitude.
3. Pedro Ortiz Armengol, *Intramuros of Manila* (Madrid: Ediciones Cultura de Hispanica, 1958).

4. Candido P. Filio, "Productivity in the Natural Resource-Based Industries," *Papers on Philippine Productivity* (Pasig, Metro Manila; National Productivity Commission, 1983), pp. 89-93.
5. Candido P. Filio, *Towards a Two-Tier Model of the Development Planning System* (Monograph presented to the participants, 19th Class, Postgraduate Course in Town and Regional Planning for Developing Countries, Technical University of Szczecin, Poland, in February 1984; for publication by the U.P. Press, Diliman, Quezon City)
6. Roy S. Dickens, Jr., and Carole E. Hill, eds. *Cultural Resources: Planning and Management* (Boulder, Colorado: Westview Press, 1978), p. 5.
7. Jaime C. Laya, "The Intramuros Restoration Project," (a lecture), p. 16.

# REFERENCES

Finsterbusch, Kurt, and C.P. Wolf, eds. 1977. *Methodology of Social Impact Assessment.* Stroudsburg, Pennsylvania: Dowden, Hutchinson, and Ross, Inc.

Laya, Jaime C., and Esperanza B. Gatbonton (introduction by Nick Joaquin). 1983. *Intramuros of Memory.* Ministry of Human Settlements/Intramuros Administration.

# APPENDIX

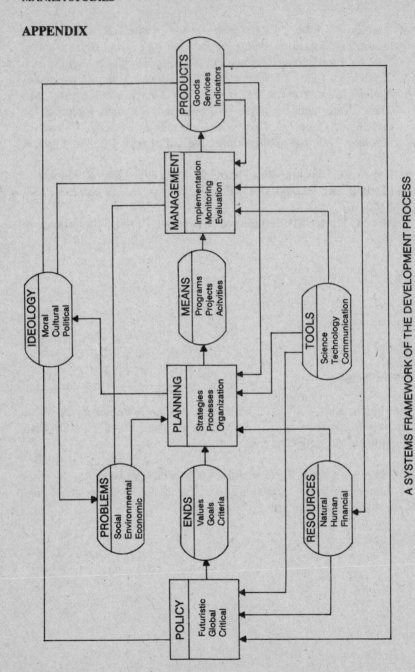

A SYSTEMS FRAMEWORK OF THE DEVELOPMENT PROCESS

# THE CREOLIZATION OF PHILIPPINE ENGLISH: EVIDENCE FOR ENGLISH-AS-A-FIRST-LANGUAGE AMONG METRO MANILA CHILDREN

ANDREW B. GONZALEZ, FSC

## Introduction

Using evidence from various language use surveys, Llamzon (1984) avers that the status of English in the Philippines at present is one of 'restriction' of domains using Moag's (1982) model to describe the cycle of English in the Philippines through its stages of transplantation, institutionalization, and now decline, so much so that the former colonial language which used to be a second language in the colony is fast becoming a foreign language for the community.

On the other hand, in 1969, Llamzon cited evidence of a widespread use of English at least among the elites of the country, so much so that he made a case for the standardization of Filipino English. For the purposes of this paper, more importantly, he cited evidence from the Catholic Educational Association of the Philippines (CEAP) schools showing that 51% of the students in these Catholic schools spoke English at home and in effect learned it at home before they started learning it more formally in school (Llamzon 1969:84).

Thus one has in the Philippines a very unusual situation which cannot be captured simplistically by a neat model — namely, that on the one hand, the domains of English in Philippine life are steadily being taken over by Pilipino and therefore the language is in a state of restriction, and on the other hand, that Philippine English, a language characterized by distinctively local features (Llamzon 1969, Alberca 1978, Gonzalez and Alberca 1978, Gonzalez, 1982, Gonzalez in press), has become at least for a certain sector of Philippine society a first language. Therefore what was once a language mixture (and therefore a pidgin) is becoming creolized as a mother tongue. The first development bodes ill for the maintenance of English in the Philippines, but the second phenomenon ensures the maintenance of English in the country, albeit in modified form and restricted to a specifiable socio-economic stratum.

The purpose of this paper is to cite further evidence going beyond Llamzon's earlier citation of the CEAP survey to show that there is indeed a small English-as-a-first-language community in the Philippines and to spell out the implications of such a fact for the maintenance or demise of English in the Philippines.

## The Evidence for Philippine English as a First Language

It should be stated from the beginning that except for the 1969 citation of Llamzon, no formal survey has ever been taken focusing only on the phenomenon of Filipinos learning English as a first language (see Gonzalez and Bautista 1986 for a critical review of language surveys in the Philippines from 1966 to 1984). The evidence must be culled from other surveys, focusing on other dimensions of language use, but including evidence for English as a home language through the usual background information accompanying such surveys. The evidence is therefore indirect, a by-product of inquiries having other objectives; it is nevertheless there and needs to be looked into and its implications drawn out in attempting to predict the fate of English in this archipelago.

### CEAP Survey (reported in 1969)

To begin with, the survey taken by the CEAP among its grade schools indicated that as many as 51% of the respondents stated that they used English at home, and by implication, that they had learned it at home as a first language prior to attending school. (I read the technical report of this survey in early 1971 but unfortunately the original technical report is no longer retrievable, even at the CEAP national office, and hence the citation is based on Llamzon's own report of it in his 1969 book.)

It should be stated first of all that children in CEAP schools constitute only a portion of the 4-5% of children attending private schools in the Philippines; this was the proportion back in 1968 or so when data was gathered (Llamzon reported it in his 1969 publication). Not all the 4-5% of students in private schools attended Catholic schools since in addition to Catholic schools, there are Protestant schools under the Association of Christian Schools and Colleges (ACSC) and the Philippine Association of Colleges and Universities (PACU), which are non-sectarian. In general, the socio-economic status (SES) of children in Catholic schools, by reason of the tuition structure, would be high and urban. (At the time, in the late 1960's (SY 1968-69), there were approximately 38,751 elementary schools in which approximately 6,701,067 pupils were enrolled.) Thus, when one cites CEAP statistics, one is really speaking of a small minority of high SES families where English is used at home. One suspects that this was mostly an urban phenomenon, largely in Metro Manila.

The other observation that should be made is that the variety of English used in such high SES homes would be what Llamzon then called 'Standard Filipino English' or what I have preferred calling 'Philippine English', that is, a variety of English with decidedly local features partly stemming from the first-language substratum of second language speakers of English and partly from local conditions and referents, the variety having undergone a process of indigenization the past seventy years and continuing to evolve at present. The features of this variety of English in formal and informal situations and in its use in the mass media (written and spoken) have already been described. If one were to use the term *pidgin* as an over-all term for a variety of a language with a mixture of elements, along a cline from a simplified grammar to a more complicated grammar, and without the social stigma attached to pidgins, then one can say that Philippine English is a form of pidgin (see Marasigan 1983 for a rapid review of the various meanings attached to *pidgins* and *creoles*). I am here distinguishing this mixture of indigenous and foreign elements from a code-switching variety of English which has sometimes been called *halo-halo* or *mix-mix*, which has likewise been described in its structural features (Bautista 1980) and its uses (Pascasio 1978, Marasigan 1983). The switching takes place at various levels of the grammatical hierarchy, from the word-level to the sentence or even paragraph levels.

The pidgin variety I am speaking of is more of an inter-language, with its manifestations most evident in the phonology (a Philippine accent), and its specific lexical usages as well as grammatical idiosyncrasies. This pidgin, it is contended here from the evidence which has been cited and which will be reinforced, has become a first-language or creole (in a process similar to Schumann's (1978) paradigm of the pidginization and creolization process for language learning). The added feature in the Philippines, however, is that for a generation of children this pidgin is now a mother tongue and therefore a creole, using the latter term in its traditional meaning of a pidgin becoming a mother tongue.

The other observation that should be made – and this is what makes the Philippine situation interesting – is that this creolized Philippine English is never learned by itself but side by side with the dominant language of the community, be it a Philippine vernacular or the fast-spreading Tagalog-based Pilipino. In other words, because of communication patterns in Philippine homes, the extended family, and among this social group, the continuing presence of household help and nursemaids or caregivers (*yayas*), the children learn an educated variety of Philippine English from the parents and relatives and siblings in school, a less educated variety of English from their *yayas* (see Bautista 1981 for a description of one variety of *yaya* English based on a Manila sample), and the dominant local language from everyone else in the community belonging to a lower SES, especially the household help. Thus no Filipino child, no matter of what SES, grows up monolingual. He is at least bilingual, and if the language of the home is not the same as the language of the community, then he grows up trilingual. The code-switching taking place and even language mixture (which needs to be documented) at a very early age widens the linguistic repertoire of the Filipino child; in many cases, this is an asset rather than a liability. The implications for language change in such a multilingual situation where multiple languages are in contact likewise have to be spelled out.

Llamzon states: 'A recent questionnaire sent out by the CEAP revealed that 51.43% of the families with children in CEAP schools in the Philippines as a whole spoke English at home. The breakdown of this figure by area is as follows: Luzon-54.53%; Visayas-46.03%; Mindanao-33.53%. This reflects a common situation, especially in the Manila area, where families speak English at home' (1969:84).

The interesting observation which may be made about this finding is that English use at home (and therefore its learning by children as a first language in a bilingual/trilingual situation) is a function of SES, urbanization, and seemingly distance from Manila—all of which are related of course since the more affluent sectors of society in the Philippines are those who are urbanized in Metro Manila.

*PNC Survey (1968)*

At about the same time as the CEAP survey, the national language policy survey among householders, teachers, and media people was conducted by the Language Study Center of Philippine Normal College (Otanes and Sibayan 1969; the survey was conducted in 1968). Drawing from a much larger population and at a lower socio-economic level, the language policy survey showed that no one reported English as a first language, although 2% of the householders and 3% of the teachers remembered learning more than one language simultaneously in childhood (see Bautista and Gonzalez 1985:3, where the survey is

362

summarized). This finding reinforces the limited scope of the CEAP survey to a group of families at the highest socio-economic level.

## Bulatao Survey (1973)

Bulatao (1973) did a survey of 500 household heads each in Manila, Naga, Tacloban, Cebu and Davao, on ethnic attitudes. The survey was conducted from January to March 1973 and focused on ethnic attitudes especially towards Muslim and Chinese residents with a total of 504 respondents in Manila.

For the purpose of this study, the completed background questionnaires yielded some interesting results with regard to first language in Manila. English is spoken by a relatively constant percentage, between 68% and 73% in each city (19); in Manila, 2% stated that it was the first language they learned whereas 60% said it was Tagalog. Again, even these 2% had exposure to Tagalog through household help and contacts in the neighborhood, but the 2% certainly confirms with another type of sample the constantly recurring percentage although low of English-language speakers as a first language learned at home.

## Sibayan Survey (1977)

Based on data gathered in 1977, reported at a RELC conference in the same year and published the following year, Sibayan used a purposive sampling of adults in Metro Manila composed of teachers at a teachers' college, a vocational-technical college, and different levels of staff at a private commercial bank, the Institute of National Language, and the general population. The sample was therefore composed of adults, teachers and parents (including professionals) to query them on view of language and identity in Manila. There were no direct measures of first languages learned but indirectly, from statements about which language(s) were used to communicate with parents and with children, one can infer the existence of English-speaking households where in effect children do learn English as a first language (though not exclusively so).

Among Tagalogs and non-Tagalogs, in communicating with their parents, the following languages and their incidence were recorded:

| LANGUAGE(S) | FREQUENCY | PERCENTAGE |
|---|---|---|
| English | 7 | 2% |
| English and Pilipino | 27 | 6% |

English and Vernacular
(other than Pilipino)                              7                    2%
English/Pilipino/Other Vernacular        21                    5%
English/Pilipino/Spanish                                              1/2%

On the language used with children, among teachers (PNC, PCAT, INL), the percentages were even bigger:

| LANGUAGE(S) | FREQUENCY | PERCENTAGE |
| --- | --- | --- |
| English | 4 | 4% |
| English and Tagalog | 21 | 10% |
| English and Vernacular | 3 | 3% |
| English/Pilipino/Vernacular | 10 | 9% |

Among non-Tagalogs speaking to their children, the languages used were:

| LANGUAGE(S) | FREQUENCY | PERCENTAGE |
| --- | --- | --- |
| English | 4 | 4% |
| English and Tagalog | 23 | 22% |
| English and Vernacular | 3 | 3% |
| English/Tagalog/Vernacular | 11 | 10% |

What these indicators point to is the presence of many households which are English-speaking and the large number of bilingual and trilingual homes in Metro Manila where English is used with parents and even more with children especially among non-Tagalogs and teachers. If one were to add all the subgroups using English alone or in combination with Pilipino and/or Vernacular, the numbers go up to 15.5% for both native Tagalogs and non-Tagalogs, 26% for teachers, and 39% for non-Tagalogs, a large percentage indeed. This is the kind of a home where children learn English as a first language; the homes are not only homes of teachers where the incidence of English language use is higher (based on the other surveys) but homes of INL staff (where predictably Pilipino is more important) and also employees (of various ranks) in a bank and in the general population (parents), thus confirming the large use of English in households in Manila, a fact that shows how the local variety of English is being spread.

## Sibayan and Segovia Survey (1978)

Sibayan and Segovia, querying teachers/professors, employers, salaried employees, and laborers, on their perceptions with regard to the relation between socio-economic advancement and language, likewise asked about native languages. Of the 248 subjects originally sampled, there were only 188 actual respondents to the question on what language the respondents considered as their native language. In this sample, no one cited English as the exclusive native language, but two out of 188 or 1% answered English and Tagalog, one from the middle-level group of salaried employees and one from the rank and file.

Again, this is a different sample, people in the actual work force, as opposed to household heads, teachers, and students (primary and secondary as well as tertiary). Only 1% professed to have English as a first language. Since this is an older group with differing educational backgrounds, the 1% is realistic since the trend of teaching English to children seems to be a postwar phenomenon. The bilingual character of this child language learning confirms, however, my earlier statement that even in these homes where the English language is spoken, no household is ever monolingual.

## Llamzon and Lee Survey (1979)

Llamzon and Lee (1979), surveying patterns of acquisition of bilingual ability and language use in three Southeast Asian countries, most likely in 1978, confined their Manila sample to 191 freshman college/university students in two public and one private college/university and 148 from freshman secondary schools in two public and one private high school.

In the private college and high school, 25% and 52%, respectively claimed English as their first language (see Bautista and Gonzalez 1985:14). For those whose first language was English, the second language learned was Tagalog. Only 2% reported Spanish and these were from the private schools.

The smaller percentage from the private college is understandable since tertiary level institutions draw from a wider clientele and a better social mix than relatively exclusive secondary schools. Admittedly, the sample is quite limited; at best, one can say that the private high school is representative of one sub-group of private secondary schools in Manila catering to a high SES class, the same group as the CEAP sample of grade schools.

The percentage (52%) in this high SES private high school claiming to have English as their mother tongue is rather large and definitely unrepresentative of the secondary school education sector. Based on the Ministry of Education, Culture and Sports statistics on survival and drop-outs (see Rimando 1983), 44 out of 100 students drop out of school after sixth grade; in high school, of the surviving 56 out of a 100, only 43 actually enter high school. At best, one can say that students in this high school belong to the highest SES groups and constitute a small sector of the entire secondary school population of the country.

The same observation can be made of the private college where 25% claimed English as their first language. Colleges draw from a wider clientele, but private high SES colleges draw from an even smaller base, although efforts are made to provide a better social mix by granting scholarships to low SES students. Twenty-five per cent would still be high, however, and unrepresentative of the tertiary level school population.

*Census Data (1980)*

As if to confirm the Sibayan data, the 1980 census on studying first languages or native languages among Filipinos (48 million in 1980) used only households (a total of 8,607,187) and showed that

Nationally          5,782 households out of 8,607,187 or .07%
National Capital Region   3,815 households out of 1,103,563 or .3%

claimed English as a mother tongue. With the NCSO national data, one is dealing with much smaller percentages, less than 1% (actually 3/10 of 1%), where the native language is supposed to be English. The figure is the most reliable one in terms of the total population since all other surveys are based on sectoral samples. The other interesting thing to note is that English-as-a-first-language households are mostly an NCR phenomenon (3815/5782 or 2/3) of the entire country, the remaining one-third scattered throughout the country, and based on the other surveys, among urban affluent and teacher families.

*Llamzon Survey (1984)*

Llamzon attempted to replicate the language policy survey of Otanes and Sibayan (1969) in 1982 only for Metro Manila and although he was unable to make direct comparisons because of the non-retrievability of the 1968 data for Metro Manila alone, he reported on the status of English in

Metro Manila in a 1984 article.

Based on a sampling of 23 communities in Metro Manila and after querying 149 householders and 115 teachers, ages 26-55, with at least a high school education, he found 6% of householders and 8.7% of teachers saying that English was the first language that they learned to speak.

The percentages are rather high, but it should be remembered that the data are confined to Metro Manila householders and teachers and that the sample is rather limited; in 1968, no such English-as-a-first-language group was reported in a national sample (much larger than the Metro Manila sample).

*Sibayan Survey (1985)*

Sibayan interviewed 186 respondents (influentials in government, business, academe, media, student leaders, from teenage to their 60's, with a median age of 43); these were key informants from seven regions including Metro Manila (NCR), La Union, Bicol, Cebu, Iloilo, Zamboanga, Cotabato. This was a largely urban sample, mostly Metro Manila (66/186) respondents.

Data were gathered from April-May 1985 and reported in July of the same year. One of the items in the background section of the questionnaire was first language(s) learned by the respondents. What the Sibayan (1985:100-102) study shows for the first time so dramatically is the extent of childhood bilingualism and multilingualism in the country. While the table (page 100) does not report breakdown by city, the realization that 66/186 respondents were Metro Manilans should give the reader an index by informal weighing of the extent of multilingualism and English as a childhood language.

FIRST LANGUAGE(S) LEARNED BY RESPONDENTS (186) NATIONAL

| | | | |
|---|---|---|---|
| English | 15/186 | 8% | (7/15 were academic faculty and administrators) |
| English/other Vernaculars | 20/186 | 10.7% | |
| English/2 other Vernaculars | 9/186 | 4.8% | |

Admittedly, the sample was composed of an elite group of influentials from different sectors; again, the report was based on national numbers rather than Metro Manila although I suppose if we weigh the

367

numbers by .77 (66/186), we can get an indication of what the Metro Manila sample is like:

FIRST LANGUAGE(S) LEARNED BY METRO MANILA RESPONDENTS

(66/186 or a weight of .77)

| | |
|---|---|
| English | 6% |
| English + 1 Vernacular | 8% |
| English + 2 Vernaculars | 3.6% |
| Total | 17.6% |

This is large, the largest among the figures covered, but the group is highly selected and constitutes the key influentials or elites of Metro Manila society. The extent of English as a first language with this group of teen-agers and adults or of English with one or two Philippine vernaculars would indicate then an English as-a-first-language group in Metro Manila larger than we suspect from the CEAP group which constituted only a small section of Metro Manila children. Unfortunately, we do not have the breakdown of CEAP school children vis-a-vis a total population of school children in Metro Manila at the time the CEAP survey was taken as a basis for comparison.

*Sibayan, Gonzalez, et al. Evaluation Study (1986)*

Sibayan, Gonzalez et al. in a national evaluation of the Bilingual Education Policy tested 568 teachers of various subjects among 16 major and one group of minor ethnolinguistic groups, of whom 46 were in Metro Manila. In the background questionnaire of the tests, 3% of the Tagalog-NCR respondents said that the first language they learned at home was English (nationally, among all groups, the average of 2.66% with highs of 9.5% for Mountain Province Ilocano groups and 6.7% for Misamis, Agusan Cebuano groups, followed by 6.5% for Cagayan Ilocano groups).

Admittedly, the sample is a small one, based on teachers from six purposively sampled schools.

**General Observations**

These different surveys reviewed show that in Metro Manila or the National Capital Region, there is a small but stable (and one gathers, increasing) minority of households (.3% or 3/10 of 1%) or roughly 3,815 households where English was learned as a first language (one surmises, not exclusively so).

If one looks at the patterns of communication of these households, one notices at least among middle and upper classes (teachers, rank-and-file and minor executives and key influentials and executives) bilingual or multilingual households where adults speak to their parents in English (among other languages), thus indicating past English-as-a-first-language learning (as high as 15.5%) and even more significantly for the future, where parents and adults talk to their children in English (26% among teachers and 39% among non-Tagalogs), thus justifying our prediction that the use of English in these households (admittedly of a middle and high SES and therefore still the minority) is increasing rather than decreasing.

The other surveys, of limited purposive samples, indicate significant percentages for key influentials (17.6%) and for teachers (8.7%) and families in private schools of high SES (6%), especially when one probes and asks not only for the language which one considers one's mother tongue and the language one learned first, to make room for bilingual child language acquisition (English and Pilipino or another Philippine language) or even trilingual child language acquisition (English, Pilipino, and a Philippine language other than Pilipino).

Beyond the scope of this study but indicated by the data as well although less clearly are similar small 'pockets' of English-language households in urban areas outside Metro Manila especially among Ilocano- and Cebuano-speaking ethnic groups.

The variety of English being used in a bilingual/trilingual setting, however, where the models speak a Philippine English in the process of standardization (what Llamzon calls Standard Filipino English at least for the educated groups) presently consists of two varieties, a basilectal and an acrolectal variety, to use standard sociolinguistic terminology, but more accurately describable (see Bautista 1981) along a cline of education or as edulects (based on the number of years and type of schooling) including the relatively low variety of yaya English (caregiver English). Three varieties of this Philippine English have been carefully described: the written and spoken English of the mass media, the spoken English and written English of Philippine elites, and the spoken English of poorly educated yayas. It is these varieties of edulects (along a cline of education) that the Filipino child is exposed to with competing Philippine languages; he learns varieties of Philippine languages as a first language side by side with other first languages of Philippine provenance.

369

## Implications

Sibayan (1978) speaking of *mix-mix* or the code-swtiching variety of English and Pilipino predicts that this code-switching variety will be the acrolectal variety of Philippine English and that this is the combination of languages being learned in English-speaking households. If such a variety is a mixed variety or one manifestation of pidgin or language mixing, then he predicts that as this is learned by children as a first language it will become creolized. He therefore concludes: 'What the challenges (or potentials) that this development will pose still have to be identified and studied. It is interesting and it suggests that the study of creolization should be receiving increased concern from many sectors—both from the academy and those in education. To ignore this is to do so at our loss.' (46)

Unless there are radical changes in the structure of Philippine society and in the country's educational system, one foresees that the number of households where English is used (side by side with other Philippine languages) and where therefore the children learn English as a first language or mother tongue in a multilingual setting will increase as the level of socio-economic development is raised and as better schools become more available to less affluent families.

It is not clear whether the creolized variety will be developed to the point where the emerging Philippine English will not be mutually intelligible with non-Philippine varieties of English. One suspects that the agencies pushing for mutual intelligibility based on standardization will be the mass media, communication with non-Filipinos (calling for a form of linguistic accommodation and moving towards the cross-country norm, English as an international auxiliary language), and exposure to a more standard form in school (which will then be an agency of decreolization in favor of standardization).

One suspects too that Metro Manila will be followed by other urban centers in the Philippines such as Baguio, Cebu and other metropolitan centers (Davao, Cagayan de Oro, Zamboanga), although what makes the situation different in these cities and will slow down standardization will be the continuing presence of a non-Tagalog Philippine language competing with Pilipino (but not with English). In turn, what Manila will have to a larger extent than these other metropolitan centers will be the continuing presence of foreign speakers, including exponents of American and British English, who will function as a social force for mutual intelligibility and slow down the indigenization process. With Moag and Llamzon, I would agree that the social domains of English are becoming restricted, but I would not agree, based on the evidence cited in this paper, that the phase of restriction will be so extensive as to make English disappear altogether. On the contrary, the patterns of use are stable (see Gonzalez and Bautista 1986) based on many surveys, with the domain of English in the school, the boardroom, international business situations, and in the homes of high SES and highly educated Filipinos who have been teaching their children English all these years (a range of 2% to 3%, with much larger percentages once one considers language combinations, English-Pilipino and/or other Vernaculars; a range of 6% to 17.6%). Other stable though not exclusive domains of English are entertainment (TV, cinema), music, drama, newspapers, and the law, science and technology in education, religion.

Focusing once more on Metro Manila, one can say that Metro Manila now and in the future will be a linguistic melting pot (with a range of 50-60% native-Tagalog speakers), the rest immigrants from outside Tagalog-speaking areas, who maintain the use of their non-Tagalog languages at least during the first generation (active and passive use) and the second generation (passive use) and who use both English and Pilipino as well as English-Pilipino-Other Philippine Language in their households, with a generation of children learning many languages as mother tongues, growing up bilingual and trilingual, and in the process code-switching and speaking a creolized variety of both English and undoubtedly Pilipino (from their parents; pidginized Pilipino-Vernacular). The community is cosmopolitan (with many foreign influences) and open (with influences from non-Tagalogs), urban, mobile, economically progressing. Spanish for practical purposes is dead (from .02% to .05%) among adults (teachers, parents) (Sibayan 1978).

But the community will set the norm for Standard Pilipino and Standard Philippine English/Standard Filipino English for the future.


## RFERENCES

Alberca, Wilfredo. 1978. The distinctive features of Philippine English of the mass media. Unpublished Ph.D. dissertation, University of Santo Tomas, Manila.

Bautista, Ma. Lourdes S. 1980. The Filipino bilingual's competence: A model based on an analysis of Tagalog-English code-switching. Canberra: The Australian National University, Pacific Linguistics Series C-No. 59.

_____ . 1981. *Yaya* English: An idiosyncratic dialect of Philippine English. Paper read at the RELC seminar on Varieties of

371

English and their Implications for English Language Teaching in Southeast Asia, Singapore, April 20-24.

_____ and Andrew Gonzalez, FSC. 1985. Language Surveys in the Philippines 1966-1984 Volume 2. Manila: Research Center, De La Salle University.

Bulatao, Rodolfo A. 1973. Ethnic attitudes in five Philippine cities. Quezon City: University of the Philippines Social Research Laboratory.

Fund for Assistance to Private Education. 1975. The FAPE Atlas Volume 1. A historical, economic, and educational profile of the Philippines. Makati, Metro Manila: FAPE.

Gonzalez, Andrew, FSC. 1982. English in the Philippine mass media. In New Englishes, ed. by J.B. Pride, 211-226. Rowley, Massachusetts: Newbury House Publishers, Inc.

_____ . In press. Studies on Philippine English. Occasional paper. Singapore: Regional Language Centre.

_____ and Ma. Lourdes S. Bautista. 1986. Language surveys in the Philippines 1966-1984 Volume 1. Manila: Research Center, De La Salle University. (To be published by the De La Salle University Press)

_____ and Wilfredo Alberca. 1978. Philippine English of the mass media. Manila: Research Center, De La Salle University.

Llamzon, Teodoro A. 1969. Standard Filipino English. Quezon City: Ateneo de Manila University Press.

_____ . 1984. The status of English in Metro Manila today. In Panagani Language planning, implementation and evaluation: Essays in honor of Bonifacio P. Sibayan on his sixty-seventh birthday, ed. by Andrew Gonzalez, 106-21. Manila: Linguistic Society of the Philippines.

_____ and Koh Beng Lee. 1979. Patterns of acquisition of bilingual ability and language use in three Southeast Asian countries. Paper read at the Fourteenth Regional Seminar, SEAMEO Regional Language Centre, Singapore.

Marasigan, Elizabeth. 1983. Code-switching and code-mixing in multilingual societies. Singapore: Singapore University Press for SEAMEO Regional Language Centre.

Moag, Rodney F. 1982. The life cycle of non-native Englishes: A case study. In the other tongue: English across cultures, ed. by Braj B. Kachru, 270-88. Urbana: University of Illinois Press.

National Census and Statistics Office. 1980. Census of population and housing — Philippines. Volume 2: National summary. Manila:

National Economic Development Authority.

Otanes, Fe and Bonifacio P. Sibayan. 1969. Language policy survey of the Philippines: Initial report. Manila: Language Study Center, Philippine Normal College.

Pascasio, Emy. 1978. Dynamics of code-switching in the business domain. *Philippine Journal of Linguistics* 9.1&2.40-50

Rimando, Tony Pe. 1983. Low survival rates in education noted. *Bulletin Today* (October 1, 1983 issue).

Schumann, John. 1978. The pidginization process. Rowley, Massachusetts: Newbury House Publishers, Inc.

Sibayan, Bonifacio P. 1978. Views on language and identity: Limited Metro Manila sample. In Language and Education in Multisectoral Societies, ed. by Arthur Yap, 3-52. Singapore: SEAMEO Regional Language Centre and Singapore University Press.

_____ . 1985. Status and role of English and Pilipino. Manila. (Manuscript of Technical Report submitted as a commissioned study, English Language Office, Cultural Affairs Office, Embassy of the United States of America.)

_____ , Andrew Gonzalez, Fe Otanes, Jose Arong, OMI, and Luke Moortgat, CICM. 1986. Eleven years of bilingual education in the Philippines (1974-1985). Manila: Linguistic Society of the Philippines. (Manuscript of Technical Report.)

_____ and Lorna Z. Segovia. 1978. Language and socio-economic development: Perceptions of a Metro Manila sample—Implications for third world countries. Paper read before the Annual National Research Council of the Philippines Meeting, Social Science Division Symposium, December 9. University of the Philippines, Quezon City.

# BILINGUALISM AND THE BILINGUAL EDUCATION PROGRAM: VIEWS OF METRO MANILA LEADERS

JUDY C. SEVILLA

A dimension of bilingualism, specifically of Pilipino (Tagalog) and English in the context of contemporary Manila, is its structured, programmed sense as embodied in the Bilingual Education Program of 1974 (referred to as BEP).

The BEP was promulgated at the start of schoolyear 1974-1975 by the then Department of Education and Culture "in order to develop a bilingual nation competent in the use of both English and Pilipino." Bilingual education was operationally defined as the *separate* use of Pilipino and English as media of instruction in definite subject areas (my italics).

I will report on one of several parallel researches carried out in 1985 to evaluate the first 10 years of BEP implementation. I will summarize part of the results of our study which was done in the second half of 1985. Our study concentrated on the respondents' level of awareness, perceptions, and utilization of the BEP in particular and bilingualism in general.

The choice of this particular group of respondents was based on the assumption that the acceptability and actual use of the national language is affected in part by the knowledge, attitudes, and language-related behaviors of influential individuals, or leaders, in the government and the non-government sectors. Consequently, the research team interviewed 33 top-level government officials of the Marcos order (referred to hereafter as GOs) and 31 leaders of non-government organizations (referred to hereafter as NGOs).

The GOs included ministers, deputy ministers, and directors of all 20 government ministries; the lowest level interviewee here held the rank of public relations officer. Other government officials interviewed came from seven support agencies (e.g., PHILCOA) and three commissions (e.g., Professional Regulation Commission).

374

On the other hand, the NGOs came from media, socio-civic organizations, sectarian or religious groups, professional and business associations, and others (including student, sports, and labor organizations).

In choosing the respondents from this group, the sectors that were thought to most feel the impact of bilingualism and/or the BEP were first listed. Then newspapers were reviewed for a full month prior to the start of data gathering in order to obtain a list of organizations, offices, or agencies belonging to each of these sectors. The final list of organizations chosen for the interview was then arrived at by random selection.

Aside from these semi-structured face-to-face interviews, background data were also obtained through structured interviews of key administrative personnel. The information provided by them pertained to language use in each of the 64 institutions, and will be integrated into the influentials' responses below.

### Summary of Findings

I will present here only the general trends observed from the data instead of the specific statistics. The first section will cover the respondents' level of awareness of the BEP; the second, their perceptions and attitudes toward the BEP and toward bilingualism in general; and the third part, their language use patterns at home and in the workplace. These will be followed by two sets of analyses: (1) the factors facilitating and hindering bilingualism, and (2) the respondents' predictions for the future of bilingualism, including the BEP.

### *Awareness of the BEP*

1. The majority of our respondents knew of the existence of a bilingual mode of instruction in our schools, although a good number were not aware of the specific policy's name, objectives, and stipulations. Slightly more GOs than NGOs expressed awareness of the policy.

2. Respondents in turn felt that few parents in general are ignorant of the policy. Certain factors were thought to be important in parents' knowledge about the BEP: parents with a high level of education, those working in education-related occupations, and those who have school-age children enrolled in schools which actively implement the BEP were expected to know more about the policy than other parents. This suggests that parents in Metro Manila (who are relatively advantaged compared to those in small cities and rural areas) are more likely to be

aware of the BEP.

3. Many of those who were unaware or unsure of the BEP's existence blamed the lack of a vigorous, effective information campaign on the Program's goals, provisions and activities. The term "bilingual education" itself seemed to have been misinterpreted to mean the combined, rather than separate, use of English and Pilipino in the classroom. Only one respondent claimed that most parents have been informed regarding the BEP's details through information drives; he was a member of the education ministry's dissemination group during the first three years of BEP implementation, and was thus highly familiar with the efforts undertaken in this direction by the Bureau of Public Schools and the Institute of National Language (now the Surian ng Wikang Pambansa).

*Perception and Attitudes toward the BEP/Bilingualism*

1. The majority of influentials interviewed believed that elementary and secondary schools have failed in their aim to produce competent bilinguals. While students even in the non-Tagalog areas now have a better grasp of spoken Pilipino, their English seems to have deteriorated noticeably. This weakening of English skills, however, may not necessarily be the effect of the BEP per se (the declining trend has been noted even before World War II), but instead may be attributed to such factors as: (a) inadequately trained teachers, (b) lack of teaching materials particularly in public schools, (c) the use of regional language in classroom teaching, (d) the poor language examples set by teachers, school administrators, parents and media in "mixing" Pilipino and English and in corrupting English, and (e) the students' own attitude of aiming merely to pass instead of improving or excelling in their classes. The greater efforts needed to learn two different language structures as well as the shrinking number of real-life situations requiring good English skills also take their toll on English competencies.

One consequence is that students suffer more in the subjects taught in English, i.e., mathematics and the so-called hard sciences, the same subjects emphasized by our high technology-oriented educational system.

Two respondents noted that socio-economic status affects command of English: not only can better-off families send their children to schools with higher standards of English skills, they also have more opportunities to use English in their daily life, rather than Pilipino or the local language. Thus, overall, the negative role of the BEP with respect to English seems to be merely contributory rather than causal.

2. Other important sources of learning bilingual skills are the home

and the media, particularly the movies and television that now reach practically all parts of the country.

3. The great majority of respondents believed that ability to communicate well in English is a definite advantage for prospective job applicants in their respective institutions. While English proficiency is preferred, it is, however, not required, particularly for lower level positions (e.g., utility men).

4. Proficiency in Pilipino is also a plus factor for job applicants in the government sector, notably those applying for employment at the grassroots level of the institution and/or in the rural areas. In these cases, respondents said, incentives might possibly be given to those who spoke Pilipino fluently.

Among the NGOs, Pilipino is likewise an advantage for better intra-institutional communication but overall is NOT considered important enough to warrant extra incentives.

5. Only two GOs and two NGOs reported having defined organizational policies regarding the use of Pilipino. In one government agency, only Pilipino was allowed to be spoken in the office, while another said that employees used English in the morning and Pilipino in the afternoon within their office. The policies mentioned by the NGOs both had to do with translation of working materials into Pilipino and/or English and did not touch at all on spoken Pilipino.

## Use of English and Pilipino

1. All the respondents are bilingual in English and Pilipino. The context of communication, however, determined which language is to be used. At home, Pilipino predominates among our largely Tagalog sample, even as both languages may be used. When with friends, GOs reported using either only Pilipino or only English, while NGOs said they tended to use *both* languages together (Taglish, or code-switching).

2. In the work setting, English and Pilipino clearly have their respective domains. English is used as the official or formal language in that it is the language of intra- and inter-office written communication as well as of formal events. English also tends to be utilized to a greater extent within top level management and when a subordinate addresses a superior.

Finally, the choice of topic also determines the language to be used, with English much preferred for technical, business, professional, or any work-related matters.

On the other hand, Pilipino and Taglish are often used within and between the middle and lower echelons of the organization and with rural or less educated target audience. These two (Pilipino and Taglish) are used during informal discussions, and when a superior addresses a subordinate. Personal matters are also more appropriately discussed in either Pilipino or Taglish.

The two exceptions to these general trends are the Surian ng Wikang Pambansa which uses Pilipino exclusively, and the Ministry of Tourism where English is used to a greater extent than in other offices because of its foreign clients.

3. More of the GOs than the NGOs thought that Pilipino should be promoted by their institution or agency; practically all of the respondents, however, voiced misgivings about the adequacy of Pilipino in their respective areas of functioning. For example, Pilipino is seen as severely deficient in technical terminology; also, it still has to evolve into a truly national language that expresses our collective thoughts, feelings and aspirations. The promotion of Pilipino is definitely not perceived as a function or priority of the organization, but primarily of the MECS.

4. On the action side, very little has actually been done by either the GOs or the NGOs to encourage Pilipino not only among their staff members but also among their target clientele. The efforts described by the respondents can be said to be rather passive and timid: celebration of "Linggo ng Wika" in August through essay-writing contests and cultural shows, sponsorship of Pilipino seminars or workshops, and translation of written materials (information bulletins, comics, etc.) from English into Pilipino.

5. The BEP implementation guidelines stress that "by 1984, all graduates of tertiary curricula should be able to pass examination in English and/or Pilipino for the practice of their professions." This proviso has obviously not been met by the educational system as well as by the testing agencies. Neither the Professional Regulation Commission nor the Civil Service Commission has been involved in any attempt to develop professional examinations in Pilipino.

6. Finally, the majority of the respondents agreed with the statement that we need a national language to develop our identity as Filipinos. Yet, they felt just as strongly that we can be nationalistic even without speaking Pilipino.

*Factors that promote and impede bilingualism*

Responses were also analyzed according to the elements that

advance the use of English and of Pilipino and those which hinder the two languages.

1. Facilitators of the use of Pilipino were perceived to be the following: (a) the rapid spread of Pilipino through mass media, particularly TV, *komiks*, and the movies; (b) grassroots or mass-based orientation of one's profession; (c) nationalist movements; (d) acceptance of Pilipino as the appropriate language for familiar or intimate communication; (e) regular observance of "Linggo ng Wika"; and (f) the enthusiasm and commitment of top-level administrators to bilingualism or the BEP, including the presence of ranking officials who are fluent in Pilipino.

2. On the other hand, obstacles to the use of Pilipino included: (a) lack of opportunities to use Pilipino, especially in non-Tagalog areas and especially for reading and writing skills; (b) the deficient educational system; (c) difficulties with the SWP-type of Pilipino; (d) lack of funds and incentives for language promotion; (e) the lower value given to Pilipino in the workplace; and (f) lack of good communication models.

3. English is perceived to be propagated easily and used widely because of the following reasons: (a) it is accepted as the language of business, technology and the professions, especially those requiring international or overseas communications; (b) English is consequently essential in "assuring" upward social and perhaps even economic mobility; and (c) there are opportunities to improve English skills, in the form of English or speech courses offered through in-house training or by speech institutes.

4. English, however, is impeded by: (a) lack of opportunities to use *good* English and the lowering standards for English over time; (b) the deficient educational system, as above; (c) lack of motivation and funds to promote good English; (d) the extra burden of learning a second language, and (e) lack of good communication models.

*Prognosis for Bilingualism (Pilipino)/the BEP*

NGOs and GOs all agreed that Pilipino will be used by increasing larger proportions of the population and in more daily situations within the next 10 years. This is expected to hold in our social, political, economic and cultural lives.

Even while English will continue to be the language of government, law, technology, business and the professions, Pilipino is predicted to make it presence felt especially in terms of oral communication. Adoption

379

of Pilipino as the single national language, however, is not expected to hamper economic development. Pilipino, on the other hand, must be given time and opportunity to evolve on its own, without being forced on unwilling citizens.

The majority of respondents think that, despite its shortcomings, the BEP is still worth pursuing. Pilipino serves to promote our cultural/national identity and unity; it is gaining social acceptance as more and more people from all social levels use it; it is gradually becoming essential as the lingua franca in our urban centers. On the other hand, proficiency in English is necessary for communication purposes in the professions and for better employment both here and abroad.

One important consideration for the GOs and the NGOs, however, is that the teaching of English and Pilipino be promoted equally, instead of at the expense of one or the other. This step implies that there will then be less difficulty in simultaneously learning two languages, and that Pilipino skills will not necessarily develop to the detriment of English. To the extent that high standards in each language can be maintained, the BEP will finally succeed in producing truly bilingual graduates.

# THE STATE OF PERFORMING ARTS CRITICISM TODAY

ROSALINDA L. OROSA

## Introduction

Of all the panelists, I may be the most unfortunate. Presumably, my distinguished colleagues did not find the need to modify their papers after the revolution, their respective topics—or rather, the treatment of their respective topics—not having called for any basic revision.

In my case, however, those four fateful days in February robbed me of my topic. Economic and political considerations immediately topped the list of priorities thus relegating the cultural to the background. Since then, newspapers have found little use for critics. In fact, since the bloodless coup and the attendant reassessment of values, no more than three reviews have come out—as if to prove that of all human beings, the artists and, by extension, the critics who write about them, are the most dispensable.

In this light, the paper I originally prepared seemed totally inapplicable to the present situation. To have changed my point of reference, however, would have wreaked havoc on my tenses, my grammar and even my sense of humor.

To solve my dilemma, I shall request the readers to assume, as I have assumed, that the current situation is fluid and tenuous and, therefore, temporary. Accordingly, I shall discuss my paper as I had written it while asking my readers to consider, as my frame of reference, the immediate past. Indeed, I would like to think that after a brief period of normalization and adjustment, most of my observations will ring true.

Jose Luna Castro's comments on music criticism in 1963 largely hold true more than two decades later. I quote:

"Music criticism in the Philippines is a pretty uncertain calling. It attracts only a few practitioners who stay on the job for one season and then pass on to devote their time to more lucrative and certainly less thankless professions. Most of those who understand music know little or nothing of the craft of writing; while reportedly most of those who can write know little about music."

Dance and theater critics also suffer from the lack of incentives Castro mentions. However, as far as articulation is concerned theater critics often have the edge because they are generally professional journalists or writers, or even playwrights themselves.

When Luna Castro wrote his journalism manual from which the quote was taken, little distinction was then being made by the public between the performing arts (music, theater and dance) and the visual arts (painting, sculpture, the graphics arts and photography). Readers usually assumed that one and the same person could evaluate a stage presentation as completely as he could a painting exhibition.

It is an encouraging sign that a distinction is now being made between the two areas of discipline. Today, a critic reviews either the visual or the performing arts, not both.

It might be logical to assume that the pioneering efforts of the *Manila Chronicle* showed postwar readers the way toward a deeper knowledge and appreciation of the arts. With the approval of publisher Oscar M. Lopez, I initiated the thrice-weekly column "Encore" which was devoted exclusively to the arts. In 1960, the *Chronicle* introduced a weekly arts page which I edited. Being experimental, the page had no budget and consequently, was short-lived.

The page was revived in 1969 as part of the "Living Section" and again I was given a free hand to edit it. By the time the *Chronicle* offices were closed on September 22, 1972, the cultural page had already acquired a personality of its own, and had become very much a part of the paper.

La Sallite Eric David, then only 19, was the visual arts critic; I was the performing arts critic. Contributors included Leonidas Benesa, Eric Torres, Roberto Chabet and Ray Albano.

Besides evaluating art exhibitions and performing arts presentations, the page covered arts festivals, endorsed and nurtured young talents, solicited in-depth articles from artists and cognoscenti, supported cultural projects, and published reprints from art magazines and interviews of established and emerging artists. In brief, it constituted a forum for the discussion and interpretation of ideas. I like to think that that particular arts page of the *Chronicle* helped to serve as a pattern for today's cultural pages.

Despite the increase in the number of critics writing today, journalism courses still do not include criticism as a separate subject in their curricula. Although a student can take any number of subjects in music, dance or drama, the writing of reviews is a craft he, perforce, must learn by himself. Further, if he has any illusions of pursuing a "career" as critic — in this country, there is no such person as a full-time reviewer — he has to contend with the fact that critics are hired on a tenuous, tentative, often arbitrary basis. Allowing for exceptions, no contracts are signed, and the hiring of a critic as well as his tenure of service will depend mostly on his personal relationship with an editor or section editor.

Under this system, one newspaper, shortly before the revolution, could actually have two or three critics reviewing one and the same play, opera or concert. The situation presented a divided front and confused readers as to who exactly was the paper's critic. Further, it weakened the impact and effectivity of each review and eventually, of the paper itself.

The fact that many non-professional journalists were allowed to serve as instant or one-performance reviewers only aggravated the confusion. An instant reviewer may have been persuaded to write on a particular show by a close friend who was participating in it, in which case the instant reviewer was not to be seen in print again until his friendship was pressed into service once more. Mere aficionados thus readily joined the ranks of seasonal and too-often incompetent reviewers whose partial and overtly adulatory pieces were aimed primarily at promoting an on-going show.

Reviews were also written upon the request of the artist himself or the sponsoring organization if the regular critic failed to write on that artist's performance or, what was an even more likely reason, if his review was a highly critical one.

Occasionally, an overtly aggressive and publicity-conscious musical artist would write up his own performances under a pseudonym, or under the by-line of one among his stable of promoters or, more audaciously still, under the by-line of a reputable critic, without that critic's knowledge or permission.

Sharp-eyed colleagues of the victimized critic would quickly discover the deception, although none of them would expose it in deference to the publisher, editor or section editor. In effect, this reverse *pakikisama* or camaraderie tolerated duplicity. There was likewise duplicity in the use of pen names. Those who wrote under their own names were at a considerable disadvantage because they were tussling with unknown adversaries. However, they could draw consolation from the thought that views expressed under assumed names lost a great deal of credibility and validity.

Certain dilettantes, writing as occasional critics for more than one paper, are in a class by themselves. Apparently obsessed with the desire to impress, they lengthily describe the performances they have seen abroad, then comment on the local presentation only at the end of their piece—almost as an afterthought.

Critics usually write their reviews while impressions are still fresh, then send their reviews, posthaste, to their respective section editors. Ideally, the reviews should appear the next day but do not. A review will appear, after a performance, anywhere from one week (at the earliest) to a full month and a week (at the latest), by which time it will have grown stale.

Under these circumstances, avid aficionados who failed to see a given performance and are consequently anxious to read the review of their favorite critic, will have no choice but to be on the look-out for it daily. (Many of these aficionados, as well as the cognoscenti, actually claim that they buy or subscribe to a newspaper only for the reviews). Naturally, the "suspense" is keener for those who are even more curious to know how the critics rated them. Unfortunately, they will not be able to ascertain the extent of their critical success—and in case of favorable reviews, to attract ticket-buyers—until too late, these reviews having come out after the show's run.

Except for plays which are staged on three or four successive weekends by certain theater groups—for example, the Philippine Educational Theater Association, Repertory Philippines, Bulwagang Gantimpala and Teatro Pilipino—most are presented on two or three successive nights (at the most) with a possible matinee or two. This often applies to music and dance offerings, although they are usually limited to a gala evening and a matinee.

Because reviews seldom appear within the brief periods of the presentations, audiences rely on press releases and word-of-mouth reports for their guide to worthwhile programs. Should there be a "repeat" months later, then press releases quote from the reviews for all the influence these can wield.

Circumstances are less adverse for visual arts critics because the exhibits they review may last for as long as a month or longer. Film critics are even more fortunate because a daily entertainment page absorbs their pieces.

In the 50's and 60's, visiting big-name artists and ensembles were given front page treatment. Thus, a concert was written up for both its news and artistic values, and the review included, therefore, human interest features quite apart from comments on the actual performance itself.

At that time, gala evenings began at nine, and at concert's end, the *Chronicle* and *Times* reviewers would rush to their respective offices to write on this or that world celebrity for the next day's front page.

In the years following the imposition of martial law, international artists and groups (for instance, Margot Fonteyn, Van Cliburn, Mstislav Rostropovich, the Cleveland Symphony, the San Francisco Opera) also landed on the front page. Eventually, however, editors allowed critics to review concerts, even by such famed individuals and companies, the following day or even later.

The claim that critics can make or unmake a Broadway show cannot quite hold in Manila because, as already mentioned, reviews come out long after a show has closed, and because they generally tend to be overly kind. In this regard, one must consider the ultra-sensitive nature of Orientals and their endemic ability to keep their perspective impersonal, clinical and detached. Owing to an exaggerated *amour-propre,* the majority of Filipino artists are offended to the soul with any adjective less than "superb" or "magnificent" and a critic who writes an uncomplimentary review may often have to contend with some officious apologist for the artist or even with the artist himself, who, in his ire, may impute malice – or envy – to that critic.

As a consequence, diplomacy, the kind that does not sacrifice integrity, becomes imperative. For instance, the critic has to guard against directly observing that the soprano "sang off-key" or was "out of tune" or "missed the pitch by a quarter of a note." The most he dares write is that the diva's attack was "tangential."

The problem of diplomacy can be especially ticklish when the discerning critic discovers plagiarism or piracy in a work – say, a ballet which is an apparent copy of a version on betamax, or a compendium of "reflections" of several taped versions. In such a case, the critic resorts to a deliberately toned-down observation such as, "The ballet appeared to have been adapted from" or "The ballet seemed largely inspired by" or "The ballet may have been derivative of" or "influenced by" the original.

Thus, the critic makes his point and achieves his purpose – as he is duty-bound to – without hurting anyone's sensibilities unduly. In the process, however, he devotes as much time reflecting on what is to be said as to figuring out how it can be said diplomatically.

How to word or phrase an unflattering conclusion is indeed an ever-recurring challenge to the critic of integrity and, therefore, credibility, because in this country, virtually everything is transacted on a personal basis, or attributed to personal reasons.

For example, a reviewer can be chatting familiarly with a performer at a cocktail or luncheon-press conference, and then write about him the following day. Further, it is not unusual for a ballerina, actor, instrumentalist (or his parent), a vocal teacher, playwright or theater director to call up a reviewer or speak to him personally, or send him a little note, or even pay him a surprise visit either in his home or office—with the expressed purpose of inviting him or enticing him to watch a performance on which his reputation, or that of an offspring, is at stake. Consequently, more than ever, the self-respecting critic musters all his objectivity to retain an unbiased view.

On the other hand, the critic might even desist, out of kindness, from reviewing an event when the things to censure far outweigh the ones to praise, lest he discourage the performers in a country where, subsidy and patronage being scarce, and marketing a problem, art and artist, perhaps more than elsewhere, find progress and development an uphill climb.

Prudence being the better part of valor, critics may thus beg off from evaluating in print, the performances of certain Philippine artists while reviewing those of their foreign counterparts.

This often leads readers to unjustifiably accuse critics of partiality or discrimination. To be sure, there are Philippine artists who are as good or even better than artists from abroad. But our own, as a rule, have yet to achieve the performance standards of the West. The reasons for this sad state are not within the province of this lecture. Western standards do appear a rather odd and "unnationalistic" gauge for local performers; nevertheless, they are inescapable because of the predominantly Western orientation of our performing arts.

Younger critics tend to be more candid than their older colleagues. Indeed, they can be savage and brutal at times. Without mincing words, one such critic dismissed a leading lady's performance thus: "She is unable to give even half of what the demanding role requires. She sadly lacks the raging electricity and the wickedness the role calls for. She giggles even when delivering the most serious lines, declaims in that screeching, irritating voice that reminds one of a clogged sinus, and walks like she is about to play a game of hopscotch all the time. (This) instead of giving insight in depicting the petty mischiefs of a flirt. Thus she fails to win the sympathy of the audience, which the character could, if properly interpreted. She also retains all the awkward body movements, unnecessary mannerisms and inflections she has carelessly displayed in previous plays. Her acting is boring; as her character herself would say: *kabagut-bagot.*'"

Two can play at this kind of game, and so, a theater director, enraged by the comments of four male critics, devoted almost all of his printed program to a lengthy refutation of the points they raised. Here is the opening salvo of his counterattack entitled: "Charlatanism Rides Again."

"I have written somewhere that—is a newspaper devoted to incompetent reviewing. With the appearance of——'s critique on my last production, my seemingly extravagant claim threatens to be one of the verities of human existence. Thus, I am persuaded to deal with the presumptuous gentlemen in order to expose the same brand of charlatanism with which the likes of ——, ——, ——, and ——, have plagued the field of theater criticism within the last three, four years."

As in any other profession, reviewing performances has its own ethics. In what way or ways can this be violated? Years before P.D. 1081, it was common for journalists on the staff of metropolitan dailies to be included on the payroll of impresarios, cultural societies and organizations which they served as press agents.

As such, they promoted individual artists and public presentations through their columns or press releases which they themselves wrote and published in the pages they edited. The practice has persisted in even more obvious guises. Thus, there are critics who are not above reviewing programs presented by the cultural institution for which they work.

There is also the matter of in-breeding. For instance, some critics, who are listed on the masthead of a magazine published by a cultural institution, review the performances presented by that institution. As another example, a cultural writer confines his ecstatic comments to the presentations of one particular theater.

These circumstances, which tend to narrow the critic's view, are neither conducive to the independent coverage of the arts nor to their growth and development. Although in-breeding may not necessarily preclude a sincere attempt on the part of the reviewer to rise above bias or partiality, how can he avoid being a captive critic when performances he reviews are sponsored by his employer, benefactor or publisher?

Indeed, there are other ways for critics not to be true to themselves or their craft. Certain critics often reflect the ideas and opinions of their own colleagues—even to the extent of lifting words, phrases and sentences (in almost the same sequencing) from them, particularly when the critics in question indicate a glaring lack of background in the areas they are reviewing.

As a final example, a "critic" once sat in a drunken stupor through half of a play. Came intermission and his friend, within my hearing, briefed him on what he had missed. When the lights dimmed for the second half of the drama, the somnolent "critic" dozed off again. Incredibly enough, his second-hand review was duly published.

At this point, one might ask: How qualified are our critics? Presumably, critics gravitate around the arts because of a natural inclination inherited from parents and other forebears, and deepened by further exposure, orientation and training in school.

Performing arts critics are expected to have a thorough grounding in at least one area of discipline, and to be conversant with the rest of the disciplines. (For instance, a critic who specializes in theater should have a grasp of music and dance.)

In view of the growing tendency to integrate the arts, a critic with a solid background in the performing arts will be much better equipped than another who has a single field of specialization. To add to the critic's burden, the performing arts are in a continuous process of accretion, change and growth. Being dynamic, they are always in transition. Lamentably, not all critics keep up with the latest movements and trends which have to be viewed within a larger framework.

Lamentably too, not all critics have the capacity to write with literacy and style.

Ultimately, the impact critics make on the performing arts depends on the editors who hire them and who formulate the cultural policy of their respective newspapers and periodicals.

Enlightened editors take a direct hand not only in the form and substance of the cultural page but also in the choice of critics. Indifferent editors, on the other hand, leave the thrust and conduct of that page, as well as the choice of critics, to the discretion of section editors. The critic is lucky if his section editor treats his copy intelligently. However, a section editor may not necessarily be informed or conversant enough with cultural matters. It is wholly possible for such a section editor—whose cultural background and literacy may leave much to be desired—to edit, cut and modify a review with obvious incompetence. The ideal situation ensues, for both the reader and the artist, when the enlightened editor and the qualified critic meet.

# BALLET EDUCATION IN METRO MANILA

LEONOR OROSA–GOQUINGCO

## The Importance of Ballet Education in Metro Manila

*Dance As A Noble Art*

Dance is a term that is wide in range.

Franklin Stevens, an American Ballet Theatre professional dancer who subsequently turned writer, goes so far as to say, "We are all dancers. We use movement to express ourselves—our hungers, pains, angers, joy, confusions, fears—long before we use words, and we understand the meanings of movement long before we understand those of words."

Similarly, we respond to music—"music in the voice"—before we understand the words spoken by the voice. Life begets movement—and dance.

Continues Stevens, "There are birds, animals, fish, amphibians, even insects, that perform courtship and battle dances of elaborate and ritual intricacy, their weavings, bobbings, advances, and retreats set in patterns as clearly marked as any seventeenth century court ceremonial dance."

Rhythm, too, is all around us, as the planets go a-circling round the sun, as night follows the day, as the seasons succeed each other, and as the sea flows and ebbs.

In brief, dance is in us and all about us, in the melding of rhythm and movement.

We, in this paper, however, refer to dance as art, and still more specifically, to dance as art in the theater, and/or by extension, in some other venue such as television, film, park, etc. Reference will cover dance as performance, spectacle, even as communication—i.e., meant to be viewed by an audience.

Dance education, as in the wider term art education, will refer to the systematic, extended, and even continuing process by which the would-be artist acquires a mastery of the tools of his art/craft/trade, often, in the case of the dancer, referred to as "technique."

A dancer's education, however, covers more than excellent technical training: it should also include ample opportunity to grow as an artist, an interpreter.

George Balanchine, considered by certain cognoscenti as the most important choreographer of modern times, says about technique:

Technique is the method or the details of procedure essential to expertness of execution in any art, says Webster. When people, even professionals, speak of dancers as good or bad technicians, they usually refer to their speed or force or physical strength. Technique of the dancer consists of the combined elements of acquired muscle strength and their complete control and coordination. Basically, it is not a question of being able to move according to one's own will, but to move where and how the dancer may be directed.

Technical perfection must be more than a means to a desired end—the perfect artistic accomplishment.

### Ballet, one of Dance's highest forms

In Italy, in past grand celebrations, music, dance and drama merged into one elaborate spectacle. So popular did such entertainment become with the nobility that in 1581, when Italian Catherine de Medici became the Queen of France, she dipped into the royal funds to subsidize the production of a "superspectacle" which is now regarded as the first ballet, the *Ballet Comique de la Reine.*

The ballet, which cost three million francs and was viewed by ten thousand guests, celebrated the betrothal of the Duc de Joyeuse to Marguerite de Lorraine, and was "choreographed" by the Italian violinist and dancing master Belgiojoso (Fr. Beaujoyeux). The lords and ladies of the court performed within the framework of the unified theme. A few of the viewers wrote in their diaries and letters that much of what they saw was boring—thus becoming the first dance critics.

In the year 1661, increasing technical demands made by innovative dancing masters led to the establishment of the Academie Royale de la Danse in Paris by Louis XIV, a school to train professional dancers, for whom dance would be a vocation, a profession, a life's work.

Jean Baptiste Lully, himself a dancer, was the director; Pierre Beauchamp, the ballet master; and the first professional ballerina produced, Lafontaine, elicited the admiration of Paris.

Today, the dancer gives his/her young life to developing skills in difficult techniques, the techniques which will enable him/her to interpret or dance the choreography for us, the spectators, the collective audience.

In its surrender of the communal/participatory character, theater dance compensatingly gained an international language and a universal appeal. Subsequently, that is. For when Lafontaine danced, her steps were still restricted by her high heeled shoes, voluminous, lengthy costumes, and tall, not-always-stable headdresses.

Male dancers for their part were free from the aforementioned encumbrances and had branched out into performing simple pirouettes and jumps.

The woman dancers soon became dissatisfied with their lack of freedom. Marie Camargo discarded her high heels, made her skirts lighter, and shortened them to the ankle. Thus she, too, could begin to jump, turn, and engage in intricate footwork.

As women gained more freedom, the dancing master/choreographer made growing technical demands and the dancers, forced by the wish to excel, extended movement into new reaches.

Towards the late eighteenth century, the female dancer began to rise — at first momentarily — onto the tips of her toes.

The delicate, ethereal look proved tremendously appealing to an age "whose temper was moving from the classic, with its myths of gods and demigods, to the romantic, with its visionary landscape of fairies, sylphs, and delicate maidens."

The Paris of 1832 saw Marie Taglioni in *La Sylphide,* and *Giselle* was only nine years away.

The first was about a magical sylph, the second about a heartbroken maiden who upon her death became a ghostly wili. Both ballets were eminently suited to pointe work, which advanced more and more.

The art of ballet and pointe work became synonymous for nearly 150 years, and except in a few cases, the male dancer's role became subordinated into that of a partner or *porteur.*

Ballet continued to develop, both technically and in dramatic quality, and its popularity extended throughout all Europe, to Russia, England, and the United States.

### Ballet — Basic Education for Would-be Dance Professional

Dance education in the Republic of the Philippines is available in private studios, in certain universities, and at the Cultural Center of the Philippines. The quality of instruction ranges from downright bad to excellent — depending on the background, teaching skills, patience and other virtues of the teacher on hand.

Instruction is available in Metro Manila in ballet, modern dance, jazz, tap, Philippine dance (frequently with the books of pioneer researcher Francisca Reyes Aquino as textbooks), Spanish dance, Chinese dance, Javanese, Hawaiian, and Tahitian dance.

The College of Music of the University of the Philippines offers courses leading to a diploma in the Creative and Performing Musical Arts (DCPMA). Offered are Asian dance courses, Philippine folk and ethnic dances, kinesiology and anatomy, and Physical Education and Recreation, which has its own two-year diploma program in dance. Electives in theater production and the broadcasting media are taken from the Theaters Arts and Mass Media programs in the university, and from the Home Economics Institute.

Dance critics can be of immense encouragement to the artists in the field of dance. Conversely, they can nip a promising career in the bud, destroy an artist's morale, or even drive an artist to suicide.

This, of course, is reprehensible. A critic can say no, *nyet*, or *non* in many ways, and the mature critic knows how say a thing kindly — in the manner that would hurt the least.

Well-qualified dance critics are rare. Little wonder, too. As Edwin Denby comments on the dance critics in U.S., in an observation which likewise pertains to this country:

"Almost all our (U.S.) dance criticism appears in the form of newspaper reviewing. But almost all papers would rather misinform the public than keep a specialized dance reporter. Even rich ones delight in skimping on costs by sending out a staff critic who covers ballet as an extra unpaid chore."

He adds:

"When people who like dancing say a critic is right they mean he is right enough and that his imaginative descriptions are generally illuminating. He can hardly be illuminating or right enough (however) unless he has a fund of knowledge about his subject. In theory, he needs to know the techniques and the historical achievements of dancing, the various ways people have looked at it and written about it, and finally he needs a workable hypothesis of what makes a dance hang together and communicate its images so they are remembered. In practice, he has to piece together what he needs unsatisfactorily; experience as a dancer and choreographer is an invaluable help to him."

Indeed, it is suggested that the critic of dance go himself through the process of learning dance. "The best organized and by far the most useful chunk of knowledge a critic has access to is that about the technique and history of classic ballet in particular, as ballet dancers learn it."

Further, the critic will have to have the gift of language — with which to describe a performance, and to point out what was remarkable about it.

Like the choreographer, the would-be dance critic will benefit from a wide background in art and in art history.

*Ballet — a very popular form in Metro Manila*

Today, modern dance is taught alongside ballet in many universities in America, as well as in other centers of dance education all over the world.

This writer, working as the pioneer Filipino choreographer, used free forms in her *Current Event* (*Dance Panorama*, St. Cecilia's Hall, St. Scholastica's College, 1939), *Lamentation* (*The Story of Man*, Philippine Women's University, 1959) and *Noli Dance Suite* (1941-58).

As a subject in Physical Education, modern dance was introduced at the University of the East and Far Eastern University in the fifties, with Carmen Ferrer Adevoso as instructor. It was also used by choreographer Manolo Rosado. A much later exponent of modern dance has been Alice Reyes who, in the seventies, organized the Alice Reyes Dance Workshop which became the Cultural Center of the Philippines Dance Company, and finally, Ballet Philippines.

As an art form, modern dance has never caught up in popularity with ballet in the Philippines, at least. Nevertheless, more and more universities are introducing the two idioms into their curricula.

The most popular dance forms and courses in the Philippines are ballet, jazz, modern dance, and ethnic dance. The first three being of foreign origin, and comparatively new, look up to schools and courses abroad as models.

In this regard, there is the Royal Ballet School in Great Britain, which incidentally also offers a three-year Teachers' course. The graduates of the school have a high employment rate, usually finding places in either the Royal ballet itself or in other companies at home or abroad.

*The Filipino is highly gifted in dance*

Filipinos are prodigiously gifted in dance.

We are a musical people and have the proper slender framework, flexibility and national grace to be enhanced still further by expert training.

Abroad, our dancers are meeting with spectacular success — Lisa Macuja, Maniya Barredo, Anna Villadolid to name a few.

Many more could make the grade, were circumstances more favorable.

*The Filipinos are currently making waves in the international ballet scene.*

Topping the list of individual accomplished dancers are Lisa Macuja, Toni Lopez Gonzales, Mary Ann Santamaria, and Anna Villadolid.

Lithe and lively Lisa, with her winsome face and elfin charm and the

393

more-serious-of-mien Mary Ann made history by graduating from the Leningrad (Vaganova) Choreographic Institute. At her graduation program at the Kirov Theatre in June 1984, Lisa rendered the Don Quixote grand *pas de deux*, with brilliant Soviet dancer Bakhtzhan Smagulov as partner. To have been assigned this role was in itself a compliment, for in the Soviet Union, only dancers of prima ballerina quality are allowed to dance it.

Lisa Macuja, reports say, not only tossed off the challenging *pas* with technical ease and flourish. Beyond this, she imbued the tried-and-true vehicle with new life and freshness. All in all, she received 11 curtain calls.

The highest tribute to Lisa, however, came in the form of an invitation from artistic director Oleg Vinogradov to join the Leningrad-Kirov Ballet Company as a soloist. She is the first foreigner ever to be invited to join this prestigious ballet group.

Young, tall (for a Filipina), long-of-limb Toni Lopez Gonzalez, previously a scholar at the Richard Thomas New York School of Dance, the American Ballet Theatre School, and the Melissa Hayden School, and a semi-finalist in the 11th International Ballet Competition in Varna, Bulgaria, once more placed the Philippines on the map when she won as one of five finalists in the First New York International Ballet Competition in June 1984.

Dance editor Jennie Schulman of New York City's *Backstage* magazine wrote: "(Her) subtle style, impeccable techniques with the softness of a dove (should have won her) at least a bronze medal (third place)." Toni also got favorable notices from the widely-read *Dance* magazine, in New York City.

Mary Ann Santamaria, after two years of assiduous work, graduated from Leningrad Choreographic Institute. At her graduation program at the 200-year-old Kirov Theatre, she danced the Cowboy's Duo, specially choreographed by Sergei Vikulov to Teleman's Andante, with Murat Tathanov. After a brief vacation in the Philippines, Mary Ann left for greener pastures in Europe to audition for several companies.

Madam Iosefavna, who had been completely won over by the two Filipinas, cited their aptitude for dance and their capacity for hard work as factors in their success. Self-discipline, too, one might add. Lisa and Mary Ann are living proof that Filipinos can make it to the top in the very specialized field of 'classic ballet,' provided they have the three aformentioned qualities.

The shy and retiring teenage daughter of Oscar and Alice Villadolid—both intellectuals and able writers—has the distinction of being the first Filipino dancer to step boldly onto the fiercely competitive turf of an international dance contest, the International Ballet Competition in Jackson, Mississippi, in 1982.

The *Clarion Ledger* of Mississippi comments: "Applause was frequent during the expressive performance of junior competitor Anna Villadolid of the Philippines, who danced the Flower Festival of Genzano *pas de deux* in the Bournoville (air-borne) style (with non-competing *balikbayan* Enrico Labayen)."

Thus, for the first time, the Philippine flag proudly joined 19 others in the auditorium at Jackson, where the names of 79 expectant, excited competitors from 20 nations were entered into the lists. This unassuming ballerina made it into the semi-finals, and was further offered a year's scholarship in the Munich Ballet Academy by Konstanze Vernon, one of the impressed judges.

### The State of Ballet Education in Metro Manila

*Ideal Conditions Attendant to Ballet Education (Russia, Canada, England, U.S.A.)*

In the Soviet Union, more than in any other country, "ballet is a direct continuation of the 19th century classic ballet, established and given form by Arthur Saint-Leon, Marius Petipa and Lev Ivanov."

The two most important ballet theaters (led by their own schools) are the *Bolshoi* in Moscow and the *Kirov* in Leningrad. These ballet schools, which are part of the state theaters, enjoy state subsidies and economic security and are considered to be the finest in the world.

The schools have a seven-year preparatory course and a three-year professional course. They are free to students who qualified in preliminary interviews, physical examinations, etc. A full high school course is taught in addition to dancing, music, art appreciation, fencing, etc. Apropos, Russian textbooks could be superior to those published anywhere in the world. Agrippina Vaganova's *Fundamentals of the Classic Dance*, translated into English by Anatole Chujoy, received universal acclaim as soon as it was published in New York in 1946.

On the efficacy of the teaching methods at the Kirov School (from which, incidentally, Filipina dancer Lisa Macuja graduated after two years of study into a soloist's rank in the Kirov Ballet), American writer Jean Ross Acocella says:

"In serious emsemble work, there is probably no greater corps de ballet in the world than the Kirov's. Here you see what you came to see, Petipa's diamonds in Vaganova's gold: the free, ample, yet perfectly disciplined flow of energy from the spine through the limbs, neck, and head--a single impulse of passion and harmony."

Other excellent ballet schools include the Royal Danish School, Copenhagen; the School of American Ballet, New York City; the national Ballet School of Canada, Ontario; and the Bavarian Training Centre, Munich.

## Conditions Prevailing in Metro Manila

Dance as a profession/vocation/way of life is still making an uphill climb in its struggle for recognition, approbation and appreciation.

The 1980 UNESCO Draft Recommendation of the Status of the Artist reads:

"Artist is taken to mean any person who creates or gives expression to, or revives works of art, who considers his artistic creation to be an essential part of his life, who contributes in this way to the development of art and culture, and who is asked to be recognized as an artist, whether or not he is bound by any relations of employment or association."

Says a writer in *Dance* magazine, April, 1984:

"It is crucial that the artist who considers his artistic creation to be an essential part of his life also realize that he is a laborer, and that his choice of profession carries with it a particular and identifiable set of conditions. Only when an artist possesses a realistic and practical professional identity can he expect to obtain government and private sector attention and support for policies and programs which will improve the way he lives his life."

The artist, as anyone else, must pay for rent, food, gas, and electricity; he must pick a neighborhood, possibly send children to school, support elderly parents, etc. Revealing, in truth, is the fact that when a ballet dancer sought the assistance of an employment service in New York City in seeking a job, the job counselor, said, "Okay, so you are a ballet dancer; but how do you earn a living?"

Apropos, the Concise Oxford English dictionaty defines "work" as "an expenditure of energy, striving, application of effort to some purpose." Purposes could include the securing of the means to provide one's (and others) with shelter, clothing, food and other basic necessities. An individual's work, further, secures for him his identity and situates him in society—i.e., gives him a measure of self-esteem.

Says John Garbett, also in *Dance* magazine of April, 1981:

"Government defines 'what you do' as paid employment. This one-dimensional definition, while serving government's purpose, ignores personal and social aspects. Our society and government make a distinction between the 'work' of an artist and the 'work' of a carpenter or a doctor. Unlike [the case of] other highly-trained professionals, such as doctors or lawyers, the public fails to see an artist's years of study, training, practice, and performance, successes and failures, or his intense discipline and commitment."

"Most people still believe that the reason actors act and dancers dance is that they 'have to' and 'love to' and not because they want [need] to earn a living as performers."

Because of the above, a highly essential part of the education of an artist as professional is the realization that he is a member of the artistic labor force, and to know how to take advantage of this collective force's political and economic clout.

The choreographer could well do with funding. For he is an artist who has to work with other professionals – dancers, musicians, composers, scenic, costume, and light designers. The choreographer, too, is in need of a theater, publicity and a marketing arm to help "sell" his product.

The choreographers in the USA have a number of organizations to fall back on – the National Endowment for the Arts and Humanities, an independent agency of the Federal government of the USA created by Public Law 89-209, passed by Congress and signed by President Lyndon Johnson into law; the National Choreographic Project; the National Corporate Fund for Dance; the Asterisk Dance Foundation; the Ford Foundation, and other foundations set up by civic and culturally concerned citizens.

After fifteen years of existence, the Dance Program of the NEA had helped the dance audience grow from 2 million to 16 million and 35 dance companies grow to more than 350.

In other countries such as the Soviet Union, the Republic of China, France, the Federal Republic of Germany, and the German Democratic Republic, among others, there is state help for the artists, the choreographer included.

While it seems to be taking the Philippine some time to follow suit and extend systematic assistance to deserving artists (dance creators/choreographers above all), it may not be a totally lost cause.

This writer can only hope that things might turn out to be better and easier on future choreographers in the Philippines than it was in her time. For herself, she can only lament, as post-modernist Trisha Brown did in *Dance* magazine, March, 1985:

"The work is fascinating. But in looking back, I regret that a dancer is not better supported at all stages of development. I'm speaking of myself and of the people who worked with me. We contributed, really, too much and received too little. That separated us from our families and deprived us of a certain fluent mobility in general society. It made us focus too long on obviously basic things, when we should have been practicing our flying."

Could the Ballet Society of the Philippines look into the matter of helping provide funds for the Filipino choreographer?

## Demonstration

Confucius says, "A picture is worth a thousand words." "Moving pictures" will be presented, together with a running commentary.

### Basic principles of Ballet

Seven essential principles have been formulated by the great masters, from their experience of disciplining the movements of their students within the classical framework. These seven principles are distinct from the seven movements of dance.

*Stance* — position taken; standing correctly.

Without the ability to stand and hold himself/herself correctly at all times, the classical dancer has little or no possibility of maintaining turn-out or following the line of dance. He/she must understand the capacity of his/her body for movement in this highly disciplined style — and he/she will get the best results when the spine has been pulled out to its straightest.

*Turn-Out* — rotary motion; bringing to view.

The 'turn-out' is an absolute necessity if the dancer aims at the perfection of a purely classical line. Its achievement requires an understanding of muscle control within the thighs, pelvis, legs and stomach in order to maintain correct placing.

The turn-out must take place within the hip-joints; the knees and thighs are rotated outwards as far as possible so that the feet turn out; each knee must keep in a natural relationship to the line of its leg and foot. Thus, it will always be directly in line with the center of the pelvis whether it faces forward or (when turned out) sideways and whether the leg is bent or straight; each foot must bend straight upwards or stretch straight downwards from the ankle towards and away from the center of the knee; thus the foot will only work at right angles to the lower leg and knee and must not roll inwards or sickle outwards at the ankle.

If these rules are at all times applied correctly, they prevent the weight from coming too far back on the heels.

Although de Valois's remark stressed the importance of perfect turn-out, she added a valuable comment for dancers who find its achievement difficult:

"It is better to sacrifice some part of the turn-out than lose the line and quality of a movement and the symmetry of the pose. It is far more important to maintain the natural relationship of the parts to the whole leg when drawing the line of dance."

*Placing*—arranging things in their proper place to achieve an ordered, balanced form.

Movement made by any dancer can be symmetric or asymmetrical. In pure classical dance, symmetry is demanded. It does not take into account the effect that emotion, mood or personal characteristics can have on the dancer's body to upset its equilibrium.

The body is basically symmetrical. The arms and legs weigh equally on each side. The crown of the head is centered over the spine and feet. The weight of the body is thus evenly balanced over the feet (the base). Turn-out once achieved, the head and torso must remain properly centered over this base even when it changes shape as weight is transferred to one foot or even more as the dancer rises through the foot to the dull pointe.

In order to keep the head and body correctly placed in relation to the legs, the spine must not be stiffened. Its natural curves, from the waist upwards, must allow the dancer to adjust his balance to every change of weight as he draws the line of dance by steps and poses.

*The Laws of Balance*—a counterpoise (of things) in order to maintain equilibrium.

There are only two laws of balance to remember. They should be applied appropriately as the dancer follows the line of dance and conforms to the other basic rules:

The Law of Opposition—Whether working or supporting, the leg in front should be balanced by the opposite arm coming forward. The dancer must be in correct alignment with hips and shoulders level and lying parallel to each other, facing the same plane and directed to one point in the personal square.

The Law of Epaulement—Whether working or supporting, the leg in front should be matched by the forward movement of the same shoulder. This law is more usually followed when a movement is to be 'shaded' as in epaulement. Dancers should study this law carefully, in relationship to stance, turn-out and placing in its first form.

*The Basic Rules of Classical Technique*—dominant custom; canon; test; normal state of things.

It is better to have a rule to break than no rules at all if chaos does not reign in the class room and on the stage.

Although an attempt can be made to set down rules for each part of the body, no one rule can be practiced for itself alone. The anatomical structure of the body is such that when one part of the body is used or one movement made, some muscles work in one way and some in another, counterposing each other to help the dancer maintain balance. For example, in order to bend the legs in *plié* some muscles relax, others stretch; or, in order to stretch the leg in *développé*, some muscles stretch and others raise the leg into position.

*Transfer of Weight* — to convey or hand over one thing or person to another place or person.

When transferring weight from one foot to the other, the dancer must be sure that the entire body goes over to the new supporting leg through the center line of balance, therefore adjustments have to be made throughout the whole body, even if only minimal ones.

The legs must be controlled at all times if the flow of movements is to be maintained. The dancer must be able to feel the fully stretched leg from hip to toe and appreciate the swift, accurate transfer of weight needed to reverse the functions of a supporting leg and a working leg. This change takes place even in the slightest movement from a first to fifth position of the feet, using a *battement tendu* or small *retire*. If the change is not accurate the dancer cannot move smoothly or maintain speed. Also, it is not possible for him to achieve that delicacy of movement which demands that no jerk and no unequal gaps be seen between the legs, particularly in such steps as *pas de bourree courus* or *suivis*.

*Co-ordination* — to bring parts into proper relationship.

The seventh and most vital principle of classical dance is co-ordination, without which no step can become part of dance.

Accuracy in classical dance is what matters and if there is to be accuracy then there must be unity and discipline. Only then will there be co-ordination.

Ninette de Valois's words sum up exactly what is required from the dancer because there must be a total response from all parts of the body if they are to move in harmony with the line of dance and the music:

"The arms and hands must always be alive and synchronize exactly with the legs and feet so that they begin together and arrive simultaneously at the finished position. They are vital elements communicating emotional significance and meaning to all forms of dance. But they must be controlled if they are to achieve that symmetry and placing demanded in classical dance. They must be controlled if they are to take part appropriately in every movement, to supply impetus and accent, and always to follow the line visualized by the head and eyes."

*Seven Basic Movements; directions for travel; adage, allegro*

When in 1723 Weaver defined his four movements of dance he was analyzing the four movements of which the body is capable, i.e., to bend, stretch, rise or raise, turn or rotate. In 1760, Noverre defined his seven movements in terms of quality of the steps his dancers had to perform.

1) *Plié* — to bend; or fold up.

Even the simplest *plié* needs the co-ordination of legs, arms and head if it is to be a dancing movement and to create a flow of line. It is the first exercise to be studied in class.

The legs are bent at three points until the *demi-plié* position is reached and at four from there to the full *plié*. In other words, the dancer bends the legs at the hip-joints, knees and ankles — and finally the feet at the metatarsal arches.

The dancer's arms are always curved except in arabesque, which means that they are bent at the arm-socket, elbow, wrist and fingers. The head can also bend or curve forwards, sidewards or backwards. The spine alone remains stretched and still though it, too, can fold up, as it were, when the dancer sinks to the floor through a *plié*.

2) *Etendre* — to stretch; or spread.

The second exercise to be studied is usually *battement tendu*, the working leg stretching throughout its length from hip to toe outwards from a closed position. The legs must also be fully stretched, but upwards, in order to regain stance after any *plié*.

The arm is fully stretched outwards from its socket only in arabesque, but should be stretched within the curve if arms, like legs, are to move freely.

If the spine is not stretched to its fullest when the dancer is standing in any of the five positions of feet, then stance is not correct. After any movement when the body has been bent, the spine must be stretched again in order to regain height.

But there is also the idea of spreading, the feeling a dancer should have when breathing deeply and stretching arms widely away from the body to give breadth, depth and height to the line of dance as it flows on. This is particularly important in such movements as *développé*, where only one leg works, and in *battements fondus*, where there must be visible equality of movement in both legs although one is working and the other supporting.

The action of bending, then stretching, accompanied by the feeling of spreading outwards, has to be practised constantly if there is to be a smooth transition from one movement to another.

3) *Relever* — to raise or lift.

The term commonly translated as 'to rise' is not the same as 'to stretch, although it may appear so to the dancer rising through the feet to *demi-pointe* and finally *sur les pointes*. Even in the earliest exercises the dancer should feel that he is raising the weight of the body into the air away from the floor, particularly the upper torso away from the pelvis at the waistline, and is not merely stretching or spreading to ease tension. This feeling of raising the weight of the body into the air is extremely important.

It is not, however, only the torso that has to be raised. The leg has to be raised into a *battement releve*. Whereas in a *développé* the leg is bent as it is raised, employing certain muscles to lift half the weight and to hold the leg at the correct height while other muscles stretch the leg outwards, in a *battement releve* the full weight and length of the leg have to be lifted and controlled at an angle away from the body and the leg stretched at the same time. The arms, too, can be lifted to various heights and at different angles. It is important always to remember that both arms and legs are raised from underneath and once in position are held by muscles lying over the limb in question.

4) *Sauter* — to jump, leap, or skip.

Any kind of jump, leap or skip (*saut*) requires the strongest possible push away from the floor so that the body, whether moving upwards in place or travelling, no matter which direction, must be seen to soar away from the floor and to be held momentarily at the height of the jump. The impetus required to propel it upwards varies a great deal and must be properly understood if the line is to be correctly drawn.

5) *Elancer* — to push with strength. *S'elancer*: to dart.

Any *elance* movement should find the dancer making a strong push away from but only just over the floor. This type of movement should never travel upwards. The difference between an *elance* and a *saute* movement is nowhere better exemplified than when dancing a *pas de basque elance*, where the dancer seems to dart over the surface like a bird, and a *grand saut de basque*, where he must soar upwards, opening the leg outwards and/or making a turn at the height of the jump.

6) *Glisse* — to step, slide or glide.

A *glisse* movement also contrasts with a *saute* or an *elance* step. It has nothing of the same exhilaration or strength. The dancer must appear to be gliding on and along the surface so that the tips of the toes scarcely leave the floor. There is no upward movement as in *saute*, nor any powerful push outwards as in an *elance* step; nor, in purely classical ballets, should there be any of the sliding or slipping which is legitimate in such *demi-caractere* ballets as *Des Patineurs* where the dancers must appear to glide on ice.

Some dancers seem to believe that *glissades* and other *glisee* movements do not require much thought. They should remember that the *glissade* is one of the most valuable preparations for many kinds of jumps. Every care should be taken to see, firstly, that it is carrying the dancer onwards in the appropriate direction from the moment it begins; secondly, that it is completed at the exact point in the flow of the line the jump or other movement must commence; and thirdly, that it gives the correct impetus to what will follow. To ensure that this will happen, the dancer must coordinate all movements of his head and arms with the step and with the music.

7) *Tourner* — go turn, or revolve.

Weaver was the first to describe the dancers' ability to turn the leg outwards from the hip because of the nature of the ball and socket joint. He noted that a similar action took place in the arm socket and that some rotation could also be made at the wrist, knee and ankle. In describing the limited rotation at these three places he was careful to add how important it was that no rotation took place at the ankle: in classical dance, as he knew it and as it is today, if any rotation occurs at the ankle there is little likelihood of the dancer maintaining balance over the supporting leg. Weaver suggested, moreover, that only very careful rotation should be made at the knee because of the danger of displacement and torn cartilages, although he allowed that such a 'flourish' added elegance to the line of the leg — just as today the *petits rond de jambe en l'air* can add brilliance.

The turn of the hand at the wrist was all-important to Weaver because so much grace and courtesy lay in the play of the hand when holding or taking off the hat, when offered to a partner or during a bow — just as today's dancers must make that simple turn of the hand at the wrist every time they stretch their arms outwards into an arabesque. The dancer should make use of these limited movements of the hand at the wrist because they give extra life and meaning to the line being followed in most *port de bras*. They should always be simple and without fuss.

The coordination of all parts of the body can be achieved only by constant practice of the rules that derive from the first seven principles already discussed and their application to the particular movement.

*Jumps and beats* are the hallmark of *allegro* or fast, lively dancing. As contributors to the well-rounded, perfectly complete technique of classical ballet, they give ballet not only excitement and brilliance, but also something without which ballet can scarcely be imagined: a vertical dimension.

A dancer must possess two qualities to jump: *elevation* and *ballon*. *Elevation* is, logically, the dancer's ability to attain height in a jump, as measured from the ground to the tips of the dancer's pointed toes in the air. *Ballon* is elasticity, or bounce such that the dancer bounds up lightly from the floor, suspends for a moment in midair, and lands softly and smoothly, ready to bounce up again like a rubber ball. The two qualities go hand in hand — one is not much good without the other — and all great jumpers have them.

Students learn the fundamentals of *allegro* at the barre, facing it and holding on with both hands for support. They start off doing little jumps in first, second, and fifth positions, paying special attention to stretching the legs and feet strongly while in the air, keeping the back straight and the shoulders down (at the beginning of the study of jumps, there is a chronic disappearance of neck into hunched shoulders), and landing *demi-plié* with the heels on the floor.

The same little jumps are done in the center. Without the barre for support, the strain in the arms, neck, and shoulders is a greater problem, and a weak back leads to a jerking movement of the upper body during the jumps. The students work to keep the upper body relaxed, to hold the arms loosely and still, to hold the back firmly — and, it is hoped, to attain some height.

It would be nice if we in the audience could identify every jump in ballet by name; it would be personally satisfying, and a lot easier than saying "those jumps in which the dancer does a sort of suspended split in the air, pushing off from one leg and landing softly on another" (*grand jetes*). Learning the name of every jump is impossible, however, for anyone but a dancer. First of all, there are so many jumps; jumps from both feet to both feet, in or into various positions jumps from one foot to another; jumps that combine other elements, such as turns; jumps from both feet to one foot, or from one foot to both feet; consecutive jumps on one foot. Big jumps, little jumps, beats. Their diversity is wondrous.

Furthermore, many jumps are just too complicated to explain in words; their descriptions would be longer than the last paragraph, and impossible for the lay person to follow. Even if you had seen a particular jump many times, you would probably never recognize it in a description.

### Pointe Work

Pointe work is dancing on the toes, literally. Beautiful pink satin slippers with satin ribbons, longed for by every child ballerina until the day she is ready to put a pair on. The epitome of technique, a badge of strength. The ballet student's "Last Frontier."

Contrary to what many people believe, the dancer really is up on her tiptoes when on pointe. People have often expressed surprise at this, assuming that the dancer is still on the flat of the toes (on half-toe) inside the shoe, with the shoe making the pointe – but not so. If you sit down and point your foot as much as possible, placing the toes lightly on the floor so that they don't buckle, and bending the knee so that the toes are directly in line with it, it will give you an idea of what the dancer stands on – not much, is it? If your foot, like most people's, is shaped so that the toes angle back toward the little toe, perhaps only two or three toes actually touch the floor in this position. Consequently, a dancer with a very square, or "chopped" foot has the best foot for pointe work, because she has a greater surface area to support her. If in addition the foot has a thick, strong ankle and a low arch – not a beautiful foot from an aesthetic point of view – it has more advantages for pointe work.

If a student is coming along nicely, she may don her first pair of pointe shoes as early as age eleven. By no means can she dance on them. At first they may be worn for about ten minutes at the end of the regular class, the student holding on the barre and doing simple exercises for rising and stepping out onto pointe. Her first priority is to learn to go up and down smoothly and quietly through all parts of the foot, to distribute the weight evenly over all toes, and to keep her knees straight. After a year, perhaps she will have strengthened her feet enough to be ready to take a beginning pointe class, a class with a barre and center floor work given immediately after a regular class, when the body is completely warmed up.

The first year or so on pointe work is agony. The beginner thinks it's never going to stop hurting, that she'll never stop having blisters and throbbing toes. When the shoes come off after class, the feet have to be pushed back into shape and circulation. The student stuffs her shoes with wads of lamb's wool or wraps her toes in rabbit's fur. Strangely, as she strengthens on pointe (and hence as the feet begin to hurt less) it becomes evident that this overstuffing is counterproductive, and she progresses to merest breath of lamb's wool or wraps the toes in a thin paper towel. The day arrives when the shoes don't hurt, when they are downright comfortable, and the lamb's wool serves not as padding but as a simple protection from rubbing.

There are new things to develop when a dancer advances to pointe work. First, of course, the muscles of the toes, the tendons of the heels, and the all-important insteps must be further strengthened and flexed, as they have not been fully developed before.

## Choreography

Choreography is the making of dances. Its chief aim is to produce something entertaining, pleasurable, even beautiful. Like painting and composing, choreography is primarily an artistic endeavor, a process of creating art for art's sake. Though it has been used for social comment or commercial purposes — just as painting and composing have — it does not really lend itself to such ends, and good choreography does not, as a rule, deal with them.

The maker of dances — the one who determines the concept, structure, and movements — is of course, the choreographer. Good choreographers, like good ballets, have certain characteristics in common. They have all been fine professional dancers — dancers of above-average, even exceptional technique and of considerable experience and exposure to ballet tradition. They all have a knowledge of and a feel for music, and some even are musicians in their own right.

But fine technique and musical ability are not enough. If choreography is an art form, then only an artist can choreograph. A virtuoso musician could not compose a fine symphony simply because he is a master technician and gifted performer, and the greatest dancer in the world cannot choreograph simply because he is a great dancer. Mr. Balanchine has said, "If I told fifty well-trained dancers to move, to dance, to entertain me, they would not know what to do." A choreographer must have that intangible creativity — or artistic genius. He cannot acquire it, no matter how long and hard he studies. He must possess it.

When we think about how most choreographers of quality ballets work, the concept of the choreographer as an artist makes sense. The idea for the ballet is the choreographer's artistic inspiration springing from a piece of music, or the qualities of a particular dancer, or perhaps some incident or feeling the choreographer has experienced. A good choreographer does not stay home in front of a mirror making a ballet and then calls rehearsals to teach it to his dancers; he calls rehearsals first, and then makes the ballet on his dancers. By moving at his direction, they keep up his inspiration, they help him work his idea out, they show him his idea for his reflection and adjustment. When everything has been arranged the way the choreographer wants it, the dancers embellish it with their own interpretation; they do not violate the music or the actual steps and gestures designed by the choreographer, but they add those touches of personal style and feeling that make a work of art come alive. As one would expect, the same piece can appear completely different when danced by two different dancers.

Finally, though you should demand coherence and competent dancing from every ballet, keep in mind that there are no formulas or set of rules for what ballet should be like, or what can or cannot be done, provided it makes artistic sense. One of the great things for the contemporary audience is that ballet is just now, after four hundred years, coming into its own as a separate art form, and therefore entering a great innovative period. A sound creative approach to choreography and a complete technique have been long established and will never be replaced, but they will undoubtedly give way to new, freer interpretations. Some already have the idea, for example, that the *corps de ballet* is merely a sort of moving scenery, or framework for soloists, is long gone. Instead, we see today in *Serenade,* for instance, that the corps is the soloists, is the basis of the ballet, and in *Allegro Brillante* that the boys' work in the corps is much more difficult than the soloists'. Once, ballet without a story, luxurious sets and costumes, and a multitudinous cast could not be imagined; now ballet is abstract, pared down to the bone, with as few as two dancers in an entire work. It is, in effect, getting closer to its own being, distilling down to its essence.

# THE SOCIAL, ECONOMIC AND CULTURAL LIFE OF MANILA IN THE 19TH CENTURY

ISAGANI R. MEDINA

As a city founded in 1571, the jurisdiction of Manila extended outside the walls, hence Extramuros, to the following *arrabales* (suburbs) forming part of the primate city: Binondo, San Jose de Trozo, Santa Cruz, Quiapo, San Miguel, Sampaloc, and Tondo. As a province, its jurisdiction covered twenty-eight towns, some of which, by late 1880's became part of the present Metro Manila area.

Manila proper and the suburban areas developed by leaps and bounds with the official opening of her port to international trade in 1834, resulting in the tremendous socio-economic changes for the Filipino. Indeed, the nineteenth century brought a great transformation from the preceding centuries of economic stagnation created by the monopolistic policy of Spain. Economic development was further retarded with the issuance of "papeletas de permiso" or passports required as early as 1784 of Manila residents when transferring from one house or from one barrio to another. This equally applied strictly to the *indios* and mestizos residing in the same city without permission from the provincial governor. In 1843, the mobility of Filipinos and mestizos going from one town or province to another without the previous knowledge of their *gobernadorcillo* or provincial governor was further controlled and violators were penalized by a fine of ₱5.00 or ten days' imprisonment.

Not only foreign but domestic trade developed with the opening of Manila to world commerce. Divisoria Market became Manila's "stomach" and "terminal" of diverse products via the Pasig River emanating from the circum-Manila area and various points of the Archipelago. Rice, sugar, and bamboo came via different transports from Pampanga. Cottage cheese, coconut wine, mats and hats came from Laguna. Hats and fresh fishes and diverse seafoods came from Bulacan. Dried fish and fresh fruits originated from Cavite. Manila itself produced a diversity of products and occupations in the various parts of Extramuros where the present street

408

names are the only mute witnesses of their bygone existence: Calles Arroceros (Rice Merchants); Labores (Embroiderers); Jaboneros (Soapmakers); Platerias (Silversmiths); Panaderos (Bakers), or Aceiteros (Ilang-ilang Oil Dealers), as Barrio Ilang-ilang in Paco supplied the flowers that produced the essential oils that commanded high prices in the Parisian perfumeries. Tondo was famous for fishing, weaving and sugar farming. Oyster shell lime was produced in Bangkusay while tuba was fermented in Tutuban, and oranges and fresh carabao's milk came from Barrio Gagalangin. Sesame and lumbang oils were extracted for the Binondo soapmakers. Quiapo was noted for its dressmaking and ambulant vendors. Sampaloc was known for its *lavanderos*, tuba and zacate grass for horse feed. Santa Ana's fame rested on its embroiderers, tiles and bricks, and even cattle. Maalat or Malate, along the Manila Bay, was known for its saltmaking, fine embroideries and weaving which allegedly | could compete with the best in Europe. Ermita was noted for its piña cloth embroideries, and Pandacan, the "Little Italy" of music lovers and an all-women orchestra ("Orquestrang Babae"), for its zacate and turkey raising.

As a consequence of this great economic changes in the life of the Filipino, a middle class of Eurasians emerged in the Filipino social pyramid. In fact, social class distinction in Philippine society during the nineteenth century was gauged by the size of one's house, construction materials used, in addition to domestic furnishings such as imported pianos, chandeliers, glassware, tableware, furniture and other luxury items which became the indices of affluence and family prestige. Pianos, for instance, were imported in 1893 worth ₱6,207.00 increasing to ₱8,378.00 the following year. Furniture pieces weighing 106,014 pounds valued at ₱42,479.00 were imported in 1893 increasing in 1894, to 429,019 pounds worth ₱33,863.00. Before the advent of the "horseless carriage" in Manila, the *carruaje* and the number of horses were other status symbols. The first shop manufacturing "carretelas bonitas, llenas de cristales, de ruedas pequeñas" was set up by a Frenchman in San Miguel, Manila in the early 1800s although it was an enterprising Yankee, Robert Hood, who thought of a "rent-a-carriage" scheme. During the seventeenth and eighteenth centuries, Spanish architectural styles were adopted gradually by the *indio* upper crust members, so that by 1850, the imposing stone and brick "bahay na bato" with galvanized iron sheet roof later, was a gauge of *principalia* and mestizo prestige.

Streets, mostly narrow, were in former times unnamed and the houses unnumbered. To avoid confusion, street names were written in thick, black letters on a white background and placed at the entrances and exits. These facilitated identification and prompt delivery of postal matter. Even stray dogs roaming the streets were ordered killed by the *bandos* of 1800 and 1814. Mail service between Manila and Cavite started as early as 1839 although postage stamps were used for the first time only some fifteen years later.

Family names were individually assigned to the Filipino households based on the official *Catálogo alfabético de apellidos*. Patronyms made it easy not only for identifying families, but also for tax payments. Failure to comply meant eight days imprisonment or a fine of three pesos. The Kagalitan family of Santa Cruz painters and sculptors, represented by "Capitan Ting" (Justiniano Asuncion), for instance, altered their *apellido* to "Asuncion." The sadistic humor of the Spaniards could be mirrored in the surnames "Utot," "Ututan," "Ung-goy," "Sipon," or "Bungi." However, the native elite who coopted with the *conquistadores*, as a special privilege retained their former names. "Lacandola," "Mojica," "Tupas," and "Rajah Matanda" were not adopted by the common tao "except by those who have a great title to possess them."

Public lighting system in Manila and suburbs using coconut oil was considered by the Ayuntamiento as early as 1814. The streets of Santa Cruz, Binondo, Quiapo, San Miguel and Sampaloc, where the more opulent Europeans and Filipinos resided were illumined by oil by the mid-century, gradually changing to the use of kerosene in the 1880s. During this time, the use of the French-invented *quinqet* (kingke) lamps was absolutely banned particularly in nipa houses to prevent the occurrence of fires. Until the close of the century, the streets of Intramuros and the suburbs were still illuminated by gaslight and at times, by coconut oil. By 1893, the Walled City and the *arrabales* were already powered by electricity with the founding of the "La Electricista."

Destructive fires had always been the foremost enemy of Intramuros and Extramuros since the time Rajah Soliman applied the "scorched earth policy," and put the primate city to flames rather than see it capitulate to the Spanish invaders. Thus, fire prevention in the Walled City and suburbia was top priority to the extent that January 17 was reserved for San Antonio Abad, the city's patron saint against fires. Corollary to this, Our Lady of Loreto in Sampaloc was declared the town's patroness and several decrees on fire prevention were passed through the years, the earliest being in 1760. The authorities also saw to it that artificial pyrotechnics like firecrackers and rockets were banned since 1764. In fact, the revised Raon's *Ordenanza del Buen Gobierno* specified that the distance between nipa houses be three feet and that spaces in between be planted with fruit trees or the sappy banana plants as deterrents in the

410

spread of fires. Binondo, as the epicenter of business, seemingly was the first suburb to have a modern street and house planning. In 1762, nipa huts were ordered removed from Binondo's main streets up to Tondo even as the lodging inns of the same inflammable materials inside Intramuros were declared illegal a year before. Suburban houses usually were built so closely together which left only a minimum of movement for fire-fighting units and panicking people in narrow *callejones* (sidestreets) during conflagrations. However, a Fire Department with four pumps was already in operation by 1800. In the 1880s, fire signals were devised to forewarn the residents of the location of fires by means of repeated fifteen or twenty bell strokes (*campanadas*). The intervening half minute, more or less, was the signal of the bell-ringer of the site of fire by the number of very strong and slow church bell sounds. One stroke meant fire was inside the Walled City; two, in Ermita or Malate; three, in Paco; four, in Arroceros; five, in Binondo; six, in Santa Cruz; seven, in Quiapo; eight, in San Miguel; nine, in San Sebastian or Sampaloc; and ten, in Tondo.

Drinking water was not available as plentiful and as convenient as today. The urban poor still depended only on surface wells and the polluted Pasig River for their daily household uses even as the Carriedo Waterworks system was inaugurated in 1878. The rich relied mostly on rain water funneled from roofs down to their *algibes* (cisterns). Earlier, all Manilans drank water coming from the springs of San Juan del Monte, transported in big bancas by sturdy *aguadores* along the wharves at the Pasig River. In fact, the teen-ager Luis Yangco started business by transporting drinking water in jars and barrels within Manila. Some enterprising men from Marikina also transported water from "El Chorrillo" (probably in the present site of Chorillo St. in Barranca) and in sitio Krus na Ligas mentioned as early as 1819, within the present U.P. campus. Water was then sold at exorbitant price of four *reales fuertes* for two jars (or at 25 centavos per jar). At the turn of the century, the "Algibe de San Fernando" supplied Manila residents daily with water which was "muy buena y barata" (very good and cheap).

Manila society was highly visible in the residential organization. Intramuros served as the politico-religous nerve center of the Spaniards in the Philippines. Within the walls or *Manila murada* was the largest Spanish community in the Islands throughout the Spanish era. Before the nineteenth century, only Spaniards and their permanent domestic helpers and carriage drivers were allowed to live there. San Miguel, originally a part of Quiapo in the late eighteenth century, was the second concentration of Spaniards and other European business magnates. It may well be the "Forbes Park," and the most fashionable district in the

Archipelago at the time. Sampaloc, noted for its elegant stone houses and printers, equally contained a large elite population.

Outside of the walls were the Filipino and Chinese communities concentrated in different sectors. The mestizos and Filipino social elite preferred Binondo, Ermita, San Jose de Trozo and Quiapo. In the 1870s, Binondo was the biggest, as it was the commercial district in the province of Manila, where Don Santiago de los Santos or Capitan Tiago in Rizal's *Noli* lived (i.e., in Calle Anloague, now Juan Luan). Trozo, Emilio Jacinto's district consisted of four barrios: San Pasual, San Jose, San Lazaro, and La Magdalena, the last two being now better known as street names. Quiapo, known for its "Cristo Negro" or "Nazareno" was the residential district of Filipino government clerks, artist and merchants. Tondo, described then as "all slums" was the major residential area of the lower Filipino working class engaged in tobacco and cigar making, fishing, and gardening for Manila's consumption.

The present Chinatown grew with the "Parian de los Sangleyes" or "Pariancillos" for the Chinese residents. At least ten sites outside the Walled City have been identified which included Meisic, a corruption of "may insik," meaning "where the Chinese are." The Parian outside the walls within cannon range on the south side of the Pasig was reserved only for the unconverted Chinese between 1581 and 1790. Binondo, on the north side of the river, served as the second Chinese sector, continuing as the "ghetto" of the main Catholic Chinese and their mestizo children. Even in death, the unbaptized Chinese or "sangleyes infieles" were excluded from the Catholic burial grounds, even as the Protestant Englishmen were interred in San Pedro Makati. Paang Bundok or La Loma, in Santa Cruz, was reserved exclusively for these unbaptized Chinese. In 1880, Carlos March, established the first funeral parlor in the Philippines — the "La Funeraria" patterned after the French model of the period at No. 3 Plaza Goiti.

Travelers in the nineteenth century Manila availed of the convenient services available. Hotel reservations were made either at the Perez-owned Hotel de Oriente in Binondo, the first of its kind in the Spanish colony. Of two storeys, with eighty-three rooms, it kept a stable good for twenty-five horses. Considered the best hotel then was "Fonda de Lala" or "Fonda Francesa" owned by Lala Ari, an Anglo-Indian, at #37 Barraca, in Binondo, good for thirty-five guests "with board and lodging including ice" for ₱2.50 daily or ₱60.00 monthly. Services at the "Hotel Ingles" and "Hotel Europa" were equally considered good. However, there were also houses for rent with prices varying according to locale. In Intramuros, rent was from ₱35.00 to ₱200.00 monthly; in the suburbs, it was only from

₱10.00 to ₱20.00. The telephone, as a public utility, though in a very limited scale was already functioning since 1890 servicing 170 clients with its main office at Intramuros and branch at Calle San Jacinto (now T. Pinpin). Telecommunications between Manila and Cavite was started in 1872 which extended north to Ilocandia and south to Bicolandia later. A decade after, the Manila-Hong Kong overseas cablegram was established via Cape Bolinao. In 1897, the domestic cable lines between Manila-Panay-Cebu started regular service. Ships sailed from Manila to Hong Kong weekly, while the Manila-Barcelona trip was monthly. However, ships coming from Japan and other Euro-Asian countries and the United States arrived irregularly. Interisland travel to the Visayas and Mindanao was mainly through steamers and sailboats. The "Ferrocarril de Manila a Dagupan," 120 miles long, the only railway line in the Archipelago, constructed mainly using Filipino manpower operated regularly just four years before the outbreak of the Philippine Revolution. There were horse-complex vehicles for hire: de-luxe carriages of various sizes and shapes such as the *quiles* and the *araña* driven by one horse and the *victoria*, by two, and of course, the ubiquitous *calesa* and *carretela*. There were five street-car lines, four of which were horse-pulled, and one which was steam-powered. The animal-driven cars traveled from Intramuros, Malate, Sampaloc and Tondo; the only steam-driven car plied from Binondo to Malabon. To avoid the traffic flow in Arroceros and Quiapo, the Puente Colgante (now Quezon Bridge), the first hanging bridge in the Far East was built. Designed by Gustave Eiffel of the Eiffel Tower fame and measuring 110 meters long and seven meters wide, it had two lanes for the carriages, and the raised middle portion was reserved for foot-travelers. Pedestrians were charged a toll fee of one *kusing* or *un cuarto* (one-half centavo), while each horse cost three *cuartos* (about two centavos). Tolls for carriages depended on the number of wheels: 6-1/14 centavos for those with four, and 3-1/8 centavos for those with only two. Traffic became heavier through the years to the extent that the daily average number of vehicles that crossed Escolta, the main street and business sector was 5,000. In the Bridge of Spain (now Jones), which linked Binondo with Intramuros, it was 6,000 daily, in the late 1880s. Twenty-five years earlier it was only 915 for Escolta, and 1,256 for the Bridge of Spain. Indeed, Calle Hormiga meaning "ant," a small sidestreet in Binondo, vividly describes the slow vehicular movement due to heavy traffic flow in Manila's busiest business center.

Banking facilities were transacted at the Banco Español Filipino de Isabel II, the first Philippine bank which issued the first paper money in 1852; and the two British-owned Chartered Bank of India, Australia and

China, and the Hong Kong and Shanghai Bank. Savings accounts of Manilans were protected through the Monte de Piedad thirty years later.

The earliest newspaper, *Del Superior Gobierno*, was sold in the streets of Manila in 1811, even as the first daily *La Esperanza* came out thirty-five years later. For the first time the reading public read news in both Tagalog and Spanish in the *Diariong Tagalog*, while news devoted exclusively to women appeared in *El Bello Sexo* at the turn of the century. By then, the Chinese in Calle Rosario were peddling illegal foreign-made pornographic pictures even as smuggling of smut literature was banned as early as 1857.

Men of leisure usually relaxed in any of these establishments: horseracing at the one-lane Manila Jockey Club from San Sebastian Church to the Quiapo Church earlier; bullfighting in Paco and in Pasay later on. Those with dramatic, discriminating tastes had at least four choices of theaters: the Teatro Filipino in Calle Echague in Quiapo; the Circo de Bilibid, the Teatro Zorilla on Calle Iris (now Recto Avenue), and the Teatro de Colon. In these playhouses, popular *zarzuelas* were staged by Filipino and Spanish playwrights as well as classical operas performed by famous visiting European artists of the time. During this time, Andres Bonifacio, also as its *apuntador* (prompter) set up the Teatro de Porvenir on Reina Regente St. where he and his brothers Procopio and Ciriaco and Macario Sakay acted in the *moro-moro*.

Movies were shown for the first time at the Salon de Pertierra at the Escolta in 1897, featuring short French films at the price of fifty centavos for a cushioned seat and thirty centavos for benches (*lunetas*).

But what appears to be the most inexpensive way of amusement was, perhaps, going to the *Museo-Biblioteca de Filipinas*, the first public library and museum inaugurated in 1891 which opened seven hours daily except on holidays when it offered service only in the mornings. On display were museum pieces in three different sections: Anthropology and Ethnology, Natural History and Fine Arts, and Philippine Products. Its average daily visitors numbered about thirty, most of whom however, were library users. Unfortunately, there were no books in the collection under the heading of Politics. One can see the significant implication of that one important subject of the politicalization of the Filipinos and the gathering mass action in the subsequent explosion of the Revolution of 1896.

Other cheaper ways of relaxation were watching people, listening to the Filipino Regimental Band, and enjoying the sunset at the Luneta; or window-shopping at the Escolta, where the Chinese merchants sold diverse luxury items from Asia, the Americas and Europe. Others went to the Jardin Botanico near the present City Hall of Manila to enjoy the rare living local and foreign botanical (later also to include zoological) specimens.

There were cafes and restaurants which served foreign wines and liquors, choice delicatessen, coffee, and even ice cream. Among the best-known in the 1870s were "La Campana" in Escolta, and "El Oriental" in Plaza San Gabriel in Binondo. Later, it was the "Fonda La Catalana." Ice during the long sultry summer was provided by the Fabrica de Hielo at No. 21 Barraca St. in Binondo some two decades before the founding of San Miguel Brewery Factory. Incidentally, a case of "Cerveza San Miguel," consisting of thirty six bottles was sold at ₱19.00 at the turn of the century. As early as the 1840s, the Americans and the British in Santa Ana exclusively enjoyed the ice supply that came from the United States. This of course, referred to the deliveries made by Frederic Tudor, the first American with James Savage, to export natural ice from Boston, to as far as the West and the East Indies, China, Australia, and to the Philippines, as early as the 1800s. As late as the middle of the nineteenth century, a British traveler wrote that:

The supply of ice during my visit to Manila was abundant, and this I believe is generally the case. It is brought from America, and to me it proved a great luxury, as no such thing had made its appearance for the three years I have been to Hong Kong. Some time previously a cargo had been imported but not paying, it was discontinued.

In the early 1880s, fish cost ₱0.12 a pound; polished rice, at ₱2.12 for 127 Spanish pounds; hens, at ₱3.75 a dozen; eggs at ₱0.25 a dozen; beef, ₱0.12 a pound; pork, at ₱0.10 a pound; and brown sugar, at ₱0.07 a pound.

Before 1898, the following labor force received these daily wages: seamstresses and laundrymen, ₱0.20; day laborers, ₱0.37; carpenters, ₱0.62; tailors and shoemakers, ₱0.75; and cigar sorters, ₱0.80. House servants and teachers, however, received a monthly pay of ₱10.00 and ₱25.00, respectively.

Economic crisis in the Philippines was greatly felt by the people with the devaluation of the Mexican silver peso (Mex) beginning in 1874, from one peso to $1.005 (U.S.). From then on, it plunged down to $0.976 in 1875; $0.776 in 1891; $0.685 in 1892; $0.531 at the outbreak of the Philippine Revolution, and to as low as $0.475 in 1897. The Great depression of the 1880's coincided with the Asiatic cholera epidemic, the rinderpest, death of coffee plants in Batangas and Cavite, the worst typhoons and earthquakes in the Philippines. Incidentally, the prosperity of Spain collapsed with the fall of Spanish wines and iron in the foreign market in 1892. The further devaluation of the Spanish *peseta* became more acute during this year, which coincided with the founding of the

Katipunan by Andres Bonifacio in Tondo, when the pound sterling increased in value to 29.62 *pesetas*. The prices of abaca and sugar, two leading Philippine export crops declined owing to lower prices in the international market. Interestingly noticeable was that the major *tulisan* attacks in Cavite and the circum-Manila areas tallied with these economic crises. The hard times forced young girls from as far as Cavite and other surrounding provinces to become prostitutes plying their trade in Manila particularly in Palomar ("pigeon-house"), the red-light district in Tondo. The peso value was reduced to only $0.531 (U.S.) when people power led by the daring Katipuneros broke out in August, 1896.

# Contributors

CARMENCITA T. AGUILAR is associate professor of political science at the University of the Philippines where she is pursuing her doctoral degree, and serving as assistant to the dean of the College of Social Sciences and Philosophy. She is also vice president of the Philippine Political Science Association, and has published papers on Philippine foreign economic policy, ethnic political development, and Philippine constitutionalism.

JOSE S. ARCILLA, S.J., archivist of the Philippine Jesuit Province, is chairperson of the History Department of Ateneo de Manila University. He has an M.A. in history from the Loyola University in Chicago, and a doctorate in philosophy and letters from the Universidad Complutense de Madrid in Spain.

BASILIO P. BALAJADIA is an associate professor in the Religious Studies Department of De La Salle University. He finished both his A.B. and M.A. in philosophy at the University of Santo Tomas, and is currently pursuing his Ph.D. in theology at DLSU. His publications include *Introduction to Biblical Anthropology*; *Study of Religion*; and *Readings in Religion, Society and Culture.*

JAIME C. BULATAO, S.J., is a professor in the Psychology Department of Ateneo. He obtained his Ph.D. in clinical psychology from Fordham University in New York, and served for four terms as president of the Psychological Association of the Philippines. His voluminous research and scholarly papers tackle a variety of subjects such as psychic and faith healing, hynopsis, transpersonal counselling, split-level Christianity, and guidance trends.

MA. LUISA T. CAMAGAY, history professor at UP, finished her Doctorat de Troisieme Cycle at the Ecole des Hautes Etudes Sciences Sociales in Paris, France. She co-authored *Philippine Community Life* with Guillermo Lazaro, and is currently writing "The Social History of Manila: 1765-1898" on a Toyota Foundation research grant.

THERESA C. CARIÑO graduated with an M.A. in Asian Studies at the UP Asian Center. At present, she is an assistant political science professor, history lecturer, and China Studies Program director at DLSU. She authored *China and the Overseas Chinese in Southeast Asia: 1949-1984*; edited *Chinese in the Philippines*; and published numerous articles, among them, "The Church in China: Report of the Montreal Conference" and "China, Japan, and the Politics of Oil."

ISAGANI R. CRUZ, noted scholar-critic on Philippine literature and culture, heads the Language and Literature Department of the DLSU Graduate School of Arts, Education and Sciences. He has a Ph.D. in English literature from the University of Maryland, and has written *Beyond Futility: The Filipino as Critic*; *Movie Times*; and *Josephine at iba pang dula*. His column, "Critic-at-large" appears regularly in *The Philippine Starweek*.

ROMEO V. CRUZ is a history professor at UP who earned his doctoral degree from the University of California at Berkeley. He has authored *America's Colonial Desk and the Philippines* and other historical articles which have seen print in scholarly journals, monographs, pamphlets and books.

J. PROSPERO E. DE VERA III finished his M.A. in social sciences, cognates in political science and history at DLSU where he was, for a time, an associate professor. He has researched and written on non-governmental organizations, local government development, and alternate model for the Philippine educational system. He is currently enrolled in the doctoral program in public administration at UP.

OPHELIA A. DIMALANTA, poet, critic and fictionist, teaches literature, literary criticism, and creative writing at the University of Santo Tomas. She has published *The Philippine Poetic*, based on her dissertation on Palanca award-winning poems, and three collections of poetry—*Montage, The Time Factor,* and *Flowing On.*

418

FERNANDO G. ELESTERIO, an associate professor in the Religious Studies Department of DLSU, holds licentiate degrees in philosophy and theology from UST, and a Ph.D. in theology from Ateneo. He has published *The Iglesia ni Kristo: Its Christology and Ecclesiology* (1977), and *Three Essays on Philippine Religious Culture* (1989).

DOREEN G. FERNANDEZ is professor of English and chairperson of the Communication Arts Department of Ateneo. She holds a Ph.D. in literature from Ateneo, and is a founding member of the Cultural Research Association of the Philippines. Her continuing research interest in Filipino culture has resulted in books and scholarly papers on local cuisine, theater and literature. She has published *The Iloilo Zarzuela: 1903-1930*; In Performance; and in collaboration with Edilberto Alegre, the two-volume *Writers and Their Milieu* and *SARAP: Essays on Philippine Food.*

CANDIDO P. FILIO who has masteral degrees in economics and mathematics studies from the University of the Philippines is associate professor at the UP Asian Center. He is a bureau member of the International Society of City and Regional Planners, and a charter member of the Philippine Institute of Environmental Planners.

EDNA F. FORMILLEZA, an M.A. graduate of the Ohio State University, is an associate economics professor at DLSU. She has published *Methods of Research, Theory and Application*; *Readings in International Economics* (co-authored with Tereso Tullao, Jr.); and *Philippine Economic History and Institutions: Notes and Comments.* She has done project/research studies on technological and engineering manpower, small- and medium-scale industries, and the Bicol River basin area.

MARCELINO A. FORONDA, JR. is professor and former chairperson of the History-Political Science Department of DLSU. An alumnus of FEU and UST, he earned a doctorate in philosophy and letters from the University of Salamanca, and took post-doctoral studies at Stanford and Notre Dame Universities. He is not only a historian, bibliographer and researcher but an essayist and poet as well. Among his many publications are *Dallang: An Introduction to Philippine Literature in Ilokano and Other Essays*; *A Filipiniana Bibliography: 1943-1982*; and *Oral History in the Philippines and Other Historical Essays.*

STELLA P. GO is an associate professor in the Behavioral Science Department, and a research associate at DLSU. She has an M.A. in sociology from the University of Hawaii (Manoa), and is currently working on her dissertation in social psychology at the Ateneo. She has undertaken major researches on basic services, community participation in national family planning programmes, and the effects of international labor contract in the Philippines.

ANDREW B. GONZALEZ, FSC is president of De La Salle University. He is also executive secretary of the Linguistic Society of the Philippines and editor of its official organ, *Philippine Journal of Linguistics*. He has a Ph.D. in linguistics from the University of California at Berkeley, and his extensive writings on language and language development have been published here and abroad. His most significant books are *Language and Nationalism: The Philippine Experience Thus Far*; *Language Surveys in the Philippines* (with Ma. Lourdes S. Bautista); and *The Role of English and Its Maintenance in the Philippines*.

LEONOR OROSA–GOQUINGCO, named National Artist in Dance in 1976, is a well-known figure in the local world of performing arts. With a B.S.E. degree, she enrolled — after World War II — in dramatics at Columbia U and Teachers' College in New York City. In subsequent U.S. visits, she took professional and teachers' courses in ballet. She is also the founder-choreographer of the Filipiñescas Dance Co. which went on seven world tours and won much acclaim. As a writer, she has contributed articles on dance in *Arts of Asia, Dance,* and other cultural magazines; and she reviews drama and dance presentations for metropolitan newspapers.

ESTRELLITA V. GRUENBERG is dean of the Graduate School of Arts, Education and Sciences of DLSU where she obtained her D.A. in Language and Literature. She also teaches literature, and is involved in a research on Philippine literary history. She has written and edited English grammar textbooks, teachers' guides, and other instructional materials. *Filipino Writers in English*, a biographical and bibliographical directory which she co-authored with her father, Florentino Valeros was published in 1987 by New Day.

MA. ELENA CHIONG-JAVIER is a research associate and assistant professor in the Behavioral Science Department of DLSU. She has an M.A. in anthropology from Ateneo, and her research work is concentrated in areas related to community participation in urban/rural development.

420

From these relevant studies, she has produced singly or jointly with other researchers-writers such publications as *Organizing Farmers for Irrigation*; *Philippine Urban Situation Analysis*; and *Economic Transactions in the Upland: The Sale of Banana and Gold Between the Iraya and the Tagalog.*

PILAR R. JIMENEZ, a Ph.D. in Philippine Studies graduate of UP, is a professor in the Behavioral Science Department of DLSU. She is also a university research associate who has written and published scholarly papers on a wide range of subjects such as fertility and ethnicity, participant observation as a qualitative research methodology, assessment of social science structures, the rural poor, and economic exchanges among tribal groups.

PATRICIA B. LICUANAN, holder of an M.A. in psychology from Cornell University and a Ph.D. in social psychology from the Pennsylvania State University, is the academic vice president of Ateneo de Manila University. She has written — from the psycho-social perspective — numerous research and scholarly papers on Filipino culture, society, politics, family, education, and economic development.

ROSARIO CRUZ LUCERO who has a Ph.D. in Philippine Studies from UP is chairperson of the Literature Department of DLSU. Besides teaching, she writes fiction in English and Pilipino, and critical essays on Philippine literature. She is presently engaged in the translation of Hiligaynon literary pieces into Tagalog and English.

ISAGANI R. MEDINA, who holds a doctoral degree in history is a full professor at UP. His exemplary scholarship in the field of local and oral history has resulted in the publication of *Filipiniana Materials in the National Library* and *Streets of Manila* which he co-authored with Luningning Ira.

ROSALINDA L. OROSA, arts and culture editor of *The Manila Times* is foremost among the country's critics on the performing arts. Aside from critical reviews, she also writes witty and perceptive informal essays on Philippine culture. She has won an NPC-ESSO Award in Journalism, and has been cited "Music Critic of the Year" by the Philippine Music Lovers' Society. Her best works — critiques, interviews, sketches, essays and profiles — have been collected and published under the titles, *What's in a (Nick) Name?* (1969) and *Above the Throng* (1980).

421

SOCORRO L. REYES, chairperson of the Political Science Department of De La Salle University, has an M.A. and a Ph.D. from DLSU and UST respectively. She has published *Political Dynamics: A Reader; The Philippines in the Year 2000: A Developmental Study;* and *Social Science Education and National Development in the Philippines.*

SOLEDAD S. REYES, chairperson of the Filipino Department of Ateneo, has an M.A. in the Sociology of Literature from Essex University, and a Ph.D. in Philippine Studies from UP. She has published *Ang Nobelang Tagalog (1905-1975): Tradisyon at Modernismo,* and *Noli Me Tangere A Century After: An Interdisciplinary Perspective;* and edited *200 Taon ni Balagtas: Mga Bagong Pananaw,* recently released by the Balagtas Bicentennial Commission.

JUDY C. SEVILLA, who is completing her Ph.D. in social ecology at the University of California (Irvine) is an assistant psychology professor at DLSU. She is also a university research associate, and has written and published "Filipino Religious Psychology: A Commentary"; *Research on the Filipino Family; Review and Prospects; Sex and the Single Filipina: The Omega Woman* (with Alex Gilandas and Ma. Cecilia Conaco); and "Indigenous Research Methods in Pilipino Psychology."

JOSE MARIA SISON, alleged founder and chairman of the Communist Party of the Philippines, finished his B.A. and M.A. degrees at UP where he was, for a brief time, a professorial lecturer on Rizal and Philippine Government. He writes essays and poetry, and edits the *Progressive Review.* He is the author of *Struggle for National Democracy* and *Philippine Society and Revolution.*

MOTOE TERAMI-WADA has been a professorial lecturer in the History and Area Studies Department of DLSU. She obtained an M.A. in Asian Studies from the East-West Center of the University of Hawaii (Honolulu), and an M.A. in Philippine Studies from UP. Aside from numerous articles on Philippine literature and culture she has written for Japanese newspapers and magazines, she has also translated and published a collection of Filipino short stories, and Edgardo Reyes *Maynila: Sa Mga Kuko ng Liwanag.*

# Participants and Delegates

| | NAME | AFFILIATION |
|---|---|---|
| 1. | ABAYA, Ma. Concepcion | Intramuros Administration |
| 2. | ABULAD, Romualdo E. | De La Salle University |
| 3. | AGPALO, Remigio | De La Salle University |
| 4. | AGUILAR, Carmencita T. | University of the Philippines |
| 5. | AGUILAR, Gemma Rosellie C. | De La Salle University |
| 6. | ALAMPAY, Belen Ma. | De La Salle University |
| 7. | ALBA, Alfonso C. | De La Salle University |
| 8. | AMON, Carmencita P. | Polytechnic University of the Philippines |
| 9. | ANDRADA, Lolita M. | Curriculum Development Division, MECS |
| 10. | ANGANGCO, Ofelia R. | Philippine Studies Association |
| 11. | ANTILLON, Loline M. | De La Salle University |
| 12. | ARAMBULO, Jesus J. | De La Salle University |
| 13. | ARANTON, Consuelo V. | Philippine Normal College |
| 14. | ARANZASO, Roberta C. | University of the East |
| 15. | ARBOLEDA, Ma. Dolores A. | De La Salle University |
| 16. | ARCILLA, S.J., Jose S. | Ateneo de Manila University |
| 17. | ARCINAS, Fe | Philippine Studies Association |
| 18. | ARENAS-VERGARA, Arturo A. | De La Salle University |
| 19. | ARGUELLES, Priscilla F. | De La Salle University |
| 20. | AZCUNA, Ma. Asuncion A. | St. Scholastica's College |
| 21. | BACAY, Virginia S. | De La Salle University |
| 22. | BALAJADIA, Basilio P. | De La Salle University |
| 23. | BASCARA, Cornelio R. | De La Salle University |
| 24. | BASSIG, Raidis J. | Intramuros Administration |
| 25. | BAUTISTA, Ma. Lourdes | De La Salle University |
| 26. | BELITA C.M., Jaime | De La Salle Univesrity |
| 27. | BERMEJO, Gerson S. | Philippine Christian University |
| 28. | BOBIS, Sonia D. | Bureau of Elementary Education, MECS |
| 29. | BRAGADO, Erlinda | De La Salle University |
| 30. | BRAWNER, Dalisay G. | Pamantasan ng Lungsod ng Maynila |
| 31. | BULATAO, S.J. Jaime C. | Ateneo de Manila University |
| 32. | CAMAGAY, Ma. Luisa T. | University of the Philippines |
| 33. | CANILLAS, Luningning T. | De La Salle University |
| 34. | CARIÑO, Theresa C. | De La Salle University |
| 35. | CARLOS, Mercedenia D. | De La Salle University |
| 36. | CARREON, Edwina S. | De La Salle University |
| 37. | CASTRO, Sandra B. | Intramuros Administration |

423

| 38. | CENIZA, Claro R. | De La Salle University |
|---|---|---|
| 39. | CONDUCTO, Joselito | University of Santo Tomas |
| 40. | CORPUZ, Carmelita C. | De La Salle University |
| 41. | CRUZ, Emerlinda G. | De La Salle University |
| 42. | CRUZ, Isagani R. | De La Salle University |
| 43. | CRUZ, Potenciano | Philippine Normal College |
| 44. | CRUZ, Romeo V. | University of the Philippines |
| 45. | CRUZ, Thelma M. | V. Mapa High School |
| 46. | DALANGIN, Carlito C. | University of Santo Tomas |
| 47. | DAROY, Ester V. | De La Salle University |
| 48. | DE GUZMAN, Raul P. | University of the Philippines, Los Baños |
| 49. | DEVEZA, Eduardo T. | De La Salle University |
| 50. | DE LA FUENTE, Benjamin C. | De La Salle University |
| 51. | DE VERA, J. Prospero E. | De La Salle University |
| 52. | DEL CASTILLO, Solita P. | Ford Foundation, Makati |
| 53. | DIAZ, Manuel | De La Salle University |
| 54. | DIMACALI, Edna Marie M. | De La Salle University |
| 55. | DIMALANTA, Ophelia A. | UST-DLSU |
| 56. | DI MARTINO, David R. | University of Nebraska at Omeka/ Pamantasan ng Lungsod ng Maynila |
| 57. | ELESTERIO, Fernando G. | De La Salle University |
| 58. | ENRIQUEZ, Emigdio A. | De La Salle University |
| 59. | ENRIQUEZ, Virgilio G. | De La Salle University |
| 60. | ERNI, Marie-Benedicte | International Committee of the Red Cross |
| 61. | ESGUERRA, Rebecca S. | De La Salle University |
| 62. | EZEH, Susan C. | University of the East |
| 63. | FABROS, George C. | De La Salle University |
| 64. | FAMA, Socorro G. | St. Scholastica's College |
| 65. | FERNANDEZ, Doreen G. | Ateneo de Manila University |
| 66. | FILIO, Candido P. | Asian Center, UP |
| 67. | FORMILLEZA, Edna F. | De La Salle University |
| 69. | FORONDA, Marcelino A. | De La Salle University |
| 70. | FORTUNATO, Teresita F. | De La Salle University |
| 71. | GACUTAN, VIOLA | Philippine Christian University |
| 72. | GALMAN, Pat G. | De La Salle University |
| 73. | GARCIA, Edmundo | University of the Philippines |
| 74. | GATAN, Fernando | De La Salle University |
| 75. | GO, Stella P. | De La Salle University |
| 76. | GONZALES, Angelita G. | De La Salle University |
| 77. | GONZALES, Lucia D. | CEU, Malolos, Bulacan |
| 78. | GONZALEZ, FSC, Andrew B. | De La Salle University |
| 79. | GOQUINGCO, Leonor O. | Ben-Lor Ballet Academy |
| 80. | GRUENBERG, Estrellita V. | De La Salle University |
| 81. | GUERRERO, Milagros C. | University of the Philippines |
| 82. | GUTIERREZ, Cecile B. | St. Scholastica's College |
| 83. | HELBLING, Jurg | IPC, Ateneo de Manila University |
| 84. | HENSON, Florante G. | De La Salle University |
| 85. | HOLMES, Margarita G. | Ateneo de Manila University |
| 86. | JACOB, Florante P. | Maryknoll College Foundation, Inc. |
| 87. | JAVIER, Ma. Elena C. | De La Salle University |
| 88. | JENISTA, Frank L. | Thomas Jefferson Cultural Center |

| 89. | JIMENEZ, Pilar R. | De La Salle University |
|---|---|---|
| 90. | KELTOS,, George M. | ICMC - ESL/CO Program |
| 91. | KRISHNASWAMY, Shantha | De La Salle University |
| 92. | LAFORTEZA, Emma C. | Phil. Business for Social Progress |
| 93. | LAGMAY, Alfredo V. | University of the Philippines |
| 94. | LANTIN, Emmanuel | De La Salle University |
| 95. | LAPEÑA, Jose Florencio Jr. | De La Salle University |
| 96. | LAPEÑA, Ma. Angeles G. | De La Salle University |
| 97. | LAQUIAN, Aprodicio A. | UNFPA-UNDP, Beijing, China |
| 98. | LICUANAN. Patricia B. | HRC, Ateneo de Manila University |
| 99. | LIM, Aurora R. | Asian Center, UP |
| 100. | LIM, Marilou S.A. | De La Salle University |
| 101. | LUCERO, Eduardo R. | De La Salle University |
| 102. | LUCERO, Rosario C. | De La Salle University |
| 103. | MAGNO, Francisco A. | De La Salle University |
| 104. | MAGPAYO, Erlinda R. | De La Salle University |
| 105. | MANDAP, Corazon V. | University of the Philippines |
| 106. | MANGAHAS, Fe B. | National Library |
| 107. | MANGAHAS, Rogelio G. | De La Salle University |
| 108. | MARAMAG, Beatriz B. | Torres High School, San Pedro, Laguna, |
| 109. | MARCO, Jesusa | De La Salle University |
| 110. | MARTINEZ, Leopoldo J. | De La Salle University |
| 111. | MEDINA, Isagani R. | U.P. Faculty Center |
| 112. | MENDOZA, Ren E. | Asian Center, UP |
| 113. | MERINO, Luis G. | Intramuros Administration |
| 114. | MILAN, Edwin S. | De La Salle University |
| 115. | MIRALLES, Teresa P. | Jose Abad Santos High School |
| 116. | MORENO, Virginia R. | U.P. Film Center |
| 117. | NATIVIDAD, Ma. Cleofe R. | De La Salle University |
| 118. | OBRA, Ven M. | De La Salle University |
| 119. | OKAMURA, Jonathan Y. | De La Salle University |
| 120. | OLOROSO, Bernadette S. | De La Salle University |
| 121. | OROSA, Rosalinda L. | The Manila Times |
| 122. | OSTERIA, Trinidad | Institute of Southeast Asian Studies |
| 123. | PALMA, Reynaldo Y. | De La Salle University |
| 124. | PANGILINAN, Stella B. | Philippine Normal College |
| 125. | PASCUAL, Teresita H. | University of the East |
| 126. | PAYUMO, Presentacion | De La Salle University |
| 127. | PERALTA, Carolina M. | Jose Abad Santos High School |
| 128. | PERNIA, Marjorie E. | De La Salle University |
| 129. | PINEDA, Imelda M. | De La Salle University |
| 130. | POLO, Lily Ann G. | University of the Philippines |
| 131. | QUEBENGCO, Carmelita | De La Salle University |
| 132. | QUIRINO, Carlos | Historian and Biographer |
| 133 | QUITO, Emerita | De La Salle University |
| 134. | RAMOS, Exaltacion L. | St. Paul College, Q.C. |
| 135. | REYES, Dolores A. | Far Eastern University |
| 136. | REYES, Emmanuel A. | De La Salle University |
| 137. | REYES, Herminia V. | De La Salle University |
| 138. | REYES, Maria S. | De La Salle University |
| 139. | REYES, Milagros R. | De La Salle University |

| 140. | REYES, Natividad T. | Philippine Normal College |
| 141. | REYES, Socorro L. | De La Salle University |
| 142. | REYES, Soledad S. | Ateneo de Manila University |
| 143. | RIVERA, Reynaldo R. | De La Salle University |
| 144. | ROMERO, Ma. Corona S. | De La Salle University |
| 145. | RONQUILLO, Teresita | Mapa High School |
| 146. | ROTOR, Nilda S. | De La Salle University |
| 147. | SANDOVAL, Prisca L. | De La Salle University |
| 148. | SANTILLAN, Antoniette D | College of the Holy Spirit |
| 149. | SAN MIGUEL, Rachel M. | De La Salle University |
| 150. | SEMBRANO, Josefina O. | De La Salle University |
| 151. | SEVILLA, Judy Carol C. | De La Salle University |
| 152. | SEVILLA, Ramon C. | De La Salle University |
| 153 | SIBAYAN, Bonifacio P. | Philippine Normal College |
| 154. | SIBAYAN, Judy | De La Salle University |
| 155. | SINHA, Aum C. | De La Salle University |
| 156. | SISON, Jose Maria | University of the Philippines |
| 157. | SORIANO, Elizabeth G. | College of the Holy Spirit |
| 158. | SUGATA, Nariko | U.P. SSP |
| 159. | SYYAP, Nora C. | De La Salle University |
| 160. | TALASTAS, Florencia M. | Pamantasan ng Lungsod ng Maynila |
| 161. | THELMO, Angeli C. | Intramuros Administration |
| 162. | TIAMSON, Alfredo | University of the Philippines |
| 163. | TIMBREZA, Florentino T. | De La Salle University |
| 164. | TIONGSON, Nicanor | UP-DLSU |
| 165. | TIROL, Marikita | De La Salle University |
| 166. | TORRES, Amaryllis | University of the Philippines |
| 167. | TULLAO, Tereso S. | De La Salle University |
| 168. | UCKELEY, Rainer | De La Salle University |
| 169. | VALEDA, Ma. Emelita P. | De La Salle University |
| 170. | VILLACORTA, Wilfrido V. | De La Salle University |
| 171. | WADA, Motoe Terami | De La Salle University |
| 172. | WIONZEK, Karl-Heinz | De La Salle University |
| 173. | ZAIDE, Ceferino A. | University of the East |